ENGL 1010

How to buy this book:

Your English Composition textbook is a compilation of articles written by English teachers for universities around the country. The entire compilation is provided free of charge through a creative commons license. You can access or even copy all the material here, for your own reference, even after the semester ends.

Different Versions:

An electronic version will be in your ENGL 1010 Blackboard page. Also, you may purchase a physical copy at the Corning Community College Bookstore. The electronic version has access to multimedia content including video, powerpoint, and interactive activities. The print version will have all the same reading material, but not include the multimedia content.

About the Author:

There are many different authors; look to the "Licenses and Attributions" section at the end of each chapter to identify contributors. This compilation was edited by Daniel Coble of Corning Community College.

Published by SUNY OER Services
Milne Library
State University of New York at Geneseo
Geneseo, NY 14454

Distributed by State University of New York Press

 July 2017

ISBN: 978-1-4384-7037-5

Contents

ENGL 1010 Rubric

This rubric corresponds with the Communications / Humanities Division's ENGL 1010 grading standards, and it indicates the essay's strengths and weaknesses. It is a holistic evaluation, not an average of the categories; different categories are weighted differently.

Student:

Essay Grade:

Requirements

Criterion	A	B	C	D	F
Fulfills all requirements of the assignment	Yes	N/A	N/A	N/a	No

Notes:

Topic, Thesis, Controlling Idea (Focus)

Criterion	A	B	C	D	F
Thesis	Significant for context	Clear topic and overall point	Clear topic and apparent purpose	Weak or overly general topic / purpose	Confusing / contradictory; doesn't fit assignment; missing
Intro	Establishes topic and seeks to engage audience	Topic established; thesis lead in	Clear, but general	Vague / too general; doesn't set up thesis	Confusing / contradictory
Conclusion	Gives reader something significant to ponder	Solid summary and final statement	Clear, but general	Vague / repetitious	Confusing / contradictory

Notes:

Organization, Coherence, Transitions (Flow)

Criterion	A	B	C	D	F
Essay Unity	Clear, logical units reinforce thesis	All units clear and logical	All units clear	At least one paragraph unified	Ideas scattered / doesn't fit assignment
Organization	Meaningful to purpose	Intentional and logical order	Clear, but mechanical	Some pattern apparent; not assigned structure	Jumbled / not clear; doesn't fit assignment
Transitions	Effectively relate ideas and reinforce order	Most are logical	Some effective; not enough or general	Only a few used; weak relation of ideas	Not enough used to link ideas; choppy
Source Integration	Signal phrases establish source and credibility	Very few dropped quotes	Numerous dropped quotes / some context	Little attempt at integration	No lead-ins / all source material dropped in

Notes:

Development (Support)

Criterion	A	B	C	D	F
Evidence and Explanation	Completes ideas and supports thesis and / or explanation	Generally effective details / logical	Clear support / some accurate explanation	Minimal support or explanation; relies on fallacies	Inadequate detail
Accurate Use of Appropriate Sources	Accurate and precise	Fits adequately with most of writer's points	Few / slight misinterpretations	Frequent inaccuracies; relies on fallacies	Largely inaccurate source use

Sentence Structure, Grammar, Mechanics, Diction (Correctness and Style)

Criterion	Content	A	B	C	D	F
Structure	· Fragments · Comma Splices · Run-on / Fused Sentences · Mixed Construction	Varied mature	Generally correct	Occasional mistakes	Frequent errors	Regular patterns of errors
Word Choice	· Style · Wrong Word · Wordiness	Going beyond common	Correct	Minor errors or repetitious	Frequent errors	Confusing
Grammar / Mechanics	· Subject-Verb agreement · Pronoun-Antecedent Agreement · Verb Forms / Tense · Spelling · Commas · Punctuation · Capitalization	Few errors, none serious	Only occasional errors	Limited error types	Various regular errors	Numerous errors

Notes:

MLA Style of Documentation

Criterion	A	B	C	D	F
Documentation	Thorough	A few paraphrased ideas / facts not cited	Quotes cited, but paraphrases generally not	Some sources credited	No attempt to credit
Format	All accurate	Occasional minor errors; no major errors	Few major errors / frequent minor errors	Major errors	No recognizable MLA format or no citation

Notes:

Separate Process Grade

Criterion	A	B	C	D	F
Process	Thorough engagement in all stages	Good, thoughtful engagement	All stages complete, some rushed or thin	Stages skipped or too general	Many stages skipped or too general

Notes:

College Reading: Active Reading

Double-Entry Response Format

Use a double-entry format to extend your thinking on a topic or to critique an author's presentation.

One very effective technique for avoiding note-bound prose is to respond to powerful quotations in what writing theorist Ann Berthoff calls the double-entry notebook form. The double-entry form shows the direct quotation on the left side of the page and your response to it on the right. There are two advantages to this technique: First, it helps you think about your subject; second, it helps you step away from your sources and discover your own approach and voice.

Double-Entry Example: Extending Thinking

Passage	Annotations
They [i.e., creative ideas] may indeed occur at times of relaxation, or in fantasy, or at other times when we alternate play with work. But what is entirely clear is that they pertain to those areas in which the person consciously has worked laboriously and with dedication. Purpose in the human being is a much more complex phenomenon than what used to be called will power. Purpose involves all levels of experience. We cannot will to have insights. We cannot will creativity. But we can will to give ourselves to the encounter with intensity of dedication and commitment. The deeper aspects of awareness are activated to the extent that the person is committed to the encounter. (Rollo May, The Courage to Create, 46)	I'm absolutely certain that Rollo May is right: Total involvement in the "encounter" of the creative process is crucial for the emergence of the Eureka moment. Unfortunately, I think, too many people are too uncomfortable about the intrusion of the disruptive "right brain" or "unconscious." They dislike the creative process because of the fear of chaos and of failure. How, then, can we encourage people to "submerge" themselves, to lose themselves in an idea or feeling, long enough to experience the Gestalt, the felt sense, the joy, the bliss, the jouissance? If students could only experience this passion for the creative process, they would learn that writing is not a boring, mechanical process of filling in completed thoughts into pre-established modes of discourse.

Double-Entry Example: Critique a Passage

Below is an example of how a double-entry format can be used to critique a document. When reading the following excerpt on the greenhouse effect, what questions do you believe a skilled reader would raise?

Passage	Annotations
The greenhouse effect is likely to change rainfall patterns, raise sea levels 4 to 7 feet by the year 2100, and increase the world's mean temperature 2.7 to 8 degrees Fahrenheit by the year 2050 (Brown and Flavin 6, 16). Everyone will suffer as irrigation and drainage systems become useless and agriculture faces its first changes in a "global climatic regime" that has changed little since farming began (Brown and Flavin 16). Some places will cease to be productive, such as the North American heartland and the Soviet Union's grain belt (Brown and Flavin 17). Although some areas, previously unproductive, will suddenly become good farmland, scientists say these climate shifts could occur so abruptly that agricultural losses would be hard to readily adjust for (Brown and Flavin 16).	On what evidence is this information based? According to the Works Cited section, this information appears in the following source: Brown, Lester R., and Christopher Flavin. "The Earth's Vital Signs." State of the World (1988): 5-7, 16-17. Critical readers would probably question the reliability of this source because the claims are so controversial and because they are not familiar with the journal. The credibility of this information could be significantly improved by "power quoting." Brown and Flavin may be correct in their dire predictions. However, chances are that critical readers such as your instructors would be more likely to believe these predictions if additional information about the authors and their research were provided or if the authors could "power quote"—that is, cite numerous other studies that reached similar conclusions.

-

Double-Entry Response Format. **Authored by**: Joe Moxley. **Located at**: https://writingcommons.org/open-text/information-literacy/critical-reading-practices/236-double-entry-response-format. **Project**: Writing Commons. **License**: *CC BY-NC-ND: Attribution-NonCommercial-NoDerivatives*

How to Annotate

An active reading strategy for articles or textbooks is **annotation**. Think for a moment about what that word means. It means to add notes (an-NOTE-tate) to text that you are reading, to offer explanation, comments or opinions to the author's words. Annotation takes practice, and the better you are at it, the better you will be at reading complicated articles.

Where to Make Notes

First, determine how you will annotate the text you are about to read.

If it is a printed article, you may be able to just write in the margins. A colored pen might make it easier to see than black or even blue.

If it is an article posted on the web, you could also use Diigo, (diigo.com) which is a highlighting and annotating tool that you can use on the website and even share your notes with your instructor. Other note-taking plug-ins for web browsers might serve a similar function.

If it is a textbook that you do not own (or wish to sell back), use post it notes to annotate in the margins.

You can also use a notebook to keep written commentary as you read in any platform, digital or print. If you do this, be sure to leave enough information about the specific text you're responding to that you can find it later if you need to. (Make notes about page number, which paragraph it is, or even short quotes to help you locate the passage again.)

What Notes to Make

Now you will annotate the document by adding your own words, phrases, and summaries to the written text. For the following examples, the article "Guniea Worm Facts" was used. (http://www.cartercenter.org/health/guinea_worm/mini_site/facts.html) was used.

Scan the document you are annotating. Some obvious clues will be apparent before you read it, such as titles or headers for sections. Read the first paragraph. Somewhere in the first (or possibly the second) paragraph should be a BIG IDEA about what the article is going to be about. In the margins, near the top, write down the big idea of the article in your own words. This shouldn't be more than a phrase or a sentence. This big idea is likely the article's thesis.

<u>Underline topic sentences or phrases</u> that express the main idea for that paragraph or section. You should never underline more than 5 words, though for large paragraphs or blocks of text, you can use brackets. (Underlining long stretches gets messy, and makes it hard to review the text later.) Write in the margin next to what you've underlined a summary of the paragraph or the idea being expressed.

Connect related ideas by drawing arrows from one idea to another. Annotate those arrows with a phrase about how they are connected.

Better to prevent than to treat later!

> Traditional removal of a Guinea worm consists of winding the worm — up to 3 feet (1 meter) long — around a small stick and manually extracting it...

> The best way to stop Guinea worm disease is to prevent people from entering sources of drinking water with an active infection...

If you encounter an idea, word, or phrase you don't understand, circle it and put a question mark in the margin that indicates an area of confusion. Write your question in the margin.

○ "Depending on the outcome of the assessment, the commission recommends to WHO which formerly endemic countries should be declared free of transmission, i.e., certified as free of the disease."-> **??
What does this mean? Who is WHO?**

Anytime the author makes a statement that you can connect with on a personal level, annotate in the margins a summary of how this connects to you. Write any comments or observations you feel appropriate to the text. You can also add your personal opinion.

○ "Guinea worm disease incapacitates victims for extended periods of time making them unable to work or grow enough food to feed their families or attend school." -> **My dad was sick for a while and couldn't work. This was hard on our family.**

Place a box around any term or phrase that emphasizes scientific language. These could be words you are not familiar with or will need to review later. Define those words in the margins.

○ "Guinea worm disease is set to become the second human disease in history, after smallpox, to be eradicated."-> **Eradicated = to put an end to, destroy**

To summarize how you will annotate text:
1. Identify the big idea
2. Underline topic sentences or main ideas
3. Connect ideas with arrows
4. Ask questions
5. Add personal notes
6. Define technical words

Like many skills, annotating takes practice. Remember that the main goal for doing this is to give you a strategy for reading text that may be more complicated and technical than what you are used to.

CC licensed content, Original

Critical Thinking

Introduction

Learning Objectives

- define critical thinking
- identify the role that logic plays in critical thinking
- apply critical thinking skills to problem-solving scenarios
- apply critical thinking skills to evaluation of information

Consider these thoughts about the critical thinking process, and how it applies not just to our school lives but also our personal and professional lives.

"Thinking Critically and Creatively"

Critical thinking skills are perhaps the most fundamental skills involved in making judgments and solving problems. You use them every day, and you can continue improving them.

The ability to think critically about a matter—to analyze a question, situation, or problem down to its most basic parts—is what helps us evaluate the accuracy and truthfulness of statements, claims, and information we read and hear. It is the sharp knife that, when honed, separates fact from fiction, honesty from lies, and the accurate from the misleading. We all use this skill to one degree or another almost every day. For example, we use critical thinking every day as we consider the latest consumer products and why one particular product is the best among its peers. Is it a quality product because a celebrity endorses it? Because a lot of other people may have used it? Because it is made by one company versus another? Or perhaps because it is made in one country or another? These are questions representative of critical thinking.

The academic setting demands more of us in terms of critical thinking than everyday life. It demands that we evaluate information and analyze myriad issues. It is the environment where our critical thinking skills can be the difference between success and failure. In this environment we must consider information in an analytical, critical manner. We must ask questions—What is the source of this information? Is this source an expert one and what makes it so? Are there multiple perspectives to consider on an issue? Do multiple sources agree or disagree on an issue? Does quality research substantiate information or opinion? Do I have any personal biases that may affect my consideration of this information?

It is only through purposeful, frequent, intentional questioning such as this that we can sharpen our critical thinking skills and improve as students, learners and researchers.

—Dr. Andrew Robert Baker, *Foundations of Academic Success: Words of Wisdom*

Defining Critical Thinking

Thinking comes naturally. You don't have to make it happen—it just does. But you can make it happen in different ways. For example, you can think positively or negatively. You can think with "heart" and you can think with rational judgment. You can also think strategically and analytically, and mathematically and scientifically. These are a few of multiple ways in which the mind can process thought.

What are some forms of thinking you use? When do you use them, and why?

As a college student, you are tasked with engaging and expanding your thinking skills. One of the most important of these skills is critical thinking. Critical thinking is important because it relates to nearly all tasks, situations, topics, careers, environments, challenges, and opportunities. It's not restricted to a particular subject area.

Critical thinking is clear, reasonable, reflective thinking focused on deciding what to believe or do. It means asking probing questions like, "How do we know?" or "Is this true in every case or just in this instance?" It involves being skeptical and challenging assumptions, rather than simply memorizing facts or blindly accepting what you hear or read.

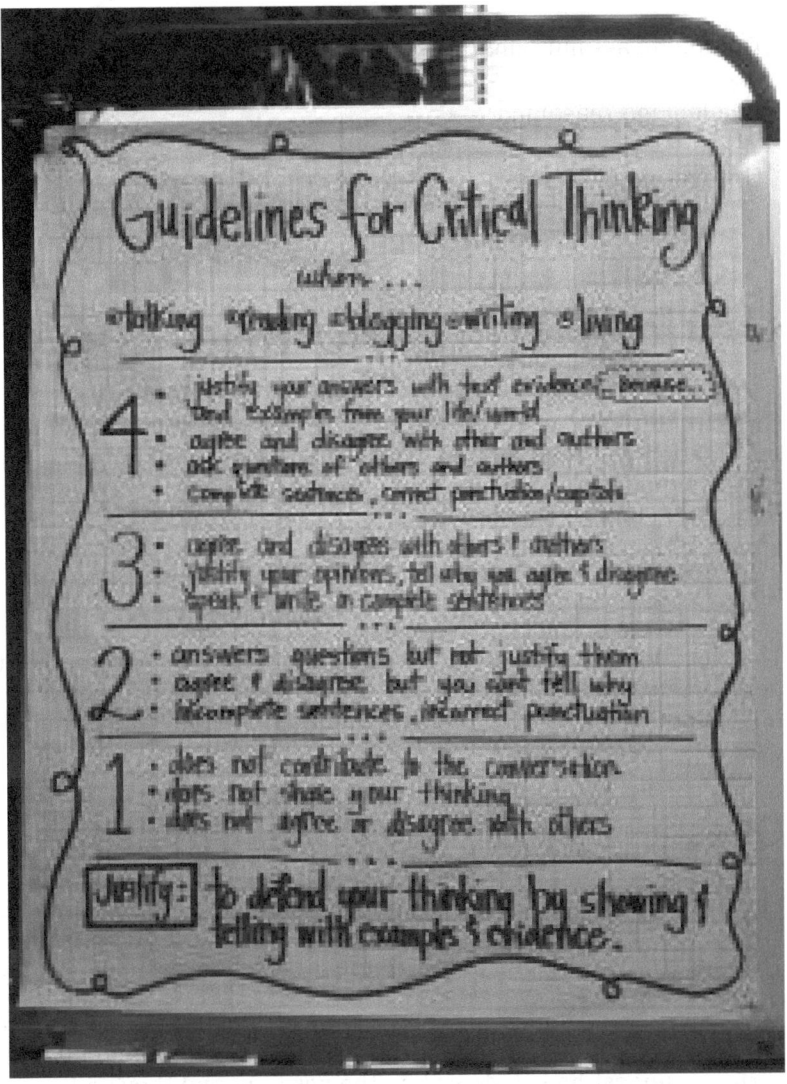

Imagine, for example, that you're reading a history textbook. You wonder who wrote it and why, because you detect certain assumptions in the writing. You find that the author has a limited scope of research focused only on a particular group within a population. In this case, your critical thinking reveals that there are "other sides to the story."

Who are critical thinkers, and what characteristics do they have in common? Critical thinkers are usually curious and reflective people. They like to explore and probe new areas and seek knowledge, clarification, and new solutions. They ask pertinent questions, evaluate statements and arguments, and they distinguish between facts and opinion. They are also willing to examine their own beliefs, possessing a manner of humility that allows them to admit lack of knowledge or understanding when needed. They are open to changing their mind. Perhaps most of all, they actively enjoy learning, and seeking new knowledge is a lifelong pursuit.

This may well be you!

No matter where you are on the road to being a critical thinker, you can always more fully develop your skills. Doing so will help you develop more balanced arguments, express yourself clearly, read critically, and absorb important information efficiently. Critical thinking skills will help you in any profession or any circumstance of life, from science to art to business to teaching.

Critical Thinking IS	Critical Thinking is NOT
Skepticism	Memorizing

Critical Thinking IS	Critical Thinking is NOT
Examining assumptions	Group thinking
Challenging reasoning	Blind acceptance of authority
Uncovering biases	

Critical Thinking and Logic

Critical thinking is fundamentally a process of questioning information and data. You may question the information you read in a textbook, or you may question what a politician or a professor or a classmate says. You can also question a commonly-held belief or a new idea. With critical thinking, anything and everything is subject to question and examination.

Logic's Relationship to Critical Thinking

The word **logic** comes from the Ancient Greek *logike*, referring to the science or art of reasoning. Using logic, a person evaluates arguments and strives to distinguish between good and bad reasoning, or between truth and falsehood. Using logic, you can evaluate ideas or claims people make, make good decisions, and form sound beliefs about the world.[1]

Questions of Logic in Critical Thinking

Let's use a simple example of applying logic to a critical-thinking situation. In this hypothetical scenario, a man has a PhD in political science, and he works as a professor at a local college. His wife works at the college, too. They have three young children in the local school system, and their family is well known in the community.

The man is now running for political office. Are his credentials and experience sufficient for entering public office? Will he be effective in the political office? Some voters might believe that his personal life and current job, on the surface, suggest he will do well in the position, and they will vote for him.

In truth, the characteristics described don't guarantee that the man will do a good job. The information is somewhat irrelevant. What else might you want to know? How about whether the man had already held a political office and done a good job? In this case, we want to ask, How much information is adequate in order to make a decision based on logic instead of assumptions?

The following questions, presented in Figure 1, below, are ones you may apply to formulating a logical, reasoned perspective in the above scenario or any other situation:

What's happening? Gather the basic information and begin to think of questions.
Why is it important? Ask yourself why it's significant and whether or not you agree.
What don't I see? Is there anything important missing?
How do I know? Ask yourself where the information came from and how it was constructed.
Who is saying it? What's the position of the speaker and what is influencing them?
What else? What if? What other ideas exist and are there other possibilities?

Questions a Critical Thinker Asks

What's Happening?
Gather the basic information and begin to think of questions

Why Is It Important?
Ask yourself why it's significant and whether or not you agree

What Don't I See?
Is there anything important missing?

Answers

How Do I Know?
Ask yourself where the information came from and how it was constructed

Who Is Saying It?
What's the position of the speaker and what is influencing them?

Pluto is not a planet

If only time were relative...

What Else? What If?
What other ideas exist and are there other possibilities?

 UBC

a place of mind

learningcommons.ubc.ca

13

Figure 1

Problem-Solving With Critical Thinking

For most people, a typical day is filled with critical thinking and problem-solving challenges. In fact, critical thinking and problem-solving go hand-in-hand. They both refer to using knowledge, facts, and data to solve problems effectively. But with problem-solving, you are specifically identifying, selecting, and defending your solution. Below are some examples of using critical thinking to problem-solve:

- Your roommate was upset and said some unkind words to you, which put a crimp in your relationship. You try to see through the angry behaviors to determine how you might best support your roommate and help bring your relationship back to a comfortable spot.

- Your campus club has been languishing on account of lack of participation and funds. The new club president, though, is a marketing major and has identified some strategies to interest students in joining and supporting the club. Implementation is forthcoming.

- Your final art class project challenges you to conceptualize form in new ways. On the last day of class when students present their projects, you describe the techniques you used to fulfill the assignment. You explain why and how you selected that approach.

- Your math teacher sees that the class is not quite grasping a concept. She uses clever questioning to dispel anxiety and guide you to new understanding of the concept.

- You have a job interview for a position that you feel you are only partially qualified for, although you really want the job and you are excited about the prospects. You analyze how you will explain your skills and experiences in a way to show that you are a good match for the prospective employer.

- You are doing well in college, and most of your college and living expenses are covered. But there are some gaps between what you want and what you feel you can afford. You analyze your income, savings, and budget to better calculate what you will need to stay in college and maintain your desired level of spending.

Problem-Solving Action Checklist

Problem-solving can be an efficient and rewarding process, especially if you are organized and mindful of critical steps and strategies. Remember, too, to assume the attributes of a good critical thinker. If you are curious, reflective, knowledge-seeking, open to change, probing, organized, and ethical, your challenge or problem will be less of a hurdle, and you'll be in a good position to find intelligent solutions.

	STRATEGIES	ACTION CHECKLIST[2]
1	Define the problem	• Identify the problem • Provide as many supporting details as possible • Provide examples • Organize the information logically

	STRATEGIES	ACTION CHECKLIST[2]
2	Identify available solutions	• Use logic to identify your most important goals • Identify implications and consequences • Identify facts • Compare and contrast possible solutions
3	Select your solution	• Use gathered facts and relevant evidence • Support and defend solutions considered valid • Defend your solution

Evaluating Information With Critical Thinking

Evaluating information can be one of the most complex tasks you will be faced with in college. But if you utilize the following four strategies, you will be well on your way to success:

Read for understanding by using text coding
Examine arguments
Clarify thinking

Cultivate "habits of mind"

Read for Understanding Using Text Coding

When you read and take notes, use a text coding strategy. (http://toolsfordifferentiation.pbworks.com/w/page/22360123/Text%20Coding).

Text coding is a way of tracking your thinking while reading. It entails marking the text and recording what you are thinking either in the margins or perhaps on Post-it notes. As you make connections and ask questions in response to what you read, you monitor your comprehension and enhance your long-term understanding of the material.

With text coding, mark important arguments and key facts. Indicate where you agree and disagree or have further questions. You don't necessarily need to read every word, but make sure you understand the concepts or the intentions behind what is written. Feel free to develop your own shorthand style when reading or taking notes. The following are a few options to consider using while coding text.

Shorthand	Meaning
!	Important
L	Learned something new
!	Big idea surfaced

Shorthand	Meaning
*	Interesting or important fact
?	Dig deeper
☐	Agree
≠	Disagree

Organizations like PBWorks and Collaborative for Teaching and Learning offer more text coding ideas as well.

Clarify Thinking

When you use critical thinking to evaluate information, you need to clarify your thinking to yourself and likely to others. Doing this well is mainly a process of asking and answering probing questions, such as the logic questions discussed earlier. Design your questions to fit your needs, but be sure to cover adequate ground. What is the purpose? What question are we trying to answer? What point of view is being expressed? What assumptions are we or others making? What are the facts and data we know, and how do we know them? What are the concepts we're working with? What are the conclusions, and do they make sense? What are the implications?

Cultivate "Habits of Mind"

"Habits of mind" are the personal commitments, values, and standards you have about the principle of good thinking. Consider your intellectual commitments, values, and standards. Do you approach problems with an open mind, a respect for truth, and an inquiring attitude? Some good habits to have when thinking critically are being receptive to having your opinions changed, having respect for others, being independent and not accepting something is true until you've had the time to examine the available evidence, being fair-minded, having respect for a reason, having an inquiring mind, not making assumptions, and always, especially, questioning your own conclusions—in other words, developing an intellectual work ethic. Try to work these qualities into your daily life.

"logic." *Wordnik*. n.d. Web. 16 Feb 2016. (https://www.wordnik.com/words/logic) ↵
"Student Success-Thinking Critically In Class and Online." *Critical Thinking Gateway*. St Petersburg
College, n.d. Web. 16 Feb 2016. ↵

Summary Writing

Process and Hints to Summary Writing

One major challenge with summary writing is deciding what to include and what to leave out. A bit of instruction on the process to follow, along with useful techniques, will have you writing expert summaries in no time.

Read the text for understanding, without editing. Make sure you understand the content, including major and minor sections, as well as the overlying message being conveyed. Look closely at topic sentences and key words repeated throughout.

Read through the material and cross out non-vital information. Underline what you believe to be the most important points, even if those points are words or phrases.

Write your summary in your own words. Follow both the organization of the original as well as its tone, though you need to make sure your own point of view is purely objective (reporting content of the text, only). Opinions should not appear in a summary. Any words or phrases from the original need to be properly documented and punctuated.

Your summary should be 15 to 20% the length of the original.

Be sure to go back when you've finished your summary and compare it to the original for accuracy.

Effective and Ineffective Summaries

Original Text

"For nearly 1,400 years Islam, though diverse in sectarian practice and ethnic tradition, has provided a unifying faith for peoples stretching from the Atlantic to the Indian Ocean and beyond. Starting in the 1500s, Western ascendancy, which culminated in colonization, eroded once glorious Muslim empires and reduced the influence of Islam. After the breakup of the Ottoman Empire following World War I and the decline of European colonial empires following World War II, Muslim nations adopted Western ideologies–communism, socialism, secular nationalism, and capitalism. Yet most Muslims remained poor and powerless. Their governments, secular regimes often backed by the West, were corrupt and repressive" (Belt 78).
Belt, Don. "The World of Islam." *National Geographic.* January 2002: 76-85. Print.

Poorly-Written Summary

Despite Western-style governments, Muslim countries are mired in deep poverty and radical governments. This despite the fact that the religion has existed for several centuries. European colonization ruined the Islamic religion for a long time. You would find it hard to imagine how many Muslims there really are out there.

Analysis

This summary:

- does not follow the order of information found in the original
- the phrase "several centuries" minimizes the historic significance of the religion

- sentence-level problems like "mired," "you would," and "out there" change the formal tone of the original to a biased, informal representation
- it is approximately half the length of the original, which is too long
- no credit is given to the original source

Well-Written Summary

For almost 1,500 years, Islam has united people globally. Western interference, through colonization and political ideologies, has not improved Muslims' lives (Belt 78).

Analysis

This summary:

- follows the order of the original
- maintains the original tone
- is approximately 20% of the original's length
- is properly documented and punctuated

Practice Summarizing

Try your hand at summarizing the following passages.

Practice Paragraph 1

"In 1925 the land aristocracy of Germany owned most of the large estates which occupied 20.2 per cent of the arable land of the country. They had 40 per cent of the land east of the Elbe River. All told, these large estates constituted but 0.4 per cent of the total number of landholdings in Germany. At the base of the pyramid were those who occupied small holdings: 59.4 per cent of the total holdings of Germany accounted for only 6.2 per cent of the arable land" (Lasswell 17).
Lasswell, Harold. *Politics: Who Gets What, When, How*. New York: Meridian Books, Inc. 1960. Print.

Practice Paragraph 2

"The Indian tribes of North and South America do not contain all the blood groups that are found in populations elsewhere. A fascinating glimpse into their ancestry is opened by this unexpected biological quirk. For the blood groups are inherited in such a way that, over a whole population, they provide some genetic record of the past. The total absence of blood group A from a population implies, with virtual certainty, that there was no blood group A in its ancestry; and similarly with blood group B. And this is in fact the state of affairs in America" (Bronowski 92).
Bronowski, J. *The Ascent of Man*. Boston: Little Brown and Company, 1973. Print.

Practice Paragraph 3

"A solenoid is an electrically energized coil that forms an electromagnet capable of performing mechanical functions. The term 'solenoid' is derived from the word 'sole' which in reference to electrical equipment means 'a part of,' or 'contained inside, or with, other electrical equipment.' The Greek word solenoides means

'Channel,' or 'shaped like a pipe.' A simple plunger-type solenoid consists of a coil of wire attached to an electrical source, and an iron rod, or plunger, that passes in and out of the coil along the axis of the spiral. A return spring holds the rod outside the coil when the current is deenergized, as shown in figure 1" (Lannon 432).

Lannon, John. *Technical Communication*. New York: Longman, 2000. Print.

College Reading: Understanding College Materials

Distinguishing Between Main Points and Sub-Claims

An effective argument contains a thesis, supporting claims, and evidence to support those claims. The thesis is the writer's central argument, or claim, and the supporting claims reinforce the validity of the thesis. When reading another writer's argument, it is important to be able to distinguish between main points and sub-claims; being able to recognize the difference between the two will prove incredibly useful when composing your own thesis-driven essays.

As you may know, a writer's thesis articulates the direction he or she will take with his or her argument. For example, let's say that my thesis is as follows: "smoking should be banned on campus because of its health and environmental repercussions." At least two things are clear from this statement: my central claim is that smoking should be banned on campus, and I will move from discussing the health impact of allowing smoking on campus to covering the environmental impact of allowing smoking on campus. These latter two ideas (the health and the environmental repercussions of allowing smoking on campus) are the author's **main points**, which function as support for the author's central claim (thesis), and they will likely comprise one or more body paragraphs of the writer's thesis-driven essay.

Let's take a look at the following diagram:

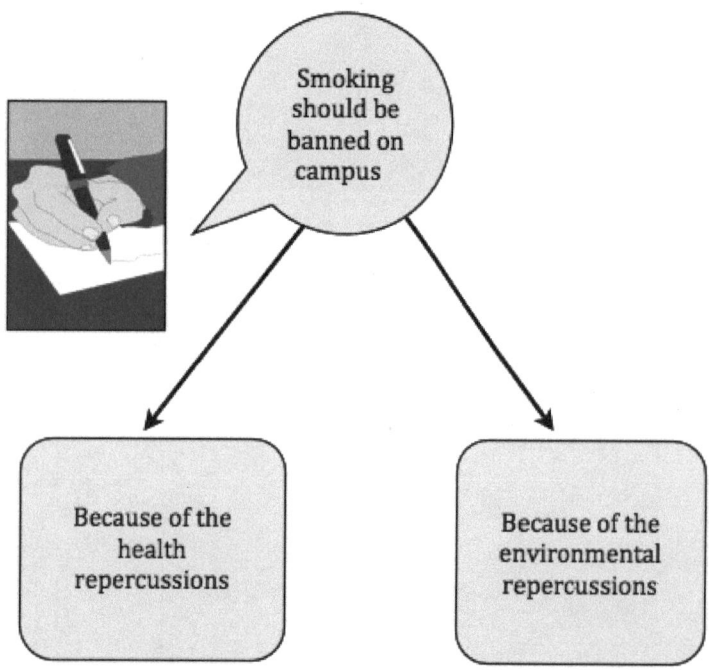

This diagram translates into the following organizational plan:

I argue that smoking should be banned on campus.
    Smoking should be banned on campus because of the health repercussions.
    Smoking should be banned on campus because of the environmental repercussions.

Points (A) and (B) will be explored in body paragraphs, will likely form the **topic sentences** of those body paragraphs, and will be supported by more claims specific to each point, or **sub-claims**. Let's return to the previous diagram and see what happens when we include sub-claims:

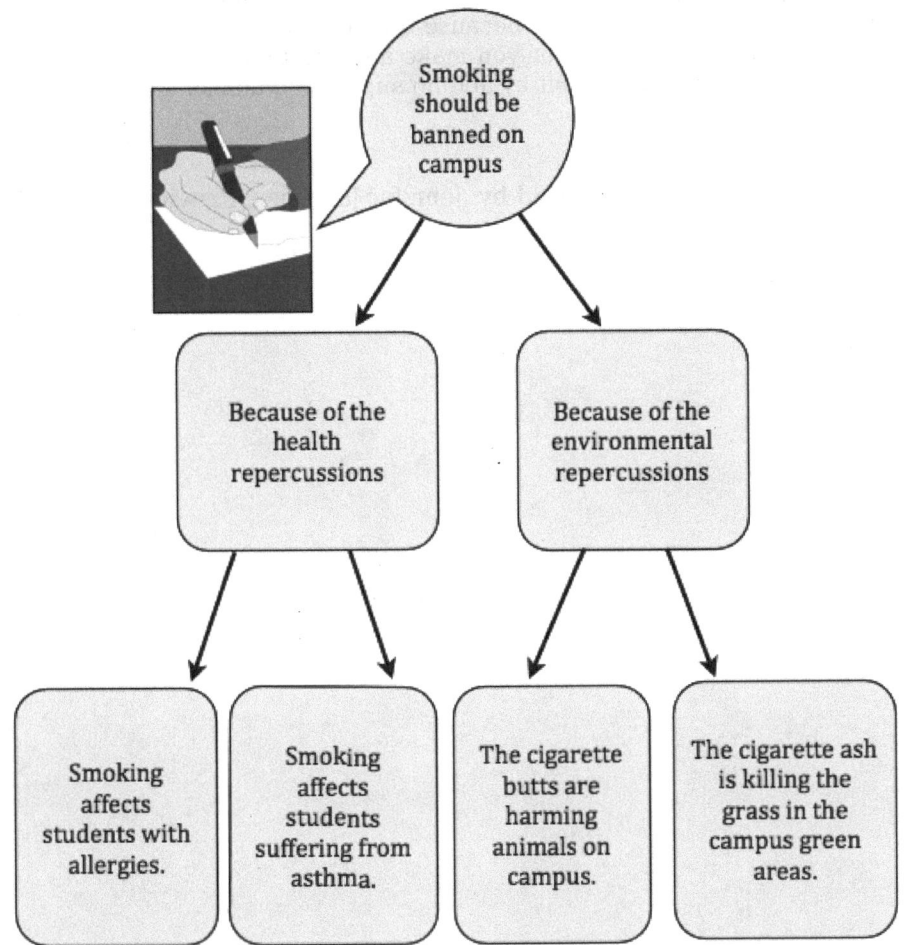

This diagram translates into the following organizational plan:

> I argue that smoking should be banned on campus.
>> Smoking should be banned on campus because of the health repercussions.
>>> Smoking affects students with allergies.
>>> Smoking affects students suffering from asthma.
>> Smoking should be banned on campus because of the environmental repercussions.
>>> The cigarette butts are harming animals on campus.
>>> The cigarette ash is killing the grass in the campus green areas.

Assertions (1) and (2) listed under each main point are the writer's sub-claims, statements that reinforce the validity of his or her main points. Think about it this way: every time a writer presents a claim, the reader likely asks, "What support do you have for that claim?" So, when the writer argues, "Smoking should be banned on campus," the reader asks, "What support do you have for that claim?" And the writer responds with, "Because I've found that there are health and environmental repercussions." Then, when the reader asks, "What support do you have for your claim that there are health and environmental repercussions to smoking on campus?" the writer can say, "Well, smoking negatively affects students suffering from asthma as well as those who have allergies, and the pollution caused by cigarettes is harming animals and killing the grass." Each major claim bolsters the writer's thesis, and each sub-claim bolsters one of the writer's major claims; additionally, the claims get increasingly specific as they move from main points to sub-claims.

Then, the writer includes evidence to support each sub-claim. For instance, if I assert that "smoking affects students with allergies," the reader would ask, "What support do you have for that claim?" And the writer might cite a poll taken on campus proving that students with allergies have suffered more when walking through smoky areas. To support the sub-claim that "smoking affects students suffering from asthma," the writer might cite a report released by Student Health Services connecting the increase of on-campus asthma attacks to on-campus smoking. Those studies function as evidence to support two of the author's sub-claims. Other evidence would be necessary to prove the validity of the writer's other sub-claims.

Whenever you, as a reader, come across an assertion in a thesis-driven text, ask yourself, "What support is the writer offering to back this claim?" You can then chart the points made by the writer by filling in the answers you locate when reading the text. If a point is missing, take note of that, because the point's absence might very well undermine the author's argument. Similarly, as a writer, whenever you make an assertion, ask yourself, "What support can I offer to back this claim?" Then bolster your argument by adding supporting claims and evidence as needed.

CC licensed content, Original

- Distinguishing Between Main Points and Sub-Claims. **Authored by**: Jennifer Janechek. **Provided by**: Writing Commons. **Located at**: https://writingcommons.org/distinguishing-between-main-points-and-sub-claims. **License**: *CC BY-NC-ND: Attribution-NonCommercial-NoDerivatives*

The Kinds of Support Authors Use

The Kinds of Support Authors Use

Writers are generally most successful with their audiences when they can skillfully and appropriately balance the three core types of appeals. These appeals are referred to by their Greek names: **logos** (the appeal to logic), **pathos** (the appeal to emotion), and **ethos** (the appeal to authority).

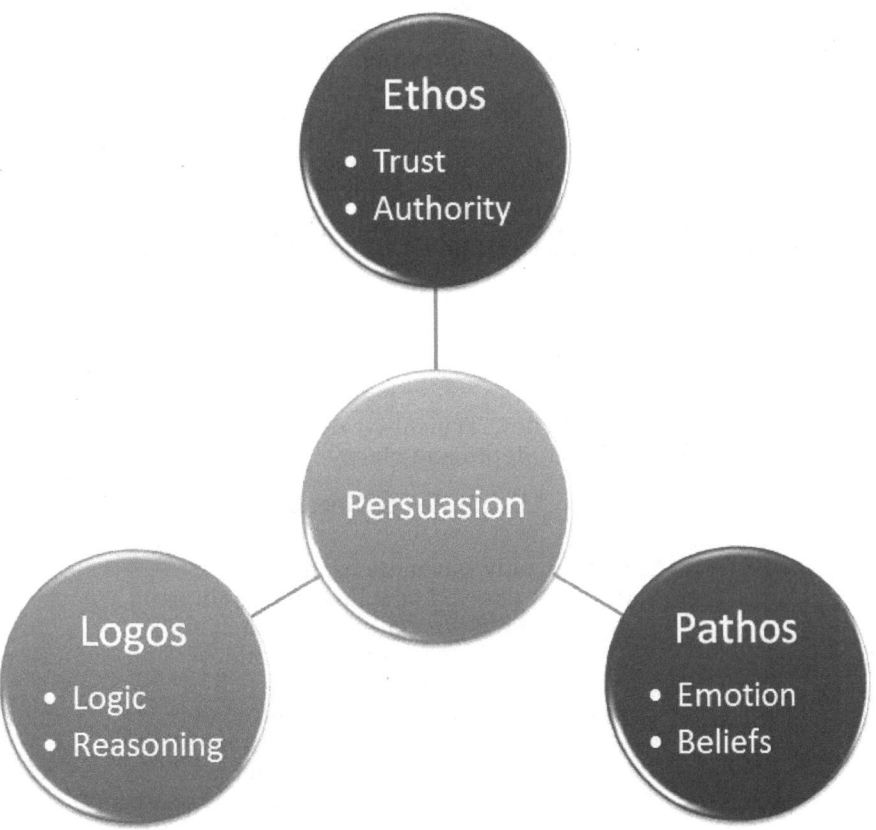

Logical Appeals

Authors using logic to support their claims will include a combination of different types of evidence. These include the following:

- established facts
- case studies
- statistics
- experiments

- analogies and logical reasoning
- citation of recognized experts on the issue

Authoritative Appeals

Authors using authority to support their claims can also draw from a variety of techniques. These include the following:

- personal anecdotes
- illustration of deep knowledge on the issue
- citation of recognized experts on the issue
- testimony of those involved first-hand on the issue

Emotional Appeals

Authors using emotion to support their claims again have a deep well of options to do so. These include the following:

- personal anecdotes
- narratives
- impact studies
- testimony of those involved first-hand on the issue

As you can see, there is some overlap on these lists. One technique might work on two or more different levels.

Most texts rely on one of the three as the primary method of support, but may also draw upon one or two others at the same time.

Using the STAR Method to Evaluate Appeals to Logic

Mapping or diagramming the arguments you read in a text may help you judge whether an appeal is adequately supported. Applying the STAR Criteria—**S**ufficiency, **T**ypicality, **A**ccuracy, and **R**elevance—is one such technique for assessing whether an argument has sufficient depth and clarity.

Measure	Question	Examples & Notes
Sufficiency	Is there *enough* evidence cited to support the conclusion?	Generally, only "strongly" and not "weakly" supported conclusions should be accepted. The more controversial a claim is, the more evidence authors should provide before expecting an audience to accept it. If the evidence is not sufficient, the author may need to modify or qualify the claim, by stating that something is true 'sometimes' rather than 'always'.
Typicality	Is the cited evidence typical or representative?	If an author makes a claim about a whole group but the evidence is based on a small or biased sample of that group, the evidence is not "typical." Similar problems stem from relying just on personal experiences (anecdotal evidence) and from "cherry picking" data by citing only the parts that support a conclusion while ignoring parts that might challenge it.

Accuracy	Is the cited evidence up to date and accurate?	Authors using polls, studies and statistics must ask whether the data were produced in a biased way and also ask whether the sample was large and representative of its target population so that results were outside the "margin of error." (**Margin of error**: If a sample is too small or not well chosen, results may be meaningless because they may represent random variation.)
Relevance	Is the cited evidence directly relevant to the claim(s) it is being used to support?	An author may supply lots of evidence, but the evidence may support something different from what the person is actually claiming. If the evidence is not relevant to the claim, the author may need to modify or qualify the claim—or even to acknowledge that the claim is indefensible.

Diagramming and Evaluating Arguments

Evaluate Unstated or Suppressed Premises As Well As Stated Ones

An unstated or suppressed premise is assumed rather than voiced outright, but is nevertheless needed for an argument to work. Consider this highly unscientific poll conducted by a TV news station. "Which do you believe

Senator Hillary Clinton is most out of touch with: illegal immigration, border security, or the American people?" The pollster is operating as if it is unquestionable that Clinton is out of touch with *something*. In other words, the question presupposes that she is "out of touch." However, this unstated premise is debatable once it is brought out into the open. Is she in fact out of touch at all?

A listener or reader who is not alert to such unstated or suppressed premises is, without realizing it, agreeing to debate on the communicator's terms—when those terms may be unfair. In fact, on more complex or serious issues it is often things people take for granted that may actually deserve the most critical scrutiny. For example, in the argument "This medication is labelled as totally natural, so it is safe for me to take it," the suppressed premise—that "natural" guarantees "safe"—is not trivial and can certainly be challenged.

Argument Diagramming

Besides recognizing the use of induction and deduction, you can use diagramming or outlining to develop an understanding of an argument's overall structure. Remember that an argument as defined here isn't a "quarrel," but rather a group of statements, some of which, the premises, are offered in support for another, the conclusion. So the first order of business in analyzing an argument is to recognize what the main claim is—the conclusion—and what other claims are being used to support it—the premises. This is much easier to do when the author is explicit about the steps in the argument, where premise and conclusion "indicator" terms appear in the text as signposts.

Words that introduce or signal an argument conclusion include *therefore, so, we may conclude/infer, thus*, and *consequently*. Words that introduce or signal argument premises include *it follows that, implies that, as a result, because* (non-causal meaning), *since, for the reason that, for, and*.[1]

When you are diagramming or outlining an argument, if the "flow" of an argument from premises to conclusion isn't readily apparent, then remember to use the above indicator terms to help you decide which claim is the conclusion and which claims are the premises. Using the indicator terms is particularly helpful because a conclusion may be stated first, last, or anywhere in between. People do all three when they write or talk in real life, so we cannot tell whether a statement is a conclusion simply by where it is positioned in the argument.

The Purpose Behind Diagramming an Argument

Diagramming or mapping someone else's argument serves a double purpose. First, the process helps you clearly see just what the other person is saying. It helps you identify the logical structure of the argument, which is necessary if you are to assess the strengths and weaknesses of the argument in order to know whether or not to accept it. Second, you develop skills of analysis that you will need in order to organize and present arguments in support of a position that *you* may want to take on some question or issue.

Steps in Diagramming an Argument

Here are the basic moves that are required in order to create a clear diagram or outline of an argument.

Identify all the claims made by the author. Since a sentence can contain multiple claims, rewrite statements so that you have one claim per sentence. Adopt some sort of numbering or labeling system for the claims. Eliminate "fluff." Ignore repetitions, assurances (assertions not backed by evidence or reasons), and information that is unrelated to the argument.

Identify which statements are premises and which statement is the main conclusion.

Recognize that there may be sub-conclusions in addition to a final or main conclusion. You may think of a sub-conclusion as the end point of a sub-argument nested inside the larger argument. Although the sub-conclusion is itself the conclusion of a nested argument, supported by premises, it also functions as a premise supporting the final or main conclusion.

Recognize that some premises are independent and others linked. If you were drawing or mapping the argument, you would be able to draw an arrow from an independent premise directly to the conclusion it supports. Linked premises, however, are multiple statements that must be combined to provide support for a conclusion. If you were drawing or mapping the argument, you would have to find some way to show that the linked premises as a group support the conclusion. You might use color coding, or underlining, or circling, or + signs—some way to connect the linked premises before drawing *one* arrow from the clustered premises to the conclusion they support.

Using the Argument's Paragraphing to Evaluate the Premises

An author must organize her material to guide the audience through her argument. One tool available to an author is the paragraph. The sentences clustered together in a paragraph should be tightly connected in terms of content. In the most common form of paragraph, the clustered sentences collectively develop an idea explicitly stated in a topic sentence. The paragraphs themselves should be placed in an order that reflects some overall plan so that the paragraphs reveal the steps or stages of the argument.

The premises may be said to be key steps or stages in the argument. A well-constructed argument therefore may use each premise as a topic sentence for a paragraph. Additionally, a premise may serve as the guiding idea for a group of paragraphs, each developing a subtopic. For example, the premise, reached by induction, that "College students overestimate the amount of binge drinking that is taking place" might introduce a cluster of three paragraphs, each showing that the overestimation varies by subgroup—with member of sororities, member of fraternities, and non-Greek populations arriving at different estimates.

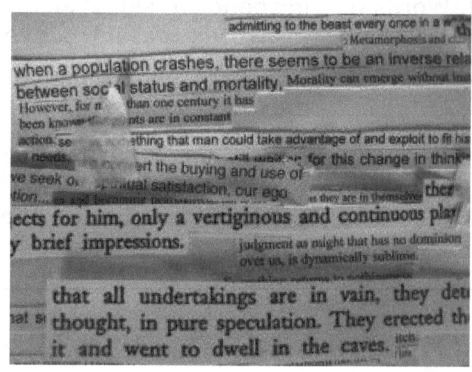

Look to see whether the author has used paragraphing-by-premise to organize her argument and outline its structure for the audience. You should also ask yourself whether any paragraphs are missing. That is, as you consider what premises serve as the foundations of the argument, be alert for the suppressed ones, the premises that the author presupposes. These unacknowledged premises may be ones that the author hopes the audience will not notice or question. In your analysis call her on it by determining where a paragraph on that premise should have appeared in the argument.

The Similarity Between Conclusions and Thesis Statements

When we talk about a paper, we usually talk about the paper's main claim as being its thesis statement. But of course a paper that just makes a claim or states an opinion but offers no supporting reasons or arguments isn't much of a paper. We would be bothered by reading an editorial in which someone stated a strong opinion on some public issue yet did nothing to justify that opinion.

When an author supports a thesis with reasons, then the thesis statement can be described as the conclusion of an argument, with the supporting reasons being that argument's premises. The argument now has a structure that can be outlined or diagrammed.

---

and often signals the introduction of a further premise, as in "You should believe Z *because* reason 1 *and* reason 2." ↵

College Reading: Understanding Rhetorical Strategies

Rhetorical Modes

We've been focusing on broad categories of reading materials so far: literature, journalism, textbooks, and academic writing. Since most of the reading (and writing!) you'll do throughout your college career falls into the "academic writing" category, this is a good point to slow down and examine the building blocks of academic writing more closely.

Rhetoric is the study of writing, and the basic types of academic writing are referred to as **rhetorical modes**.

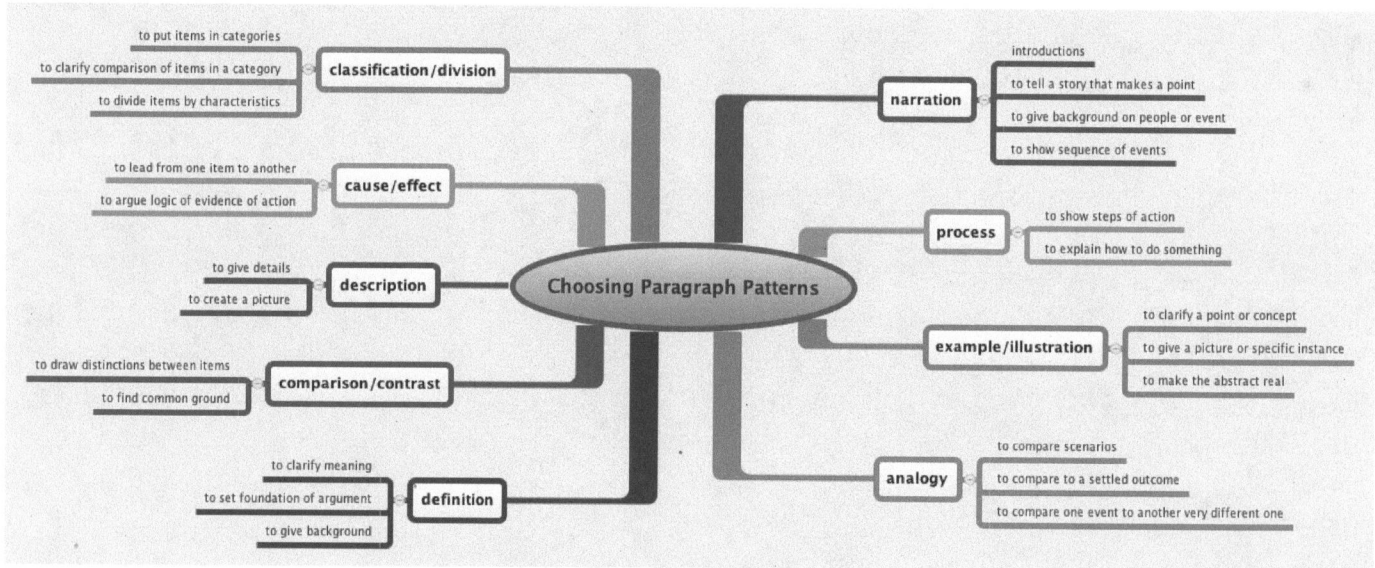

As you can see in the chart above, different styles of non-fiction writing serve different purposes. It's quite possible that a single text—or even a single paragraph—will contain multiple rhetorical modes, each used to serve a distinct purpose in support of the article's thesis.

Consider nine of the most common types of rhetorical modes. What might lead an author to select one type of writing over another? How might each be used differently to serve the purpose of a text?

Narration

The purpose of **narration** is to tell a story or relate an event. Narration is an especially useful tool for sequencing or putting details and information into some kind of logical order, usually chronological.

Literature uses narration heavily, but it also can be useful in non-fiction, academic writing for strong impact.

Description

The purpose of description is to recreate, invent, or visually present a person, place, event, or action so that the reader can picture that which is being described. It is heavily based on **sensory details**: what we experience through our five senses.

Example

It's common to see examples used in all kinds of situations—an idea can be considered too general or abstract until we see it in action. An **exemplification essay** extends this idea even further: it carries one or more examples into great detail, in order to show the details of a complex problem in a way that's easy for readers to understand.

Definition

In the vocabulary section we talked about word definitions in depth. A **definition essay** takes the concept of "definition" more broadly, moving beyond a dictionary definition to deeply examine a word or concept as we actually use and understand it.

Process Analysis

Analyzing a process can also be thought of as "how-to" instruction. Technical writing includes a lot of process analysis, for instance. Academic writing can incorporate process analysis to show how an existing problem came to be, or how it might be solved, by following a clear series of steps.

Division/Classification

Classification takes one large concept, and divides it into individual pieces. A nice result from this type of writing is that it helps the reader to understand a complex topic by focusing on its smaller parts. This is particularly useful when an author has a unique way of dividing up the concepts, to provide new insight into the ways it might be viewed.

Comparison/Contrast

Comparison focuses on **similarities** between things, and contrast focuses on their **differences**. We innately make comparisons all the time, and they appear in many kinds of writings. The goal of comparison and contrast in academic essays is generally to show that one item is superior to another, based on a set of evaluations included as part of the writing.

Cause/Effect

If narration offers a sequence of events, cause/effect essays offer an explanation about why that sequence matters. Cause/effect writing is particularly powerful when the author can provide a cause/effect relationship that the reader wasn't expecting, and as a result see the situation in a new light.

Problem/Solution

This type of academic writing has two equally important tasks: clearly identifying a problem, and then providing a logical, practical solution for that problem. Establishing that a particular situation IS a problem can sometimes be a challenge–many readers might assume that a given situation is "just the way it is," for instance.
CC licensed content, Shared previously

Evaluating Appeals to Ethos, Logos, and Pathos

Introduction

As a reader and a listener, it is fundamental that you be able to recognize how writers and speakers depend upon **ethos**, **logos**, and **pathos** in their efforts to communicate. As a communicator yourself, you will benefit from being able to see how others rely upon ethos, logos, and pathos so that you can apply what you learn from your observations to your own speaking and writing.

Evaluate an Appeal to Ethos

When you evaluate an appeal to **ethos**, you examine how successfully a speaker or writer establishes authority or credibility with her intended audience. You are asking yourself what elements of the essay or speech would cause an audience to feel that the author is (or is not) trustworthy and credible.

A good speaker or writer leads the audience to feel comfortable with her knowledge of a topic. The audience sees her as someone worth listening to—a clear or insightful thinker, or at least someone who is well-informed and genuinely interested in the topic.

Some of the questions you can ask yourself as you evaluate an author's ethos may include the following:

- Has the writer or speaker cited her sources or in some way made it possible for the audience to access further information on the issue?
- Does she demonstrate familiarity with different opinions and perspectives?
- Does she provide complete and accurate information about the issue?
- Does she use the evidence fairly? Does she avoid selective use of evidence or other types of manipulation of data?
- Does she speak respectfully about people who may have opinions and perspectives different from her own?
- Does she use unbiased language?
- Does she avoid excessive reliance on emotional appeals?
- Does she accurately convey the positions of people with whom she disagrees?
- Does she acknowledge that an issue may be complex or multifaceted?
- Does her education or experience give her credibility as someone who should be listened to on this issue?

Some of the above questions may strike you as relevant to an evaluation of logos as well as ethos—questions about the completeness and accuracy of information and whether it is used fairly. In fact, illogical thinking and the misuse of evidence may lead an audience to draw conclusions not only about the person making the argument but also about the logic of an argument.

Recognizing a Manipulative Appeal to Ethos

In a perfect world, everyone would tell the truth and we could depend upon the credibility of speakers and authors. Unfortunately, that is not always the case. You would expect that news reporters would be objective and tell new stories based upon the facts. Janet Cooke, Stephen Glass, Jayson Blair, and Brian Williams all lost their jobs for plagiarizing or fabricated part of their news stories. Janet Cooke's Pulitzer Prize was revoked after it was discovered that she made up "Jimmy," an eight-year old heroin addict (Prince, 2010). Brian Williams was fired as anchor of the NBC Nightly News for exaggerating his role in the Iraq War.

Others have become infamous for claiming academic degrees that they didn't earn as in the case of Marilee Jones. At the time of discovery, she was Dean of Admissions at Massachusetts Institute of Technology (MIT). After 28 years of employment, it was determined that she never graduated from college (Lewin, 2007). However, on her website (http://www.marileejones.com) she is still promoting herself as "a sought after speaker, consultant and author" (para. 1) and "one of the nation's most experienced College Admissions Deans" (para. 2).

Beyond lying about their own credentials, authors may employ a number of tricks or fallacies to lure you to their point of view. Some of the more common techniques are described below. Others may be found in the appendix. When you recognize these fallacies being committed you should question the credibility of the speaker and the legitimacy of the argument. If you use these when making your own arguments, be aware that they may undermine or destroy your credibility.

Fallacies That Misuse Appeals to Ethos

Ad hominem: attacking the person making an argument rather than the argument itself.
> Example: "Of course that doctor advocates vaccination—he probably owns stock in a pharmaceutical company."

False authority: relying on claims of expertise when the claimed expert (a) lacks adequate background/credentials in the relevant field, (b) departs in major ways from the consensus in the field, or (c) is biased, e.g., has a financial stake in the outcome.
> Example: "Dr. X is an engineer, and *he* doesn't believe in global warming."

Guilt by association: linking the person making an argument to an unpopular person or group.
> Example: "My opponent is a card-carrying member of the ACLU."

Poisoning the well: undermining an opponent's credibility before he or she gets a chance to speak.
> Example: "The prosecution is going to bring up a series or so-called experts who are getting a lot of money to testify here today."

Transfer fallacy: associating the argument with someone or something popular or respected; hoping that the positive associations will "rub off" onto the argument.
> Examples: In politics, decorating a stage with red, white, and blue flags and bunting; in advertising, using pleasant or wholesome settings as the backdrop for print or video ads.

Name-calling: labeling an opponent with words that have negative connotations in an effort to undermine the opponent's credibility.
> Example: "These rabble-rousers are nothing but feminazis."

Plain folk: presenting yourself as (or associating your position with) ordinary people with whom you hope your audience will identify; arguers imply that they or their supporters are trustworthy because they are 'common people' rather than members of the elite.
> Example: "Who would you vote for—someone raised in a working-class neighborhood who has the support of Joe the Plumber or some elitist whose daddy sent him to a fancy school?"

Testimonial fallacy: inserting an endorsement of the argument by someone who is popular or respected but who lacks expertise or authority in the area under discussion.
> Example: "I'm not a doctor, but I play one on TV"—a famous example of a celebrity endorsement for a cough syrup (Deis, 2011, n.p.).

The most general structure of this argument runs something like the following: Person A claims that Person A is a respected scientist or other authority; therefore, the claim they make is true.

Evaluate an Appeal to Logos

When you evaluate an appeal to **logos**, you consider how logical the argument is and how well-supported it is in terms of evidence. You are asking yourself what elements of the essay or speech would cause an audience to believe that the argument is (or is not) logical and supported by appropriate evidence.

To evaluate whether the evidence is appropriate, apply the **STAR** criteria: how **S**ufficient, **T**ypical, **A**ccurate, and **R**elevant is the evidence?

Recognizing a Manipulative Appeal to Logos

Diagramming the argument can help you determine if an appeal to logos is manipulative. Are the premises true? Does the conclusion follow logically from the premises? Is there sufficient, typical, accurate, and relevant evidence to support inductive reasoning? Is the speaker or author attempting to divert your attention from the real issues? These are some of the elements you might consider while evaluating an argument for the use of logos.

Pay particular attention to numbers, statistics, findings, and quotes used to support an argument. Be critical of the source and do your own investigation of the "facts." Maybe you've heard or read that half of all marriages in America will end in divorce. It is so often discussed that we assume it must be true. Careful research will show that the original marriage study was flawed, and divorce rates in America have steadily declined since 1985 (Peck, 1993). If there is no scientific evidence, why do we continue to believe it? Part of the reason might be that it supports our idea of the dissolution of the American family.

Fallacies that misuse appeals to logos or attempt to manipulate the logic of an argument are discussed below. Other fallacies of logos may be found in the appendix.

Fallacies That Misuse Appeals to Logos

Hasty generalization: jumping to conclusions based upon an unrepresentative sample or insufficient evidence.
> Example: "10 of the last 14 National Spelling Bee Champions have been Indian American. Indian Americans must all be great spellers!"

Appeal to ignorance—true believer's form: arguing along the lines that if an opponent can't prove something *isn't* the case, then it is reasonable to believe that it *is* the case; transfers the burden of proof away from the person making the claim (the proponent).
> Example: "You can't prove that extraterrestrials *haven't* visited earth, so it is reasonable to believe that they *have* visited earth."

Appeal to ignorance—skeptic's form: confusing absence of evidence with evidence of absence; assumes that if you cannot *now* prove something exists, then it is shown that it doesn't exist.
> Example: "There's no proof that starting classes later in the day will improve the performance of our high school students; therefore, this change in schedule will not work."

Begging the question: circular argument because the premise is the same as the claim that you are trying to prove.
> Example: "This legislation is sinful because it is the wrong thing to do."

False dilemma: misuse of the either/or argument; presenting only two options when other choices exist
> Example: "Either we pass this ordinance or there will be rioting in the streets."

Post hoc ergo propter hoc: Latin phrase meaning "after this, therefore because of this"; confuses correlation with causation by concluding that an event preceding a second event must be the cause of that second event.
> Example: "My child was diagnosed with autism after receiving vaccinations. That is proof that vaccines are to blame."

Non-sequitur: Latin for "does not follow"; the conclusion cannot be inferred from the premises because there is a break in the logical connection between a claim and the premises that are meant to support it, either because a premise is untrue (or missing) or because the relationship between premises does not support the deduction stated in the claim.
> Example (untrue premise):"If she is a Radford student, she is a member of a sorority. She is a Radford student. Therefore she is a member of a sorority."

Smoke screen: avoiding the real issue or a tough question by introducing an unrelated topic as a distraction; sometimes called a **red herring**.
> Example: "My opponent says I am weak on crime, but I have been one of the most reliable participants in city council meetings."

Straw man: pretending to criticize an opponent's position but actually misrepresenting his or her view as simpler and/or more extreme than it is and therefore easier to refute than the original or actual position; unfairly undermines credibility of *claim* if not *source* of claim.
> Example: "Senator Smith says we should cut back the Defense budget. His position is that we should let down our defenses and just trust our enemies not to attack us!"

The red herring is as much a debate tactic as it is a logical fallacy. It is a fallacy of distraction, and is committed when a listener attempts to divert an arguer from his argument by introducing another topic. This can be one of the most frustrating, and effective, fallacies to observe. The fallacy gets its name from fox hunting, specifically from the practice of using smoked herrings, which are red, to distract hounds from the scent of their quarry. Just as a hound may be prevented from catching a fox by distracting it with a red herring, so an arguer may be prevented from proving his point by distracting him with a tangential issue.

Evaluate an Appeal to Pathos

People may be uninterested in an issue unless they can find a personal connection to it, so a communicator may try to connect to her audience by evoking emotions or by suggesting that author and audience share attitudes, beliefs, and values—in other words, by making an appeal to **pathos**. Even in formal writing, such as academic books or journals, an author often will try to present an issue in such a way as to connect to the feelings or attitudes of his audience.

When you evaluate pathos, you are asking whether a speech or essay arouses the audience's interest and sympathy. You are looking for the elements of the essay or speech that might cause the audience to feel (or not feel) an emotional connection to the content.

An author may use an audience's attitudes, beliefs, or values as a kind of foundation for his argument—a layer that the writer knows is already in place at the outset of the argument. So one of the questions you can ask yourself as you evaluate an author's use of pathos is whether there are points at which the writer or speaker makes statements assuming that the audience shares his feelings or attitudes. For example, in an argument about the First Amendment, does the author write as if he takes it for granted that his audience is religious?

Recognizing a Manipulative Appeal to Pathos

Up to a certain point, an **appeal to pathos** can be a legitimate part of an argument. For example, a writer or speaker may begin with an anecdote showing the effect of a law on an individual. This anecdote will be a means of gaining an audience's attention for an argument in which she uses evidence and reason to present her full case as to why the law should/should not be repealed or amended. In such a context, engaging the emotions, values, or beliefs of the audience is a legitimate tool whose effective use should lead you to give the author high marks.

An appropriate appeal to **pathos** is different than trying to unfairly play upon the audience's feelings and emotions through fallacious, misleading, or excessively emotional appeals. Such a **manipulative** use of pathos may alienate the audience or cause them to "tune out". An example would be the American Society for the Prevention of Cruelty to Animals (ASPCA) commercials featuring the song *In the Arms on an Angel* and footage of abused animals. Even Sarah McLachlan, the singer and spokesperson featured in the commercials admits that she changes the channel because they are too depressing (Brekke, 2014).

Even if an appeal to pathos is not manipulative, such an appeal should complement rather than replace reason and evidence-based argument. In addition to making use of pathos, the author must establish her credibility (**ethos**) and must supply reasons and evidence (**logos**) in support of her position. An author who essentially replaces logos and ethos with pathos alone should be given low marks.

See below for the most common fallacies that misuse appeals to pathos.

Fallacies That Misuse Appeals to Pathos

Appeal to fear: using scare tactics; emphasizing threats or exaggerating possible dangers.
　　Example: "Without this additional insurance, you could find yourself broke and homeless."
Appeal to guilt and **appeal to pity**: trying to evoke an emotional reaction that will cause the audience to behave sympathetically even if it means disregarding the issue at hand.
　　Example: "I know I missed assignments, but if you fail me, I will lose my financial aid and have to drop out."
Appeal to popularity (bandwagon): urging audience to follow a course of action because "everyone does it."
　　Example: "Nine out of ten shoppers have switched to Blindingly-Bright-Smile Toothpaste."
Slippery Slope: making an unsupported or inadequately supported claim that "One thing inevitably leads to another." This may be considered a fallacy of logos as well as pathos but is placed in this section because it often is used to evoke the emotion of fear.
　　Example: "We can't legalize marijuana; if we do, then the next thing you know people will be strung out on heroin."
Appeal to the people: also called **stirring symbols** fallacy; the communicator distracts the readers or listeners with symbols that are very meaningful to them, with strong associations or connotations.
　　Example: This fallacy is referred to in the sentence "That politician always wraps himself in the flag."
Appeal to tradition: people have been done it a certain way for a long time; assumes that what has been customary in past is correct and proper.
　　Example: "A boy always serves as student-body president; a girl always serves as secretary."
Loaded-Language and other emotionally charged uses of language: using slanted or biased language, including God terms, devil terms, euphemisms, and dysphemisms.
　　Example: In the sentence "Cutting access to food stamps would encourage personal responsibility," the god term is "personal responsibility." It might seem as if it would be hard to argue against "personal responsibility" or related god terms such as "independence" and "self-reliance." However, it would require a definition of "personal responsibility," combined with evidence from studies of people's behavior in the face of food stamp or other benefit reductions, to argue that cutting access to food stamps would lead to the intended results.

Here is an example of a common logical fallacy known as the ad hominem argument, which is Latin for "argument against the person" or "argument toward the person." Basically, an ad hominem argument goes like this: Person 1 makes claim X. There is something objectionable about Person 1. Therefore claim X is false.

Conclusion

Fallacies can crop up whenever definitions, inferences, and facts are at issue. Once we become familiar with fallacies we may start to see them everywhere. That can be good and bad. Since persuasion is ever-present, it is good to be on guard against various hidden persuaders. But whether a persuasive strategy is considered fallacious may be dependent on context. Editorials and advertisements—both political and commercial—frequently use such strategies as transfer and appeals to popularity. We need to be critically aware of the techniques of persuasion being used on us, but since we *expect* advertisements, political speeches, and editorials on public policy or ethical issues to try to sway us emotionally, perhaps only extreme examples deserve to be judged harshly for being fallacious.

In addition, something that looks as if it is a fallacy may turn out not to be on closer examination. For example, not everything that smacks of slippery slope is fallacious. There are indeed some *genuine* slippery slopes, where an initial decision or action may have both great and inevitable repercussions. So whether that fallacy has been committed depends upon what the author has done (or failed to do) to support his claim. Similarly, while personal attacks (*ad hominem*) in most cases are unfair and considered fallacious, there are special situations in which a person's character may be directly relevant to his or her qualifications. For example, when somebody is running for political office or for a judgeship, casting doubt on his or her character may be appropriate—*if* one has facts to back it up—since it relates to job expectations. But wholesale character assassination remains a rhetorical ploy of the propagandist or demagogue.

Public domain content

- The Logical Structure of Arguments. **Provided by**: Radford University. **Located at**: http://lcubbison.pressbooks.com/chapter/core-201-analyzing-arguments/. **Project**: Core Curriculum Handbook. **License**: *Public Domain: No Known Copyright*

Logical Fallacies

Defining Fallacy

Fallacies are errors or tricks of reasoning. We call a fallacy an *error* of reasoning if it occurs accidentally; we call it a *trick* of reasoning if a speaker or writer uses it in order to deceive or manipulate his audience. Fallacies can be either **formal** or **informal**.

Whether a fallacy is an error or a trick, whether it is formal or informal, its use undercuts the validity and soundness of any argument. At the same time, fallacious reasoning can damage the credibility of the speaker/writer and improperly manipulate the emotions of the audience/reader.

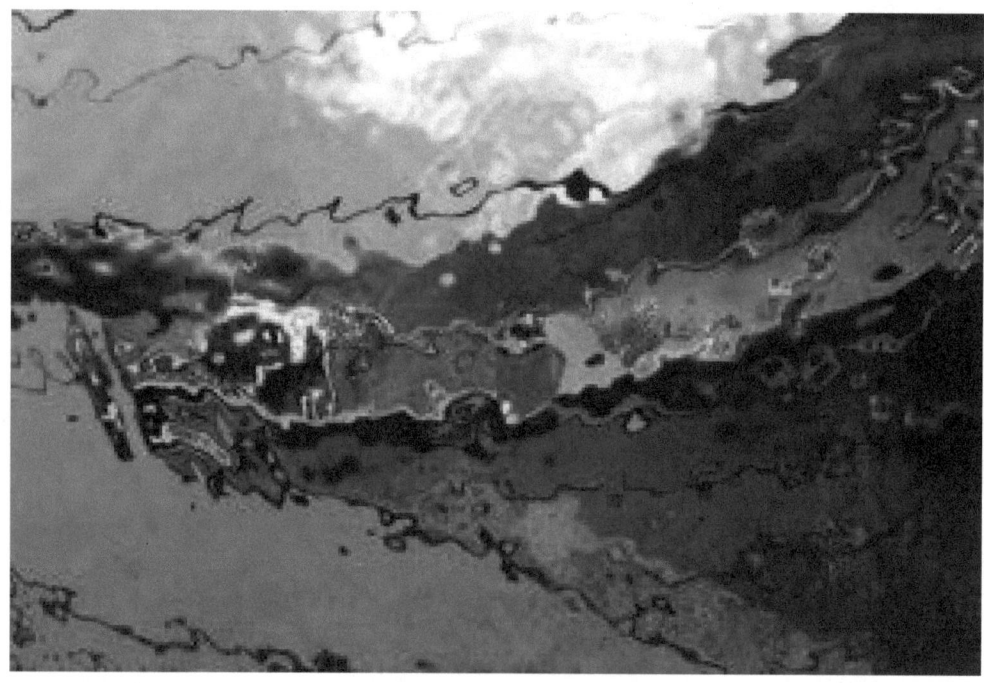

Formal Fallacies

Most **formal fallacies** are errors of logic: the conclusion doesn't really "follow from" (is not supported by) the premises. Either the premises are untrue or the argument is invalid. Below is an example of an invalid deductive argument.

> **Premise**: All black bears are omnivores.
>
> **Premise**: All raccoons are omnivores.
>
> **Conclusion**: All raccoons are black bears.

Bears are a subset of omnivores. Raccoons also are a subset of omnivores. But these two subsets do not overlap, and that fact makes the conclusion illogical. The argument is invalid—that is, the relationship between the premises doesn't support the conclusion.

Recognizing Formal Fallacies

"Raccoons are black bears" is instantaneously recognizable as fallacious and may seem too silly to be worth bothering about. However, that and other forms of poor logic play out on a daily basis, and they have real world consequences. Below is an example of a fallacious argument:

Premise: All Arabs are Muslims.

Premise: All Iranians are Muslims.

Conclusion: All Iranians are Arabs.

This argument fails on two levels. First, the premises are untrue because although many Arabs and Iranians are Muslim, not all are. Second, the two ethnic groups are sets that do not overlap; nevertheless, the two groups are confounded because they (largely) share one quality in common. One only has to look at comments on the web to realize that the confusion is widespread and that it influences attitudes and opinions about U.S. foreign policy.

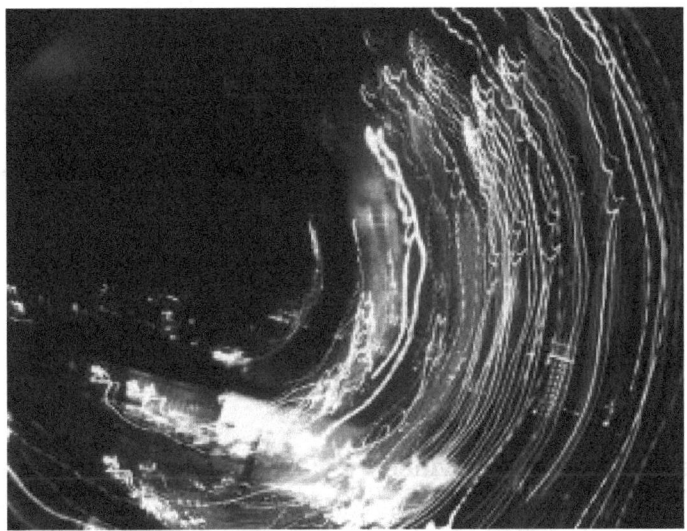

Informal Fallacies

Informal fallacies take many forms and are widespread in everyday discourse. Very often they involve bringing irrelevant information into an argument or they are based on assumptions that, when examined, prove to be incorrect. Formal fallacies are created when the relationship between premises and conclusion does not hold up or when premises are unsound; informal fallacies are more dependent on misuse of language and of evidence.

It is easy to find fairly well-accepted lists of informal fallacies, but that does not mean that it is always easy to spot them. Some moves are always fallacious; others may be allowable given the context.

Using Ethos, Logos, and Pathos to Test Arguments for Fallacies

One way to go about evaluating an argument for fallacies is to return to the concept of the three fundamental appeals: **ethos**, **logos**, and **pathos**.

As a quick reminder,

Fallacies of ethos relate to credibility. These fallacies may unfairly build up the credibility of the author (or his allies) or unfairly attack the credibility of the author's opponent (or her allies). Some fallacies give an unfair advantage to the claims of the speaker or writer or an unfair disadvantage to his opponent's claims. These are **fallacies of logos**. **Fallacies of pathos** rely excessively upon emotional appeals, attaching positive associations to the author's argument and negative ones to his opponent's position.

Conclusion

Both formal and informal fallacies are errors of reasoning, and if a speaker or writer relies on such fallacies, even unintentionally, she undercuts her argument. For example, if someone defines a key term in her argument in an ambiguous, vague, or circular way, her argument will appear very weak to a critical audience.

In addition, when listeners or readers spot questionable reasoning or unfair attempts at audience manipulation, more than their evaluation of the author's argument (*logos*) may be compromised. Their evaluation of the credibility of the speaker (*ethos*), and perhaps their ability to connect with that speaker on the level of shared values (*pathos*), also may be compromised. At the very least, the presence of fallacies will suggest to an audience that the speaker or writer lacks argumentative skill.

- **Ethos** is an argument that appeals to ethics, authority, and/or credibility
- **Logos** is an argument that appeals to logic
- **Pathos** is an argument that appeals to emotion

Once you have refreshed your memory of the basics, you may begin to understand how ethos, logos, and pathos can be used appropriately to strengthen your argument or inappropriately to manipulate an audience through the use of fallacies. Classifying fallacies as fallacies of ethos, logos, or pathos will help you both to understand their nature and to recognize them when you encounter them. Please keep in mind, however, that some fallacies may fit into multiple categories.

Inductive and Deductive Reasoning

Two Ways of Understanding

We have two basic approaches for how we come to believe something is true.

The first way is that we are exposed to several different examples of a situation, and from those examples, we conclude a general truth. For instance, you visit your local grocery store daily to pick up necessary items. You notice that on Friday, two weeks ago, all the clerks in the store were wearing football jerseys. Again, last Friday, the clerks wore their football jerseys. Today, also a Friday, they're wearing them again. From just these observations, you can conclude that on **all** Fridays, these supermarket employees will wear football jerseys to support their local team.

This type of pattern recognition, leading to a conclusion, is known as **inductive reasoning**.

Knowledge can also move the opposite direction. Say that you read in the news about a tradition in a local grocery store, where employees wore football jerseys on Fridays to support the home team. This time, you're starting from the overall rule, and you would expect individual evidence to support this rule. Each time you visited the store on a Friday, you would expect the employees to wear jerseys.

Such a case, of starting with the overall statement and then identifying examples that support it, is known as **deductive reasoning**.

deductive
reasoning

General
Principle

Special
Case

inductive
reasoning

The Power of Inductive Reasoning

You have been employing **inductive reasoning** for a very long time. Inductive reasoning is based on your ability to recognize meaningful patterns and connections. By taking into account both examples and your understanding of how the world works, induction allows you to conclude that something is likely to be true. By using induction, you move from specific data to a generalization that tries to capture what the data "mean."

Imagine that you ate a dish of strawberries and soon afterward your lips swelled. Now imagine that a few weeks later you ate strawberries and soon afterwards your lips again became swollen. The following month, you ate yet another dish of strawberries, and you had the same reaction as formerly. You are aware that swollen lips can be a sign of an allergy to strawberries. Using induction, you conclude that, more likely than not, you are allergic to strawberries.

   Data: After I ate strawberries, my lips swelled (1st time).

   Data: After I ate strawberries, my lips swelled (2nd time).

   Data: After I ate strawberries, my lips swelled (3rd time).

   Additional Information: Swollen lips after eating strawberries may be a sign of an allergy.

   Conclusion: Likely I am allergic to strawberries.

Inductive reasoning can never lead to absolute certainty. Instead, induction allows you to say that, given the examples provided for support, the claim more likely than not is true. Because of the limitations of inductive reasoning, a conclusion will be more credible if multiple lines of reasoning are presented in its support.

The results of inductive thinking can be skewed if relevant data are overlooked. In the previous example, inductive reasoning was used to conclude that I am likely allergic to strawberries after suffering multiple instances of my lips swelling. Would I be as confident in my conclusion if I were eating strawberry shortcake on each of those occasions? Is it reasonable to assume that the allergic reaction might be due to another ingredient besides strawberries?

This example illustrates that inductive reasoning must be used with care. When evaluating an inductive argument, consider

- the amount of the data,
- the quality of the data,
- the existence of additional data,
- the relevance of necessary additional information, and
- the existence of additional possible explanations.

The Power of Deductive Reasoning

Deductive reasoning is built on two statements whose logical relationship should lead to a third statement that is an unquestionably correct conclusion, as in the following example.

All raccoons are omnivores.
This animal is a raccoon.
This animal is an omnivore.

If the first statement is true (All raccoons are omnivores) and the second statement is true (This animal is a raccoon), then the conclusion (This animal is an omnivore) is unavoidable. If a group must have a certain quality, and an individual is a member of that group, then the individual must have that quality.

Going back to the example from the opening of this page, we could frame it this way:

Grocery store employees wear football jerseys on Fridays.
Today is Friday.
Grocery store employees will be wearing football jerseys today.

Unlike inductive reasoning, deductive reasoning allows for certainty as long as certain rules are followed.

Evaluating the Truth of a Premise

A formal argument may be set up so that, on its face, it looks logical. However, no matter how well-constructed the argument is, the additional information required must be true. Otherwise any inferences based on that additional information will be invalid.

Inductive reasoning can often be hidden inside a deductive argument. That is, a generalization reached through inductive reasoning can be turned around and used as a starting "truth" a deductive argument. For instance,

Most Labrador retrievers are friendly.
Kimber is a Labrador retriever.
Therefore, Kimber is friendly.

In this case we cannot know for certain that Kimber is a friendly Labrador retriever. The structure of the argument may look logical, but it is based on observations and generalizations rather than indisputable facts.

Methods to Evaluate the Truth of a Premise

One way to test the accuracy of a premise is to apply the same questions asked of inductive arguments. As a recap, you should consider

- the amount of the data,
- the quality of the data,
- the existence of additional data,
- the relevance of the additional data, and
- the existence of additional possible explanations.

Determine whether the starting claim is based upon a sample that is both representative and sufficiently large, and ask yourself whether all relevant factors have been taken into account in the analysis of data that leads to a generalization.

Another way to evaluate a premise is to determine whether its source is credible.

- Are the authors identified?
- What is their background?
- Was the claim something you found on an undocumented website?
- Did you find it in a popular publication or a scholarly one?
- How complete, how recent, and how relevant were the studies or statistics discussed in the source?

Identifying a Conversation

An important part of research writing (and many other kinds of writing) is identifying when sources are "speaking" to each other. When researching a particular topic, you will likely collect many sources that seem to discuss the same thing. Sometimes the authors of these sources will explicitly know about each other and reference one another in their own texts. This is common in academic writing, where explicit conversations between different scholars are expected and valued. A long works cited page in an academic article might indicate that the author is having a long conversation with many other authors of other sources, some of whom might not still be publishing. For instance, there are many scholars over many generations who have conversed with each other in print about *Hamlet,* and each new author adds a unique perspective to the conversation, even though some of the speakers can no longer respond. However, not all conversations in which sources "speak" to each other can be identified so easily, and instead might be seen as "speaking" to each other indirectly. Sometimes it is up to a researcher who is reading all of these sources that seem to talk about the same thing to identify when that is happing and to explain it to an audience. This is one of the primary goals of academic research—to identify conversations between sources and to show how they might interact with each other.

Many Speakers and Conversations

When writers mention "conversations" and sources "speaking" to one another, they are referring to the ways that many voices shape how communities see a topic. For instance, there are many writers today who are having a conversation about the topic of global warming, even if they don't actually know all the other writers who are part of the conversation. Climatologists, meteorologists, ecologists, sociologists, politicians, bloggers, priests, and corporate CEOs are all kinds of people involved in a written conversation on the topic of global warming. Of course, there are many smaller textual conversations within this larger one, as well as smaller groups or communities of speakers within this larger group. The climatologists, meteorologists, ecologists, and sociologists might be said to encompass part of an academic community conversing about global warming through scientific research, while the others might make up different groups. Even further, the climatologists, meteorologists, and ecologists might be said to encompass a certain kind of scientific conversation group more interested in the natural processes of the Earth, while the sociologists might be part of a different kind of academic group that focuses on human activity. Because of this fracturing of conversation groups—called "discourse communities"—and the many mini-conversations going on, it is sometimes the goal of a researcher like yourself to bring them together in one written work that puts them "in conversation" with each other.

For example, if you were interested in writing a paper about workplace inequalities between men and women, you would have many different speakers and conversations to look at. For instance, you might find that newspaper reporters, lawyers, psychologists, and government researchers all published various documents (stories, court proceedings, research, reports, etc.) about this topic. And, since writing can be preserved over long periods (unlike a face-to-face conversation), you are also dealing with speakers from across time. You might, for instance, want to discuss the ways different scientific writers saw the role of women in America in the 1950's and today. Scientific research on gender in the 1950's, as we know, is not the same as it is today. As a researcher, you might imagine yourself putting an author of a source on gender from the 1950's and an author of a source on gender from today in a room together. They would have different things to say about gender and the workplace, to be sure. The researcher from today might complicate the work of the researcher from the 1950's, or build on it, or disregard it. In addition to different speakers in the conversation, there would also be many different smaller conversations going on within the larger one of gender inequalities in the workplace. For example, some authors might write about salary inequalities in higher education, while others might focus more on cases of sexual harassment at work. Although both topics are related to the conversation of gender inequalities in the workplace, your paper might not need to address both subtopics (or mini-conversations).

Putting It All Together

Sometimes your role as a researcher is to figure out when and how sources seem to be dealing with the same thing, and decide how that changes what you know about the topic. When what you know about a topic changes because of how two sources talk about the same thing, writers might refer to that as a "conversation" between the two authors that you read. That change can be explained for your audience to show a "conversation"—an interaction—between two sources that might be separated by decades, miles, discourse communities, or even languages.

There are many ways to put sources together to make a conversation. You might think of it like a puzzle, except that you have some control over how the pieces are shaped. The above example of a research paper on gender inequalities only puts two sources in conversation, and they are both scientific puzzle pieces. However, there are many other voices in the conversation on gender that might fit into the puzzle. Deciding what kinds of sources are speaking to each other about a topic dictates the kind of puzzle you are building. Since it is probably impossible to identify all the conversations on a topic, you must make decisions about which ones are pieces in your puzzle, and which ones aren't. As a rule of thumb, you'll probably want to look for speakers whose topics are very closely related. However, you may also want to keep in mind that as a researcher you have the ability to build a puzzle that mobilizes science, art, history, and your aunt Jean into a new kind of conversation about a topic. As long as you can show your audience how each speaker changes what you know about a topic—as long as you can show the "conversation" between them—the puzzle is yours to design. Your audience, though, will determine its credibility, and so you will want to make sure you consider how they would build the puzzle themselves. If, for instance, you ignore in your research paper (your puzzle) a long conversation between many respected authorities on your topic, you should have a good reason for doing so, or your audience may find you lacking credibility.

It is important to remember that some authors have already put themselves into conversation with other sources, and some have not. When authors refer to other works, they are building a conversation puzzle in their own writing. Many times, this should act as a signpost to you as a researcher, directing you towards a conversation going on between sources. Other times, though, some sources will discuss the same topic and have never heard of each other. This happens often in large conversations where many different discourse communities with many different values all talk about the same thing. For instance, a scientific researcher might not be interested in responding to a blogger on the effects of global warming, since they might value different things or belong to communities that only want to talk to other members of that community. As a researcher, you might identify all of the conversations within one discourse community—for instance all of the scholarly discourse about Hamlet—or show how many communities all say something about a given topic—say, global warming. Identifying which sources are in conversation with each other is not enough though. As a researcher, you will also have to explain how they are in conversation. Do they challenge each other? Complicate? Extend? Ignore? Support? These are the kinds of questions you should seek to answer when putting your puzzle together. Deciding on these questions will require that you are familiar with many works on your given topic, and how they are all voices in a conversation that is taking place in your research.

Research: Understanding Sources

Types of Research Sources

Types of Research Sources

It is a well-known cliché: we live in an information age. Information has become a tangible commodity capable of creating and destroying wealth, influencing public opinion and government policies and effecting social change. As writers and citizens, we have unprecedented access to different kinds of information from different sources. Writers who hope to influence their audiences needs to know what research sources are available, where to find them, and how to use them.

Primary and Secondary Sources Definition of Primary Sources

Let us begin with the definition of primary and secondary sources. A primary research sources is one that allows you to learn about your subject "first-hand." Primary sources provide direct evidence about the topic under investigation. They offer us "direct access" to the events or phenomena we are studying. For example, if you are researching the history of World War II and decide to study soldiers' letters home or maps of battlefields, you are working with primary sources. Similarly, if you are studying the history of your home town in a local archive that contains documents pertaining to that history, you are engaging in primary research. Among other primary sources and methods are interviews, surveys, polls, observations, and other similar "first-hand" investigative techniques.

The fact that primary sources allow us "direct access" to the topic does not mean that they offer an objective and unbiased view of it. It is therefore important to consider primary sources critically and, if possible, gather multiple perspectives on the same event, time period, or questions, from multiple primary sources.

Definition of Secondary Sources

Secondary sources describe, discuss, and analyze research obtained from primary sources or from other secondary sources. Using the previous example about World War II, if you read other historians' accounts of it, government documents, maps and other written documents, you are engaging in secondary research. Some types of secondary sources with which you are likely to work include books, academic journals, popular magazines and newspapers, websites and other electronic sources. The same source can be both primary and secondary, depending on the nature and purpose of the project.

For example, if you study a culture or group of people by examining texts they produce, you are engaging in primary research. On the other hand, if that same group published a text analyzing some external event, person, or issue and if your focus is not on the text's authors but on their analysis, you would be doing secondary research. Secondary sources often contain descriptions and analyses of primary sources. Therefore, accounts, descriptions, and interpretations of research subjects found in secondary sources are at least one step further removed from what can be found in primary sources about the same subject. And while primary sources do not give us a completely objective view of reality, secondary sources, inevitably add an extra layer of opinion and interpretation to the views and ideas found in primary sources. As we have mentioned many times throughout this book, all texts are rhetorical creations, and writers make choices about what to include and what to omit. As researchers, we need to understand that and not to rely on either primary or secondary sources blindly.

Print and Electronic Sources

Researcher have at their disposal both printed and electronic sources. Before the advent of the Internet, most research papers were written based with the use of printed sources only. Until fairly recently, one of the main stated goals of research writing instruction was to give students practice in the use of the library. Libraries are venerable institutions, and therefore printed sources have traditionally been seen (with good reason, usually) as more solid and reliable than those found on the Internet.

With the growing popularity of the Internet and other computerized means of storing and communicating information, traditional libraries faced serious competition for clients. It has become impractical if not impossible for researchers to ignore the massive amount of information available to them on the Internet or from other online sources. As a result, it is not uncommon for many writers beginning a research project to begin searching online rather than at a library or a local archive. For example, several times in the process of writing this book, when I found myself in need of information, fast, I opened my web browser and researched online.

With the popularity of the Internet ever increasing, it has become common practice for many student writers to limit themselves to online research and to ignore the library. While there are some cases when a modified version of such an approach to searching may be justifiable (more about that later), it is clear that by using only online research sources, a writer severely limits his or her options.

This section of the chapter covers three areas. First, we will discuss the various types of printed and online sources as well the main similarities and differences between them. Next, I'd like to offer some suggestions on using your library effectively and creatively. Finally, we will the topic of conducting online searches, including methods of evaluating information found on the Internet.

Know your Library

It is likely that your college or university library consists of two parts. One is the brick and mortar building, often at a central location on campus, where you can go to look for books, magazines, newspapers, and other publications. The other part is online. Most good libraries keep a collection of online research databases which are supported, at least in part, by your tuition and fees, and to which only people who are affiliated with the college or the university that subscribes to these databases have access. Let us begin with the brick and mortar library. If you have not yet been to your campus library, visit it soon. Larger colleges and universities usually have several libraries that may specialize in different academic disciplines. As you enter the, you are likely to find a circulation desk (place where you can check out materials) and a reference desk. Behind a reference desk, work reference librarians. Instead of wandering around the library alone, hoping to hit the research sources that you need for your project, it is a good idea to talk to a reference librarian at the beginning of every research project, especially if you are at a loss for a topic or research materials. Your brick and mortar campus library is likely to house the following types of materials:

- Books (these include encyclopedias, dictionaries, indexes, and so on)
- Academic Journals
- Popular magazines
- Newspapers
- Government documents
- A music and film collection (on CDs, VHS tapes, and DVDs)
- A CD-Rom collection
- A microfilm and microfiche collection
- Special collections, such as ancient manuscripts or documents related to local history and culture.

According to librarian Linda M. Miller, researchers need to "gather relevant information about a topic or research question thoroughly and efficiently. To be thorough, it helps to be familiar with the kinds of resources that the library holds, and the services it provides to enable access to the holdings of other libraries." (2001, 61). Miller's idea is a simple one, yet it is amazing how many inexperienced writers prefer to use the first book or journal they come across in the library in their writing and do not take the time to learn what the library has to offer. Here are some practical steps that will help you to learn about your library:

- Take a tour of the library with your class or other groups if such tours are available. While such group tours are generally less effective that conducting your own searches or a topic that interests you, they will give you a good introduction to the library and, perhaps, give you a chance to talk to a librarian.

- Check your library's website to see if online "virtual" tours are available. At James Madison University where I work, the librarians have developed a series of interactive online activities and quizzes which anyone wishing to learn about the JMU libraries can take in their spare time.
- Talk to reference librarians! They are, truly, your best source of information. They will not get mad at you if you ask them too many questions. Not only are they paid to answer your questions, but most librarians love what they do and are eager to share their expertise with others.
- Go from floor to floor and browse the shelves. Learn where different kinds of materials are located and what they look like.
- Pay attention to the particulars of your campus library's architecture. I am an experienced library user, but it look me some time, after I arrived at my university for the first time, to figure out that our library building has an annex and that to get to that annex I had to take a different elevator from that which would lead me to the main floors.
- Use the library not only as a source of knowledge, but also as a source of entertainment and diversion. I like going to the library to browse through new fiction acquisitions. Many campus libraries also have excellent film and music collections.

The items on the list above will help you to acquire a general understanding of your campus library. However, the only way to gain an in-depth and meaningful knowledge of your library is to use is for specific research and writing projects. No matter how attentive you are during a library tour or, on your own, going from floor to floor and learning about all the different resources your library has to offer, it is during searchers that you conduct for your research projects, that you will become most interested and involved in what you are doing. Here, therefore, is an activity which combines a practical purpose of finding research sources for a research project with a somewhat more far- reaching purpose of learning as much as you can about your campus library.

Cyber-library

Besides the brick and mortar buildings, virtually all college and university libraries have a web space which is a gateway to more documents, resources, and information than any library building can house. From that website, you can not only to conduct a search of your library collection, but also access millions of articles, electronic books, and other resources available on the Internet.

I hasten to add that, usually, when trying to access most of those materials, it is a good idea to conduct a search from your campus library page rather than from your favorite search engine. There are three reasons for that. Firstly, most of the materials which you will find through your library site are accessible to paying subscribers only, and cannot be found via any search engine. Secondly, online library searches return organized and categorized results, complete with the date of publication and source—something that cannot be said about popular search engines. Finally, by searching online databases, we can be reasonably sure that the information we retrieve is reliable. So, what might you expect to find on your library's website?

In addition to the link to the library catalog, there is a "Super Search" link, a link called "Databases A-Z," a "Journal Locator," "Research Guides," and "Ebooks." There are also links to special collections and to the featured or new electronic databases to which the library has recently subscribed.

The titles of most of these links are self-explanatory. Obviously, the link to the library catalog allows you to search your brick and mortar library's collection. A journal locator search will tell you what academic journals, popular magazines, and newspapers are available at your library.

However, where a link like "Research Guides" will take you, is a little less obvious. Research guide websites are similar to the database homepages, except that, in addition to database links, they often offer direct connections to academic journals and other relevant online resources on the research subject. Searching online is a skill that can only be learned through frequent practice and critical reflection. Therefore, in order to become a proficient user of your library's electronic resources, you will need to visit the library's website often and conduct many searches. Although the web sites of most libraries are organized according to similar principles and offer similar types of resources, it will be up to you as a researcher and learner to find out what your school library has to offer and to learn to use those resources. I hope that the following activities will help you in that process.

The most user-friendly option is "Super Search." It allows you to search all areas of the above types, plus any not mentioned, at the same time.

CC licensed content, Original

- Modifications and Revisions. **Authored by**: Dann Coble. **Provided by**: Corning Community College. **Project**: ENGL 1010 OER Project. **License**: *CC BY-NC-SA: Attribution-NonCommercial-ShareAlike*

CC licensed content, Shared previously

- Methods of Discovery: Finding and Evaluating Research Sources. **Authored by**: Pavel Zemliansky. **Located at**: http://methodsofdiscovery.net. **License**: *CC BY-NC-SA: Attribution-NonCommercial-ShareAlike*

Distinguishing Scholarly Journals from Other Periodicals

Journals, magazines, and newspapers are important sources for up-to-date information in all disciplines. It is often difficult to distinguish between the various levels of scholarship found in the collection. In this guide we have divided the criteria for evaluating periodical literature into four categories:

- Scholarly
- Substantive News/General Interest
- Popular
- Sensational

Definitions:

- **Scholarly or peer-reviewed journal articles** are written by scholars or professionals who are experts in their fields. In the sciences and social sciences, they often publish research results.
- **Substantive news articles** are reliable sources of information on events and issues of public concern.
- **Popular articles** reflect the tastes of the general public and are often meant as entertainment.
- **Sensational articles** intend to arouse strong curiosity, interest, or reaction. They are not factually accurate.

Keeping these definitions in mind, and realizing that none of the lines drawn between types of journals can ever be totally clear cut, the general criteria are as follows.

Scholarly

Scholarly journals are also called academic, peer-reviewed, or refereed journals. (Strictly speaking, peer-reviewed (also called refereed) journals refer only to those scholarly journals that submit articles to several other scholars, experts, or academics (peers) in the field for review and comment. These reviewers must agree that the article represents properly conducted original research or writing before it can be published.)

What to look for:

- Scholarly journal articles often have an abstract, a descriptive summary of the article contents, before the main text of the article.
- Scholarly journals generally have a sober, serious look. They often contain many graphs and charts but few glossy pages or exciting pictures.
- Scholarly journals always cite their sources in the form of footnotes or bibliographies. These bibliographies are generally lengthy and cite other scholarly writings.
- Articles are written by a scholar in the field or by someone who has done research in the field. The affiliations of the authors are listed, usually at the bottom of the first page or at the end of the article–universities, research institutions, think tanks, and the like. The language of scholarly journals is that of the discipline covered. It assumes some technical background on the part of the reader.

- The main purpose of a scholarly journal is to report on original research or experimentation in order to make such information available to the rest of the scholarly world. Many scholarly journals, though by no means all, are published by a specific professional organization.

Examples of Scholarly Journals

- American Economic Review
- Applied Geography
- Archives of Sexual Behavior
- JAMA: The Journal of the American Medical Association
- Journal of Marriage and the Family (published by the National Council on Family Relations)
- Journal of Theoretical Biology
- Modern Fiction Studies

Substantive News or General Interest

These periodicals may be quite attractive in appearance, although some are in newspaper format. Articles are often heavily illustrated, generally with photographs.

What to look for:

- News and general interest periodicals sometimes cite sources, though more often do not. Articles may be written by a member of the editorial staff, a scholar or a freelance writer.
- The language of these publications is geared to any educated audience. There is no specialty assumed, only interest and a certain level of intelligence. They are generally published by commercial enterprises or individuals, although some emanate from specific professional organizations. The main purpose of periodicals in this category is to provide information, in a general manner, to a broad audience of concerned citizens.

Examples of Substantive News or General Interest Periodicals

- The Economist
- National Geographic
- The New York Times
- Scientific American
- Vital Speeches of the Day

Popular

Popular periodicals come in many formats, although often slick and attractive in appearance with lots of color graphics (photographs, drawings, etc.). These publications do not cite sources in a bibliography. Information published in popular periodicals is often second or third hand and the original source is rarely mentioned.

Articles are usually very short and written in simple language. The main purpose of popular periodicals is to entertain the reader, to sell products (their own or their advertisers), or to promote a viewpoint.

Examples of Popular Periodicals

- Ebony
- Parents
- People
- Weekly
- Readers Digest
- Sports Illustrated
- Vogue

Sensational

Sensational periodicals come in a variety of styles, but often use a newspaper format. Their language is elementary and occasionally inflammatory or sensational. They assume a certain gullibility in their audience.

The main purpose of sensational magazines seems to be to arouse curiosity and to cater to popular superstitions. They often do so with flashy headlines designed to astonish (e.g., Half- man Half-woman Makes Self Pregnant).

Examples of Sensational Periodicals

- Globe
- National Examiner
- Star
- Weekly World News

Another example of sensational material is what is commonly referred to on social media as "clickbait." With this in mind, be careful when using items found online via sites like Buzzfeed.

For More Information on Individual Periodical Titles

There are reference books which describe and evaluate periodicals. For evaluations of specific periodicals, use:

LaGuardia, Cheryl, ed., with Bill and Linda Sternberg Katz. Magazines for Libraries. 17th ed. New York: Bowker, 2009.

An annotated listing by subject of over 6,000 periodicals. Each entry gives name of periodical, beginning publication date, publisher, editor, address, price and such information as indexing, size, and level of audience. Short abstracts describe the scope, political slant, and other aspects of the publication. Arrangement is topical, bringing magazines and journals on like subjects together. To find an individual title, use the title index at the end of the volume.

Research: Finding Strong Sources

Introduction to Research Process

Have you heard about the dangers of dihydrogen monoxide? Did you know that it is commonly found in many household products, is readily available, but can also cause severe burns, erosion, corrosion, and is the major component in acid rain? Jennifer Abel from *Consumer Affairs* tells us, "search online for information about dihydrogen monoxide, and you'll find a long list of scary and absolutely true warnings about it: used by the nuclear power industry, vital to the production of everything from pesticides to Styrofoam, present in tumors removed from cancer patients, and guaranteed fatal to humans in large quantities."

Are you starting to feel like something is not quite right about this information? What exactly *is* DHMO? How can it be found so easily, yet pose so many risks? If you haven't tried it already, do a quick Google search for dihydrogen monoxide. Aside from the dhmo.org website, what other search results do you see?

Source Reliability

You probably found the Wikipedia page titled "Dihydrogen Monoxide Hoax" (https://en.wikipedia.org/wiki/Dihydrogen_monoxide_hoax) or a Snopes.com article debunking the circulating myths. It turns out that dihydrogen monoxide is really just a fancy way of referencing water, or H_2O, and is certainly something we don't want to ban or protest against. This new context about the real meaning of DHMO certainly provides amusing insight into the "horrors" you read about on the DHMO website: Does it enhance athletic performance? Can it improve your marriage? What are its overdose symptoms?

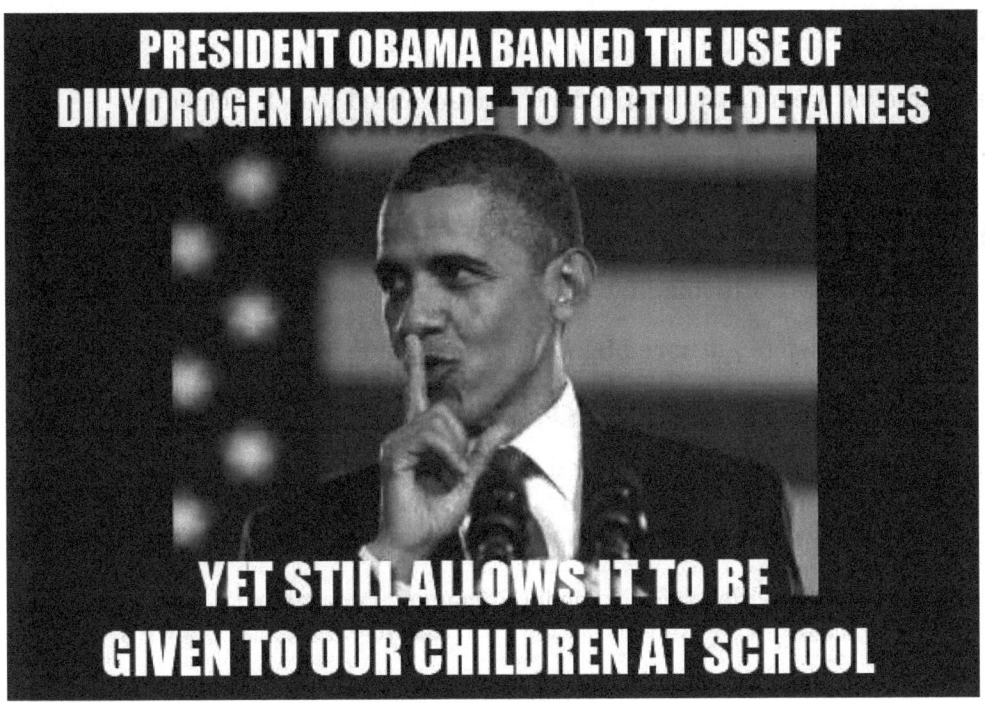

A funny meme depicting how easy it is to misrepresent information and give people the wrong impression. While Obama did prohibit waterboarding as a torture technique, banning water in schools would have obvious disastrous consequences.

Nowadays, we are surrounded with so much readily available information at our fingertips, that it is sometimes hard to differentiate fact from fiction. Of course, not everything you read on the internet is true, but how do you know what's a good source to rely on for personal information in your life? How about for an academic essay?

In this section, you'll learn about tools you can use and steps you can follow in order to find credible information. You'll learn how to find information, evaluate it, integrate it, and document it correctly for your research paper.

These skills will help you excel in your academic writing, but also pave the way for a more critical eye when hearing or reading about any newfound information.

USING SOURCES IN RESEARCH

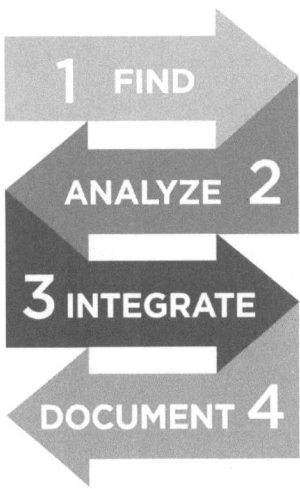

Learning Outcomes

- Evaluate and practice preliminary, intermediate, and advanced search techniques
- Evaluate and practice methods of analysis to assess the quality and reliability of a source
- Evaluate issues of plagiarism and academic dishonesty
- Evaluate and practice MLA document formatting and citation practices

How to Find Sources

Finding Print Resources

Print resources include a vast array of documents and publications. Regardless of your topic, you will consult some print resources as part of your research. (You will use electronic sources as well, but it is not wise to limit yourself to electronic sources only, because some potentially useful sources may be available only in print form.) Table 11.1 "Library Print Resources" lists different types of print resources available at public and university libraries.

Table 11.1 Library Print Resources

Resource Type	Description	Example(s)
Reference works	Reference works provide a summary of information about a particular topic. Almanacs, encyclopedias, atlases, medical reference books, and scientific abstracts are examples of reference works. In some cases, reference books may not be checked out of a library. Note that reference works are many steps removed from original primary sources and are often brief, so these should be used only as a starting point when you gather information.	• *The World Almanac and Book of Facts 2010* • *Diagnostic and Statistical Manual* published by the American Psychiatric Association
Nonfiction books	Nonfiction books provide in-depth coverage of a topic. Trade books, biographies, and how-to guides are usually written for a general audience. Scholarly books and scientific studies are usually written for an audience that has specialized knowledge of a topic.	• *The Low-Carb Solution: A Slimmer You in 30 Days* • *Carbohydrates, Fats and Proteins: Exploring the Relationship Between Macronutrient Ratios and Health Outcomes*
Periodicals and news sources	These sources are published at regular intervals—daily, weekly, monthly, or quarterly. Newspapers, magazines, and academic journals are examples. Some periodicals provide articles on subjects of general interest, while others are more specialized.	• *New York Times* • *PC Magazine* • *JAMA, The Journal of the American Medical Association*
Government publications	Federal, state, and local government agencies publish information on a variety of topics. Government publications include reports, legislation, court documents, public records, statistics, studies, guides, programs, and forms.	• The *Census 2000 Profile* • *The Business Relocation Package* published by the Philadelphia Chamber of Commerce

Resource Type	Description	Example(s)
Business and nonprofit publications	Businesses and nonprofit organizations produce publications designed to market a product, provide background about the organization, provide information on topics connected to the organization, or promote a cause. These publications include reports, newsletters, advertisements, manuals, brochures, and other print documents.	• A company's instruction manual explaining how to use a specific software program • A news release published by the Sierra Club

Some of these resources are also widely available in electronic format. In addition to the resources noted in the table, library holdings may include primary texts such as historical documents, letters, and diaries.

Writing at Work

Businesses, government organizations, and nonprofit organizations produce published materials that range from brief advertisements and brochures to lengthy, detailed reports. In many cases, producing these publications requires research. A corporation's annual report may include research about economic or industry trends. A charitable organization may use information from research in materials sent to potential donors.

Regardless of the industry you work in, you may be asked to assist in developing materials for publication. Often, incorporating research in these documents can make them more effective in informing or persuading readers.

Tip

As you gather information, strive for a balance of accessible, easy-to-read sources and more specialized, challenging sources. Relying solely on lightweight books and articles written for a general audience will drastically limit the range of useful, substantial information. On the other hand, restricting oneself to dense, scholarly works could make the process of researching extremely time-consuming and frustrating.

Tip

Knowing the right keywords can sometimes make all the difference in conducting a successful search. If you have trouble finding sources on a topic, consult a librarian to see whether you need to modify your search terms.

Using Periodicals, Indexes, and Databases

Library catalogs can help you locate book-length sources, as well as some types of nonprint holdings, such as CDs, DVDs, and audio books. To locate shorter sources, such as magazine and journal articles, you will need to use a periodical index or an online periodical database. These tools index the articles that appear in newspapers, magazines, and journals. Like catalogs, they provide publication information about an article and often allow users to access a summary or even the full text of the article.

Print indexes may be available in the periodicals section of your library. Increasingly, libraries use online databases that users can access through the library website. A single library may provide access to multiple periodical databases. These can range from general news databases to specialized databases. Table 11.2 "Commonly Used Indexes and Databases" describes some commonly used indexes and databases.

Table 11.2 Commonly Used Indexes and Databases

Resource	Format	Contents
New York Times Index	Print	Guide to articles published in the *New York Times*

Resource	Format	Contents
ProQuest	Online	Database that archives content from newspapers, magazines, and dissertations
Psychlit, PsycINFO	Online	Databases that archive content from journals in psychology and psychiatry
Business Source Complete	Online	Database that archives business-related content from magazines and journals
MEDLINE, PubMed	Online	Databases that archive articles in medicine and health
EBSCOhost	Online	General database that provides access to articles on a wide variety of topics

Writing at Work

Periodicals databases are not just for students writing research papers. They also provide a valuable service to workers in various fields. The owner of a small business might use a database such as Business Source Premiere to find articles on management, finance, or trends within a particular industry. Health care professionals might consult databases such as MedLine to research a particular disease or medication. Regardless of what career path you plan to pursue, periodicals databases can be a useful tool for researching specific topics and identifying periodicals that will help you keep up with the latest news in your industry.

Consulting a Reference Librarian

Sifting through library stacks and database search results to find the information you need can be like trying to find a needle in a haystack. If you are not sure how you should begin your search, or if it is yielding too many or too few results, you are not alone. Many students find this process challenging, although it does get easier with experience. One way to learn better search strategies is to consult a reference librarian.

Reference librarians are intimately familiar with the systems libraries use to organize and classify information. They can help you locate a particular book in the library stacks, steer you toward useful reference works, and provide tips on how to use databases and other electronic research tools. Take the time to see what resources you can find on your own, but if you encounter difficulties, ask for help. Many university librarians hold virtual office hours and are available for online chatting.

Tip

One way to refine your keyword search is to use Boolean operators. These operators allow you to combine keywords, find variations on a word, and otherwise expand or limit your results. Here are some of the ways you can use Boolean operators:

- Combine keywords with **and** or **+** to limit results to citations that include both keywords—for example, **diet + nutrition**.
- Combine keywords with **not** or **-** to search for the first word without the second. This can help you eliminate irrelevant results based on words that are similar to your search term. For example, searching for **obesity not childhood** locates materials on obesity but excludes materials on childhood obesity.
- Enclose a phrase in quotation marks to search for an exact phrase, such as "**morbid obesity**."
- Use parentheses to direct the order of operations in a search string. For example, since Type II diabetes is also known as adult-onset diabetes, you could search **(Type II or adult-onset) and diabetes** to limit your search results to articles on this form of the disease.
- Use a wildcard symbol such as **#**, **?**, or **$** after a word to search for variations on a term. For instance, you might type **diabet#** to search for information on diabetes and diabetics. The specific symbol used varies with different databases.

Finding and Using Electronic Resources

With the expansion of technology and media over the past few decades, a wealth of information is available to you in electronic format. Some types of resources, such as a television documentary, may only be available electronically. Other resources—for instance, many newspapers and magazines—may be available in both print and electronic form. The following are some of the electronic sources you might consult:

- Online databases
- CD-ROMs
- Popular web search engines
- Websites maintained by businesses, universities, nonprofit organizations, or government agencies
- Newspapers, magazines, and journals published on the web
- E-books
- Audio books
- Industry blogs
- Radio and television programs and other audio and video recordings
- Online discussion groups

The techniques you use to locate print resources can also help you find electronic resources efficiently. Libraries usually include CD-ROMs, audio books, and audio and video recordings among their holdings. You can locate these materials in the catalog using a keyword search. The same Boolean operators used to refine database searches can help you filter your results in popular search engines.

Using Internet Search Engines Efficiently

When faced with the challenge of writing a research paper, some students rely on popular search engines as their first source of information. Typing a keyword or phrase into a search engine instantly pulls up links to dozens, hundreds, or even thousands of related websites—what could be easier? Unfortunately, despite its apparent convenience, this research strategy has the following drawbacks to consider:

- **Results do not always appear in order of reliability.** The first few hits that appear in search results may include sites whose content is not always reliable, such as online encyclopedias that can be edited by any user. Because websites are created by third parties, the search engine cannot tell you which sites have accurate information.
- **Results may be too numerous for you to use.** The amount of information available on the web is far greater than the amount of information housed within a particular library or database. Realistically, if your web search pulls up thousands of hits, you will not be able to visit every site—and the most useful sites may be buried deep within your search results.
- **Search engines are not connected to the results of the search.** Search engines find websites that people visit often and list the results in order of popularity. The search engine, then, is not connected to any of the results. When you cite a source found through a search engine, you do not need to cite the search engine. Only cite the source.

A general web search can provide a helpful overview of a topic and may pull up genuinely useful resources. To get the most out of a search engine, however, use strategies to make your search more efficient. Use multiple keywords and Boolean operators to limit your results. Click on the Advanced Search link on the homepage to find additional options for streamlining your search. Depending on the specific search engine you use, the following options may be available:

- Limit results to websites that have been updated within a particular time frame.
- Limit results by language or country.
- Limit results to scholarly works available online.
- Limit results by file type.
- Limit results to a particular domain type, such as .edu (school and university sites) or .gov (government sites). This is a quick way to filter out commercial sites, which can often lead to more objective results.

Use the Bookmarks or Favorites feature of your web browser to save and organize sites that look promising.
CC licensed content, Original

- Revisions. **Authored by**: Dann Coble. **Provided by**: Corning Community College. **Project**: ENGL 1010 OER

Project. **License**: *CC BY-SA: Attribution-ShareAlike*

Electronic Sources

Print Sources or Electronic?

In the early years of the Internet, there was a wide-spread mistrust of the World Wide Web and the information it had to offer. While some of this mistrust is still present, including among writing teachers and students, the undeniable fact is that the authority of the Internet as a legitimate and reliable source of information has increased considerably in recent years. For example, academic journals in almost every discipline compliment their printed volumes with web versions, and some have gone completely online. These online journals employ the same rigorous submission review processes as their printed counterparts. Complete texts of academic and other books are sometimes available on the Internet. Respected specialized databases and government document collections are published entirely and exclusively online.

Print and electronic sources are not created equal, and, although online and other electronic texts are gaining ground rather quickly as legitimate research resources, there is still a wide-spread, and often justified, opinion among academics and other writers that printed materials make better research sources. Some materials that are available in some libraries simply cannot be found online and vice versa.

For example, if you are a Shakespeare scholar wishing to examine manuscripts from the Elizabethan times, you will not find them online. To get to them, you will have to visit the Folger Shakespeare Library in Washington, DC, or a similar repository of scholarship on Shakespeare. On the other hand, if you are researching the Creative Commons movement which is a community dedicated to reforming copyright laws in this country, then your best bet is to begin your search on the Internet at http://www.creativecommons.org/. Surely, after reading the website, you will need to augment your research by reading other related materials, both online and in print, but in this case, starting online rather than in the library is a reasonable idea.

As a researching writer, you should realize that, inherently, printed and electronic sources are not bad or good. Both kinds can be reliable and unreliable, although with printed materials, publishers and libraries take care of not letting utterly unreliable works through to readers. Both kinds can be appropriate and inappropriate for a specific research project. It is up to researchers and writers to learn how to select both print and electronic sources judiciously and how to evaluate them for their reliability and appropriateness for these writers' research and writing purposes.

Determining the Suitability and Reliability of Research Sources

Much of the discussion about the relative value of printed and electronic, especially Internet, sources revolves around the issue of reliability. When it comes to libraries, the issue is more or less clear. Libraries keep books, journals, and other publications that usually undergo a rigorous pre and post-publication review process. It is a fairly safe bet that your campus library contains very few or no materials which are blatantly unreliable or false, unless those materials are kept there precisely to demonstrate their unreliability and falsehood.

As a faculty member, I am sometimes asked by my university librarians to recommend titles in my academic field which, I feel, our university library should have. Of course, my opinion, as well as the opinions of my colleagues, do not provide a one- hundred-percent guarantee against errors and inaccurate facts, we use our experience and knowledge in the field to recommend certain titles and omit certain others.

These faculty recommendations are the last stage in the long process before a publication gets to a campus library. Before that, every book, journal article, or other material undergoes a stringent review from the publisher's editors and other readers. And while researchers still need to use sound judgment in deciding which library sources to use in their project, the issue is usually one of relevance and suitability for a specific research project and specific research questions rather than one of whether the information presented in the source is truthful or not.

The same is true of some electronic sources. Databases and other research sources published on CD-ROMs, as well as various online research websites which accompany many of contemporary writing textbooks, for example, are subject to the same strict review process as their printed counterparts. Information contained in specialized academic and professional databases is also screened for reliability and correctness.

If, as we have established, most of the materials which you are likely to come across in your campus library are generally trustworthy, then your task as a researcher is to determine the appropriateness of the information which these books, journals, and other materials contain, for your particular research project. It is a simple question, really: will my research sources help me answer the research questions that I am posing in my project? Will they help me learn as much as I can about my topic and create a rhetorically effective and interesting text for my readers? Consider the following example.

Recently, the topic of the connection between certain anti-depressant drugs and suicidal tendencies among teenagers that take those drugs has received a lot of coverage in the media. Suppose that you are interested in researching this topic further. Suppose also that you want not only to give statistical information about the problem in your paper, but also to study first-hand accounts of the people, who have been negatively affected by the anti-depressants.

When you come to your campus library, you have no trouble locating the latest reports and studies that give you a general overview of your topic, including rates of suicidal behavior in teenagers who took the drugs, tabulated data on the exact relationships between the dosage of the drugs and the changes in the patients' moods, and so on. All this may be useful information, and there is a good chance that, as a writer, you will still find a way to use it in your paper. You could, for example, provide the summary of the statistics in order to introduce the topic to your readers. However, this information does not fulfill your research purpose completely. You set out to find out, first-hand, what it is like to be a teenager whose body and mind are affected by the anti-depressants, yet the printed materials that you have found so far offer no such insight. They fulfill your goal only partially.

To find such first- hand accounts, then, you will either have to keep looking in the library or to conduct interviews with the people who have affected by these drugs, if you can locate such people. The library website of the University of California at Berkeley offers a comprehensive list of criteria for critical evaluation of all research sources which I find very useful. The expanded list of criteria and examples can be found at http://www.lib.berkeley.edu/TeachingLib/Guides/Evaluation.html.

Suitability of Sources

Determine how suitable a particular source is for your current research project. To do this, consider the following factors:

Scope

What topics and subtopics does the source cover? Is it a general overview of your subject or it is a specialized resource?

Audience

Who is the intended audience for the text? If the text itself is too basic or too specialized, it may not match the expectations and needs of your own target audience.

Timeliness

When was the source published? Does it represent the latest information, theories, and views on the subject? Bear in mind, though, that if you are conducting a historical investigation, you will probably need to consult older materials, too.

Authority

What the credentials of the author or authors of the sources? This may be particularly important when you use Internet sources since a lot of materials by various authors are posted online. As a part of your evaluation of the source's authority, you should also pay attention to the kinds of external sources that were used during its creation. Look through the bibliography or list of works cited attached to the text. Not only will it help you determine how reliable and suitable the source is, but it may also provide you with further leads for your own research. Try asking the above questions of any source you are using for a research project you are currently conducting.

Reliability of Internet Sources

Charles Lowe, the author of the essay "The Internet Can be a Wonderful Place, But...," offers the following opinion of the importance of the Internet as a research source for contemporary researchers:

> "To a generation raised in the electronic media culture, the Internet is an environment where you feel more comfortable, more at home than the antiquated libraries and research arenas of the pre-electronic, print culture. To you, instructors just don't get it when they advise against using the Internet for research or require the bulk of the sources for a research paper to come from the library" (129-130).

Indeed, the Internet has become the main source of information not only for college students, but also for a lot of people outside of the academe. And while I do not advise you to stay away from the Internet when researching and I generally do not require my own students to use primarily printed sources, I do know that working with Internet sources places additional demands on the researcher and the writer.

Because much of the Internet is a democratic, open space, and because anyone with a computer can post materials online, evaluating online sources is not always easy. A surprisingly large number of people believe much of the information on the Internet, even if this information is blatantly misleading or if its authors have a self-serving agenda. In the chapter of this book dedicated to research and writing in academic disciplines, we discussed how authority of a text can influence its reception by the readers. I think many students uncritically accept information they find on the internet because some of the sites on which this information appears look and sound very authoritative. Used to believing the published word, inexperienced writers often fall for such information as legitimate research data.

So, what are some of strategies you can use to determine that reliability? The key to successful evaluation of Internet research sources, as any other research sources, is application of your critical reading and thinking skills. In order to determine the reliability of every source, including online sources, it is generally useful to conduct a basic rhetorical analysis of that source. When deciding whether to use a particular website as a research source, every writer should ask and answer the following questions:

- Who is the author (or, authors) of the website and the materials presented on it?
- What is known about the site's author or authors and its publishers and their agendas and goals?
- What is the purpose of the website?
- Who is the target audience of the website
- How do the writing style and the design of the website contribute to (or detract from) its meaning?

Website Authors and Publishers

Just like with a printed source, first, we need to consider the author and the publisher of a website. Lowe whom I mentioned earlier suggest that first we need to look at the tag in the website's URL. Whether it is a ".com," a ".org," a ".net, "or a ".edu" site can offer useful clues about the types of materials located on the site and about their credibility. In addition to the three most common URL tags which are listed above, websites of military organizations use the extension ".mil" while websites hosted in other countries have other tags which are usually abbreviations of those countries' names. Sites of government agencies end in ".gov."

For example, most sites hosted in Great Britain have the tag "uk" which stands for "United Kingdom." Websites out of Italy usually have the tag "it," and so on. Typically, a ".com" site is set up to sell or promote a product or service. Therefore, if you are researching Nike shoes, you will probably not want to rely on http://www.nike.com/ if you want to get a more or less unbiased review of the product. While Nike's website may provide some useful information about the products it sells, the site's main purpose is to sell Nike's goods, playing up the advantages of their products their competitors'.

Keep in mind that not all ".com" websites try to sell something. Sometimes, academics and other professionals obtain ".com" addresses because they are easy to obtain. For example, the professional website Charles Lowe whose work I mentioned earlier is located at http://www.cyberdash.com/.Political candidates running for office also often choose ".com" addresses for their campaign websites. In every case, you need to apply your critical reading skills and your judgment when evaluating a website. The ".org" sites usually belong to organizations, including political groups. These sites can present some specific challenges to researchers trying to evaluate their credibility and usefulness for their research.

To understand these challenges, let us consider the ".org" sites of two political research organizations, also known as "think tanks." One is the conservative Heritage Foundation (http://www.heritage.org), and the traditionally liberal Center for National Policy (http://www.cnponline.org). Both sites have "About" pages intended to explain to their readers the goals and purposes of the organizations they represent. The Heritage Foundation's site, contains the following information:

> ...The Heritage Foundation is a research and educational institute – a think tank – whose mission is to formulate and promote conservative public policies based on the principles of free enterprise, limited government, individual freedom, traditional American values, and a strong national defense. (http://www.heritage.org/about)

This statement can tell a researcher a lot about the research articles and other materials contained in the site. It tells us that the authors of the site are not neutral, nor do they pretend to be. Instead, they are advancing a particular political agenda, and so, when used as research sources, the writings on the site should not be seen as unbiased "truths", but as arguments. The same is true of the Center for National Policy's website, although its authors choose a different rhetorical strategy explaining their political leanings to the readers. They write:

> The Center for National Policy (CNP) is a non-profit, non-partisan public policy organization located in Washington, DC. Founded in 1981, the Center's mission is to engage national leaders with new policy options and innovative programs designed to advance progressive ideas in the interest of all Americans (http://www.cnponline.org/people_and_programs.html).

It takes further study of the Center's website, as well as a certain knowledge of the American political scene to realize that the organization is leaning towards the left of the political spectrum. The websites of both organizations contain an impressive amount of research, commentaries, and other materials designed to advance the groups' causes.

When evaluating ".org" sites, it is important to realize that they belong to organizations, and each organization has a purpose or a cause. Therefore, each organizational website will try to advance that cause and fulfill that purpose by publishing appropriate materials. Even if the research and arguments presented on those sites are solid (and they often are), there is no such thing as an unbiased and disinterested source.

This is especially true of political and social organizations whose sole purpose is to promote agendas. The Internet addresses ending in ".edu" are rather self- explanatory—they belong to universities and other educational institutions. On these sites, we can expect academic articles and other writings, as well as, often, papers and other works created by students. These websites are also useful resources if you are looking for information on a specific college or university. Be aware, though, that typically any college faculty member or student can obtain web space from their institution and publish materials of their own choosing on that space. Thus, some of the texts that appear on ".edu" sites may be personal rather than academic.

In recent years, some political research organizations have begun to use web addresses with the "edu" tag. One of these organizations is The Brookings Institution, whose address is http://www.brookings.edu. Government websites which end in ".gov" can be useful sources of information on the latest legislation and other regulatory documents. The website with a "dot net" extension can belong to commercial organizations or online forums.

Website Content

Now that we have established principles for evaluating the authors and publishers of web materials, let us look at the content of the writing. As I have stated above, like all writing, web writing is argumentative, therefore it is important to recognize that authors of web texts work to promote their agendas or highlight the events, organizations, and opinions that they consider right, important, and worthy of public attention. Different writers work from different assumption and try to reach different audiences. Websites of political organizations are prime examples of that.

Activity: Evaluating the Content of Websites

Go to one of the following websites:

- The Heritage Foundation (http://www.heritage.org)
- The Center for National Policy (http://www.cnponline.org)
- The Brookings Institution (http://www.brookings.edu)
- The American Enterprise Institute (http://www.aei.org)
- Or choose another website suggested by your instructor. Browse through the content of the site have to offer and consider the following questions:

Answer the following questions about the site:

- What is the purpose of the site?
- What is its intended audience? How do we know?
- What are the main subjects discussed on the sites?
- What assumptions and biases do the authors of the publications on the site seem to have? How do we know?
- What research methods and sources do the authors of these materials use
- How does research help the writers of the site state their case?

Apply the same analysis to any online sources you are using for one of your research projects.

Website Design and Style

The style and layout of any text is a part of that text's message, and online research sources are no exception. Well-designed and written websites add to the ethos (credibility) of their authors while badly designed and poorly written ones detract from it. Sometimes, however, a website with a good-looking design can turn out to be an unreliable or unsuitable research source.

In Place of a Conclusion: Do not Accept A Source Just because it Sounds or Looks Authoritative

Good writers try to create authoritative texts. Having authority in their writing helps them advance their arguments and influence their audiences. To establish such authority, writers use a variety of methods. As has been discussed throughout this chapter, it is important for any researcher to recognize authoritative and credible research sources. On the other hand, it is also important not to accept authoritative sources without questioning them. After all, the purpose of every researcher piece of writing is to create new views and new theories on the subject, not to repeat the old ones, however good and well-presented those old theories may be. Therefore, when working with reliable and suitable research sources, consider them solid foundations which will help you to achieve a new understanding of your subject, which will be your own. Applying the critical source evaluation techniques laid out in this chapter will help you to accomplish this goal.

- Revisions. **Authored by**: Dann Coble. **Provided by**: Corning Community College. **Project**: ENGL 1010 OER Project. **License**: *CC BY-SA: Attribution-ShareAlike*

CC licensed content, Shared previously

- Methods of Discovery: Finding and Evaluating Research Sources. **Authored by**: Pavel Zemliansky. **Located at**: http://methodsofdiscovery.net. **License**: *CC BY-SA: Attribution-ShareAlike*

Evaluating Research Resources

Evaluating Research Resources

As you gather sources, you will need to examine them with a critical eye. Smart researchers continually ask themselves two questions: "Is this source relevant to my purpose?" and "Is this source reliable?" The first question will help you avoid wasting valuable time reading sources that stray too far from your specific topic and research questions. The second question will help you find accurate, trustworthy sources.

Determining Whether a Source Is Relevant

At this point in your research process, you may have identified dozens of potential sources. It is easy for writers to get so caught up in checking out books and printing out articles that they forget to ask themselves how they will use these resources in their research. Now is a good time to get a little ruthless. Reading and taking notes takes time and energy, so you will want to focus on the most relevant sources.

To weed through your stack of books and articles, skim their contents. Read quickly with your research questions and subtopics in mind. Table 11.3 "Tips for Skimming Books and Articles" explains how to skim to get a quick sense of what topics are covered. If a book or article is not especially relevant, put it aside. You can always come back to it later if you need to.

Table 11.3 Tips for Skimming Books and Articles

Tips for Skimming Books	Tips for Skimming Articles
1. Read the dust jacket and table of contents for a broad overview of the topics covered. 2. Use the index to locate more specific topics and see how thoroughly they are covered. 3. Flip through the book and look for subtitles or key terms that correspond to your research.	1. Skim the introduction and conclusion for summary material. 2. Skim through subheadings and text features such as sidebars. 3. Look for keywords related to your topic. 4. Journal articles often begin with an abstract or summary of the contents. Read it to determine the article's relevance to your research.

Determining Whether a Source Is Reliable

All information sources are not created equal. Sources can vary greatly in terms of how carefully they are researched, written, edited, and reviewed for accuracy. Common sense will help you identify obviously questionable sources, such as tabloids that feature tales of alien abductions, or personal websites with glaring typos. Sometimes, however, a source's reliability—or lack of it—is not so obvious. For more information about source reliability, see Chapter 12 "Writing a Research Paper".

To evaluate your research sources, you will use critical thinking skills consciously and deliberately. You will consider criteria such as the type of source, its intended purpose and audience, the author's (or authors') qualifications, the publication's reputation, any indications of bias or hidden agendas, how current the source is, and the overall quality of the writing, thinking, and design.

Evaluating Types of Sources

The different types of sources you will consult are written for distinct purposes and with different audiences in mind. This accounts for other differences, such as the following:

- How thoroughly the writers cover a given topic
- How carefully the writers research and document facts
- How editors review the work
- What biases or agendas affect the content

A journal article written for an academic audience for the purpose of expanding scholarship in a given field will take an approach quite different from a magazine feature written to inform a general audience. Textbooks, hard news articles, and websites approach a subject from different angles as well. To some extent, the type of source provides clues about its overall depth and reliability.

High-Quality Sources

These sources provide the most in-depth information. They are researched and written by subject matter experts and are carefully reviewed.

- Scholarly books and articles in scholarly journals
- Trade books and magazines geared toward an educated general audience, such as *Smithsonian Magazine* or *Nature*
- Government documents, such as books, reports, and web pages
- Documents posted online by reputable organizations, such as universities and research institutes
- Textbooks and reference books, which are usually reliable but may not cover a topic in great depth

Varied-Quality Sources

These sources are often useful. However, they do not cover subjects in as much depth as high-quality sources, and they are not always rigorously researched and reviewed. Some, such as popular magazine articles or company brochures, may be written to market a product or a cause. Use them with caution.

- News stories and feature articles (print or online) from reputable newspapers, magazines, or organizations, such as *Newsweek* or the Public Broadcasting Service
- Popular magazine articles, which may or may not be carefully researched and fact checked
- Documents published by businesses and nonprofit organizations

Questionable Sources

These sources should be avoided. They are often written primarily to attract a large readership or present the author's opinions and are not subject to careful review.

- Loosely regulated or unregulated media content, such as Internet discussion boards, blogs, free online encyclopedias, talk radio shows, television news shows with obvious political biases, personal websites, and chat rooms

Tip

Free online encyclopedias and wikis may seem like a great source of information. They usually appear among the first few results of a web search. They cover thousands of topics, and many articles use an informal, straightforward writing style. Unfortunately, these sites have no control system for researching, writing, and reviewing articles. Instead, they rely on a community of users to police themselves. At best, these sites can be a starting point for finding other, more trustworthy sources. Never use them as final sources.

Evaluating Credibility and Reputability

Even when you are using a type of source that is generally reliable, you will still need to evaluate the author's credibility and the publication itself on an individual basis. To examine the author's credibility—that is, how much you can believe of what the author has to say—examine his or her credentials. What career experience or academic study shows that the author has the expertise to write about this topic?

Keep in mind that expertise in one field is no guarantee of expertise in another, unrelated area. For instance, an author may have an advanced degree in physiology, but this credential is not a valid qualification for writing about psychology. Check credentials carefully.

Just as important as the author's credibility is the publication's overall reputability. Reputability refers to a source's standing and reputation as a respectable, reliable source of information. An established and well-known newspaper, such as the *New York Times* or the *Wall Street Journal*, is more reputable than a college newspaper put out by comparatively inexperienced students. A website that is maintained by a well-known, respected organization and regularly updated is more reputable than one created by an unknown author or group.

If you are using articles from scholarly journals, you can check databases that keep count of how many times each article has been cited in other articles. This can be a rough indication of the article's quality or, at the very least, of its influence and reputation among other scholars.

Checking for Biases and Hidden Agendas

Whenever you consult a source, always think carefully about the author's or authors' purpose in presenting the information. Few sources present facts completely objectively. In some cases, the source's content and tone are significantly influenced by biases or hidden agendas.

Bias refers to favoritism or prejudice toward a particular person or group. For instance, an author may be biased against a certain political party and present information in a way that subtly—or not so subtly—makes that organization look bad. Bias can lead an author to present facts selectively, edit quotations to misrepresent someone's words, and distort information.

Hidden agendas are goals that are not immediately obvious but influence how an author presents the facts. For instance, an article about the role of beef in a healthy diet would be questionable if it were written by a representative of the beef industry—or by the president of an animal-rights organization. In both cases, the author would likely have a hidden agenda.

As Jorge conducted his research, he read several research studies in which scientists found significant benefits to following a low-carbohydrate diet. He also noticed that many studies were sponsored by a foundation associated with the author of a popular series of low-carbohydrate diet books. Jorge read these studies with a critical eye, knowing that a hidden agenda might be shaping the researchers' conclusions.

Using Current Sources

Be sure to seek out sources that are current, or up to date. Depending on the topic, sources may become outdated relatively soon after publication, or they may remain useful for years. For instance, online social networking sites have evolved rapidly over the past few years. An article published in 2002 about this topic will not provide current information. On the other hand, a research paper on elementary education practices might refer to studies published decades ago by influential child psychologists.

When using websites for research, check to see when the site was last updated. Many sites publish this information on the homepage, and some, such as news sites, are updated daily or weekly. Many nonfunctioning links are a sign that a website is not regularly updated. Do not be afraid to ask your professor for suggestions if you find that many of your most relevant sources are not especially reliable—or that the most reliable sources are not relevant.

Evaluating Overall Quality by Asking Questions

When you evaluate a source, you will consider the criteria previously discussed as well as your overall impressions of its quality. Read carefully, and notice how well the author presents and supports his or her statements. Stay actively engaged—do not simply accept an author's words as truth. Ask questions to determine each source's value. Checklist 11.1 lists ten questions to ask yourself as a critical reader.

Checklist 11.1

Source Evaluation

- Is the type of source appropriate for my purpose? Is it a high-quality source or one that needs to be looked at more critically?
- Can I establish that the author is credible and the publication is reputable?
- Does the author support ideas with specific facts and details that are carefully documented? Is the source of the author's information clear? (When you use secondary sources, look for sources that are not too removed from primary research.)
- Does the source include any factual errors or instances of faulty logic?
- Does the author leave out any information that I would expect to see in a discussion of this topic?
- Do the author's conclusions logically follow from the evidence that is presented? Can I see how the author got from one point to another?
- Is the writing clear and organized, and is it free from errors, clichés, and empty buzzwords? Is the tone objective, balanced, and reasonable? (Be on the lookout for extreme, emotionally charged language.)
- Are there any obvious biases or agendas? Based on what I know about the author, are there likely to be any hidden agendas?
- Are graphics informative, useful, and easy to understand? Are websites organized, easy to navigate, and free of clutter like flashing ads and unnecessary sound effects?
- Is the source contradicted by information found in other sources? (If so, it is possible that your sources are presenting similar information but taking different perspectives, which requires you to think carefully about which sources you find more convincing and why. Be suspicious, however, of any source that presents facts that you cannot confirm elsewhere.)

Writing at Work

The critical thinking skills you use to evaluate research sources as a student are equally valuable when you conduct research on the job. If you follow certain periodicals or websites, you have probably identified publications that consistently provide reliable information. Reading blogs and online discussion groups is a great way to identify new trends and hot topics in a particular field, but these sources should not be used for substantial research.

Research: How to Use Sources Effectively

Listening to Sources, Talking to Sources

Principle 1: Listen to your sources

Excerpt from student essay

These insights from cognitive science enable us to critically assess the claims made on both sides of the education reform debate. On one hand, they cast doubt on the claims of education reformers that measuring teachers' performance by student test scores is the best way to improve education....

At the same time, opponents of education reform should acknowledge that these research findings should prompt us to take a fresh look at how we educate our children. While Stan Karp of Rethinking Schools is correct when he argues that "data-driven formulas [based on standardized testing] lack both statistical credibility and a basic understanding of the human motivations and relation- ships that make good schooling possible"[1], it doesn't necessarily follow that all education reform proposals lack merit. Challenging standards, together with specific training in emotional self-regulation, will likely enable more students to succeed.

Have you ever had the maddening experience of arguing with someone who twisted your words to make it seem like you were saying something you weren't? Novice writers sometimes inadvertently misrepresent their sources when they quote very minor points from an article or even positions that the authors of an article disagree with. It often happens when students approach their sources with the goal of finding snippets that align with their own opinion. For example, the passage above contains the phrase "measuring teachers' performance by student test scores is the best way to improve education." An inexperienced writer might include that quote in a paper without making it clear that the author(s) of the source actually dispute that very claim. Doing so is not intentionally fraudulent, but it reveals that the paper-writer isn't really thinking about and responding to claims and arguments made by others. In that way, it harms his or her credibility.

Academic journal articles are especially likely to be misrepresented by student writers because their literature review sections often summarize a number of contrasting viewpoints. For example, sociologists Jennifer C. Lee and Jeremy Staff wrote a paper in which they note that high-schoolers who spend more hours at a job are more likely to drop out of school.[2] However, Lee and Staff 's analysis finds that working more hours doesn't actually make a student more likely to drop out. Instead, the students who express less interest in school are both more likely to work a lot of hours *and* more likely to drop out. In short, Lee and Staff argue that disaffection with school causes students to drop-out, not working at a job. In reviewing prior research about the impact of work on dropping out, Lee and Staff write "Paid work, especially when it is considered intensive, reduces grade point averages, time spent on homework, educational aspirations, and the likelihood of completing high school."[3] If you included that quote without explaining how it fits into Lee and Staff 's actual argument, you would be misrepresenting that source.

Principle 2: Provide context

Another error beginners often make is to drop in a quote without any context. If you simply quote, "Students begin preschool with a set of self-regulation skills that are a product of their genetic inheritance and their family environment" (Willingham, 2011, p.24), your reader is left wondering who Willingham is, why he or she is included here, and where this statement fits into his or her larger work. The whole point of incorporating sources is to situate your own insights in the conversation. As part of that, you should provide some kind of context the first time you use that source. Some examples:

Willingham, a cognitive scientist, claims that ...

Research in cognitive science has found that ... (Willingham, 2011).

Willingham argues that "Students begin preschool with a set of self-regulation skills that are a product of their genetic inheritance and their family environment" (Willingham, 2011, p.24). Drawing on findings in cognitive science, he explains "..."

As the second example above shows, providing a context doesn't mean writing a brief biography of every author in your bibliography—it just means including some signal about why that source is included in your text.

Even more baffling to your reader is when quoted material does not fit into the flow of the text. For example, a novice student might write,

Schools and parents shouldn't set limits on how much teenagers are allowed to work at jobs. "We conclude that intensive work does not affect the likelihood of high school dropout among youths who have a high propensity to spend long hours on the job" (Lee and Staff, 2007, p. 171). Teens should be trusted to learn how to manage their time.

The reader is thinking, who is this sudden, ghostly "we"? Why should this source be believed? If you find that passages with quotes in your draft are awkward to read out loud, that's a sign that you need to contextualize the quote more effectively. Here's a version that puts the quote in context:

Schools and parents shouldn't set limits on how much teenagers are allowed to work at jobs. Lee and Staff 's carefully designed study found that "intensive work does not affect the likelihood of high school dropout among youths who have a high propensity to spend long hours on the job" (2007, p. 171). Teens should be trusted to learn how to manage their time.

In this latter example, it's now clear that Lee and Staff are scholars and that their empirical study is being used as evidence for this argumentative point. Using a source in this way invites readers to check out Lee and Staff's work for themselves if they doubt this claim.

Many writing instructors encourage their students to contextualize their use of sources by making a "quotation sandwich"; that is, introduce the quote in some way and then follow it up with your own words. If you've made a bad habit of dropping in unintroduced quotes, the quotation sandwich idea may help you improve your skills, but in general you don't need to approach every quote or paraphrase as a three-part structure to have well integrated sources. You should, however, avoid ending a paragraph with a quotation. If you're struggling to figure out what to write after a quote or close paraphrase, it may be that you haven't yet figured out what role the quote is playing in your own analysis. If that happens to you a lot, try writing the whole first draft in your own words and then incorporate material from sources as you revise.

Principle 3: Use sources efficiently

Some student writers are in a rut of only quoting whole sentences. Some others get overly enamored of extended block quotes and the scholarly look they give to the page. These aren't the worst sins of academic writing, but they get in the way of one of the key principles of writing with sources: shaping quotes and paraphrases efficiently. Efficiency follows from the second principle, because when you fully incorporate sources into your own explicit argument, you zero in on the phrases, passages, and ideas that are relevant to your points. It's a very good sign for your paper when most quotes are short (key terms, phrases, or parts of sentences) and the longer quotes (whole sentences and passages) are clearly justified by the discussion in which they're embedded. Every bit of every quote should feel indispensable to the paper. An overabundance of long quotes usually means that your own argument is undeveloped. The most incandescent quotes will not hide that fact from your professor.

Also, some student writers forget that quoting is not the only way to incorporate sources. Paraphrasing and summarizing are sophisticated skills that are often more appropriate to use than direct quoting. The first two paragraphs of the example passage above do not include any quotations, even though they are both clearly focused on presenting the work of others. Student writers may avoid paraphrasing out of fear of plagiarizing, and it's true that a poorly executed paraphrase will make it seem like the student writer is fraudulently claiming the wordsmithing work of others as his or her own. Sticking to direct quotes seems safer. However, it is worth your time to master paraphrasing because it often helps you be more clear and concise, drawing out only those elements that are relevant to the thread of your analysis.

For example, here's a passage from a hypothetical paper with a block quote that is fully relevant to the argument but, nevertheless, inefficient:

Drawing on a lifetime of research, Kahneman concludes our brains are prone to error:[4]

> System 1 registers the cognitive ease with which it processes information, but it does not generate a warning signal when it becomes unreliable. Intuitive answers come to mind quickly and confidently, whether they originate from skills or from heuristics. There is no simple way for System 2 to distinguish between a skilled and a heuristic response. Its only recourse is to slow down and attempt to construct an answer on its own, which it is reluctant to do because it is indolent. Many suggestions of System 1 are casually endorsed with minimal checking, as in the bat-and-ball problem.

While people can get better at recognizing and avoiding these errors, Kahneman suggests, the more robust solutions involve developing procedures within organizations to promote careful, effortful thinking in making important decisions and judgments.

Even a passage that is important to reference and is well contextualized in the flow of the paper will be inefficient if it introduces terms and ideas that aren't central to the analysis within the paper. Imagine, for example, that other parts of this hypothetical paper use Kahneman's other terms for System 1 (fast thinking) and System 2 (slow thinking); the sudden encounter of "System 1" and "System 2" would be confusing and tedious for your reader. Similarly, the terms "heuristics" and "bat-and-ball problem" might be unfamiliar to your reader. Their presence in the block quote just muddies the waters. In this case, a paraphrase is a much better choice. Here's an example passage that uses a paraphrase to establish the same points more clearly and efficiently:

> Drawing on a lifetime of research, Kahneman summarizes that our brains are prone to error because they necessarily rely on cognitive shortcuts that may or may not yield valid judgments. We have the capacity to stop and examine our assumptions, Kahneman points out, but we often want to avoid that hard work. As a result, we tend to accept our quick, intuitive responses. While people can get better at recognizing and avoiding these errors, Kahneman suggests that the more robust solutions involve developing procedures within organizations to promote careful, effortful thinking in making important decisions and judgments.

Not only is the paraphrased version shorter (97 words versus 151), it is clearer and more efficient because it highlights the key ideas, avoiding specific terms and examples that aren't used in the rest of the paper.

Whether you choose a long quote, short quote, paraphrase or summary depends on the role that the source in playing in your analysis. The trick is to make deliberate, thoughtful decisions about how to incorporate ideas and words from others.

Paraphrasing, summarizing, and the mechanical conventions of quoting take a lot of practice to master. If you suspect that you're in a quoting rut, try out some new ways of incorporating sources.

Principle 4: Choose precise verbs of attribution

It's time to get beyond the all-purpose "says." And please don't look up "says" in the thesaurus and substitute verbs like "proclaim" (unless there was actually a proclamation) or "pronounce" (unless there was actually a pronouncement). Here are 15 useful alternatives:

- claims
- asserts
- relates
- recounts
- complains
- reasons
- proposes
- suggests (if the author is speculating or hypothesizing)
- contests (disagrees)
- concludes
- shows
- argues
- explains
- indicates
- points out

More precise choices like these carry a lot more information than "says", enabling you to relate more with fewer words. For one thing, they can quickly convey what kind of idea you're citing: a speculative one ("postulates")? A conclusive one ("determines")? A controversial one ("counters")? You can further show how you're incorporating these sources into your own narrative. For example, if you write that an author "claims" something, you're presenting yourself as fairly neutral about that claim. If you instead write that the author "shows" something, then you signal to your reader that you find that evidence more convincing. "Suggests" on the other hand is a much weaker endorsement.

Using Sources Creatively

When writing papers that require the use of outside source material, it is often tempting to cite only direct quotations from your sources. If, however, this is the only method of citation you choose, your paper will become nothing more than a series of quotations linked together by a few connecting words. Your paper will seem to be a collection of others' thoughts and will contain little thinking on your part.

To avoid falling into this trap, follow a few simple pointers:

- **Avoid using long quotations merely as space-fillers**. While this is an attractive option when faced with a ten-page paper, the overuse of long quotations gives the reader the impression you cannot think for yourself.
- **Don't use only direct quotations**. Try using paraphrases in addition to your direct quotations. To the reader, the effective use of paraphrases indicates that you took the time to think about the meaning behind the quote's words.
- When introducing direct quotations, try to **use a variety of verbs in your signal phrases**. Don't always rely on stock verbs such as "states" or "says." Think for a little while about the purpose of your quotation and then choose a context-appropriate verb.

Also, when using direct quotations try qualifying them in a novel or interesting manner. Depending on the system of documentation you're using, the signal phrases don't always have to introduce the quotation.

For example, instead of saying:

"None of them knew the color of the sky" is the opening line of Stephen Crane's short story, "The Open Boat" (339). This implies the idea that "all sense of certainty" in the lives of these men is gone (Wolford 18).

Try saying:

"None of them knew the color of the sky," the opening line of Stephen Crane's, "The Open Boat," implies that "all sense of certainty" in the lives of these men is gone (Crane 339; Wolford 18).

The combination of these two sentences into one is something different. It shows thought on the writer's part in how to combine direct quotations in an interesting manner.

Conclusion

Like so many things in adult life, writing in college is often both more liberating and burdensome than writing in high school and before. On the one hand, students might have felt in their high-school experiences that their own opinions didn't matter in academic writing, and that they can't make any claims that aren't exactly paralleled by a pedigreed quotation. Writing papers based on their own insights and opinions can seem freeing in contrast.

At the same time, a college student attending full time may be expected to have original and well-considered ideas about pre-Columbian Latin American history, congressional redistricting, sports in society, post-colonial literatures, and nano-technology, all in about two weeks. Under these conditions, it's easy to see why some would long for the days when simple, competent reporting did the job.

You probably won't have an authentic intellectual engagement with *every* college writing assignment, but approaching your written work as an opportunity to dialogue with the material can help you find the momentum you need to succeed with this work.

---

http://www.rethinkingschools.org/archive/26_03/26_03_karp.shtm ↵
Lee, J.C. and Jeremy Staff, "When Work Matters: The Varying Impact of Work Intensity on High School Drop Out," *Sociology of Education* 80, no. 2 (2007): 158-178. ↵
Ibid., 159. ↵

Kahneman, Thinking, Fast and Slow, 416-7. ↵

CC licensed content, Original

- Revisions and Adaptations. **Authored by**: Dann Coble. **Provided by**: Corning community College. **Project**: ENGL 1010 OER Project. **License**: *CC BY-NC-SA: Attribution-NonCommercial-ShareAlike*

CC licensed content, Shared previously

- Using Sources Creatively section. **Authored by**: Heather Logan. **Provided by**: University of Richmond Writing Center. **Located at**: http://writing2.richmond.edu/writing/wweb/creatsrc.html. **License**: *CC BY-NC-ND: Attribution-NonCommercial-NoDerivatives*
- Listening to Sources, Talking to Sources. **Authored by**: Amy Guptill. **Provided by**: The College at Brockport, SUNY. **Located at**: http://textbooks.opensuny.org/writing-in-college-from-competence-to-excellence/. **Project**: Writing in College: From Competence to Excellence. **License**: *CC BY-NC-SA: Attribution-NonCommercial-ShareAlike*
- Image of context is king. **Authored by**: Rebecca Jackson. **Located at**: https://flic.kr/p/tkdaSh. **License**: *CC BY-NC-ND: Attribution-NonCommercial-NoDerivatives*
- Image of three communicators. **Authored by**: Paul Shanks. **Located at**: https://flic.kr/p/Ckunu. **License**: *CC BY-NC: Attribution-NonCommercial*
- Revision and Adaptation. **Provided by**: Lumen Learning. **License**: *CC BY-NC-SA: Attribution-NonCommercial-ShareAlike*

Using Sources

Beginning writers sometimes attempt to transform a pile of note cards into a formal research paper without any intermediary step. This approach presents problems. The writer's original question and thesis may be buried in a flood of disconnected details taken from research sources. The first draft may present redundant or contradictory information. Worst of all, the writer's ideas and voice may be lost. An effective research paper focuses on the writer's ideas—from the question that sparked the research process to how the writer answers that question based on the research findings. Before beginning a draft, or even an outline, good writers pause and reflect. They ask themselves questions such as the following:

- How has my thinking changed based on my research? What have I learned?
- Was my working thesis on target? Do I need to rework my thesis based on what I have learned?
- How does the information in my sources mesh with my research questions and help me answer those questions? Have any additional important questions or subtopics come up that I will need to address in my paper?
- How do my sources complement each other? What ideas or facts recur in multiple sources?
- Where do my sources disagree with each other, and why?

Selecting Useful Information

When you conduct research, you keep an open mind and seek out many promising sources. You take notes on any information that looks like it might help you answer your research questions. Often, new ideas and terms come up in your reading, and these, too, find their way into your notes. You may record facts or quotations that catch your attention even if they did not seem immediately relevant to your research question. By now, you have probably amassed an impressively detailed collection of notes.

You will not use all of your notes in your paper.

Good researchers are thorough. They look at multiple perspectives, facts, and ideas related to their topic, and they gather a great deal of information. Effective writers, however, are selective. They determine which information is most relevant and appropriate for their purpose. They include details that develop or explain their ideas—and they leave out details that do not. The writer, not the pile of notes, is the controlling force. The writer shapes the content of the research paper.

Writing at Work

When you create workplace documents based on research, selectivity remains important. A project team may spend months conducting market surveys to prepare for rolling out a new product, but few managers have time to read the research in its entirety. Most employees want the research distilled into a few well-supported points. Focused, concise writing is highly valued in the workplace.

Identify Information That Supports Your Thesis

Systematically looking through your notes will help you. Begin by identifying the notes that clearly support your thesis. Mark or group these, either physically or using the cut-and-paste function in your word-processing program. As you identify the crucial details that support your thesis, make sure you analyze them critically. Ask the following questions to focus your thinking:

- **Is this detail from a reliable, high-quality source? Is it appropriate for me to cite this source in an academic paper?** The bulk of the support for your thesis should come from reliable, reputable sources. If most of the details that support your thesis are from less-reliable sources, you may need to do additional research or modify your thesis.
- **Is the link between this information and my thesis obvious—or will I need to explain it to my readers?** Remember, you have spent more time thinking and reading about this topic than your audience. Some connections might be obvious to both you and your readers. More often, however, you will need to provide the analysis or explanation that shows how the information supports your thesis. As you read through your notes, jot down ideas you have for making those connections clear.
- **What personal biases or experiences might affect the way I interpret this information?** No researcher is 100 percent objective. We all have personal opinions and experiences that influence our reactions to what we read and learn. Good researchers are aware of this human tendency. They keep an open mind when they read opinions or facts that contradict their beliefs.

Tip

It can be tempting to ignore information that does not support your thesis or that contradicts it outright. However, such information is important. At the very least, it gives you a sense of what has been written about the issue. More importantly, it can help you question and refine your own thinking so that writing your research paper is a true learning process.

CC licensed content, Original

Synthesizing Sources

Synthesis is something you already do in your everyday life. For example, if you are shopping for a new car, the research question you are trying to answer is, "Which car should I buy"? You explore available models, prices, options, and consumer reviews, and you make comparisons. For example: Car X costs more than car Y but gets better mileage. Or: Reviewers A, B, and C all prefer Car X, but their praise is based primarily on design features that aren't important to you. It is this analysis *across* sources that moves you towards an answer to your question.

Early in an academic research project you are likely to find yourself making initial comparisons—for example, you may notice that Source A arrives at a conclusion very different from that of Source B—but the task of synthesis will become central to your work when you begin drafting your research paper or presentation.

Remember, when you synthesize, you are not just compiling information. You are organizing that information around a specific argument or question, and this work—your own intellectual work—is central to research writing.

Below are some questions that highlight ways in which the act of synthesizing brings together ideas and generates new knowledge.

How do the sources speak to your specific argument or research question?

Your argument or research question is the main unifying element in your project. Keep this in the forefront of your mind when you write about your sources. Explain how, specifically, each source supports your central claim/s or suggests possible answers to your question. For example: Does the source provide essential background information or a definitional foundation for your argument or inquiry? Does it present numerical data that supports one of your points or helps you answer a question you have posed? Does it present a theory that might be applied to some aspect of your project? Does it present a recognized expert's insights on your topic?

How do the sources speak to each other?

Sometimes you will find explicit dialogue between sources (for example, Source A refutes Source B by name), and sometimes you will need to bring your sources into dialogue (for example, Source A does not mention Source B, but you observe that the two are advancing similar or dissimilar arguments). Attending to interrelationships among sources is at the heart of the task of synthesis.

Begin by asking: What are the points of agreement? Where are there disagreements?

But be aware that you are unlikely to find your sources in pure positions of "for" vs. "against." You are more likely to find agreement in some areas and disagreement in other areas. You may also find agreement but for different reasons—such as different underlying values and priorities, or different methods of inquiry.

Where are there, or aren't there, information gaps?

Where is the available information unreliable (for example, it might be difficult to trace back to primary sources), or limited, (for example, based on just a few case studies, or on just one geographical area), or difficult for non-specialists to access (for example, written in specialist language, or tucked away in a physical archive)?

Does your inquiry contain sub-questions that may not at present be answerable, or that may not be answerable without additional primary research—for example, laboratory studies, direct observation, interviews with witnesses or participants, etc.?

Or, alternatively, is there a great deal of reliable, accessible information that addresses your question or speaks to your argument or inquiry?

In considering these questions, you are engaged in synthesis: you are conducting an overview assessment of the field of available information and in this way generating composite knowledge.

Remember, synthesis is about pulling together information from a range of sources in order to answer a question or construct an argument. It is something you will be called upon to do in a wide variety of academic, professional, and personal contexts. Being able to dive into an ocean of information and surface with meaningful conclusions is an essential life skill.

Synthesis Notes

Synthesis notes are a strategy for taking and using reading notes that bring together—synthesize—what we read with our thoughts about our topic in a way that lets us integrate our notes seamlessly into the process of writing a first draft. Six steps will take us from reading sources to a first draft.

When we read, it is easy to take notes that don't help us build our own arguments when we move from note-taking to writing. In high school, most of us learned to take notes that summarize readings. Summarizing works well when the purpose of our notes is to help us memorize information quickly for a test. When we read in preparation for writing a research-supported argument, however, summarizing is inefficient because our notes don't reflect how our sources fit into our argument. We have to return to our sources and try to recall why and how we saw them contribute to our thinking.

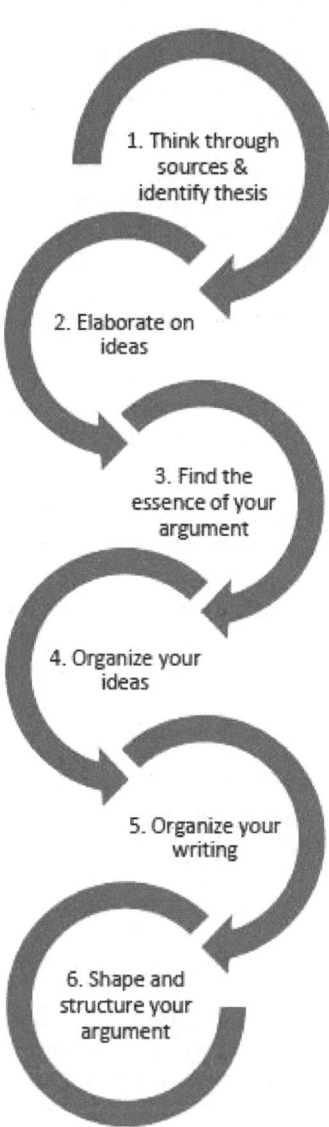

1. Think through sources & identify thesis

2. Elaborate on ideas

3. Find the essence of your argument

4. Organize your ideas

5. Organize your writing

6. Shape and structure your argument

Thinking through your sources

Step 1: As you read, keep in mind your purpose. Why are you reading this source? About what will you be writing? Write down your thoughts on how the text fits in with what you are currently thinking about your topic; if you did not begin your research with ideas, start thinking and building as you read. Try to make complete sentences. Often, you may summarize or paraphrase a bit of what the text is saying as you refer to it in the context of your own thinking, but do not just summarize what the text says. Capture what you think as you read: your reactions, how it is helpful, how it is relevant. Incorporate any quotes you find especially helpful, but rather than simply copying the quote, write about and around the quote.

Repeat step 1 for each source you think you may use to build your argument.

Identifying your thesis: Whether or not you began with firm ideas about your topic, your reading – and, more precisely, your thinking as you read – will be the source of new ideas. Your thesis, then, will emerge during your reading as the product of how all of your reading and thinking comes together to create a position you can support, with your sources and with your own well-informed argumentation. Even if you began your research holding a clear position on your topic, give your thesis permission to change as you read. Not doing so limits your capacity to learn and grow through your reading and, moreover, risks leaving you unable to support your thesis with your sources.

When you feel as though you have read and thought enough to develop a position on your topic that your sources can support, and that you can stand behind, take note of that position as your thesis. Know, though, that your thesis may still grow and change as you continue to read, think, and draft if you find your sources leading you to support a different position.

Elaborating on your ideas

Step 2: When you are ready to begin writing, refer back to your synthesis notes. Look at the first point and write a short paragraph about that thought or observation. If your synthesis notes are in complete sentences, you may cut and paste those sentences into your new paragraphs or revise and build from them to reflect how your thinking has changed and grown. Then move to the next note and, again, write a short paragraph about that observation. These sections of writing do not need to be connected; that will come later. Do not worry about writing a coherent paper; just focus on one idea or observation at a time.

If you get stuck – if you cannot figure out how a particular note fits into your argument or if it no longer fits—skip that note and move to the next one. You can return to these unused notes later when you may find that you now have something to say about them or that they simply are not part of your argument.

You may find it helpful to color-code your synthesis notes to remind yourself of what material you have and have not used. Remember, too, to include in-text citations to your original source material as you write.

When you reach the end of your notes, you should have a list of short paragraphs constituting much of your argument.

Finding the essence of your argument

Step 3: Read back through your short paragraphs and, in a separate document or on a separate sheet of paper, summarize each paragraph in a single phrase or sentence. If you cannot summarize a paragraph with a single phrase, try to revise the paragraph so that it focuses on just one idea. Give each paragraph and its corresponding summary phrase a number so that you can match the paragraph to its summary phrase.

Organizing your ideas

Step 4: Now we will organize the writing we did in step 2. Looking only at the list of summary phrases, rearrange them until they can be read as a logical, coherent paragraph from top to bottom. This paragraph should summarize your argument. If you find that a phrase fails to fit, set it aside. If you find a gap where you need an additional sentence to provide a logical connection between two of your phrases, write in that sentence.

Organizing your writing

Step 5: Return to your short paragraphs and rearrange them so that they match the order of the summary phrases that you have just organized. If you set aside any phrases, set aside their corresponding paragraphs—you may not end up using those paragraphs. If you had to write any new phrases, add those phrases in their place in-between paragraphs; you can expand these phrases into full paragraphs in the next step.

Shaping and structuring your argument

Step 6: Now, take these organized paragraphs and bring them together into a coherent argument. When you read your organized paragraphs, the ideas from each paragraph should flow logically into the next. Add transitions to make those connections explicit. Revise your paragraphs to make the logic of your argument more clear. Delete sentences that are no longer relevant in their new context or add sentences if you need to more fully explain an idea. Expand any added phrases into more complete connecting paragraphs.

At this stage, you may need to refer back to your source material to flesh out any gaps in your argument, or you may find that you need to consult new source material for the same purpose, but your draft should make clear what additional information you need and where it goes. You will also want to add an introduction and conclusion summarizing and drawing out the main points of your argument. Nevertheless, you have produced a first draft from your reading notes without ever going through the painful steps of wondering where and how to begin writing.

Research: Documentation

Academic Integrity

What is Academic Integrity?

Academic Integrity is defined as the honest and responsible pursuit of scholarship. Academic integrity is characterized by

- completing exams and other academic assignments in an honest way
- presenting truthful and accurate data and research information in academic assignments
- avoiding plagiarism by properly incorporating and acknowledging sources

Academic Dishonesty

In all academic work, students are expected to submit materials that are their own and are to include attribution for any ideas or language that are not their own. Examples of dishonest conduct include, but are not limited to:

- Cheating including **giving and receiving information in examinations**.
- Falsification of data, results or sources.
- **Collusion**, such as working with another person when independent work is assigned.
- Plagiarism.
- **Submitting the same paper** or report for assignments in more than one course without permission (self-plagiarism).

Cheating

Cheating is the most well-known academically dishonest behavior. Cheating includes more than just copying a neighbor's answers on an exam or peeking at a cheat sheet or storing answers on your phone. Giving or offering information in examinations is also dishonest. Turning in someone else's work as your own is also considered cheating.

Collusion

Collusion, such as working with another person or persons when independent work is assigned, is considered academic dishonesty. While it is fine to work in a team if your professor specifically requires or allows it, be sure to communicate about guidelines on permissible collaboration if you are unsure (including how to attribute the contributions of others).

> **True Story:** In 2012, 125 Harvard students (http://en.wikipedia.org/wiki/2012_Harvard_cheating_scandal) were investigated for working together on a take-home final exam. The only rule on the exam was not to work together. Almost half of those students were determined to have cheated, and forced to withdraw from school for a year.

Falsifying Results and Misrepresentation

Falsifying results in studies or experiments is a serious breach of academic honesty. Students are sometimes tempted to make up results if their study or experiment does not produce the results they hoped for. But getting caught has major consequences.

Misrepresenting yourself or your research is, by definition, dishonest. Misrepresentation might include inflating credentials, claiming that a study proves something that it does not, or leaving out inconvenient and/or contradictory results.

> **True Story:** An undergraduate at the University of Kansas claimed to be a researcher and promoted his (unfortunately incorrect) research on how much a Big Mac would cost if the U.S. raised minimum wage. His study was picked up by the Huffington Post, NY Times, and other major news outlets, who then had to publish retractions.

Plagiarism

Plagiarism occurs when you present another person's ideas, intentionally or unintentionally, as your own. In the *MLA Style Manual and Guide to Scholarly Publishing*, Joseph Gibaldi likens plagiarism to "intellectual theft," because it "gives the impression that you wrote or thought something that you in fact borrowed from someone, and to do so is a violation of professional ethics" (165). It is your responsibility as the student to avoid plagiarizing. As a scholar you are expected to credit the sources of the ideas that you use in your own work.

How Can You Avoid Academic Dishonesty?

- Start your assignments early and stay on track with due dates.
- Ask for help from your professor.
- Join a study group.
- Take careful notes as you do your research and organize your sources.
- Work with a Librarian or the Writing Center to integrate and cite your sources and avoid plagiarism.
- Prioritize your integrity!

Know What Needs a Citation

The key to avoiding plagiarism is to make sure you give credit where credit is due. This may be credit for something somebody said, wrote, emailed, drew, or implied. You need to give credit to:

- Words or ideas presented in a magazine, book, newspaper, song, TV program, movie, web page, computer program, letter, advertisement, or any other medium
- Information you gain through interviewing or conversing with another person face-to-face, over the phone, or in writing
- Exact words or a unique phrase that you copy
- Diagrams, illustrations, charts, pictures, or other visual materials that you reprint
- Any electronically available media, including images, audio, video, or other media, that you reuse or repost.

Ultimately, you must cite any source of information you use in your paper that doesn't originate with you. You do **NOT** need to cite:

- your own ideas and opinions
- your own words
- common knowledge

Examples of common knowledge include:

- Basic facts: there are 365 days in a year, the earth orbits the sun, the molecular structure of water (H_2O), etc.
- Very well-known quotes: "A rose by any other name would smell as sweet" or "ask not what your country can do for you, ask what you can do for your country." You still have to use quotation marks and indicate who said the quote (Romeo in Shakespeare's Romeo and Juliet, and John F. Kennedy, respectively), but you do not need to include the source in your bibliography.
- Subject-specific common knowledge: There is information in specific disciplines or branches of knowledge that is considered common knowledge. A good indicator of what constitutes common knowledge is if you see the information in 4 or 5 articles or books and it does not need a citation. Until you become familiar

with what is considered common knowledge in your major area of study, it is best to play it safe and cite your sources or ask your professor.

CC licensed content, Shared previously

- What is Academic Integrity? and paragraph on plagiarism from Module 1 of the Academic Integrity Tutorial. **Provided by**: University of Maryland University College. **Located at**: http://www.umuc.edu/students/academic-integrity/tutorial.cfm/vailtutor/. **License**: *CC BY-SA: Attribution-ShareAlike*
- Academic Integrity Tutorial, examples of Academic Dishonesty. **Provided by**: DiMenna-Nyselius Library, Fairfield University. **Located at**: http://librarybestbets.fairfield.edu/c.php?g=476878&p=3314732. **License**: *CC BY-NC-SA: Attribution-NonCommercial-ShareAlike*
- Revision and Adaptation. **Provided by**: Lumen Learning. **License**: *CC BY-NC-SA: Attribution-NonCommercial-ShareAlike*
- Walk, Talk, Cook, Eat: A Guide to Using Sources. **Authored by**: Cynthia R. Haller. **Located at**: http://www.saylor.org/site/wp-content/uploads/2013/01/writing-spaces-readings-on-writing-vol-2.pd. **Project**: Writing Spaces. **License**: *CC BY-NC-SA: Attribution-NonCommercial-ShareAlike*

Paraphrasing

Introduction

Recall from the video in the opening of this section that "Sparky Sweets, PhD" didn't use any direct quotes from *Animal Farm*, even for capturing the book's thesis idea. Instead, he cast the main idea in unique language, which both made it memorable and also demonstrated his deep understanding of the concept. Read on for advice on paraphrasing effectively, from Texas A&M University.

When you paraphrase, you recast someone else's words into an entirely new form. A good paraphrase doesn't simply substitute synonyms for the original words but substantially rewrites the passage—without changing its meaning or emphasis. Always cite anything you paraphrase; failure to cite someone else's ideas, even if you reword them, is plagiarism.

When to Paraphrase

There are many reasons to use a paraphrase as opposed to a direct quotation. You might need to paraphrase in any of the following situations:

- The ideas in the original passage are more important than the style or authority of the author.
- The ideas are more memorable than the author's language.
- The original language is difficult to comprehend or highly technical.
- A quotation is too long and/or wordy.
- The original passage needs to be clarified.
- The source of a quotation is unknown.

Writing a Paraphrase

First, re-read the original work to be sure you understand it. Then, set it aside and write what you think it means in your own words. Putting the original out of sight is helpful since it frees you from the temptation to merely rearrange the words or substitute a synonym or two. A successful paraphrase will typically involve several of the following: changing word order or sentence structure, combining related ideas, eliminating jargon or wordiness, simplifying the original, and using synonyms for key terms. If the original uses a very distinct term or phrase that you don't want to eliminate (or simply can't improve upon), use the term or phrase in quotation marks and incorporate it into your paraphrase. Finally, check to be sure you haven't altered the meaning of the original.

Incorporating a Paraphrase

It's important to integrate the paraphrase smoothly into the rest of your writing. A useful technique is to begin by acknowledging the source of the material. For instance, when paraphrasing a researcher named John Doe, you might say, "According to Doe . . ." or "As researcher Doe stated . . ." You can also give information about the source: "According to John Doe, a prominent statistician, the idea of . . ." You may also want to provide context to help your reader understand why you're including the paraphrased material: "Researcher John Doe reached a similar conclusion when he stated that . . ." Finally, be sure to cite the original.

Sample Paraphrase

Original quotation from President Kennedy's inaugural address: "And so, my fellow Americans: ask not what your country can do for you—ask what you can do for your country. My fellow citizens of the world: ask not what America will do for you, but what together we can do for the freedom of man."

Paraphrase: In the closing of his inaugural address, President Kennedy implored both Americans and people from other nations to put aside their personal interests in order to work for the common good.

Checklist

- Does the paraphrase consist entirely of your own words?
- Did you do more than just substitute synonyms or change the sentence structure?
- Did you make it clear that you are using someone else's thoughts?
- Did you keep the general meaning and emphasis of the original?
- Did you correctly cite the paraphrase?

MLA General Format

MLA General Format

Summary:

MLA (Modern Language Association) style is most commonly used to write papers and cite sources within the liberal arts and humanities. This resource, updated to reflect the *MLA Handbook* (8th ed.), offers examples for the general format of MLA research papers, in-text citations, endnotes/footnotes, and the Works Cited page.

Writers who properly use MLA also build their credibility by demonstrating accountability to their source material. Most importantly, the use of MLA style can protect writers from accusations of plagiarism, which is the purposeful or accidental uncredited use of source material by other writers.

If you are asked to use MLA format, be sure to consult the *MLA Handbook* (8th edition). Publishing scholars and graduate students should also consult the *MLA Style Manual and Guide to Scholarly Publishing* (3rd edition). The *MLA Handbook* is available in most writing centers and reference libraries; it is also widely available in bookstores, libraries, and at the MLA web site. See the Additional Resources section of this handout for a list of helpful books and sites about using MLA style.

Paper Format

The preparation of papers and manuscripts in MLA style is covered in chapter four of the MLA Handbook, and chapter four of the *MLA Style Manual*. Below are some basic guidelines for formatting a paper in *MLA style*.

General Guidelines

- Type your paper on a computer and print it out on standard, white 8.5 x 11-inch paper.
- Double-space the text of your paper, and use a legible font (e.g. Times New Roman). Whatever font you choose, MLA recommends that the regular and italics type styles contrast enough that they are recognizable one from another. The font size should be 12 pt.
- Leave only one space after periods or other punctuation marks (unless otherwise instructed by your instructor).
- Set the margins of your document to 1 inch on all sides.
- Indent the first line of paragraphs one half-inch from the left margin. MLA recommends that you use the Tab key as opposed to pushing the Space Bar five times.
- Create a header that numbers all pages consecutively in the upper right-hand corner, one-half inch from the top and flush with the right margin. (Note: Your instructor may ask that you omit the number on your first page. Always follow your instructor's guidelines.)
- Use italics throughout your essay for the titles of longer works and, only when absolutely necessary, providing emphasis.
- If you have any endnotes, include them on a separate page before your Works Cited page. Entitle the section Notes (centered, unformatted).

Formatting the First Page of Your Paper

- Do not make a title page for your paper unless specifically requested.
- In the upper left-hand corner of the first page, list your name, your instructor's name, the course, and the date. Again, be sure to use double-spaced text.
- Double space again and center the title. Do not underline, italicize, or place your title in quotation marks;

write the title in Title Case (standard capitalization), not in all capital letters.
- Use quotation marks and/or italics when referring to other works in your title, just as you would in your text: *Fear and Loathing in Las Vegas* as Morality Play; Human Weariness in "After Apple Picking"
- Double space between the title and the first line of the text.
- Create a header in the upper right-hand corner that includes your last name, followed by a space with a page number; number all pages consecutively with Arabic numerals (1, 2, 3, 4, etc.), one-half inch from the top and flush with the right margin. (Note: Your instructor or other readers may ask that you omit last name/page number header on your first page. Always follow instructor guidelines.)

Here is a sample of the first page of a paper in MLA style:

Catlin 1

Beth Catlin

Professor Elaine Bassett

English 106

3 August 2009

Andrew Carnegie: The Father of Middle-Class America

For decades Americans couldn't help but love the red-headed, fun-loving Little Orphan Annie. The image of the little girl moving so quickly from poverty to wealth provided hope for the poor in the 1930s, and her story continues to be a dream of what the future just might hold. The rags-to-riches phenomenon is the heart of the American Dream. And few other people have embodied this phenomenon as much as Andrew Carnegie did in the late 1800s and early 1900s. His example and industry caused him to become the father of middle-class America.

Andrew Carnegie can be looked to as an ideal example of a poor immigrant making his way up to become leader of the capitalist world. Carnegie was born into a poor working-class family in Scotland. According to the PBS documentary "The Richest Man in the World: Andrew Carnegie," the Industrial Revolution was difficult on Carnegie's father, causing him to lose his weaving business. The Carnegie family was much opposed to the idea of a privileged class, who gained their wealth simply by inheritance ("Richest"). This type of upbringing played a large factor in Andrew Carnegie's destiny. In order to appease his mother's desire for material benefits, and perhaps in an effort to heal his father's wounds, Carnegie rejected poverty and cleaved to prosperity.

Carnegie's character was ideal for gaining wealth. His mother taught him to "look after the pennies, and the pounds will take care of themselves;" he later turned this proverb into "watch the costs, and the profits take care of themselves" ("Richest"). Such thrift was integral to his future success. He also believed that "all is well since all goes better" ("Richest"). His theory

The First Page of an MLA Paper

Section Headings

Writers sometimes use Section Headings to improve a document's readability. These sections may include individual chapters or other named parts of a book or essay.

Essays

MLA recommends that when you divide an essay into sections that you number those sections with an Arabic number and a period followed by a space and the section name.

> Early Writings
> The London Years
> Traveling the Continent

Final Years

Books

MLA does not have a prescribed system of headings for books (for more information on headings, please see page 146 in the *MLA Style Manual and Guide to Scholarly Publishing*, 3rd edition). If you are only using one level of headings, meaning that all of the sections are distinct and parallel and have no additional sections that fit within them, MLA recommends that these sections resemble one another grammatically. For instance, if your headings are typically short phrases, make all of the headings short phrases (and not, for example, full sentences). Otherwise, the formatting is up to you. It should, however, be consistent throughout the document.

If you employ multiple levels of headings (some of your sections have sections within sections), you may want to provide a key of your chosen level headings and their formatting to your instructor or editor.

Sample Section Headings

The following sample headings are meant to be used only as a reference. You may employ whatever system of formatting that works best for you so long as it remains consistent throughout the document.

Numbered:

Soil Conservation
      Erosion
      Terracing
Water Conservation
Energy Conservation

Formatted, unnumbered:

Level 1 Heading: bold, flush left

Level 2 Heading: italics, flush left

Level 3 Heading: centered, bold

Level 4 Heading: centered, italics

Level 5 Heading: underlined, flush left
All rights reserved content

MLA In-Text Citation

MLA In-Text Citations: The Basics

Summary:

MLA (Modern Language Association) style is most commonly used to write papers and cite sources within the liberal arts and humanities. This resource, updated to reflect the *MLA Handbook* (8th ed.), offers examples for the general format of MLA research papers, in-text citations, endnotes/footnotes, and the Works Cited page.

Basic in-text citation rules

In MLA style, referring to the works of others in your text is done by using what is known as **parenthetical citation**. This method involves placing relevant source information in parentheses after a quote or a paraphrase.

General Guidelines

- The source information required in a parenthetical citation depends (1.) upon the source medium (e.g. Print, Web, DVD) and (2.) upon the source's entry on the Works Cited (bibliography) page.
- Any source information that you provide in-text must correspond to the source information on the Works Cited page. More specifically, whatever signal word or phrase you provide to your readers in the text, must be the first thing that appears on the left-hand margin of the corresponding entry in the Works Cited List.

In-text citations: Author-page style

MLA format follows the author-page method of in-text citation. This means that the author's last name and the page number(s) from which the quotation or paraphrase is taken must appear in the text, and a complete reference should appear on your Works Cited page. The author's name may appear either in the sentence itself or in parentheses following the quotation or paraphrase, but the page number(s) should always appear in the parentheses, not in the text of your sentence. For example:

Wordsworth stated that Romantic poetry was marked by a "spontaneous overflow of powerful feelings" (263).

Romantic poetry is characterized by the "spontaneous overflow of powerful feelings" (Wordsworth 263). Wordsworth extensively explored the role of emotion in the creative process (263).

Both citations in the examples above, (263) and (Wordsworth 263), tell readers that the information in the sentence can be located on page 263 of a work by an author named Wordsworth. If readers want more information about this source, they can turn to the Works Cited page, where, under the name of Wordsworth, they would find the following information:

Wordsworth, William. *Lyrical Ballads*. Oxford UP, 1967.

In-text citations for print sources with known author

For Print sources like books, magazines, scholarly journal articles, and newspapers, provide a signal word or phrase (usually the author's last name) and a page number. If you provide the signal word/phrase in the sentence, you do not need to include it in the parenthetical citation.
Human beings have been described by Kenneth Burke as "symbol-using animals" (3).
Human beings have been described as "symbol-using animals" (Burke 3).

These examples must correspond to an entry that begins with Burke, which will be the first thing that appears on the left-hand margin of an entry in the Works Cited:

Burke, Kenneth. *Language as Symbolic Action: Essays on Life, Literature, and Method*. Berkeley: U of California P, 1966.

In-text citations for print sources by a corporate author

When a source has a corporate author, it is acceptable to use the name of the corporation followed by the page number for the in-text citation. You should also use abbreviations (e.g., nat'l for national) where appropriate, so as to avoid interrupting the flow of reading with overly long parenthetical citations.

In-text citations for print sources with no known author

When a source has no known author, use a shortened title of the work instead of an author name. Place the title in quotation marks if it's a short work (such as an article) or italicize it if it's a longer work (e.g. plays, books, television shows, entire Web sites) and provide a page number.
We see so many global warming hotspots in North America likely because this region has "more readily accessible climatic data and more comprehensive programs to monitor and study environmental change . . ." ("Impact of Global Warming" 6).

In this example, since the reader does not know the author of the article, an abbreviated title of the article appears in the parenthetical citation which corresponds to the full name of the article which appears first at the left-hand margin of its respective entry in the Works Cited. Thus, the writer includes the title in quotation marks as the signal phrase in the parenthetical citation in order to lead the reader directly to the source on the Works Cited page. The Works Cited entry appears as follows:

"The Impact of Global Warming in North America." *Global Warming: Early Signs*. 1999. http://www.climatehotmap.org/. Accessed 23 Mar. 2009.

We'll learn how to make a Works Cited page in a bit, but right now it's important to know that parenthetical citations and Works Cited pages allow readers to know which sources you consulted in writing your essay, so that they can either verify your interpretation of the sources or use them in their own scholarly work.

Author-page citation for classic and literary works with multiple editions

Page numbers are always required, but additional citation information can help literary scholars, who may have a different edition of a classic work like Marx and Engels's *The Communist Manifesto*. In such cases, give the page number of your edition (making sure the edition is listed in your Works Cited page, of course) followed by a semicolon, and then the appropriate abbreviations for volume (vol.), book (bk.), part (pt.), chapter (ch.), section (sec.), or paragraph (par.). For example:
Marx and Engels described human history as marked by class struggles (79; ch. 1).

Citing authors with same last names

Sometimes more information is necessary to identify the source from which a quotation is taken. For instance, if two or more authors have the same last name, provide both authors' first initials (or even the authors' full name if different authors share initials) in your citation. For example:
Although some medical ethicists claim that cloning will lead to designer children (R. Miller 12), others note that the advantages for medical research outweigh this consideration (A. Miller 46).

Citing a work by multiple authors

For a source with two authors, list the authors' last names in the text or in the parenthetical citation:
Best and Marcus argue that one should read a text for what it says on its surface, rather than looking for some hidden meaning (9).
The authors claim that surface reading looks at what is "evident, perceptible, apprehensible in texts" (Best and Marcus 9).

Corresponding works cited entry:

Best, David, and Sharon Marcus. "Surface Reading: An Introduction." *Representations*, vol. 108, no. 1, Fall 2009, pp. 1-21. JSTOR, doi:10.1525/rep.2009.108.1.1

For a source with three or more authors, list only the first author's last name, and replace the additional names with et al.
According to Franck et al., "Current agricultural policies in the U.S. are contributing to the poor health of Americans" (327).
The authors claim that one cause of obesity in the United States is government-funded farm subsidies (Franck et al. 327).

Corresponding works cited entry:

Franck, Caroline, et al. "Agricultural Subsidies and the American Obesity Epidemic." *American Journal of Preventative Medicine*, vol. 45, no. 3, Sept. 2013, pp. 327-333.

Citing multiple works by the same author

If you cite more than one work by a particular author, include a shortened title for the particular work from which you are quoting to distinguish it from the others. Put short titles of books in italics and short titles of articles in quotation marks.

Citing two articles by the same author:
Lightenor has argued that computers are not useful tools for small children ("Too Soon" 38), though he has acknowledged elsewhere that early exposure to computer games does lead to better small motor skill development in a child's second and third year ("Hand-Eye Development" 17).

Citing two books by the same author:
Murray states that writing is "a process" that "varies with our thinking style" (*Write to Learn* 6). Additionally, Murray argues that the purpose of writing is to "carry ideas and information from the mind of one person into the mind of another" (*A Writer Teaches Writing* 3).

Additionally, if the author's name is not mentioned in the sentence, you would format your citation with the author's name followed by a comma, followed by a shortened title of the work, followed, when appropriate, by page numbers:
Visual studies, because it is such a new discipline, may be "too easy" (Elkins, "Visual Studies" 63).

Citing multivolume works

If you cite from different volumes of a multivolume work, always include the volume number followed by a colon. Put a space after the colon, then provide the page number(s). (If you only cite from one volume, provide only the page number in parentheses.)
. . . as Quintilian wrote in *Institutio Oratoria* (1: 14-17).

Citing the Bible

In your first parenthetical citation, you want to make clear which Bible you're using (and underline or italicize the title), as each version varies in its translation, followed by book (do not italicize or underline), chapter and verse. For example:
Ezekiel saw "what seemed to be four living creatures," each with faces of a man, a lion, an ox, and an eagle (*New Jerusalem Bible*, Ezek. 1.5-10).

If future references employ the same edition of the Bible you're using, list only the book, chapter, and verse in the parenthetical citation.

Citing indirect sources

Sometimes you may have to use an indirect source. An indirect source is a source cited in another source. For such indirect quotations, use "qtd. in" to indicate the source you actually consulted. For example:
Ravitch argues that high schools are pressured to act as "social service centers, and they don't do that well" (qtd. in Weisman 259).

Note that, in most cases, a responsible researcher will attempt to find the original source, rather than citing an indirect source.

Citing non-print or sources from the Internet

With more and more scholarly work being posted on the Internet, you may have to cite research you have completed in virtual environments. While many sources on the Internet should not be used for scholarly work (reference the OWL's Evaluating Sources of Information resource) (http://owl.english.purdue.edu/owl/resource/553/01/), some Web sources are perfectly acceptable for research. When creating in-text citations for electronic, film, or Internet sources, remember that your citation must reference the source in your Works Cited.

Sometimes writers are confused with how to craft parenthetical citations for electronic sources because of the absence of page numbers, but often, these sorts of entries do not require any sort of parenthetical citation at all. For electronic and Internet sources, follow the following guidelines:

- Include in the text the first item that appears in the Work Cited entry that corresponds to the citation (e.g. author name, article name, website name, film name).
- You do not need to give paragraph numbers or page numbers based on your Web browser's print preview function.
- Unless you must list the Web site name in the signal phrase in order to get the reader to the appropriate entry, do not include URLs in-text. Only provide partial URLs such as when the name of the site includes, for example, a domain name, like *CNN.com* or *Forbes.com* as opposed to writing out http://www.cnn.com or http://www.forbes.com.

Miscellaneous non-print sources

Werner Herzog's *Fitzcarraldo* stars Herzog's long-time film partner, Klaus Kinski. During the shooting of *Fitzcarraldo*, Herzog and Kinski were often at odds, but their explosive relationship fostered a memorable and influential film.
During the presentation, Jane Yates stated that invention and pre-writing are areas of rhetoric that need more attention.

In the two examples above "Herzog" from the first entry and "Yates" from the second lead the reader to the first item each citation's respective entry on the Works Cited page:

Herzog, Werner, dir. *Fitzcarraldo*. Perf. Klaus Kinski. Filmverlag der Autoren, 1982.

Yates, Jane. "Invention in Rhetoric and Composition." Gaps Addressed: Future Work in Rhetoric and Composition, CCCC, Palmer House Hilton, 2002.

Electronic sources

One online film critic stated that *Fitzcarraldo* "has become notorious for its near-failure and many obstacles" (Taylor, "Fitzcarraldo").
The *Purdue OWL* is accessed by millions of users every year. Its "MLA Formatting and Style Guide" is one of the most popular resources (Russell et al.).

In the first example, the writer has chosen not to include the author name in-text; however, two entries from the same author appear in the Works Cited. Thus, the writer includes both the author's last name and the article title in the parenthetical citation in order to lead the reader to the appropriate entry on the Works Cited page (see below). In the second example, "Russell et al." in the parenthetical citation gives the reader an author name followed by the abbreviation "et al.," meaning, "and others," for the article "MLA Formatting and Style Guide." Both corresponding Works Cited entries are as follows:

Taylor, Rumsey. "Fitzcarraldo." *Slant*, 13 Jun. 2003, www.slantmagazine.com/film/review/fitzcarraldo/.

Russell, Tony, et al. "MLA Formatting and Style Guide." *The Purdue OWL*, 2 Aug. 2016, owl.english.purdue.edu/owl/resource/747/01/.

Multiple citations

To cite multiple sources in the same parenthetical reference, separate the citations by a semi-colon:
. . . as has been discussed elsewhere (Burke 3; Dewey 21).

Time-based media sources

When creating in-text citations for media that has a runtime, such as a movie or podcast, include the range of hours, minutes and seconds you plan to reference, like so (00:02:15-00:02:35).

When a citation is not needed

Common sense and ethics should determine your need for documenting sources. You do not need to give sources for familiar proverbs, well-known quotations or common knowledge. Remember, this is a rhetorical choice, based on audience. If you're writing for an expert audience of a scholarly journal, for example, they'll have different expectations of what constitutes common knowledge.

All rights reserved content

MLA Formatting Quotations

MLA Formatting Quotations

Summary:

MLA (Modern Language Association) style is most commonly used to write papers and cite sources within the liberal arts and humanities. This resource, updated to reflect the *MLA Handbook* (8th ed.), offers examples for the general format of MLA research papers, in-text citations, endnotes/footnotes, and the Works Cited page.

When you directly quote the works of others in your paper, you will format quotations differently depending on their length. Below are some basic guidelines for incorporating quotations into your paper. Please note that all pages in MLA should be **double-spaced**.

Short quotations

To indicate short quotations (fewer than four typed lines of prose or three lines of verse) in your text, enclose the quotation within double quotation marks. Provide the author and specific page citation (in the case of verse, provide line numbers) in the text, and include a complete reference on the Works Cited page. Punctuation marks such as periods, commas, and semicolons should appear after the parenthetical citation. Question marks and exclamation points should appear within the quotation marks if they are a part of the quoted passage but after the parenthetical citation if they are a part of your text.

For example, when quoting short passages of prose, use the following examples:
According to some, dreams express "profound aspects of personality" (Foulkes 184), though others disagree.
According to Foulkes's study, dreams may express "profound aspects of personality" (184).
Is it possible that dreams may express "profound aspects of personality" (Foulkes 184)?

When short (fewer than three lines of verse) quotations from poetry, mark breaks in short quotations of verse with a slash, (/), at the end of each line of verse (a space should precede and follow the slash).
Cullen concludes, "Of all the things that happened there / That's all I remember" (11-12).

Long quotations

For quotations that are more than four lines of prose or three lines of verse, place quotations in a free-standing block of text and omit quotation marks. Start the quotation on a new line, with the entire quote indented **½ inch** from the left margin; maintain double-spacing. Only indent the first line of the quotation by an additional quarter inch if you are citing multiple paragraphs. Your parenthetical citation should come **after** the closing punctuation mark. When quoting verse, maintain original line breaks. (You should maintain double-spacing throughout your essay.)

For example, when citing more than four lines of prose, use the following examples:
Nelly Dean treats Heathcliff poorly and dehumanizes him throughout her narration:
They entirely refused to have it in bed with them, or even in their room, and I had no more sense, so, I put it on the landing of the stairs, hoping it would be gone on the morrow. By chance, or else attracted by hearing his voice,

it crept to Mr. Earnshaw's door, and there he found it on quitting his chamber. Inquiries were made as to how it got there; I was obliged to confess, and in recompense for my cowardice and inhumanity was sent out of the house. (Bronte 78)

When citing long sections (more than three lines) of poetry, keep formatting as close to the original as possible.
In his poem "My Papa's Waltz," Theodore Roethke explores his childhood with his father:
The whiskey on your breath
Could make a small boy dizzy;
But I hung on like death:
Such waltzing was not easy.
We Romped until the pans
Slid from the kitchen shelf;
My mother's countenance
Could not unfrown itself. (quoted in Shrodes, Finestone, Shugrue 202)

When citing two or more paragraphs, use block quotation format, even if the passage from the paragraphs is less than four lines. Indent the first line of each quoted paragraph an extra quarter inch.
In "American Origins of the Writing-across-the-Curriculum Movement," David Russell argues,
Writing has been an issue in American secondary and higher education since papers and examinations came into wide use in the 1870s, eventually driving out formal recitation and oral examination. . . .
From its birth in the late nineteenth century, progressive education has wrestled with the conflict within industrial society between pressure to increase specialization of knowledge and of professional work (upholding disciplinary standards) and pressure to integrate more fully an ever-widerning number of citizens into intellectually meaningful activity within mass society (promoting social equity). . . . (3)

Adding or omitting words in quotations

If you add a word or words in a quotation, you should put brackets around the words to indicate that they are not part of the original text.
Jan Harold Brunvand, in an essay on urban legends, states, "some individuals [who retell urban legends] make a point of learning every rumor or tale" (78).

If you omit a word or words from a quotation, you should indicate the deleted word or words by using ellipsis marks, which are three periods (. . .) preceded and followed by a space. For example:
In an essay on urban legends, Jan Harold Brunvand notes that "some individuals make a point of learning every recent rumor or tale . . . and in a short time a lively exchange of details occurs" (78).

Please note that brackets are not needed around ellipses unless adding brackets would clarify your use of ellipses.

When omitting words from poetry quotations, use a standard three-period ellipses; however, when omitting one or more full lines of poetry, space several periods to about the length of a complete line in the poem:
These beauteous forms,
Through a long absence, have not been to me
As is a landscape to a blind man's eye:
. . . .
Felt in the blood, and felt along the heart;
And passing even into my purer mind,
With tranquil restoration . . . (22-24, 28-30)

MLA Works Cited Page

MLA Formatting and Style Guide

Summary:

MLA (Modern Language Association) style is most commonly used to write papers and cite sources within the liberal arts and humanities. This resource, updated to reflect the *MLA Handbook* (8th ed.), offers examples for the general format of MLA research papers, in-text citations, endnotes/footnotes, and the Works Cited page.

The following overview should help you better understand how to cite sources using MLA eighth edition, including the list of works cited and in-text citations.

Please use the example at the bottom of this page to cite the Purdue OWL in MLA.

Creating a Works Cited list using the eighth edition

MLA has turned to a style of documentation that is based on a general method that may be applied to every possible source, to many different types of writing. But since texts have become increasingly mobile, and the same document may be found in several different sources, following a set of fixed rules is no longer sufficient.

The current system is based on a few principles, rather than an extensive list of specific rules. While the handbook still gives examples of how to cite sources, it is organized according to the process of documentation, rather than by the sources themselves. This process teaches writers a flexible method that is universally applicable. Once you are familiar with the method, you can use it to document any type of source, for any type of paper, in any field.

Here is an overview of the process:

When deciding how to cite your source, start by consulting the list of core elements. These are the general pieces of information that MLA suggests including in each Works Cited entry. In your citation, the elements should be listed in the following order:

Author.
Title of source.
Title of container,
Other contributors,
Version,
Number,
Publisher,
Publication date,
Location.

Each element should be followed by the punctuation mark shown here. Earlier editions of the handbook included the place of publication, and required punctuation such as journal editions in parentheses, and colons after issue numbers. In the current version, punctuation is simpler (just commas and periods separate the elements), and information about the source is kept to the basics.

Author

Begin the entry with the author's last name, followed by a comma and the rest of the name, as presented in the work. End this element with a period.

Said, Edward W. *Culture and Imperialism.* Knopf, 1994.

Title of source

The title of the source should follow the author's name. Depending upon the type of source, it should be listed in italics or quotation marks.

A book should be in italics:

Henley, Patricia. *The Hummingbird House.* MacMurray, 1999.

A website should be in italics:

Lundman, Susan. "How to Make Vegetarian Chili." *eHow,* www.ehow.com/how_10727_make-vegetarian-chili.html.*

A periodical (journal, magazine, newspaper article) should be in quotation marks:

Bagchi, Alaknanda. "Conflicting Nationalisms: The Voice of the Subaltern in Mahasweta Devi's Bashai Tudu." *Tulsa Studies in Women's Literature,* vol. 15, no. 1, 1996, pp. 41-50.

A song or piece of music on an album should be in quotation marks:

Beyoncé. "Pray You Catch Me." *Lemonade,* Parkwood Entertainment, 2016, www.beyonce.com/album/lemonade-visual-album/.

*The eighth edition handbook recommends including URLs when citing online sources. For more information, see the "Optional Elements" section below.

Title of container

Unlike earlier versions, the eighth edition refers to containers, which are the larger wholes in which the source is located. For example, if you want to cite a poem that is listed in a collection of poems, the individual poem is the source, while the larger collection is the container. The title of the container is usually italicized and followed by a comma, since the information that follows next describes the container.

Kincaid, Jamaica. "Girl." *The Vintage Book of Contemporary American Short Stories,* edited by Tobias Wolff, Vintage, 1994, pp. 306-07.

The container may also be a television series, which is made up of episodes.

"94 Meetings." *Parks and Recreation,* created by Greg Daniels and Michael Schur, performance by Amy Poehler, season 2, episode 21, Deedle-Dee Productions and Universal Media Studios, 2010.

The container may also be a website, which contains articles, postings, and other works.

Zinkievich, Craig. Interview by Gareth Von Kallenbach. *Skewed & Reviewed,* 27 Apr. 2009, www.arcgames.com/en/games/star-trek-online/news/detail/1056940-skewed-%2526-reviewed-interviews-craig. Accessed 15 Mar. 2009.

In some cases, a container might be within a larger container. You might have read a book of short stories on *Google Books,* or watched a television series on *Netflix.* You might have found the electronic version of a journal on JSTOR. It is important to cite these containers within containers so that your readers can find the exact source that you used.

"94 Meetings." *Parks and Recreation,* season 2, episode 21, NBC, 29 Apr. 2010. *Netflix,* www.netflix.com/watch/70152031?trackId=200256157&tctx=0%2C20%2C0974d361-27cd-44de-9c2a-2d9d868b9f 64-12120962.

Langhamer, Claire. "Love and Courtship in Mid-Twentieth-Century England." *Historical Journal,* vol. 50, no. 1, 2007, pp. 173-96. *ProQuest,* doi:10.1017/S0018246X06005966. Accessed 27 May 2009.

Other contributors

In addition to the author, there may be other contributors to the source who should be credited, such as editors, illustrators, translators, etc. If their contributions are relevant to your research, or necessary to identify the source, include their names in your documentation.

Note: In the eighth edition, terms like editor, illustrator, translator, etc., are no longer abbreviated.

Foucault, Michel. *Madness and Civilization: A History of Insanity in the Age of Reason.* Translated by Richard Howard, Vintage-Random House, 1988.

Woolf, Virginia. *Jacob's Room.* Annotated and with an introduction by Vara Neverow, Harcourt, Inc., 2008.

Version

If a source is listed as an edition or version of a work, include it in your citation.

The Bible. Authorized King James Version, Oxford UP, 1998.

Crowley, Sharon, and Debra Hawhee. *Ancient Rhetorics for Contemporary Students.* 3rd ed., Pearson, 2004.

Number

If a source is part of a numbered sequence, such as a multi-volume book, or journal with both volume and issue numbers, those numbers must be listed in your citation.

Dolby, Nadine. "Research in Youth Culture and Policy: Current Conditions and Future Directions." *Social Work and Society: The International Online-Only Journal,* vol. 6, no. 2, 2008, www.socwork.net/sws/article/view/60/362. Accessed 20 May 2009.

"94 Meetings." *Parks and Recreation,* created by Greg Daniels and Michael Schur, performance by Amy Poehler, season 2, episode 21, Deedle-Dee Productions and Universal Media Studios, 2010.

Quintilian. *Institutio Oratoria.* Translated by H. E. Butler, vol. 2, Loeb-Harvard UP, 1980.

Publisher

The publisher produces or distributes the source to the public. If there is more than one publisher, and they are all are relevant to your research, list them in your citation, separated by a forward slash (/).

Klee, Paul. *Twittering Machine.* 1922. Museum of Modern Art, New York. *The Artchive,* www.artchive.com/artchive/K/klee/twittering_machine.jpg.html. Accessed May 2006.

Women's Health: Problems of the Digestive System. American College of Obstetricians and Gynecologists, 2006.

Daniels, Greg and Michael Schur, creators. *Parks and Recreation.* Deedle-Dee Productions and Universal Media Studios, 2015.

Note: the publisher's name need not be included in the following sources: periodicals, works published by their author or editor, a Web cite whose title is the same name as its publisher, a Web cite that makes works available but does not actually publish them (such as *YouTube*, *WordPress*, or *JSTOR*).

Publication date

The same source may have been published on more than one date, such as an online version of an original source. For example, a television series might have aired on a broadcast network on one date, but released on *Netflix* on a different date. When the source has more than one date, it is sufficient to use the date that is most relevant to your use of it. If you're unsure about which date to use, go with the date of the source's original publication.

In the following example, Mutant Enemy is the primary production company, and "Hush" was released in 1999. This is the way to create a general citation for a television episode.

"Hush." *Buffy the Vampire Slayer,* created by Joss Whedon, performance by Sarah Michelle Gellar, season 4, Mutant Enemy, 1999.

However, if you are discussing, for example, the historical context in which the episode originally aired, you should cite the full date. Because you are specifying the date of airing, you would then use WB Television Network (rather than Mutant Enemy), because it was the network (rather than the production company) that aired the episode on the date you're citing.

"Hush." Buffy the Vampire Slayer, created by Joss Whedon, performance by Sarah Michelle Gellar, season 4, episode 10, WB Television Network, 14 Dec. 1999.

Location

You should be as specific as possible in identifying a work's location.

An essay in a book, or an article in journal should include page numbers.

Adiche, Chimamanda Ngozi. "On Monday of Last Week." *The Thing around Your Neck,* Alfred A. Knopf, 2009, pp. 74-94.

The location of an online work should include a URL.

Wheelis, Mark. "Investigating Disease Outbreaks Under a Protocol to the Biological and Toxin Weapons Convention." *Emerging Infectious Diseases*, vol. 6, no. 6, 2000, pp. 595-600, wwwnc.cdc.gov/eid/article/6/6/00-0607_article. Accessed 8 Feb. 2009.

A physical object that you experienced firsthand should identify the place of location.

Matisse, Henri. *The Swimming Pool.* 1952, Museum of Modern Art, New York.

Optional elements

The eighth edition is designed to be as streamlined as possible. The author should include any information that helps readers easily identify the source, without including unnecessary information that may be distracting. The following is a list of select optional elements that should be part of a documented source at the writer's discretion.

Date of original publication:

If a source has been published on more than one date, the writer may want to include both dates if it will provide the reader with necessary or helpful information.

Erdrich, Louise. *Love Medicine.* 1984. Perennial-Harper, 1993.

City of publication:

The seventh edition handbook required the city in which a publisher is located, but the eighth edition states that this is only necessary in particular instances, such as in a work published before 1900. Since pre-1900 works were usually associated with the city in which they were published, your documentation may substitute the city name for the publisher's name.

Thoreau, Henry David. *Excursions.* Boston, 1863.

Date of access:

When you cite an online source, the *MLA Handbook* recommends including a date of access on which you accessed the material, since an online work may change or move at any time.

Bernstein, Mark. "10 Tips on Writing the Living Web." *A List Apart: For People Who Make Websites,* 16 Aug. 2002, alistapart.com/article/writeliving. Accessed 4 May 2009.

URLs:

As mentioned above, while the eighth edition recommends including URLs when you cite online sources, you should always check with your instructor or editor and include URLs at their discretion.

DOIs:

A DOI, or digital object identifier, is a series of digits and letters that leads to the location of an online source. Articles in journals are often assigned DOIs to ensure that the source is locatable, even if the URL changes. If your source is listed with a DOI, use that instead of a URL.

Alonso, Alvaro, and Julio A. Camargo. "Toxicity of Nitrite to Three Species of Freshwater Invertebrates." *Environmental Toxicology*, vol. 21, no. 1, 3 Feb. 2006, pp. 90-94. *Wiley Online Library,* doi: 10.1002/tox.20155.

Creating in-text citations using the eighth edition

The in-text citation is a brief reference within your text that indicates the source you consulted. It should properly attribute any ideas, paraphrases, or direct quotations to your source, and should direct readers to the entry in the list of works cited. For the most part, an in-text citation is the **author's name and page number (or just the page number, if the author is named in the sentence) in parentheses**:
Imperialism is "the practice, the theory, and the attitudes of a dominating metropolitan center ruling a distant territory" (**Said 9**).

or
According to **Edward W. Said**, imperialism is defined by "the practice, the theory, and the attitudes of a dominating metropolitan center ruling a distant territory" (**9**).
Work Cited
Said, Edward W. *Culture and Imperialism.* Knopf, 1994.

When creating in-text citations for media that has a runtime, such as a movie or podcast, include the range of hours, minutes and seconds you plan to reference, like so (00:02:15-00:02:35).

Again, your goal is to attribute your source and provide your reader with a reference without interrupting your text. Your readers should be able to follow the flow of your argument without becoming distracted by extra information.

Final thoughts about the eighth edition

The current MLA guidelines teach you a widely applicable skill. Once you become familiar with the core elements that should be included in each entry in the Works Cited list, you will be able to create documentation for any type of source. While the handbook still includes helpful examples that you may use as guidelines, you will not need to consult it every time you need to figure out how to cite a source you've never used before. If you include the core elements, in the proper order, using consistent punctuation, you will be fully equipped to create a list of works cited on your own.

How to Cite the Purdue OWL in MLA

Entire Website

The Purdue OWL. Purdue U Writing Lab, 2016.

Individual Resources

Contributors' names and the last edited date can be found in the orange boxes at the top of every page on the OWL.

Contributors' names. "Title of Resource." *The Purdue OWL,* Purdue U Writing Lab, Last edited date.

Russell, Tony, et al. "MLA Formatting and Style Guide." *The Purdue OWL.* Purdue U Writing Lab, 2 Aug. 2016.
All rights reserved content

Annotated Bibliographies

What is an Annotated Bibliography?

An annotated bibliography is a list of citations to books, articles, and documents. Each citation is followed by a brief (usually about 150 words) descriptive and evaluative paragraph, the annotation. The purpose of the annotation is to inform the reader of the relevance, accuracy, and quality of the sources cited.

Annotations vs. Abstracts

Abstracts are the purely descriptive summaries often found at the beginning of scholarly journal articles or in periodical indexes. Annotations are descriptive and critical; they expose the author's point of view, clarity and appropriateness of expression, and authority.

The Process

Creating an annotated bibliography calls for the application of a variety of intellectual skills: concise exposition, succinct analysis, and informed library research.

First, locate and record citations to books, periodicals, and documents that may contain useful information and ideas on your topic. Briefly examine and review the actual items. Then choose those works that provide a variety of perspectives on your topic.

Cite the book, article, or document using the appropriate style.

Write a concise annotation that summarizes the central theme and scope of the book or article. Include one or more sentences that (a) evaluate the authority or background of the author, (b) comment on the intended audience, (c) compare or contrast this work with another you have cited, or (d) explain how this work illuminates your bibliography topic.

Critically Appraising the Book, Article, or Document

Critically appraise and analyze the sources for your bibliography. For information on the author's background and views, ask at the reference desk for help finding appropriate biographical reference materials and book review sources.

Style for Annotated Bibliographies

When you write an annotated bibliography for a course or in preparation for a thesis advisor, consider that the professionalism of the product is a direct reflection of the quality of the paper that will result. Therefore, be stylistically conscientious, following these tips:

- Begin by listing complete bibliographic information (author, year, source name, publisher, etc.) just as you would on the References page at the end of a paper.
- Provide a sentence or two describing the contents of the source.
- Summarize the various relevant topic areas that the source discusses.
- Avoid vague phrasing and empty sentences. Weed out any generic sentences such as "This source is very useful because it has tons of really good information."
- Use present tense and future tense verbs to facilitate the immediacy of the information and the actual future use of sources.
- Discuss the exact way that you will use the source (e.g., for background information, data, graphics, as a bibliographic tool).
- Carefully judge the value of the source, considering, for example, its level of detail, bias, or the timeliness of its data.
- Note if the source's text or bibliography will lead you to other sources.
- Comment on anything that you find especially noteworthy about a source—is it controversial? definitive? political? new?
- Format the annotated bibliography so that each description is clearly associated with the proper source.

Sample Annotated Bibliography Entry for a Journal Article

This example uses the MLA format for the journal citation. NOTE: Standard MLA practice requires double spacing within citations.

Waite, Linda J., Frances Kobrin Goldscheider, and Christina Witsberger. "Nonfamily Living and the Erosion of Traditional Family Orientations Among Young Adults." *American Sociological Review* 51.4 (1986): 541-554. Print.

The authors, researchers at the Rand Corporation and Brown University, use data from the National Longitudinal Surveys of Young Women and Young Men to test their hypothesis that nonfamily living by young adults alters their attitudes, values, plans, and expectations, moving them away from their belief in traditional sex roles. They find their hypothesis strongly supported in young females, while the effects were fewer in studies of young males. Increasing the time away from parents before marrying increased individualism, self-sufficiency, and changes in attitudes about families. In contrast, an earlier study by Williams cited below shows no significant gender differences in sex role attitudes as a result of nonfamily living.

College Writing: Parts of the Essay

How to Write an Engaging Introduction

In what ways does your opening engage your reader?

Writers who produce engaging openings keep their audience in mind from the very first sentence. They consider the tone, pace, delivery of information, and strategies for getting the reader's attention. Many teachers generally recommend that students write their introductions last, because oftentimes introductions are the hardest paragraphs to write.

They're difficult to write first because you have to consider what the reader needs to know about your topic before getting to the thesis. So, I, like other instructors, suggest writing them last—even after the conclusion—though it's always a good idea to write with a working thesis in mind. Here are some general principles to consider when writing an introduction.

Avoid opening with cosmic statements.

Think about the term "cosmic." What does it mean? "Far out." Do you want your introductions to be "far out" (in a bad way)? Then avoid beginning your papers with a cosmic statement—a generalization, an overly broad idea. Publishers say that the first one or two sentences make or break a submission: if the first two sentences are poorly written or are uninteresting, they won't keep reading. Consider what your target audience would think if the first two lines were so broad that they really meant nothing at all. Here is a list of a few phrases that signify cosmic statements and that are often seen in the emerging level of student writing:

- From the beginning of time . . .
- Ever since the dawn of time . . .
- Since man first walked the earth . . .
- There are two sides to every issue.
- There are many controversial issues over which people disagree.

That's just a short list; there are many more cosmic phrases. But you can see from these examples that they preface statements that are so broad they will either lead into an incorrect or bland statement or will disconnect the reader from the real point that you want to make. Let's take the first cosmic phrase from this list and finish it:

From the beginning of time, people have been tattooing each other.

Though the writer might think this is a good broad statement to introduce a paper on tattooing practices, it's too broad—not to mention historically incorrect. How might we revise this cosmic statement so that it's more engaging?

Tattooing practices have widely varied over the past few centuries.

Though still pretty broad, this statement is at least accurate. Consider, though, how we might draw the reader in even more:

Imagine you're in a tattoo parlor, and you're about to get a tattoo for the first time. You look over and see the tattoo artist coming at you with a piece of glass. How would you feel? Well, tattooing practices have only become standardized in the last two centuries.

By incorporating narrative into the introduction, the writer can engage the reader and entice him or her to continue reading. Note that narrative doesn't suit all genres of writing, though. More formal assignments may ask you to construct an introduction without figurative language or narrative. Think about the requirements of your assignment and your rhetorical situation when crafting your introduction.

Avoid opening with a dictionary definition.

Just like it's important to avoid using cosmic statements in your introductions, it's also important to avoid starting your papers with a dictionary definition. If your paper topic is abortion, for instance, your reader doesn't need to know what Merriam Webster considers abortion to be; he or she needs to know what broader idea will lead him or her to your thesis. So don't look to dictionary.com for a snazzy opener; you won't find one there.

Before writing the first line of your introduction, it's a good idea to write out the thesis. You will need to build up to that thesis statement: the purpose of the introduction paragraph is to give the reader the information he or she needs to understand the thesis statement.

Wade your reader in to your paper.

Why is it important to gradually move your reader through your introduction toward your thesis? Let's say that you're showing your friend this great new lake you've discovered. When you reach the edge, do you push your friend in or do you wade into the lake with him? Perhaps you'd push your friend in, but you don't want to shove your reader into your paper. You want to wade him or her into your paper, gradually taking him or her to the thesis statement.

If you write your introduction paragraph last, you will be familiar with your argument and its direction. You can then use this knowledge to structure your introduction paragraph, asking yourself questions like, "What details do I include in my body paragraphs (so that I avoid bringing them in to the paper too soon)?" and "What background information, either about the greater conversation surrounding this topic or about the topic's historical context, might my reader need to appreciate my thesis?"

Let's take a look at an example of an introduction paragraph that shoves the reader into the paper:

Tattooing practices have varied widely over the past few centuries. Indeed, tattooing has become much safer. Whereas in the nineteenth century tattooing was performed with sharp instruments like glass in countries such as Africa, in the twenty-first century tattooing is performed with sanitary needles.

This introduction can't really stand on its own as a paragraph, anyway; it's far too short. How might we add material to this paragraph (revise it) so that it gradually brings the reader to the thesis?

Imagine you're in a tattoo parlor, and you're about to get a tattoo for the first time. You look over and see the tattoo artist coming at you with a piece of glass. How would you feel? Well, tattooing practices have only become standardized in the last two centuries. In fact, in the nineteenth century, some tattoo artists used sharp instruments like shards of glass to mark the skin. Yet with the public focus in the modern world on health and healthful practices, tattooing practices have evolved accordingly. Whereas in the nineteenth century tattooing was performed in unsanitary, dangerous ways, in the twenty-first century tattooing is performed with sanitary needles, demonstrating a shift in ideas regarding health in public opinion.

Whereas the first introduction galloped into the thesis statement, this paragraph wades the reader into the paper. Guiding the reader toward your thesis statement will also help him or her better understand the context for your particular topic, thereby giving him or her a greater stake in your writing.

Ultimately, then, I suggest you practice writing your introduction last. If it doesn't work for you, then switch back to writing it first. But writing it last may help you avoid writing two introduction paragraphs or foregrounding your argument too much. Overall, consider the progression of ideas in your introduction: you should move from global to local, from the general (but not over-generalized) to the specific (your thesis statement).

Attracting Interest in Your Introductory Paragraph

Your introduction should begin with an engaging statement devised to provoke your readers' interest. In the next few sentences, introduce them to your topic by stating general facts or ideas about the subject. As you move deeper into your introduction, you gradually narrow the focus, moving closer to your thesis. Moving smoothly and logically from your introductory remarks to your thesis statement can be achieved using a funnel technique, as illustrated in the diagram in Figure 9.1 "Funnel Technique".

Figure 9.1 Funnel Technique

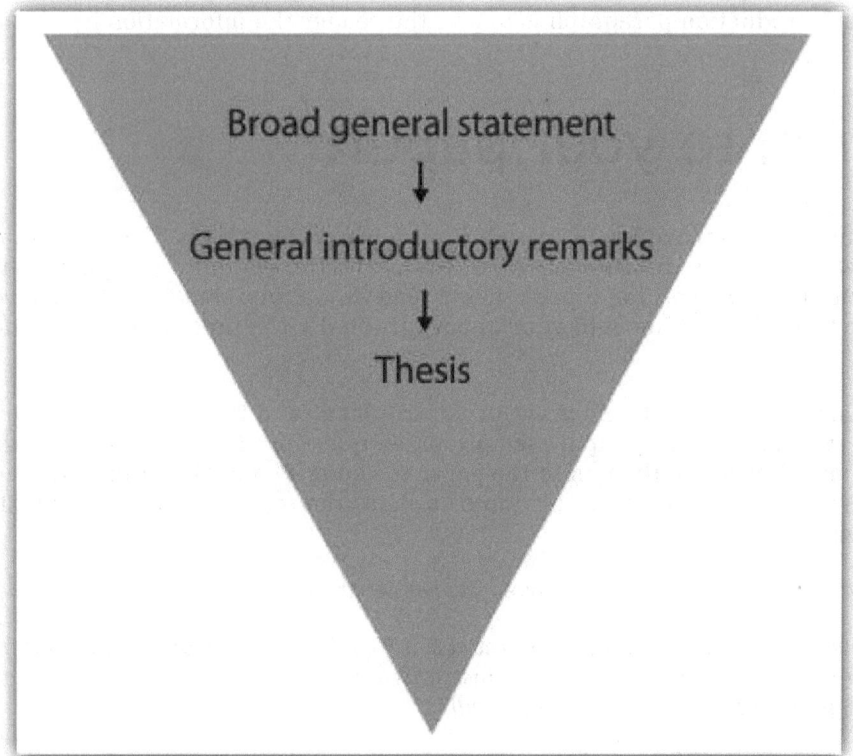

CC licensed content, Shared previously

- How to Write an Engaging Introduction. **Authored by**: Jennifer Janechek. **Provided by**: Writing Commons. **Located at**: https://writingcommons.org/how-to-write-an-engaging-introduction. **License**: *CC BY-NC-ND: Attribution-NonCommercial-NoDerivatives*
- Writing Introductory and Concluding Paragraphs. **Authored by**: Saylor Academy. **Located at**: http://www.saylor.org/courses/engl002/. **License**: *CC BY-NC-SA: Attribution-NonCommercial-ShareAlike*

How to Write a Compelling Conclusion

In what manner have you reiterated your ideas? What have you left your reader to think about at the end of your paper? How does your paper answer the "So what?" question?

As the last part of the paper, conclusions often get the short shrift. We instructors know (not that we condone it)—many students devote a lot less attention to the writing of the conclusion. Some students might even finish their conclusion thirty minutes before they have to turn in their papers. But even if you're practicing desperation writing, don't neglect your conclusion; it's a very integral part of your paper.

Think about it: Why would you spend so much time writing your introductory material and your body paragraphs and then kill the paper by leaving your reader with a dud for a conclusion? Rather than simply trailing off at the end, it's important to learn to construct a compelling conclusion—one that both reiterates your ideas and leaves your reader with something to think about.

The Reiteration

In the first part of the conclusion, you should spend a brief amount of time summarizing what you've covered in your paper. This reiteration should not merely be a restatement of your thesis or a collection of your topic sentences but should be a condensed version of your argument, topic, and/or purpose.

Let's take a look at an example reiteration from a paper about offshore drilling:

Ideally, a ban on all offshore drilling is the answer to the devastating and culminating environmental concerns that result when oil spills occur. Given the catastrophic history of three major oil spills, the environmental and economic consequences of offshore drilling should now be obvious.

Now, let's return to the thesis statement in this paper so we can see if it differs from the conclusion:

As a nation, we should reevaluate all forms of offshore drilling, but deep water offshore oil drilling, specifically, should be banned until the technology to stop and clean up oil spills catches up with our drilling technology. Though some may argue that offshore drilling provides economic advantages and would lessen our dependence on foreign oil, the environmental and economic consequences of an oil spill are so drastic that they far outweigh the advantages.

Since the author has already discussed the environmental and economic concerns associated with oil drilling, there's no need to be passive about the assertion; the author thus moves from presenting oil spills as a problem to making a statement that a ban on offshore drilling is the answer to this problem. Moreover, the author provides an overview of the paper in the second sentence of the conclusion, recapping the main points and reminding the reader that he or she should now be willing to acknowledge his or her position as viable. Though you may not always want to take this aggressive of an approach (i.e., saying something should be obvious to the reader), the key is to summarize your main ideas without "plagiarizing" yourself (repeating yourself word for word). Indeed, you may take the approach of rather saying, "The reader can now, given the catastrophic history of three major oil spills, see the environmental and economic consequences of oil drilling." For more information about summary, please refer to the textbook piece on incorporating sourced material into your essays.

As you can thus see, reiteration is **not** restatement. Summarize your paper in one to two sentences (or even three or four, depending on the length of the paper), and then move on to answering the "So what?" question.

Leaving Your Reader with Something to Think About: Answering the "So what?" Question

The bulk of your conclusion should answer the "So what?" question. Have you ever had an instructor write "So what?" at the end of your paper? You might have been offended, but the instructor was not saying that he or she did not care about your paper; rather, he or she was pointing to the fact that your paper leaves the reader with nothing new to think about. You cannot possibly spend an entire paragraph summarizing your paper topic, nor does your reader want to see an entire paragraph of summary, so you should craft something juicy—some new tidbit that serves as an extension of your original ideas.

There are a variety of ways that you can answer the "So what?" question. The following are just a few types of "endnotes":

The Call to Action

The **call to action** can be used at the end of a variety of papers, but it works best for persuasive papers, such as social action papers and Rogerian argument essays (essays that begin with a problem and move toward a solution, which serves as the author's thesis). Any time your purpose in writing an essay is to change your reader's mind or you want to get your reader to do something, the call to action is the way to go. Basically, the call to action asks your reader, after having progressed through a brilliant and coherent argument, to do something or believe a certain way. Following the reiteration at which we previously looked, here comes a call to action:

We have advanced technology that allows deepwater offshore drilling, but we lack the advanced technology that would manage these spills effectively, As such, until cleanup and prevention technology are available we should, as gatekeepers of our coastal shores and defenders of marine wildlife, ban offshore drilling—or, at the very least, demand a moratorium on all offshore oil drilling.

This call to action requests that the reader—remember, you need to identify your audience/reader before you begin writing—consider a ban on offshore drilling. Whether the author wants the reader to actually enact the ban or just to come to his or her side of the fence, he or she is asking the reader to do or believe something new based upon the information he or she just received.

The Contextualization

The contextualization places the author's local argument, topic, or purpose in a more global context so that the reader can see the larger purpose for the piece—or where the piece fits into the larger conversation. Whereas writers do research for papers so that they enter into specific conversations, they provide their readers with a contextualization in their conclusions so that they acknowledge the broader dialogue that contains that local conversation. For instance, if we were to return to the paper on offshore drilling, rather than proposing a ban on offshore drilling (a call to action), we might provide the reader with a contextualization:

We have advanced technology that allows deepwater offshore drilling, but we lack the advanced technology that would manage these spills effectively. Thus, one can see the need to place environmental concerns at the forefront of the political arena. Many politicians have already done so, including So-and-so and So-and-so.

Rather than asking the reader to do or believe something, this conclusion answers the "So what?" question by showing the reader why this specific conversation about offshore drilling matters in the larger conversation about politics and environmentalism.

The Twist

The twist leaves the reader with a contrasting idea to consider. For instance, if I were to write a paper that argued that the media was responsible for the poor body image of adolescent females, I might, in the last few lines of the conclusion, give the reader a twist:

While the media is certainly responsible for the majority of American girls' body image issues, parents sometimes affect the way girls perceive themselves more than the media does.

While this contrasting idea does not negate the writer's original argument (why would you want to do that?), it does present an alternative contrasting idea to weigh against the original argument. The twist is kind of like a cliffhanger, as it's sure to leave the reader saying, "Hmm . . ."

The Suggestion of Possibilities for Future Research

This approach to answering the "So what?" question is best for projects that you want to turn into a larger, ongoing project—or, if you want to suggest possibilities for future research for someone else (your reader) who might be interested in that topic. This approach involves pinpointing various directions which your research may take if someone were to extend the ideas included in your paper. Remember, research is a conversation, so it's important to consider how your piece fits into this conversation and how others might use it in their own conversations. For example, if we were to suggest possibilities for future research based on this recurring example of the paper on offshore drilling, the conclusion might end with something like this:

I have just explored the economic and environmental repercussions of offshore drilling based on the examples we have of three major oil spills over the past thirty years. Future research might uncover more economic and environmental consequences of offshore drilling, as such consequences will become clearer as the effects of the BP oil spill become more pronounced.

Suggesting opportunities for future research involve the reader in the paper, just like the call to action does. Who knows, the reader may be inspired by your brilliant ideas and may want to use your piece as a jumping-off point!

Whether you use a **call to action**, a **twist**, a **contextualization**, or whether you **suggest future possibilities for research**, it's important to answer the "So what?" question so that your reader stays interested in your topic until the very end of the paper. And, perhaps more importantly, leaving your reader with something juicy to consider makes it more likely that the reader will remember your piece of writing. Why write just to end your paper with a dud? Give your conclusion some love: reiterate and then answer the "So what?" question.

Writing a Conclusion

It is not unusual to want to rush when you approach your conclusion, and even experienced writers may fade. But what good writers remember is that it is vital to put just as much attention into the conclusion as in the rest of the essay. After all, a hasty ending can undermine an otherwise strong essay.

A conclusion that does not correspond to the rest of your essay, has loose ends, or is unorganized can unsettle your readers and raise doubts about the entire essay. However, if you have worked hard to write the introduction and body, your conclusion can often be the most logical part to compose.

The Anatomy of a Strong Conclusion

Keep in mind that the ideas in your conclusion must conform to the rest of your essay. In order to tie these components together, restate your thesis at the beginning of your conclusion. This helps you assemble, in an orderly fashion, all the information you have explained in the body. Repeating your thesis reminds your readers of the major arguments you have been trying to prove and also indicates that your essay is drawing to a close. A strong conclusion also reviews your main points and emphasizes the importance of the topic.

The construction of the conclusion is similar to the introduction, in which you make general introductory statements and then present your thesis. The difference is that in the conclusion you first paraphrase, or state in different words, your thesis and then follow up with general concluding remarks. These sentences should progressively broaden the focus of your thesis and maneuver your readers out of the essay.

Many writers like to end their essays with a final emphatic statement. This strong closing statement will cause your readers to continue thinking about the implications of your essay; it will make your conclusion, and thus your essay, more memorable. Another powerful technique is to challenge your readers to make a change in either their thoughts or their actions. Challenging your readers to see the subject through new eyes is a powerful way to ease yourself and your readers out of the essay.

Tip

When closing your essay, do not expressly state that you are drawing to a close. Relying on statements such as *in conclusion, it is clear that, as you can see*, or *in summation* is unnecessary and can be considered trite.

Tip

It is wise to avoid doing any of the following in your conclusion:

- Introducing new material
- Contradicting your thesis
- Changing your thesis
- Using apologies or disclaimers

Introducing new material in your conclusion has an unsettling effect on your reader. When you raise new points, you make your reader want more information, which you could not possibly provide in the limited space of your final paragraph.

Contradicting or changing your thesis statement causes your readers to think that you do not actually have a conviction about your topic. After all, you have spent several paragraphs adhering to a singular point of view. When you change sides or open up your point of view in the conclusion, your reader becomes less inclined to believe your original argument.

By apologizing for your opinion or stating that you know it is tough to digest, you are in fact admitting that even you know what you have discussed is irrelevant or unconvincing. You do not want your readers to feel this way. Effective writers stand by their thesis statement and do not stray from it.

The Three-Story Thesis

You have no doubt been drilled on the need for a thesis statement and its proper location at the end of the introduction. And you also know that all of the key points of the paper should clearly support the central driving thesis. Indeed, the whole model of the five-paragraph theme hinges on a clearly stated and consistent thesis. However, some students are surprised—and dismayed—when some of their early college papers are criticized for not having a good thesis. Their professor might even claim that the paper doesn't have a thesis when, in the author's view it clearly does. So, what makes a good thesis in college?

A good thesis is non-obvious. High school teachers needed to make sure that you and all your classmates mastered the basic form of the academic essay. Thus, they were mostly concerned that you had a clear and consistent thesis, even if it was something obvious like "sustainability is important." A thesis statement like that has a wide-enough scope to incorporate several supporting points and concurring evidence, enabling the writer to demonstrate his or her mastery of the five-paragraph form. Good enough! When they can, high school teachers nudge students to develop arguments that are less obvious and more engaging. College instructors, though, fully expect you to produce something more developed.

A good thesis is arguable. In everyday life, "arguable" is often used as a synonym for "doubtful." For a thesis, though, "arguable" means that it's worth arguing: it's something with which a reasonable person might disagree. This arguability criterion dovetails with the non-obvious one: it shows that the author has deeply explored a problem and arrived at an argument that legitimately needs 3, 5, 10, or 20 pages to explain and justify. In that way, a good thesis sets an ambitious agenda for a paper. A thesis like "sustainability is important" isn't at all difficult to argue for, and the reader would have little intrinsic motivation to read the rest of the paper. However, an arguable thesis like "sustainability policies will inevitably fail if they do not incorporate social justice," brings up some healthy skepticism. Thus, the arguable thesis makes the reader want to keep reading.

A good thesis is well specified. Some student writers fear that they're giving away the game if they specify their thesis up front; they think that a purposefully vague thesis might be more intriguing to the reader. However, consider movie trailers: they always include the most exciting and poignant moments from the film to attract an audience. In academic papers, too, a well specified thesis indicates that the author has thought rigorously about an issue and done thorough research, which makes the reader want to keep reading. Don't just say that a particular policy is effective or fair; say what makes it is so. If you want to argue that a particular claim is dubious or incomplete, say why in your thesis.

A good thesis includes implications. Suppose your assignment is to write a paper about some aspect of the history of linen production and trade, a topic that may seem exceedingly arcane. And suppose you have constructed a well supported and creative argument that linen was so widely traded in the ancient Mediterranean that it actually served as a kind of currency.[1] That's a strong, insightful, arguable, well specified thesis. But which of these thesis statements do you find more engaging?

Version A: Linen served as a form of currency in the ancient Mediterranean world, connecting rival empires through circuits of trade.

Version B: Linen served as a form of currency in the ancient Mediterranean world, connecting rival empires through circuits of trade. The economic role of linen raises important questions about how shifting environmental conditions can influence economic relationships and, by extension, political conflicts.

Putting your claims in their broader context makes them more interesting to your reader and more impressive to your professors who, after all, assign topics that they think have enduring significance. Finding that significance for yourself makes the most of both your paper and your learning.

How do you produce a good, strong thesis? And how do you know when you've gotten there? Many instructors and writers find useful a metaphor based on this passage by Oliver Wendell Holmes, Sr.[2]:

There are one-story intellects, two-story intellects, and three-story intellects with skylights. All fact collectors who have no aim beyond their facts are one-story men. Two-story men compare, reason, generalize using the labor of fact collectors as their own. Three-story men idealize, imagine, predict—their best illumination comes from above the skylight.

One-story theses state inarguable facts. Two-story theses bring in an arguable (interpretive or analytical) point. Three-story theses nest that point within its larger, compelling implications.[3]

The biggest benefit of the three-story metaphor is that it describes a process for building a thesis. To build the first story, you first have to get familiar with the complex, relevant facts surrounding the problem or question. You have to be able to describe the situation thoroughly and accurately. Then, with that first story built, you can layer on the second story by formulating the insightful, arguable point that animates the analysis. That's often the most effortful part: brainstorming, elaborating and comparing alternative ideas, finalizing your point. With that specified, you can frame up the third story by articulating why the point you make matters beyond its particular topic or case.

For example, imagine you have been assigned a paper about the impact of online learning in higher education. You would first construct an account of the origins and multiple forms of online learning and assess research findings about its use and effectiveness. If you've done that well, you'll probably come up with a well considered opinion that wouldn't be obvious to readers who haven't looked at the issue in depth. Maybe you'll want to argue that online learning is a threat to the academic community. Or perhaps you'll want to make the case that online learning opens up pathways to college degrees that traditional campus-based learning does not. In the course of developing your central, argumentative point, you'll come to recognize its larger context; in this example, you may claim that online learning can serve to better integrate higher education with the rest of society, as online learners bring their educational and career experiences together.

Example 1

To outline this example:

- **First story**: Online learning is becoming more prevalent and takes many different forms.
- **Second story**: While most observers see it as a *transformation* of higher education, online learning is better thought of an *extension* of higher education in that it reaches learners who aren't disposed to participate in traditional campus-based education.
- **Third story**: Online learning appears to be a promising way to better integrate higher education with other institutions in society, as online learners integrate their educational experiences with the other realms of their life, promoting the freer flow of ideas between the academy and the rest of society.

Example 2

Here's another example of a three-story thesis:[4]

- **First story**: Edith Wharton did not consider herself a modernist writer, and she didn't write like her modernist contemporaries.
- **Second story**: However, in her work we can see her grappling with both the questions and literary forms that fascinated modernist writers of her era. While not an avowed modernist, she did engage with modernist themes and questions.
- **Third story**: Thus, it is more revealing to think of modernism as a conversation rather than a category or practice.

Example 3

Here's one more example:

- **First story**: Scientists disagree about the likely impact in the U.S. of the light brown apple moth (LBAM), an agricultural pest native to Australia.
- **Second story**: Research findings to date suggest that the decision to spray pheromones over the skies of several southern Californian counties to combat the LBAM was poorly thought out.
- **Third story**: Together, the scientific ambiguities and the controversial response strengthen the claim that industrial-style approaches to pest management are inherently unsustainable.

A thesis statement that stops at the first story isn't usually considered a thesis. A two-story thesis is usually considered competent, though some two-story theses are more intriguing and ambitious than others. A thoughtfully crafted and well informed three-story thesis puts the author on a smooth path toward an excellent paper.

The Organizational Statement

Sometimes, an organization statement will be used in conjunction with a thesis. An organizational statement is a map that tells readers what they should expect to read in an essay. It introduces the two or three main pieces of evidence that the author will use to support the essay's position. While not required in a thesis, organizational statements can make for stronger thesis statements.

An organizational statement can take the form of a separate sentence or can be attached to a thesis in a single sentence, as seen in the examples below. The organizational elements appear in bold text:

Movies produced in the mid-1950s used obsessive behavior to depict teenage romance as something dangerous that should be avoided. Obsessive behavior was viewed as **rebellious, uncontrollable, and harmful**, both to the teenagers and to the people who loved them.

Since obsessive behavior was viewed as **rebellious, uncontrollable, and dangerous**, movies produced in the mid-1950s used it to depict teenage romance as something that should be avoided for the sake of young adults and the people who loved them.

Notice how the second version, above, strengthens the original thesis by appearing as part of the same sentence.

Evidence in the body of an essay should be presented in the same order in which it appears in an organizational statement. In the example above, it means the paper would have to discuss rebelliousness, an uncontrollable nature, and danger (as they relate to obsessive teenage romance in film) *in that order*.

Ways to Revise Your Thesis

You can cut down on irrelevant aspects and revise your thesis by taking the following steps:

Pinpoint and replace all nonspecific words, such as *people, everything, society,* or *life,* with more precise words in order to reduce any vagueness.**Working thesis:** Young people have to work hard to succeed in life.**Revised thesis:** Recent college graduates must have discipline and persistence in order to find and maintain a stable job in which they can use and be appreciated for their talents. The revised thesis makes a more specific statement about success and what it means to work hard. The original includes too broad a range of people and does not define exactly what success entails. By replacing those general words like *people* and *work hard,* the writer can better focus his or her research and gain more direction in his or her writing.

Clarify ideas that need explanation by asking yourself questions that narrow your thesis. **Working thesis:** The welfare system is a joke. **Revised thesis:** The welfare system keeps a socioeconomic class from gaining employment by alluring members of that class with unearned income, instead of programs to improve their education and skill sets. *A joke* means many things to many people. Readers bring all sorts of backgrounds and perspectives to the reading process and would need clarification for a word so vague. This expression may also be too informal for the selected audience. By asking questions, the writer can devise a more precise and appropriate explanation for *joke.* The writer should ask himself or herself questions similar to the 5WH questions. (See Chapter 8 "The Writing Process: How Do I Begin?" for more information on the 5WH questions.) By incorporating the answers to these questions into a thesis statement, the writer more accurately defines his or her stance, which will better guide the writing of the essay.

Replace any linking verbs with action verbs. Linking verbs are forms of the verb *to be,* a verb that simply states that a situation exists. **Working thesis:** Kansas City schoolteachers are not paid enough. **Revised thesis:** The Kansas City legislature cannot afford to pay its educators, resulting in job cuts and resignations in a district that sorely needs highly qualified and dedicated teachers. The linking verb in this working thesis statement is the word *are.* Linking verbs often make thesis statements weak because they do not express action. Rather, they connect words and phrases to the second half of the sentence. Readers might wonder, "Why are they not paid enough?" But this statement does not compel them to ask many more questions. The writer should ask himself or herself questions in order to replace the linking verb with an action verb, thus forming a stronger thesis statement, one that takes a more definitive stance on the issue:

- Who is not paying the teachers enough?
- What is considered "enough"?
- What is the problem?
- What are the results

Omit any general claims that are hard to support. **Working thesis:** Today's teenage girls are too sexualized. **Revised thesis:** Teenage girls who are captivated by the sexual images on MTV are conditioned to believe that a woman's worth depends on her sensuality, a feeling that harms their self-esteem and behavior. It is true that some young women in today's society are more sexualized than in the past, but that is not true for all girls. Many girls have strict parents, dress appropriately, and do not engage in sexual activity while in middle school and high school. The writer of this thesis should ask the following questions:

- Which teenage girls?
- What constitutes "too" sexualized?
- Why are they behaving that way?
- Where does this behavior show up?
- What are the repercussions?

For more see Fabio Lopez-Lazaro "Linen." In Encyclopedia of World Trade from Ancient Times to the Present. Armonk: M.E. Sharpe, 2005.
http://corp.credoreference.com/component/booktracker/edition/9668.html ↵
Oliver Wendell Holmes Sr., *The Poet at the Breakfast Table* (New York: Houghton & Mifflin, 1892) ↵
The metaphor is extraordinarily useful even though the passage is annoying. Beyond the sexist language of the time, it displays condescension toward "fact-collectors" which reflects a general modernist tendency to elevate the abstract and denigrate the concrete. In reality, data-collection is a creative and demanding craft, arguably more important than theorizing. ↵
Drawn from Jennifer Haytock, *Edith Wharton and the Conversations of Literary Modernism* (New York: Palgrave-MacMillan, 2008). ↵

- The three-story thesis: from the ground up. **Authored by**: Amy Guptill. **Provided by**: The College at Brockport, SUNY. **Located at**: http://textbooks.opensuny.org/writing-in-college-from-competence-to-excellence/. **License**: *Public Domain: No Known Copyright*
- Image of pagoda corner. **Authored by**: Takashi Hososhima. **Located at**: https://flic.kr/p/gGhtya. **License**: *CC BY-SA: Attribution-ShareAlike*
- Revision and Adaptation. **Provided by**: Lumen Learning. **License**: *CC BY-SA: Attribution-ShareAlike*
- What are thesis and organizational statements?. **Authored by**: Angela Francis. **Provided by**: CUNY Academic Commons. **Located at**: https://bacwritingfellows.commons.gc.cuny.edu/for-students/what-are-thesis-and-organizational-statements/. **License**: *CC BY-NC-SA: Attribution-NonCommercial-ShareAlike*
- Successful Writing Section 9.1: Developing a Strong, Clear Thesis Statement. **Authored by**: Anonymous. **Located at**: http://2012books.lardbucket.org/books/successful-writing/s13-01-developing-a-strong-clear-thes.html. **License**: *CC BY-NC-SA: Attribution-NonCommercial-ShareAlike*

The Well-Structured Paragraph

Paragraphs Are Unified by a Single Purpose or Theme

Regardless of whether a paragraph is deductively or inductively structured, readers can generally follow the logic of a discussion better when a paragraph is unified by a single purpose. Paragraphs that lack a central idea and that wander from subject to subject are apt to confuse readers, making them wonder what they should pay attention to and why.

To ensure that each paragraph is unified by a single idea, Francis Christensen, in Notes Toward a New Rhetoric (NY: Harper & Row, 1967), has suggested that we number sentences according to their level of generality. According to Christensen, we would assign a 1 to the most general sentence and then a 2 to the second most general sentence, and so on. Christensen considers the following paragraph, which he excerpted from Jacob Bronowski's The Common Sense of Science, to be an example of a subordinate pattern because the sentences become increasingly more specific as the reader progresses through the paragraph:

> The process of learning is essential to our lives.
> All higher animals seek it deliberately.
> They are inquisitive and they experiment.
> An experiment is a sort of harmless trial run of some action which we shall have to make in the real world; and this, whether it is made in the laboratory by scientists or by fox-cubs outside their earth.
> The scientist experiments and the cub plays; both are learning to correct their errors of judgment in a setting in which errors are not fatal.
> Perhaps this is what gives them both their air of happiness and freedom in these activities.

Christensen is quick to point out that not all paragraphs have a subordinate structure. The following one, which he took from Bergen Evans's Comfortable Words, is an example of what Christensen considers a coordinate sequence:

> He [the native speaker] may, of course, speak a form of English that marks him as coming from a rural or an unread group.
> But if he doesn't mind being so marked, there's no reason why he should change.
> Samuel Johnson kept a Staffordshire burr in his speech all his life.
> In Burns' mouth the despised lowland Scots dialect served just as well as the "correct" English spoken by ten million of his southern contemporaries.
> Lincoln's vocabulary and his way of pronouncing certain words were sneered at by many better educated people at the time, but he seemed to be able to use the English language as effectively as his critics.

Paragraphs Flow When Information Is Logical

Paragraphs provide a visual representation of your ideas. When revising your work, evaluate the logic behind how you have organized the paragraphs.

Question whether your presentation would appear more logical and persuasive if you rearranged the sequence of the paragraphs. Next, question the structure of each paragraph to see if sentences need to be reordered. Determine whether you are organizing information deductively or according to chronology or according to some sense of what is most and least important. Ask yourself these five questions:

How is each paragraph organized? Do I place my general statement or topic sentence near the beginning or the end of each paragraph? Do I need any transitional paragraphs or transitional sentences?

As I move from one idea to another, will my reader understand how subsequent paragraphs relate to my main idea as well as to previous paragraphs? Should any paragraphs be shifted in their order in the text? Should a later paragraph be combined with the introductory paragraph?

Should the existing paragraphs be cut into smaller segments or merged into longer ones? If I have a concluding paragraph, do I really need it?

Will readers understand the logical connections between paragraphs? Do any sentences need to be added to clarify the logical relationship between ideas? Have I provided the necessary forecasting and summarizing sentences that readers will need to understand how the different ideas relate to each other? Have I been too blatant about transitions? Are all of the transitional sentences and paragraphs really necessary or can the reader follow my thoughts without them?

Paragraphs Often Follow Deductive Organization

Your goals for the opening sentences of your paragraphs are similar to your goals for writing an introduction to a document. In the beginning of a paragraph, clarify the purpose. Most paragraphs in academic and technical discourse move deductively-that is, the first or second sentence presents the topic or theme of the paragraph and the subsequent sentences illustrate and explicate this theme.

Notice, in particular, how Chris Goodrich cues readers to the purpose of his paragraph (and article) in the first sentence of his essay "Crossover Dreams":

Norman Cantor, New York University history professor and author, most recently, of Inventing the Middle Ages, created a stir this spring when he wrote a letter to the newsletter of the American Historical Association declaring that "no historian who can write English prose should publish more than two books with a university press-one for tenure, and one for full professor After that (or preferably long before) work only in the trade market." Cantor urged his fellow scholars to seek literary agents to represent any work with crossover potential. And he didn't stop there: As if to be sure of offending the entire academic community, Cantor added, "If you are already a full professor, your agent should be much more important to you than the department chair or the dean."

Paragraphs Use Inductive Structure for Dramatic Conclusions or Varied Style

While you generally want to move from the known to the new, from the thesis to its illustration or restriction, you sometimes want to violate this pattern. Educated readers in particular can be bored by texts that always present information in the same way.

For example, how Valerie Steele's anecdotal tone and dialogue in the opening sentences of her essay on fashion in academia prepare the reader for her thesis:

Once, when I was a graduate student at Yale, a history professor asked me about my dissertation. "I'm writing about fashion," I said.

That's interesting. Italian or German?"

It took me a couple of minutes, as thoughts of Armani flashed through my mind, but finally I realized what he meant. "Not fascism," I said. "Fashion. As in Paris."

"Oh." There was a long silence, and then, without another word, he turned and walked away.

Fashion still has the power to reduce many academics to embarrassed or indignant silence. Some of those to whom I spoke while preparing this article requested anonymity or even refused to address the subject. ("The F-Word." Lingua Franca April 1991: 17–18.)

Paragraph Transitions

Effective paragraph transitions signal to readers how two consecutive paragraphs relate to each other. The transition signals the relationship between the "new information" and the "old information."

For example, the new paragraph might

- elaborate on the idea presented in the preceding paragraph
- introduce a related idea
- continue a chronological narrative
- describe a problem with the idea presented in the preceding paragraph
- describe an exception to the idea presented in the preceding paragraph
- describe a consequence or implication of the idea presented in the preceding paragraph

Effective paragraph transitions signal to readers how two consecutive paragraphs relate to each other. The transition signals the relationship between the "new information" and the "old information."

For example, the new paragraph might

- elaborate on the idea presented in the preceding paragraph
- introduce a related idea
- continue a chronological narrative
- describe a problem with the idea presented in the preceding paragraph
- describe an exception to the idea presented in the preceding paragraph
- describe a consequence or implication of the idea presented in the preceding paragraph

Let's consider a few examples (drawn from published books and articles of paragraph transitions that work. The examples below reproduce paragraph endings and openings. Pay attention to how each paragraph opening signals to readers how the paragraph relates to the one they have just finished reading. Observe the loss in clarity when transitional signals are removed.

Example 1:

Part of the Paragraph	Example Quote
Paragraph ending	[...]Once his system was applied to all acts of manual labor, Taylor assured his followers, it would bring about a restructuring not only of industry but of society, creating a utopia of perfect efficiency.
Paragraph Opening with transitional cues	Taylor's system is **still** very much with us; it **remains** the ethic of industrial manufacturing. [...]
Paragraph opening *without* transitional cues	Taylor's system is the ethic of present-day industrial manufacturing. [...]

The transitional sentence signals that the new paragraph will seek to demonstrate that the phenomenon described in the preceding paragraph (Taylorism) is ongoing: it is "still" with us and "remains" the dominant workplace ethic. Compare this sentence with the one directly beneath it ("paragraph opening without transitional cues"). With this version, readers are left on their own to infer the connection.

Example 2:

Part of the Paragraph	Example Quote
Paragraph ending	[...]"I was a lit major in college, and used to be [a] voracious book reader," he wrote. "What happened?" He speculates on the answer: "What if I do all my reading on the web not so much because the way I read has changed, i.e. I'm just seeking convenience, but because the way I THINK has changed?
Paragraph opening with transitional cues	Bruce Friedman, who blogs regularly about the use of computers in medicine, also has described how the Internet has altered his mental habits. [...]
Paragraph opening *without* transitional cues	Bruce Friedman, who blogs regularly about the use of computers in medicine, has described how the Internet has altered his mental habits. [...]

The transitional sentence signals that the new paragraph will provide another example of the phenomenon (changed mental habits) described in the preceding paragraph. In this example, the word "also" serves an important function. Notice that without this transitional cue the relationship between the two paragraphs becomes less clear.

Example 3:

Part of the Paragraph	Example Quote
Paragraph Ending	[...] The camera-as-narrator is the usual viewpoint in film. It can be used continuously, appearing to reflect reality, and making few mental demands on the viewer. The passive camera seems to be a trustworthy witness, and so the viewer relies upon its apparent omniscience.
Paragraph opening with transitional cues	**But** the illusion of objectivity is a rhetorical device exploited by the filmmaker. [...]
Paragraph opening *without* transitional cues	The illusion of objectivity is a rhetorical device exploited by the filmmaker. [...]

The transitional sentence signals that the new paragraph will challenge the assumption described in the preceding paragraph. The single transitional term "but" signals this relationship. Notice the drop-off in clarity when the transitional term is omitted.

Example 4:

Part of the Paragraph	Example Quote
Paragraph Ending	[...] If the story concerns social crisis or disorder, more frequently than not this response will come from sources of official authority: the police quell the rioting, labor and management leaders reach an agreement, the State Department approves or condemns the latest coup d'état in South America. The press in this way establishes a subtle relation between narrative order and the perception or representation of political order.
Paragraph opening with transitional cues	Todd Gitlin makes a similar point in commenting on the "orderliness" of television news. [...]

Paragraph opening _without_ transitional cues	Todd Gitlin comments on the "orderliness" of television news. [...]

The transitional sentence signals that the new paragraph will further explore the idea expressed in the preceding paragraph. The phrase "makes a similar point" signals this relationship. Without this transitional phrase, the connection between the two paragraphs can still be inferred, but it is now much less clear.

As the above examples illustrate, effective paragraph transitions signal relationships between paragraphs.

Below are some terms that are often helpful for signaling relationships among ideas.

Relationship Type	Signal Words
Chronology	before, next, earlier, later, during, after, meanwhile, while, until, then, first, second
Comparison	also, similarly, likewise, in the same way, in the same manner
Contrast	however, but, in contrast, still, yet, nevertheless, even though, although
Clarity	for example, for instance, in other words
Continuation	and, also, moreover, additionally, furthermore, another, too
Consequence	as a result, therefore, for this reason, thus, consequently
Conclusion	in conclusion, in summary, to sum up

* The examples of transitional sentences are from:

Parker, Ian. "Absolute Powerpoint." New Yorker. 28 May 2001: 76-87.
Carr, Nicholas. "Is Google Making Us Stupid?" Atlantic Monthly. Jul/Aug2008: 56-63.
Harrington, John. The Rhetoric of Film. New York: Holt, Rinehart and Winston, 1973.
Spurr, David. The Rhetoric of Empire. Durham, N. C.: Duke University Press, 1993.

Anatomy of a Well-Cited Paragraph

Writing a paragraph with the sources properly cited can seem a tricky task at first, but the process is straightforward enough, especially when we analyze an example. Writing a sound paragraph is really just a matter of thinking clearly about a topic you have researched and transferring that thinking to the page. To illustrate, a tidy sample paragraph follows, with the sources properly documented in the author-year system. Next, the genesis of the paragraph is analyzed.

> The millions of species of plants and animals on the earth have a phenomenal influence on the human species. Not only do they provide a substantial amount of our food, they are of great value in medicine and science. Over 60 percent of the purchases we make at the pharmacy contain substances that are derived from wild organisms (Myers 2008). Studies of plants and animals have led to discoveries in virtually all of the sciences, from biology and chemistry to psychology and astronomy (Wilson 2001). Furthermore, plants and animals are vital to the maintenance of our ecosystem. Their diversity and balance directly control food webs, nutrient diversity, supplies of fresh water, climate consistency, and waste disposal (Eberly 1988). Finally, many species act as barometers of our environment. The salmon, for example, is extremely sensitive to changes in the condition of the water in which it lives. Any abnormality in population or behavior of fish usually indicates some type of chemical imbalance in the water. The same is true of butterflies and their responses to the environment within prominent agricultural areas. Clearly, the millions of species of plants and animals in the world are vital to the continued thriving of the human population.

Now let's walk through the paragraph and its use of sources. The first two sentences assert the author's personal view about the value of the world's species (a view shaped by his research, no doubt), which he is about to back up by using three recent sources. Next, the author cites a journal article (Myers) from which he extracted a statistic ("over 60 percent of the purchases we make at the pharmacy"). Without this source cited, the reader might believe that the author estimated loosely or simply relied on his memory for the statistic.

The next source (Wilson) is cited because the paper author borrowed a general claim from a textbook by Wilson. The author was at first not sure whether to cite the source, but he wisely decided that he should because he realized that he had in fact had Wilson's book open to a particular page and referred to it as he wrote the sentence. The next source (Eberly) is cited because the author had browsed through a whole chapter of Eberly's book in order to compose the list in the sentence, usually using Eberly's exact section headings from the chapter as the list members.

The final examples of the salmon and the butterfly were based directly on the author's personal experience of working at a fish hatchery for a summer, so documenting sources was not an issue. The fact that the author finds a way to tie this experiential knowledge in with his research is testimony to the fact that he is *thinking* as he writes the paragraph. He blends his sources, but he does not allow them to do the thinking for him. More evidence of the author's control over his material resides in his transparent mid-paragraph transition sentence (beginning with "Furthermore"), his labeling of species as "barometers" of the environment a few sentences later, and his closing sentence, which wraps up the paragraph's ideas neatly by making an affirmative and confident statement that backs up his topic sentence and examples.

Not every paragraph should look exactly like this, of course, but every paragraph should be written with the same kind of conscientiousness about how, when, and why the sources are cited.

Regardless of whether a paragraph is deductively or inductively structured, readers can generally follow the logic of a discussion better when a paragraph is unified by a single purpose. Paragraphs that lack a central idea and that wander from subject to subject are apt to confuse readers, making them wonder what they should pay attention to and why.

To ensure that each paragraph is unified by a single idea, Francis Christensen, in Notes Toward a New Rhetoric (NY: Harper & Row, 1967), has suggested that we number sentences according to their level of generality. According to Christensen, we would assign a 1 to the most general sentence and then a 2 to the second most general sentence, and so on. Christensen considers the following paragraph, which he excerpted from Jacob Bronowski's The Common Sense of Science, to be an example of a subordinate pattern because the sentences become increasingly more specific as the reader progresses through the paragraph:

> The process of learning is essential to our lives.
> All higher animals seek it deliberately.
> They are inquisitive and they experiment.
> An experiment is a sort of harmless trial run of some action which we shall have to make in the real world; and this, whether it is made in the laboratory by scientists or by fox-cubs outside their earth.
> The scientist experiments and the cub plays; both are learning to correct their errors of judgment in a setting in which errors are not fatal.
> Perhaps this is what gives them both their air of happiness and freedom in these activities.

Christensen is quick to point out that not all paragraphs have a subordinate structure. The following one, which he took from Bergen Evans's Comfortable Words, is an example of what Christensen considers a coordinate sequence:

> He [the native speaker] may, of course, speak a form of English that marks him as coming from a rural or an unread group.
> But if he doesn't mind being so marked, there's no reason why he should change.
> Samuel Johnson kept a Staffordshire burr in his speech all his life.
> In Burns' mouth the despised lowland Scots dialect served just as well as the "correct" English spoken by ten million of his southern contemporaries.
> Lincoln's vocabulary and his way of pronouncing certain words were sneered at by many better educated people at the time, but he seemed to be able to use the English language as effectively as his critics.

Paragraphs Flow When Information Is Logical

Paragraphs provide a visual representation of your ideas. When revising your work, evaluate the logic behind how you have organized the paragraphs.

Question whether your presentation would appear more logical and persuasive if you rearranged the sequence of the paragraphs. Next, question the structure of each paragraph to see if sentences need to be reordered. Determine whether you are organizing information deductively or according to chronology or according to some sense of what is most and least important. Ask yourself these five questions:

How is each paragraph organized? Do I place my general statement or topic sentence near the beginning or the end of each paragraph? Do I need any transitional paragraphs or transitional sentences?

As I move from one idea to another, will my reader understand how subsequent paragraphs relate to my main idea as well as to previous paragraphs? Should any paragraphs be shifted in their order in the text? Should a later paragraph be combined with the introductory paragraph?

Should the existing paragraphs be cut into smaller segments or merged into longer ones? If I have a concluding paragraph, do I really need it?

Will readers understand the logical connections between paragraphs? Do any sentences need to be added to clarify the logical relationship between ideas? Have I provided the necessary forecasting and summarizing sentences that readers will need to understand how the different ideas relate to each other? Have I been too blatant about transitions? Are all of the transitional sentences and paragraphs really necessary or can the reader follow my thoughts without them?

Paragraphs Often Follow Deductive Organization

Your goals for the opening sentences of your paragraphs are similar to your goals for writing an introduction to a document. In the beginning of a paragraph, clarify the purpose. Most paragraphs in academic and technical discourse move deductively–that is, the first or second sentence presents the topic or theme of the paragraph and the subsequent sentences illustrate and explicate this theme.

Notice, in particular, how Chris Goodrich cues readers to the purpose of his paragraph (and article) in the first sentence of his essay "Crossover Dreams":

Norman Cantor, New York University history professor and author, most recently, of Inventing the Middle Ages, created a stir this spring when he wrote a letter to the newsletter of the American Historical Association declaring that "no historian who can write English prose should publish more than two books with a university press–one for tenure, and one for full professor After that (or preferably long before) work only in the trade market." Cantor urged his fellow scholars to seek literary agents to represent any work with crossover potential. And he didn't stop there: As if to be sure of offending the entire academic community, Cantor added, "If you are already a full professor, your agent should be much more important to you than the department chair or the dean."

Paragraphs Use Inductive Structure for Dramatic Conclusions or Varied Style

While you generally want to move from the known to the new, from the thesis to its illustration or restriction, you sometimes want to violate this pattern. Educated readers in particular can be bored by texts that always present information in the same way.

For example, how Valerie Steele's anecdotal tone and dialogue in the opening sentences of her essay on fashion in academia prepare the reader for her thesis:

Once, when I was a graduate student at Yale, a history professor asked me about my dissertation. "I'm writing about fashion," I said.

That's interesting. Italian or German?"

It took me a couple of minutes, as thoughts of Armani flashed through my mind, but finally I realized what he meant. "Not fascism," I said. "Fashion. As in Paris."

"Oh." There was a long silence, and then, without another word, he turned and walked away.

Fashion still has the power to reduce many academics to embarrassed or indignant silence. Some of those to whom I spoke while preparing this article requested anonymity or even refused to address the subject. ("The F-Word." Lingua Franca April 1991: 17–18.)

Paragraph Transitions

Effective paragraph transitions signal to readers how two consecutive paragraphs relate to each other. The transition signals the relationship between the "new information" and the "old information."

For example, the new paragraph might

- elaborate on the idea presented in the preceding paragraph
- introduce a related idea
- continue a chronological narrative
- describe a problem with the idea presented in the preceding paragraph
- describe an exception to the idea presented in the preceding paragraph
- describe a consequence or implication of the idea presented in the preceding paragraph

---

Effective paragraph transitions signal to readers how two consecutive paragraphs relate to each other. The transition signals the relationship between the "new information" and the "old information."

For example, the new paragraph might

- elaborate on the idea presented in the preceding paragraph
- introduce a related idea
- continue a chronological narrative
- describe a problem with the idea presented in the preceding paragraph
- describe an exception to the idea presented in the preceding paragraph
- describe a consequence or implication of the idea presented in the preceding paragraph

Let's consider a few examples (drawn from published books and articles of paragraph transitions that work. The examples below reproduce paragraph endings and openings. Pay attention to how each paragraph opening signals to readers how the paragraph relates to the one they have just finished reading. Observe the loss in clarity when transitional signals are removed.

Example 1:

Part of the Paragraph	Example Quote
Paragraph ending	[…]Once his system was applied to all acts of manual labor, Taylor assured his followers, it would bring about a restructuring not only of industry but of society, creating a utopia of perfect efficiency.
Paragraph Opening with transitional cues	Taylor's system is **still** very much with us; it **remains** the ethic of industrial manufacturing. […]
Paragraph opening *without* transitional cues	Taylor's system is the ethic of present-day industrial manufacturing. […]

The transitional sentence signals that the new paragraph will seek to demonstrate that the phenomenon described in the preceding paragraph (Taylorism) is ongoing: it is "still" with us and "remains" the dominant workplace ethic.Compare this sentence with the one directly beneath it ("paragraph opening without transitional cues"). With this version, readers are left on their own to infer the connection.

Example 2:

Paragraph ending	[...]"I was a lit major in college, and used to be [a] voracious book reader," he wrote. "What happened?" He speculates on the answer: "What if I do all my reading on the web not so much because the way I read has changed, i.e. I'm just seeking convenience, but because the way I THINK has changed?
Paragraph opening with transitional cues	Bruce Friedman, who blogs regularly about the use of computers in medicine, also has described how the Internet has altered his mental habits. [...]
Paragraph opening *without* transitional cues	Bruce Friedman, who blogs regularly about the use of computers in medicine, has described how the Internet has altered his mental habits. [...]

The transitional sentence signals that the new paragraph will provide another example of the phenomenon (changed mental habits) described in the preceding paragraph. In this example, the word "also" serves an important function. Notice that without this transitional cue the relationship between the two paragraphs becomes less clear.

Example 3:

Paragraph Ending	[...] The camera-as-narrator is the usual viewpoint in film. It can be used continuously, appearing to reflect reality, and making few mental demands on the viewer. The passive camera seems to be a trustworthy witness, and so the viewer relies upon its apparent omniscience.
Paragraph opening with transitional cues	**But** the illusion of objectivity is a rhetorical device exploited by the filmmaker. [...]
Paragraph opening *without* transitional cues	The illusion of objectivity is a rhetorical device exploited by the filmmaker. [...]

The transitional sentence signals that the new paragraph will challenge the assumption described in the preceding paragraph. The single transitional term "but" signals this relationship. Notice the drop-off in clarity when the transitional term is omitted.

Example 4:

Paragraph Ending	[...] If the story concerns social crisis or disorder, more frequently than not this response will come from sources of official authority: the police quell the rioting, labor and management leaders reach an agreement, the State Department approves or condemns the latest coup d'état in South America. The press in this way establishes a subtle relation between narrative order and the perception or representation of political order.
Paragraph opening with transitional cues	Todd Gitlin makes a similar point in commenting on the "orderliness" of television news. [...]
Paragraph opening *without* transitional cues	Todd Gitlin comments on the "orderliness" of television news. [...]

The transitional sentence signals that the new paragraph will further explore the idea expressed in the preceding paragraph. The phrase "makes a similar point" signals this relationship. Without this transitional phrase, the connection between the two paragraphs can still be inferred, but it is now much less clear.

As the above examples illustrate, effective paragraph transitions signal relationships between paragraphs.

Below are some terms that are often helpful for signaling relationships among ideas.

Chronology	before, next, earlier, later, during, after, meanwhile, while, until, then, first, second
Comparison	also, similarly, likewise, in the same way, in the same manner
Contrast	however, but, in contrast, still, yet, nevertheless, even though, although
Clarity	for example, for instance, in other words
Continuation	and, also, moreover, additionally, furthermore, another, too
Consequence	as a result, therefore, for this reason, thus, consequently
Conclusion	in conclusion, in summary, to sum up

* The examples of transitional sentences are from:

Parker, Ian. "Absolute Powerpoint." New Yorker. 28 May 2001: 76-87.
Carr, Nicholas. "Is Google Making Us Stupid?" Atlantic Monthly. Jul/Aug2008: 56-63.
Harrington, John. The Rhetoric of Film. New York: Holt, Rinehart and Winston, 1973.
Spurr, David. The Rhetoric of Empire. Durham, N. C.: Duke University Press, 1993.

Anatomy of a Well-Cited Paragraph

Writing a paragraph with the sources properly cited can seem a tricky task at first, but the process is straightforward enough, especially when we analyze an example. Writing a sound paragraph is really just a matter of thinking clearly about a topic you have researched and transferring that thinking to the page. To illustrate, a tidy sample paragraph follows, with the sources properly documented in the author-year system. Next, the genesis of the paragraph is analyzed.

The millions of species of plants and animals on the earth have a phenomenal influence on the human species. Not only do they provide a substantial amount of our food, they are of great value in medicine and science. Over 60 percent of the purchases we make at the pharmacy contain substances that are derived from wild organisms (Myers 2008). Studies of plants and animals have led to discoveries in virtually all of the sciences, from biology and chemistry to psychology and astronomy (Wilson 2001). Furthermore, plants and animals are vital to the maintenance of our ecosystem. Their diversity and balance directly control food webs, nutrient diversity, supplies of fresh water, climate consistency, and waste disposal (Eberly 1988). Finally, many species act as barometers of our environment. The salmon, for example, is extremely sensitive to changes in the condition of the water in which it lives. Any abnormality in population or behavior of fish usually indicates some type of chemical imbalance in the water. The same is true of butterflies and their responses to the environment within prominent agricultural areas. Clearly, the millions of species of plants and animals in the world are vital to the continued thriving of the human population.

Now let's walk through the paragraph and its use of sources. The first two sentences assert the author's personal view about the value of the world's species (a view shaped by his research, no doubt), which he is about to back up by using three recent sources. Next, the author cites a journal article (Myers) from which he extracted a statistic ("over 60 percent of the purchases we make at the pharmacy"). Without this source cited, the reader might believe that the author estimated loosely or simply relied on his memory for the statistic.

The next source (Wilson) is cited because the paper author borrowed a general claim from a textbook by Wilson. The author was at first not sure whether to cite the source, but he wisely decided that he should because he realized that he had in fact had Wilson's book open to a particular page and referred to it as he wrote the sentence. The next source (Eberly) is cited because the author had browsed through a whole chapter of Eberly's book in order to compose the list in the sentence, usually using Eberly's exact section headings from the chapter as the list members.

The final examples of the salmon and the butterfly were based directly on the author's personal experience of working at a fish hatchery for a summer, so documenting sources was not an issue. The fact that the author finds a way to tie this experiential knowledge in with his research is testimony to the fact that he is *thinking* as he writes the paragraph. He blends his sources, but he does not allow them to do the thinking for him. More evidence of the author's control over his material resides in his transparent mid-paragraph transition sentence (beginning with "Furthermore"), his labeling of species as "barometers" of the environment a few sentences later, and his closing sentence, which wraps up the paragraph's ideas neatly by making an affirmative and confident statement that backs up his topic sentence and examples.

Not every paragraph should look exactly like this, of course, but every paragraph should be written with the same kind of conscientiousness about how, when, and why the sources are cited.

Bringing Elements of a Paper Together

What Logical Plan Informs Your Paper's Organization?

Why is it important to organize a paper logically?

Academic writing—like many types of writing—is typically more effective when the writer's ideas are presented logically. For the sake of clarity and cohesiveness, a logical plan should inform the paper's organization from beginning to end at the global (big picture) and local (zoomed in) levels. The target audience is more likely to become engaged, and maintain their engagement, when the conversation is clearly organized and purposefully presented.

Organizational structures that work:

- **Graphic organizers**
  - **Web:** Draw a circle in the middle of a page and write your thesis inside. In a series of circles around the thesis, fill in ideas for the introduction, the main point of each body paragraph, and the conclusion. Then number the circles appropriately.
  - **Cluster or mind map:** Begin with the topic in the center and map out a series of main ideas in connected ovals; continue to draw more ovals and cluster the details around each main idea.
- **Outlines**
  - **Traditional, formal outline:** This organizational plan typically begins with a thesis statement and lays out your paper's content in detail, using a standard outline format. Working outline: This plan generally begins with a working thesis followed by an organized, but less formal, presentation of ideas. Strategic reorganization of the outline takes place as your paper develops.
  - **Reverse outline:** Outlining is done after a draft of the paper has been written. The writer extracts the main idea from each paragraph, determines what steps need to be taken to present the ideas logically, and reorganizes appropriately.

What can be done to construct a logical plan?

- Experiment with different organizational structures and choose one that works in harmony with your writing style, as well as the requirements of the assignment.
- Develop a well-organized thesis or working thesis—ideas that are clearly-presented in the thesis generally support clearly-presented ideas in the body of your paper.
- Treat the paper as a living document. Systematically reevaluate the success, or failure, of the organizational plan and reorganize as needed to keep the paper "breathing."

Moving Beyond the Five-Paragraph Theme

One of the major transitions between high-school writing and college writing involves a wider set of options of how to organize an essay. Choosing the right structure is up to you, and depends on the application of critical thinking skills to select the best fit for your purpose.

In high school, the SAT and other standardized testing formats value a very formulaic, rigid approach to essay writing. Some students who have mastered that form, and enjoyed a lot of success from doing so, assume that college writing is simply more of the same. The skills that go into a very basic kind of essay—often called the five-paragraph theme—are indispensable. If you're good at the five-paragraph theme, then you're good at identifying a clear and consistent thesis, arranging cohesive paragraphs, organizing evidence for key points, and situating an argument within a broader context through the intro and conclusion.

In college you need to build on those essential skills. The five-paragraph theme, as such, is bland and formulaic; it doesn't compel deep thinking. Your professors are looking for a more ambitious and arguable thesis, a nuanced and compelling argument, and real-life evidence for all key points, all in an organically-structured paper.

Figures 3.1 and 3.2 contrast the standard five-paragraph theme and the organic college paper. The five-paragraph theme, outlined in Figure 3.1, is probably what you're used to: the introductory paragraph starts broad and gradually narrows to a thesis, which readers expect to find at the very end of that paragraph. In this idealized format, the thesis invokes the magic number of three: three reasons why a statement is true. Each of those reasons is explained and justified in the three body paragraphs, and then the final paragraph restates the thesis before gradually getting broader. This format is easy for readers to follow, and it helps writers organize their points and the evidence that goes with them. That's why you learned this format.

Figure 3.2, in contrast, represents a paper on the same topic that has the more organic form expected in college. The first key difference is the thesis. Rather than simply positing a number of reasons to think that something is true, it puts forward an arguable statement: one with which a reasonable person might disagree. An arguable thesis gives the paper purpose. It surprises readers and draws them in. You hope your reader thinks, "Huh. Why would they come to that conclusion?" and then feels compelled to read on. The body paragraphs, then, build on one another to carry out this ambitious argument. In the classic five-paragraph theme (Figure 3.1) it hardly matters which of the three reasons you explain first or second. In the more organic structure (Figure 3.2) each paragraph specifically leads to the next.

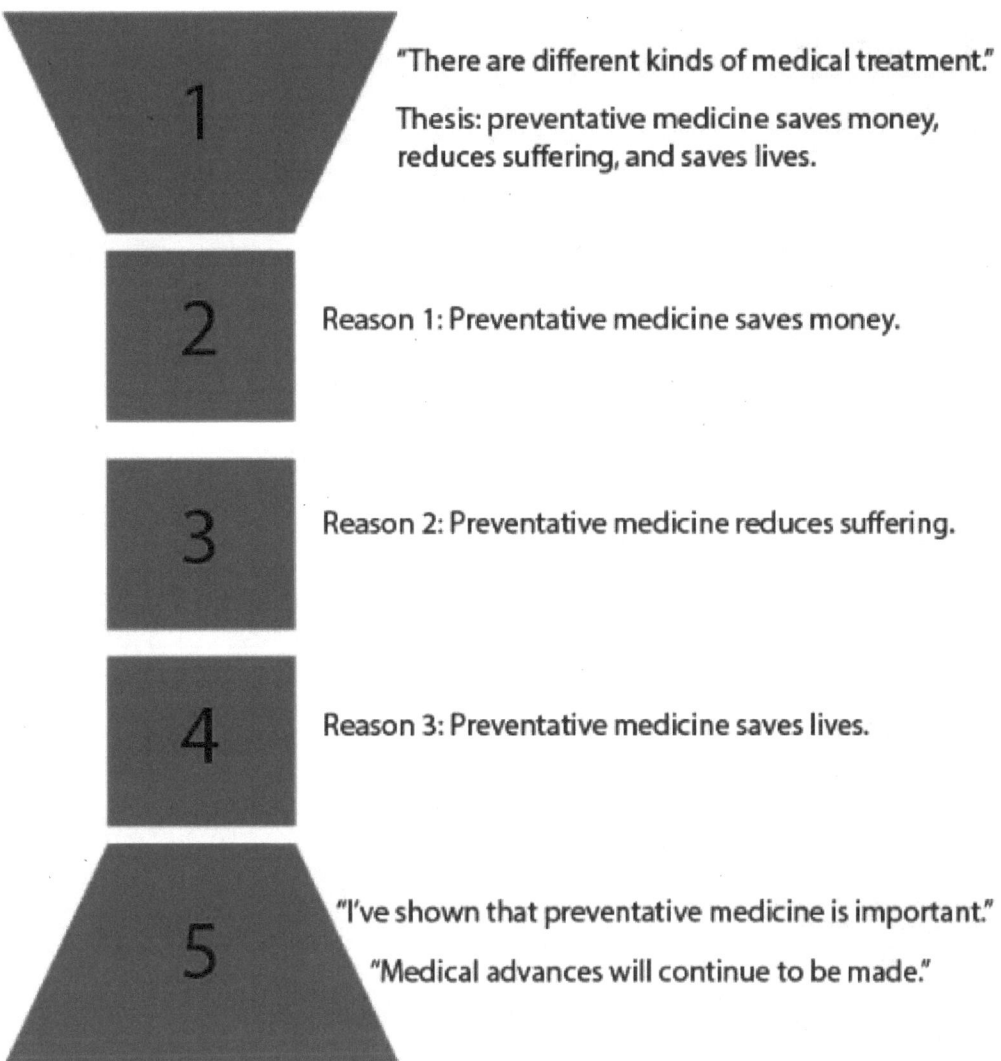

Figure 3.1, The five-paragraph "theme"

The last key difference is seen in the conclusion. Because the organic essay is driven by an ambitious, non-obvious argument, the reader comes to the concluding section thinking "OK, I'm convinced by the argument. What do you, author, make of it? Why does it matter?" The conclusion of an organically structured paper has a real job to do. It doesn't just reiterate the thesis; it explains why the thesis matters.

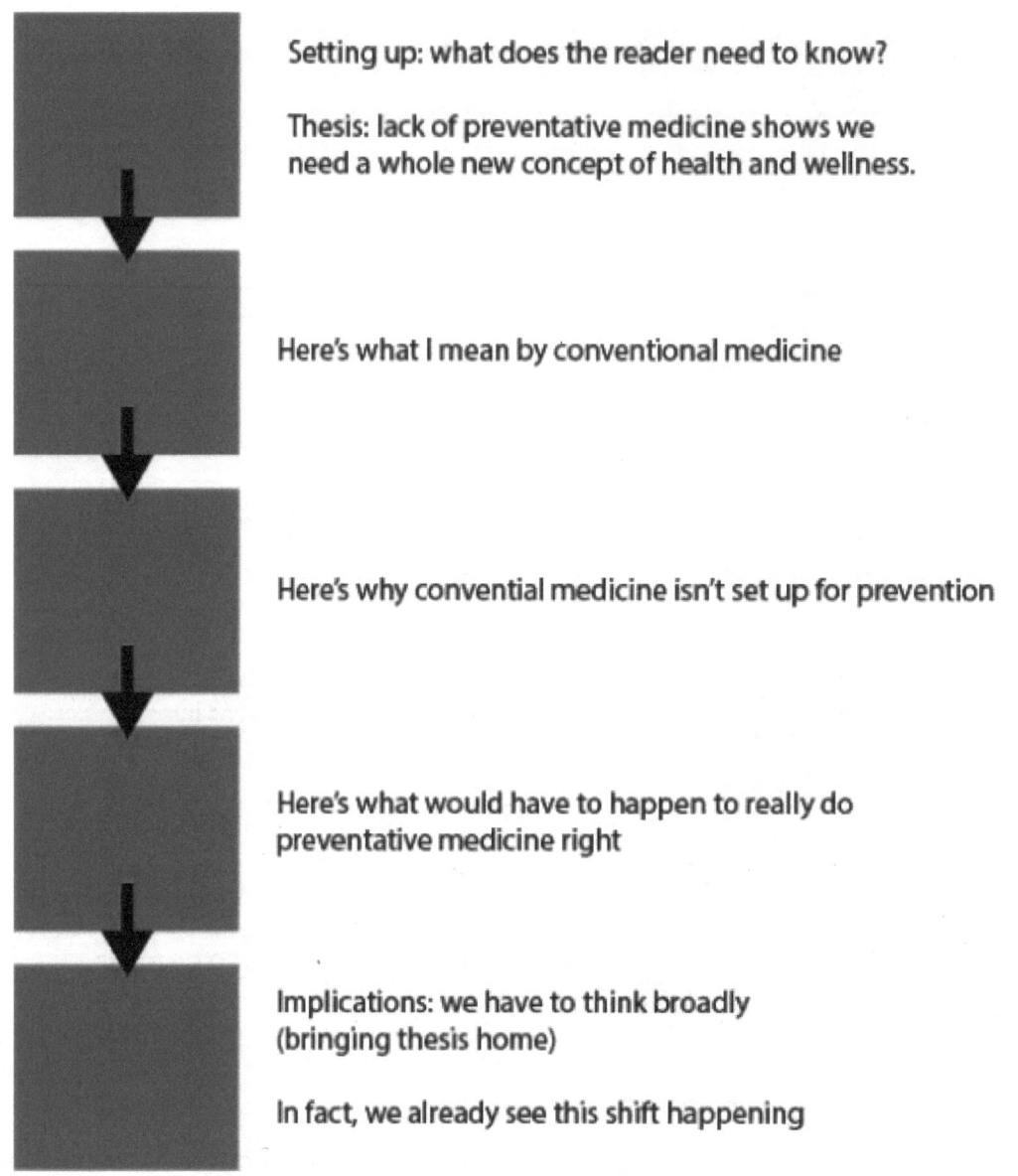

Setting up: what does the reader need to know?

Thesis: lack of preventative medicine shows we need a whole new concept of health and wellness.

Here's what I mean by conventional medicine

Here's why convential medicine isn't set up for prevention

Here's what would have to happen to really do preventative medicine right

Implications: we have to think broadly (bringing thesis home)

In fact, we already see this shift happening

Figure 3.2, The organic college paper

The substantial time you spent mastering the five-paragraph form in Figure 3.1 was time well spent; it's hard to imagine anyone succeeding with the more organic form without the organizational skills and habits of mind inherent in the simpler form. But if you assume that you must adhere rigidly to the simpler form, you're blunting your intellectual ambition. Your professors will not be impressed by obvious theses, loosely related body paragraphs, and repetitive conclusions. They want you to undertake an ambitious independent analysis, one that will yield a thesis that is somewhat surprising and challenging to explain.

General to Specific (Deductive)

Provide thesis and forecasting statements in the introduction to help busy readers focus.

Approximately 100,000 books and millions of journal articles are published each year in the United States (see Bowker Annual). Digital Archivists estimate the size of the Deep Web at over 7.5 billion documents. The Internet

Archive has archived 10 billion pages of the Open Web–over 100 terabytes of information. Now that the Internet has made it possible for just about anyone to publish and potentially reach millions of readers, we are truly overwhelmed by information.

Hook Your Readers – Get to the Point!

Accordingly, writers are under increasing pressure to get to the point, to grab the prospective reader's attention and deliver the goods. In many writing contexts, across genres, readers expect writers to define the purpose, organization, and significance of a document in a thesis statement that is provided in the introduction. As a result, most documents follow a deductive organization in which the authors make a general statement and then support it with specific examples. In other words, writers summarize their thesis and often forecast how they've organized a document. Here, for example, is a headline from today's newspaper:

"Self-Amputation. Frustrated Man Plans to Cut Off His Legs Online" by Paul Eng (ABCNEWS.COM)

This headline is designed to hook readers, enticing them to read the essay. Now, in the past–that is, long ago (read after the Ice Age but before the Internet)–readers may have given writers several pages to get to the point. Nowadays, you've got seconds. Literally seconds. The time it takes to click onto something more informative or entertaining.

Prior research has examined how marital relationships can result in separation and divorce due to Internet addiction. This paper examines how the ability to form romantic and sexual relationships over the Internet can result in marital separation and possible divorce. The ACE Model (Anonymity, Convenience, Escape) of Cybersexual Addiction provides a workable framework to help explain the underlying cyber-cultural issues increasing the risk of virtual adultery. Finally, the paper outlines specific interventions that focus on strategies for rebuilding trust after a cyberaffair, ways to improve marital communication, and finally how to educate couples on ways to continue commitment.

Here's another example of an introduction that gets right to the point, extracted from "Blinded by Junk Food":

Over indulging in fat-filled snack foods may heighten the risk of developing advanced age-related muscular degeneration, the leading cause of blindness and vision impairment in the United States for those over 55, researchers at the Massachusetts Eye and Ear Infirmary said in a new study.

By the way, you should know that readers expect you to provide deductive summaries throughout a document, particularly in lengthy documents. Each time you begin a new section, consider:

> Providing a quick, perhaps one-sentence review of what you've discussed.
> Explaining ways the new topic relates to what has been discussed.
> Explaining how one section relates to another section.

Specific to General (Inductive)

Use an inductive organizational structure to surprise readers or to address controversial topics.

While writers are under increasing pressure to organize information deductively, they can–and do–write inductively. Typically, writers employ a more inductive style when the topic is controversial or when they wish to surprise readers.

Controversial Issues

When writing documents that address controversial issues or matters that threaten the beliefs of their readers, writers may find it strategic to place their arguments in their conclusions rather than their introductions.

Surprise Readers

Readers of novels expect to be delighted with surprise endings. In contrast, readers of nonfiction don't expect the surprise ending, so they can be especially appreciative of a carefully constructed surprise. Note below, for example, the way Dianne Lynch surprises you with the line, "you are using the Internet to fight back"–a line in direct juxtaposition to the first 122 words of her short essay "Afghan Women Reach Out Via the Web."

- You can't laugh or talk aloud in public, and even your shoes must make no sound. Wearing cosmetics or showing your ankles is punishable by whipping; women have had their fingers amputated for wearing nail polish.
- You paint the windows of your house black so you cannot be seen from the outside. You are forbidden from walking on your balcony or in your backyard. It has been years since the sun shone on your face. And all public references to you have disappeared.
- You are a woman in Afghanistan today, living under the regime of the Islamic fundamentalist Taliban.
- And if you are one of the nearly 2,000 women who belong to The Revolutionary Association of the Women of Afghanistan, or RAWA, you are using the Internet to fight back.

When writing essays for school contexts, be sure to check whether your instructor will permit an inductive organization. While an inductive approach can be an effective strategic approach, some readers–particularly in academic and business contexts–define "good writing" as writing that follows a deductive structure.

Provide Metalanguage to Highlight Your Organization

Use metalanguage to help your readers understand your organization and reasoning. Clarify logical relationships, temporal relationships, and spatial relationships by using metalanguage.

The term "metalanguage" refers to language that helps writers explain relationships between ideas or words that explain how texts are presented. Phrases like "for example," "as a result," and "therefore" are examples of metalanguage. Like an impatient TV watcher clicking through hundreds of channels, readers tend to be impatient, always ready to put their work aside.

As a result, throughout a document, you must ensure that readers will understand how different ideas relate to one another. You don't want your readers to ask

- "So what?"
- "Who cares?"
- "Jeez, just what is this text about?"
- "What's going on in the world today?" i.e., tangential thoughts.

Successful writers maintain a sense of their readers' likely responses to their documents. Just as writers commonly summarize their message in their introductions, highlighting its significance, writers frequently repeat their main ideas throughout a document, reminding readers of what's been discussed, what will follow, and how new information relates to old information. Your essay shouldn't be a spinning top, wandering from one topic to another–not if you want readers (or a good grade), anyway. Of course, peppering your language with metadiscourse–such as "thus," "therefore," "consequently," and so on–will not provide logic. By itself, metalanguage cannot provide missing logic; it merely provides the glue to help readers better understand how ideas cohere.

Below is a list of common metalanguage terms. Ideally, your ideas relate so well that you do not need extensive metalanguage.

Transitional Cues	Common Transitions

To guide readers	• You might first conclude • Please consider the possibility that • As you recall • Consider now
To order ideas and structure texts	• To begin...next...furthermore • First, second, third...
To place emphasis	• More importantly • Without doubt • Surprisingly • Remarkably
To provide examples	• For example • For instance • In fact • Additionally • Also • Similarly • In other words
To show logical connections	• If...then • Consequently • However • Furthermore • Hence • As a result • On the other hand... • In contrast • Nonetheless • Still • While
To hedge	• Perhaps • We may conclude • Possibly • This suggest • It may seem
To summarize	• In conclusion... • To summarize • As a result • As I have demonstrated

- Specific to General (Inductive). **Provided by**: Writing Commons. **Located at**: https://writingcommons.org/open-text/writing-processes/organize/organize-structure/124-specific-to-general-inductive. **License**: *CC BY-NC-ND: Attribution-NonCommercial-NoDerivatives*
- Provide Metalanguage to Highlight Your Organization. **Authored by**: Joe Moxley. **Provided by**: Writing Commons. **Located at**: https://writingcommons.org/open-text/writing-processes/organize/organize-structure/126-provide-metalanguage-to-highlight-your-organization. **License**: *CC BY-NC-ND: Attribution-NonCommercial-NoDerivatives*

College Writing: The Writing Process

Introduction to Writing Process

Why is it necessary to evaluate the process of writing?

Differing Purposes of High School and College

College may look and feel similar to high school, and, for the most part, you already know how to perform your student role within this setting. However, there are some fundamental differences. The most obvious ones are that high school is mandatory (to a certain point), freely available, and a legal right. They have to offer you the opportunity, regardless of your grades.

College, on the other hand, is optional, costly, and performance-based. Most institutions will dismiss you if your grades don't meet a certain minimum. But college is different in more subtle ways as well, including ways in which you're expected to behave as an independent thinker and learner.

Students drive their own learning

The assumption behind high-school instruction is that the teacher is the engine of learning. Consequently, a lot of time is spent in direct face-to-face instruction. Homework is for further practice to reinforce material from that day. Teachers will often tell students what each night's homework assignment is, follow up on missing work, and closely track students' progress.

The assumption behind college instruction, in contrast, is that students are the engine of learning, and that most of the significant learning happens **outside of class** while students are working through a dense reading or other challenging intellectual task on their own.

Most college classes meet only 1-3 times a week for a total of about 3 hours. Consequently, college instructors think of class meetings as an opportunity to prepare you for the heavy-lifting that you'll be doing on your own. Sometimes that involves direct instruction (how to solve a particular kind of problem or analyze a particular kind of text). More often, though, professors want to provide you with material not contained in the reading or facilitate active learning experiences based on what you read. The assumption is that all students have the skill and self-motivation to carefully read all the assigned texts. Professors lay out a path for learning—much like how personal trainers develop exercise routines—but it is up to students (and athletes) to do the difficult work themselves.

College Writing Is Different

Professors look at you as independent junior scholars and imagine you writing as someone who has a genuine, driving interest in tackling a complex question. They envision you approaching an assignment without a pre-existing thesis. They expect you to look deep into the evidence, consider several alternative explanations, and work out an original, insightful argument that you actually care about.

This kind of scholarly approach usually entails writing a rough draft, through which you work out an ambitious thesis and the scope of your argument, and then starting over with a wholly rewritten second draft containing a mostly complete argument anchored by a refined thesis. In that second round, you'll discover holes in the argument that should be remedied, counter-arguments that should be acknowledged and addressed, and important implications that should be noted. When the paper is substantially complete, you'll go through it again to tighten up the writing and ensure clarity. Writing a paper isn't about getting the "right answer" and adhering to basic conventions; it's about joining an academic conversation with something original to say, borne of rigorous thought.

The Writing Process

This amount of work devoted to mastering a writing project can seem daunting, at first. Break it into smaller tasks, following the stages of the Writing Process, makes it a lot more manageable, and even enjoyable.

THE WRITING PROCESS

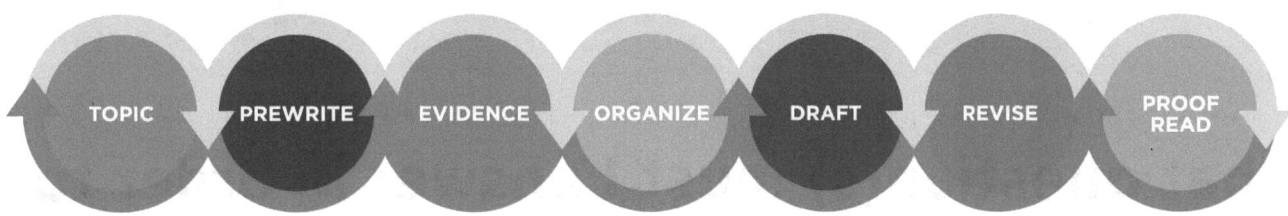

Through this module, we will examine each of these stages of the writing process in detail, and evaluate how each helps further establish you as a critical thinker, writer, and scholar.

Where to Start a Paper

Starting a paper is almost always the hardest part of the writing process. Consider these questions as you prepare to start your paper. It may even be helpful to write out your answers.

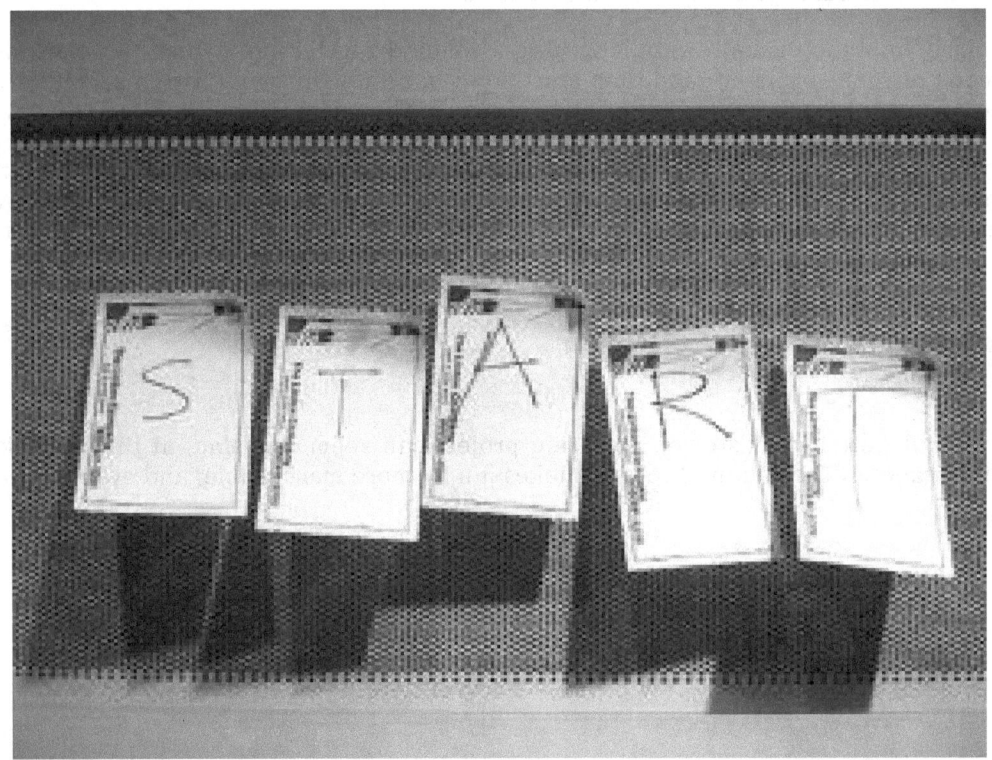

What question(s) must I answer in order to fulfill the assignment?

What "code words" does my assignment contain? (Code words could be abstract terms such as "concepts of freedom" and "system of belief," or they could be terms that demand a certain task of you, such as "analyze," "compare," "explore reasons for," etc.)

Which areas of my readings or sources are still unclear to me? How necessary are they for writing a first draft?

Who is the audience for this paper? Don't always assume that you're writing for your professor; s/he may want you to write for people unfamiliar with the topic. If you're in doubt, ask your professor. What are the most important things that my audience needs to know?

What are a few main points that I want to convey in this paper?

Are any of these points contradictory or overly vague? (For example, if you wrote "I want to show how factories in Japan and America are both similar and different," your goals are probably too broad; "Macbeth was both good and evil" could be easily read as a contradictory statement.)

Can I refine any of these goals? (For instance, for the second example above, you might decide to focus on how Macbeth was a good man who fell because of his lust for power.)

Can I support my main ideas? Are they unsupported speculations and opinions? Depending on the type of paper, opinions might be acceptable. Generally, professors look for support from readings and other academic sources–when in doubt, ask.

Choosing and Developing Topics

Part of what separates good writers from great writers is the ability to organize and relate multiple ideas in one place. We will explore how the concept of "topics" (or, to use the traditional term, **topoi**) has developed and how you might begin to practice developing your own topics.

Finding a Place to Stand

Though it seems particularly pressing in our current social media, online-all-the-time culture, the idea of "information overload" has troubled humans for centuries. Despite these concerns, many of our ancestors found productive ways to manage information overload. And their strategies remain helpful today. With the *topoi* (a word that refers to "topics" but that also means "places"), ancient **rhetoricians**, including Aristotle and Cicero, developed techniques that writers used to gather, categorize, and identify important topics worthy of discussion. *Topoi* have two functions that are still important now: organizing information and exploring common features in sets of information.

First, *topoi* were used to organize information. Using notebooks, rhetoricians gathered research material including common sayings, overheard quotes, everyday opinions, annotations on texts, and insights. After collecting these materials over time, a rhetor would begin to see similar ideas repeat and begin to make relationships with other ideas. These similarities would form "headings" that grouped together related sayings or sentiments. This form of *topoi* would later develop into what became called **commonplace books**. Not unlike your computer's web browser and the multiple "bookmarks" you might collect, these books helped writers and speakers collect and organize information so they could prepare talks and write texts. Commonplaces were the "storehouses" of information that helped rhetors engage with civic and cultural life.

The second use of *topoi* identified similar features or "places" that occurred in arguments. So-called **common topics** were those general features shared in any idea or argument regardless of the content of that argument, including definition, relationship, and/or division. For instance, ancient rhetoricians might ask "Is the argument about a definition?" If they discovered that a definition was, in fact, controversial, then they knew they could follow certain common patterns and use common strategies. Other common topics included comparison, cause-and-effect contradictions, and antecedent/consequence.

These common features provided a structure for any arguments. The structure helped the writer identify what types of arguments might be available and which arguments were likely to be less successful. It gave them a "place to stand," so to speak. It's clear that this way of thinking remains with us today: we often describe someone's argument as staking a "position" within a debate or controversy.

Out of a few initial questions, rhetoricians have developed many topics in many cultures. For instance, the commonplace that "America is the best nation on Earth" is frequently repeated to stake a position and develop an argument. Or, consider a topic like "voting laws": you could easily collect various sources that present both common topics and special topics. Common topic issues of cause and effect (perceived voter fraud and revisions of voting laws) or definition (what defines a legal voter registration?) easily give way to special topics found in deliberative discussions (what makes for *good* elections laws? What is *expedient* for ensuring an inclusive voting system?) And, frequently, the shared commonplace that "voting is the lifeblood of democracy" helps ground and sustain many relevant arguments on the topic.

So *topoi* help rhetors organize and explore research material. That kind of organization can help us develop our own positions on current issues.

CC licensed content, Shared previously

Prewriting and Rhetorical Context

During the pre-writing stage, also known as the brainstorming stage, a writer seeks to generate and develop ideas about a topic.

Techniques and strategies

- using free mental associations that might eventually lead to written notes or outlines
- creating a personal inventory of interests and fascinations, likes and dislikes
- conducting online or print catalog searches using keywords and questions
- using the inductive or deductive reasoning process to identify a manageable topic
- reading a text that addresses a similar topic; perhaps reading the table of contents, index, and chapter headings and subheadings to gain insight on the topic
- creating a uniform set of questions to be answered about a topic (e.g. the "five Ws and an H" model: Who? What? When? Where? Why? How?)
- writing handwritten notes—organized or disorganized—on a note card, on paper, or in electronic form
- writing a preliminary outline—formal or informal—about the intended topic and subtopics
- creating a graphic organization of ideas (e.g. Venn diagram or circle clusters)
- writing a draft of the thesis or hypothesis with an outline of key supporting details
- creating a very rough draft of the opening paragraph that includes a topical overview

Starting off on the right foot

The term "pre-writing" may be a bit misleading because writing can and often does occur at this critical stage. For example, written notes and outlines, including graphic organizers, can serve as a record of one's ideas and the sources of those ideas. A preliminary thesis or hypothesis could inform the process and the product.

Many people do brainstorm via their thoughts without recording those ideas and sources in permanent form prior to the next steps in the writing process. Most emerging writers, however, need to record their pre-writing ideas in permanent form so that those ideas can clearly inform and guide the thinking and writing process, resulting in a coherent, well-organized product or text.

Many students — and some teachers — want to skip the pre-writing stage because they see it as unnecessarily burdensome and time-consuming. However, teachers who dismiss the pre-writing stage as being completely unnecessary are performing a disservice to many of their students. Pre-writing is an essential part of the entire writing process because it enables the writer to begin documenting the process by which the eventual product will be formed and evaluated. It is part of a procedure that is necessary for accountability and reliability. Most professions include accountability and reliability in their standard operating procedures as written reports of preparatory work for use by the practitioner and for potential legal documentation and reference. Writers are no less responsible for accountability for their work than are lawyers and medical personnel.

Resources

Skipping the pre-writing stage is like taking a vacation without first choosing a destination: If you don't know where you're going, how will you get there? Fortunately, pre-writing can take many forms, and there are strategies that suit every type of writer.

The strategies and processes used in the pre-writing stage not only help the writer formulate a topic and solidify ideas, they also serve as a kind of rehearsal for the rest of the writing process. As the writer uses the vocabulary associated with a particular topic, he or she becomes more well-versed in the subject and is able to express ideas with more confidence, organization, and clarity. All of this brings to mind the old joke, "How do you get to Carnegie Hall?"

The answer, of course: "Practice. Practice. Practice."

Just as a musician must practice his instrument in order to achieve his goal, the practice undertaken during the pre-writing stage guides the writer toward a specific goal: developing a well-defined topic that will eventually be couched in the language of a succinct thesis or hypothesis.

Any piece of writing is shaped by external factors before the first word is ever set down on the page. These factors are referred to as the **rhetorical situation**, or **rhetorical context**, and are often presented in the form of a pyramid.

Rhetorical Context

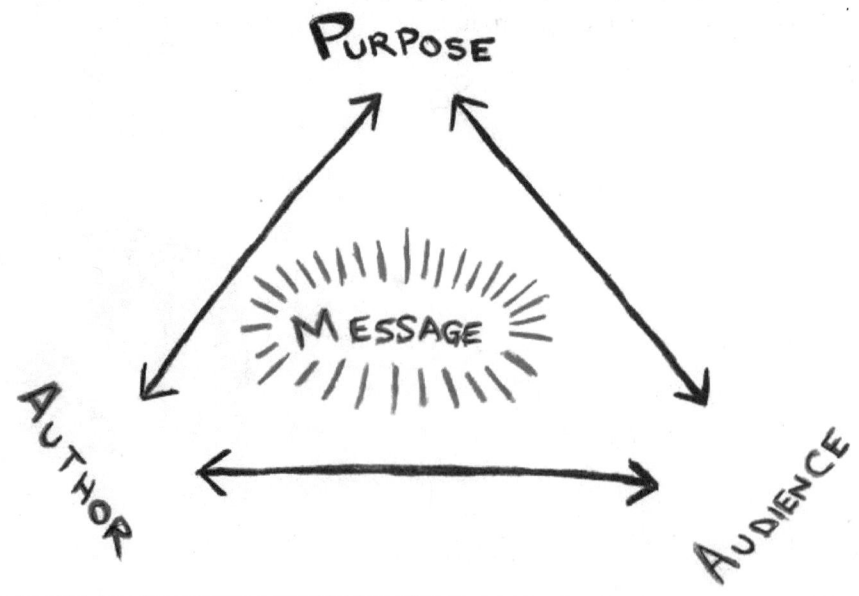

The three key factors-purpose, author, and audience-all work together to influence what the text itself says, and how it says it. Let's examine each of the three in more detail.

Purpose

Any time you are preparing to write, you should first ask yourself, "Why am I writing?" All writing, no matter the type, has a purpose. Purpose will sometimes be given to you (by a teacher, for example), while other times, you will decide for yourself. As the author, it's up to you to make sure that purpose is clear not only for yourself, but also-especially-for your audience. If your purpose is not clear, your audience is not likely to receive your intended message.

There are, of course, many different reasons to write (e.g., to inform, to entertain, to persuade, to ask questions), and you may find that some writing has more than one purpose. When this happens, be sure to consider any conflict between purposes, and remember that you will usually focus on one main purpose as primary.

Bottom line: Thinking about your purpose before you begin to write can help you create a more effective piece of writing.

Why Purpose Matters

If you've ever listened to a lecture or read an essay and wondered "so what" or "what is this person talking about," then you know how frustrating it can be when an author's purpose is not clear. By clearly defining your purpose before you begin writing, it's less likely you'll be that author who leaves the audience wondering.
If readers can't identify the purpose in a text, they usually quit reading. You can't deliver a message to an audience who quits reading.
If a teacher can't identify the purpose in your text, they will likely assume you didn't understand the assignment and, chances are, you won't receive a good grade.

Useful Questions

Consider how the answers to the following questions may affect your writing:

- What is my primary purpose for writing? How do I want my audience to think, feel, or respond after they read my writing?
- Do my audience's expectations affect my purpose? Should they?
- How can I best get my point across (e.g., tell a story, argue, cite other sources)?
- Do I have any secondary or tertiary purposes? Do any of these purposes conflict with one another or with my primary purpose?

Audience

In order for your writing to be maximally effective, you have to think about the audience you're writing for and adapt your writing approach to their needs, expectations, backgrounds, and interests. Being aware of your audience helps you make better decisions about what to say and how to say it. For example, you have a better idea if you will need to define or explain any terms, and you can make a more conscious effort not to say or do anything that would offend your audience.

Sometimes you know who will read your writing - for example, if you are writing an email to your boss. Other times you will have to guess who is likely to read your writing - for example, if you are writing a newspaper editorial. You will often write with a primary audience in mind, but there may be secondary and tertiary audiences to consider as well.

What to Think About

When analyzing your audience, consider these points. Doing this should make it easier to create a profile of your audience, which can help guide your writing choices.

Background-knowledge or Experience — In general, you don't want to merely repeat what your audience already knows about the topic you're writing about; you want to build on it. On the other hand, you don't want to talk over their heads. Anticipate their amount of previous knowledge or experience based on elements like their age, profession, or level of education.

Expectations and Interests — Your audience may expect to find specific points or writing approaches, especially if you are writing for a teacher or a boss. Consider not only what they *do* want to read about, but also what they *do not* want to read about.

Attitudes and Biases — Your audience may have predetermined feelings about you or your topic, which can affect how hard you have to work to win them over or appeal to them. The audience's attitudes and biases also affect their expectations - for example, if they expect to disagree with you, they will likely look for evidence that you have considered their side as well as your own.

Demographics — Consider what else you know about your audience, such as their age, gender, ethnic and cultural backgrounds, political preferences, religious affiliations, job or professional background, and area of residence. Think about how these demographics may affect how much background your audience has about your topic, what types of expectations or interests they have, and what attitudes or biases they may have.

Applying Your Analysis to Your Writing

Here are some general rules about writing, each followed by an explanation of how audience might affect it. Consider how you might adapt these guidelines to your specific situation and audience. (Note: This is not an exhaustive list. Furthermore, you need not follow the order set up here, and you likely will not address all of these approaches.)[1]

Add information readers need to understand your document / omit information readers don't need. Part of your audience may know a lot about your topic, while others don't know much at all. When this happens, you have to decide if you should provide explanation or not. If you don't offer explanation, you risk alienating or confusing those who lack the information. If you offer explanation, you create more work for yourself and you risk boring those who already know the information, which may negatively affect the larger view those readers have of you and your work. In the end, you may want to consider how many people need an explanation, whether those people are in your primary audience (rather than a secondary audience), how much time you have to complete your writing, and any length limitations placed on you.

Change the level of the information you currently have. Even if you have the right information, you might be explaining it in a way that doesn't make sense to your audience. For example, you wouldn't want to use highly advanced or technical vocabulary in a document for first-grade students or even in a document for a general audience, such as the audience of a daily newspaper, because most likely some (or even all) of the audience wouldn't understand you.

Add examples to help readers understand. Sometimes just changing the level of information you have isn't enough to get your point across, so you might try adding an example. If you are trying to explain a complex or abstract issue to an audience with a low education level, you might offer a metaphor or an analogy to something they are more familiar with to help them understand. Or, if you are writing for an audience that disagrees with your stance, you might offer examples that create common ground and/or help them see your perspective.

Change the level of your examples. Once you've decided to include examples, you should make sure you aren't offering examples your audience finds unacceptable or confusing. For example, some teachers find personal stories unacceptable in academic writing, so you might use a metaphor instead.

Change the organization of your information. Again, you might have the correct information, but you might be presenting it in a confusing or illogical order. If you are writing a paper about physics for a physics professor who has his or her PhD, chances are you won't need to begin your paper with a lot of background. However, you probably would want to include background information in the beginning of your paper if you were writing for a fellow student in an introductory physics class.

Strengthen transitions. You might make decisions about transitions based on your audience's expectations. For example, most teachers expect to find topic sentences, which serve as transitions between paragraphs. In a shorter piece of writing such as a memo to co-workers, however, you would probably be less concerned with topic sentences and more concerned with transition words. In general, if you feel your readers may have a hard time making connections, providing transition words (e.g., "therefore" or "on the other hand") can help lead them.

Write stronger introductions - both for the whole document and for major sections. In general, readers like to get the big picture up front. You can offer this in your introduction and thesis statement, or in smaller introductions to major sections within your document. However, you should also consider how much time your audience will have to read your document. If you are writing for a boss who already works long hours and has little or no free time, you wouldn't want to write an introduction that rambles on for two and a half pages before getting into the information your boss is looking for.

Create topic sentences for paragraphs and paragraph groups. A topic sentence (the first sentence of a paragraph) functions much the same way an introduction does – it offers readers a preview of what's coming and how that information relates to the overall document or your overall purpose. As mentioned earlier, some readers will expect topic sentences. However, even if your audience isn't expecting them, topic sentences can make it easier for readers to skim your document while still getting the main idea and the connections between smaller ideas.

Change sentence style and length. Using the same types and lengths of sentences can become boring after a while. If you already worry that your audience may lose interest in your issue, you might want to work on varying the types of sentences you use.

Use graphics, or use different graphics. Graphics can be another way to help your audience visualize an abstract or complex topic. Sometimes a graphic might be more effective than a metaphor or step-by-step explanation. Graphics may also be an effective choice if you know your audience is going to skim your writing quickly; a graphic can be used to draw the reader's eye to information you want to highlight. However, keep in mind that some audiences may see graphics as inappropriate.

Author

The final unique aspect of anything written down is who it is, exactly, that does the writing. In some sense, this is the part you have the most control over–it's you who's writing, after all! You can harness the aspects of yourself that will make the text most effective to its audience, for its purpose.

Analyzing yourself as an author allows you to make explicit why your audience should pay attention to what you have to say, and why they should listen to you on the particular subject at hand.

Questions for Consideration

- What personal motivations do you have for writing about this topic?
- What background knowledge do you have on this subject matter?
- What personal experiences directly relate to this subject? How do those personal experiences influence your perspectives on the issue?
- What formal training or professional experience do you have related to this subject?
- What skills do you have as a communicator? How can you harness those in this project?
- What should audience members know about you, in order to trust what you have to tell them? How will you convey that in your writing?

(Rules adapted from David McMurrey's online text, *Power Tools for Technical Communication*) ↵

Connecting Research to the Process

THE RESEARCH PROCESS

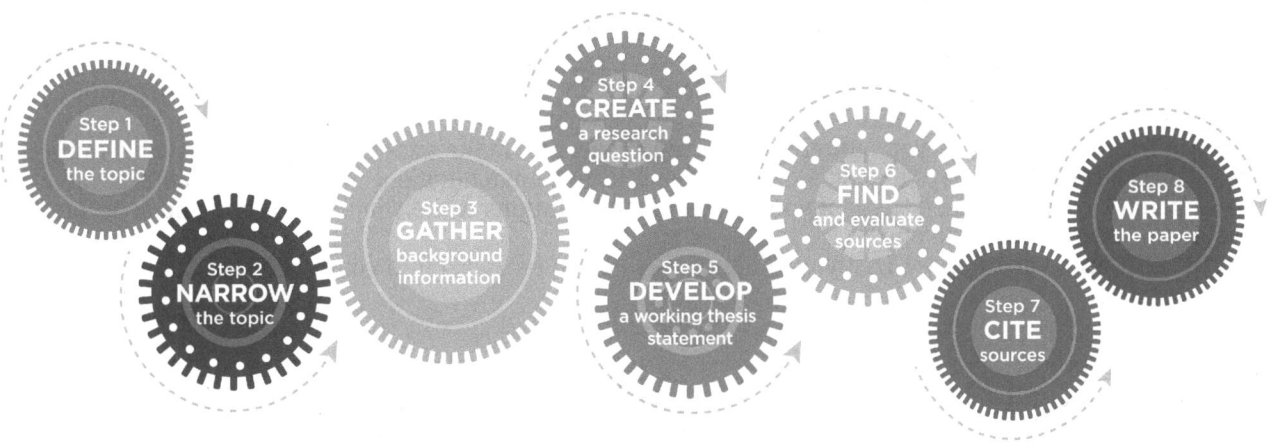

The research process is not a linear process in which you must complete step one before moving on to step two or three. You don't need to put off writing your paper until you've gathered all of your sources, in fact, you may want to start writing as soon as possible and adjust your search, thesis statement, and writing as you continue to work through the research process. For that reason, consider the following research process as a guideline to follow as your work through your paper. You can (and should!) revisit the steps as many times as needed to create a finished product.

Decide on the topic, or carefully consider the topic that has been assigned.

Narrow the topic in order to narrow search parameters. When you go to a professional sports event, concert, or event at a large venue, your ticket has three items on it: the section, the row, and the seat number. You go in that specific order to pinpoint where you are supposed to sit. Similarly, when you decide on a topic, you often start large and must narrow the focus; you move from general subject, to a more limited topic, to a specific focus or issue. The reader does not want a cursory look at the topic; she wants to walk away with some newfound knowledge and deeper understanding of the issue. For that, details are essential. For example, suppose you want to explore the topic of autism. You might move from:

- **General topic:** special needs in a classroom
- **Limited topic:** autistic students in a classroom setting
- **Specific focus:** how technology can enhance learning for autistic students

Do background research, or pre-research. Begin by figuring out what you know about the topic, and then fill in any gaps you may have on the basics by looking at more general sources. This is a place where general Google searches, Wikipedia, or another encyclopedia-style source will be most useful. Once you know the basics of the topic, start investigating that basic information for potential sources of conflict. Does there seem to be disagreement about particular aspects of the topic? For instance, if you're looking at a

Civil War battle, are there any parts of the battle that historians seem to argue about? Perhaps some point to one figure's failing as a reason for a loss, and some point instead to another figure's spectacular success as a reason his side won?

Create a research question. Once you have narrowed your topic so that is manageable, it is time to generate research questions about your topic. Create thought-provoking, open-ended questions, ones that encourage debate. Decide which question addresses the issue that concerns you—that will be your main research question. Secondary questions will address the who, what, when, where, why, and how of the issue. As an example:

- o **Main question:** Does the media stereotype women in such a way that women do not believe they can be leaders?
- o **Secondary questions:** How can more women get involved in politics? Why aren't more women involved in politics? What role do media play in discouraging women from being involved? How many women are involved in politics at a state or national level? How long do they typically stay in politics, and for what reasons do they leave?

Next, "answer" the main research question to create a **working thesis statement**. The thesis statement is a single sentence that identifies the topic and shows the direction of the paper while simultaneously allowing the reader to glean the writer's stance on that topic. A working thesis performs four main functions:

Narrows the subject to the single point that readers should understand

Names the topic and makes a significant assertion about that topic

Conveys the purpose

Provides a preview of how the essay will be arranged (usually).

Determine what kind of sources are best for your argument.

- o How many sources will you need? How long should your paper be? Will you need primary or secondary sources? Where will you find the best information?

Create a bibliography as you gather and reference sources. Make sure you are using credible and relevant sources. It's always a good idea to utilize reference management programs like Zotero, Mendeley, or EndNote so you can keep track of your research and citations while you are working and searching, instead of waiting until the end.

Write and edit your paper! Lastly, you'll incorporate the research into your own writing and properly cite your sources.

Finding Items for a Topic

Today, the commonplace books that rhetoricians once maintained to organize and develop topics for their own use have been replaced by books, libraries, television, radio, and the Internet. A lot of the work done by people in the media, government, business, and academia comes down to taming the flow of information that's now faster than ever. As an academic reader and writer, you're joining that effort. One of your goals should be to become a critical thinker and writer who possesses the skills to organize, explore, and develop topics on your own. You can gain those skills with practice. Lots of practice.

To help that practice, you can use some tools you're already familiar with and some others that may be new to you.

Students sometimes believe they really don't know what to write and argue about. When the Internet was developing a few years ago as a common communication medium, a lot of commentators believed it would make being an informed researcher and citizen easier: after all, having access to the Internet means having access to more information than anyone has ever had access to before in human history. But the problem is that having access to the Internet means having access to more information than anyone has ever had access to before in human history. To start looking for and working with a topic, for instance, your first inclination might be to use Google and simply "search" for a term. If we tried to look for information on voting laws, though, we'd get a return of over 32,000,000 items in less than a second.

There are two problems with this approach (at least).

First, the quality of the items should cause us some doubt. This basic search returns wikipedia articles, news stories, government agency sources, and even a non-profit organization website. While some of these might be helpful, the items have neither given us a detailed "place" to begin our topic nor a clear "place" to stand.

Our second problem concerns the amount of information. We just can't sift through 32 million items, so we need a tool that does some of the selecting and organizing for us. Google News is one example of just such a tool. This site allows us to better focus on a topic as it unfolds in real time. If we use our "voting laws" search term, Google News and its "Realtime Coverage" option posts the most recent news articles in the subject, provides investigative "in depth" articles, makes available opinion pieces, and even includes a timeline for articles published on the topic. These features give us places for specific types of items, and they help us because they are already loosely organized and defined.

Next Steps

Sites like Google News are great places to *begin* research on a topic because they provide a range of different types of items and a helpful model for how to organize those items. On the other hand, these sites are bad places to *end* your research. Google News, for instance, does not capture **scholarly resources**. These sources are often vital to provide even more in-depth and focused coverage on topics.

For the purposes of beginning your research topic, however, selecting a range of articles from an array of sources will help you explore the various "places" contained in any topic. For instance, a typical news story is usually brief and only has room to offer minimal information. The common topics most likely to occur here are those best used to communicate basic facts: cause-effect, definition, and/or antecedent/consequence. An investigative journalism essay, a longer piece taking much more time to develop and much more space for coverage, will be better suited for more nuanced kinds of common topics such as contradictions, limits, and/or similarity/difference. More particular examples, such as YouTube videos of a politician's speeches, might offer exposure to those "special topics" found in deliberative, judicial, and ceremonial discourses. Opinion essays or "op-eds" might offer access to commonplaces and a good place to see how they are used.

But whichever source types you use, you should know that any well-researched paper will be supported by a balance of items from many different media, viewpoints, and levels of expertise.

ShareAlike

- Thesis statement information, Pot of Gold, Information Literacy Tutorial. **Provided by**: Notre Dame. **Located at**: http://library.nd.edu/instruction/potofgold/investigating/?page=10. **License**: *CC BY-NC-SA: Attribution-NonCommercial-ShareAlike*
- Steps 2-4 in the Research Process come from Chapter 1: Writing and Research in the Academic Sphere and Chapter 2: Research Proposals and Thesis Statements. **Authored by**: Denise Snee, Kristin Houlton, and Nancy Heckel. Edited by Kimberly Jacobs.. **Project**: Research, Analysis, and Writing. **License**: *CC BY-NC-SA: Attribution-NonCommercial-ShareAlike*
- Revision and Adaptation. **Provided by**: Lumen Learning. **License**: *CC BY-NC-SA: Attribution-NonCommercial-ShareAlike*
- The Research Process graphic. **Authored by**: Kim Louie for Lumen Learning. **License**: *CC BY: Attribution*
- Choosing and Developing Topics. **Authored by**: Jay Jordan. **Provided by**: University of Utah, University Writing Program. **Project**: Open2010. **License**: *CC BY-NC-SA: Attribution-NonCommercial-ShareAlike*
- Image of overwhelming menu options. **Authored by**: Ian Muttoo. **Located at**: https://flic.kr/p/7nrU1S. **License**: *CC BY-SA: Attribution-ShareAlike*

Getting a Rough Draft Completed

From Outlining to Drafting

So far we've presented "organizing" and "drafting" as two separate steps on the writing process continuum. While there are distinct differences between the two stages, the line between these steps is the muddiest of the entire writing process. Ideally, as you're working on an essay project, you won't be able to draw a clear line between when you stop working on organizing and start working on your first essay draft.

Remember from the previous section that there are several different kinds of outlines:

- Roman or Arabic Numeral (highly structured)
- bullet point (loosely structured)
- mind map
- timeline
- PowerPoint

Roman Numeral Outline

Thesis statement: E-mail and internet monitoring, as currently practiced, is an invasion of employees' rights in the workplace.

    I. The situation: Over 80% of today's companies monitor their employees.
        To prevent fraudulent activities, theft, and other workplace related violations.
        To more efficiently monitor employee productivity.
        To prevent any legal liabilities due to harassing or offensive communications.
    II. What are employees' privacy rights when it comes to electronic monitoring and surveillance in the workplace?
        American employees have basically no legal protection from mean and snooping bosses.
            There are no federal or State laws protecting employees.
            Employees may assert privacy protection for their own personal effects.
        Most managers believe that there is no right to privacy in the workplace.
            Workplace communications should be about work; anything else is a misuse of company equipment and company time
            Employers have a right to prevent misuse by monitoring employee communications

Arabic Numeral Outline

Bullet Point Outline

Set up – introduce the characters, world building, normal life

Event One – the first incident that causes this journey to begin

Reaction – In the beginning, she is always reacting to the events around her.

Event Two – Something else big happens that changes the story

Proactive – This is where she begins to take matters in her own hands. She is no longer reacting. She is making decisions.

Event Three – Something else happens usually increasing the stakes more and more.

Resolution – She has decided what she'll do and takes steps to make it happen

Even Four – The stakes are as high as they'll get now. This is the black moment.

The End – wrap it up quickly. Show how she has changed or not. A glimpse at her new life.

Mind Map Outline

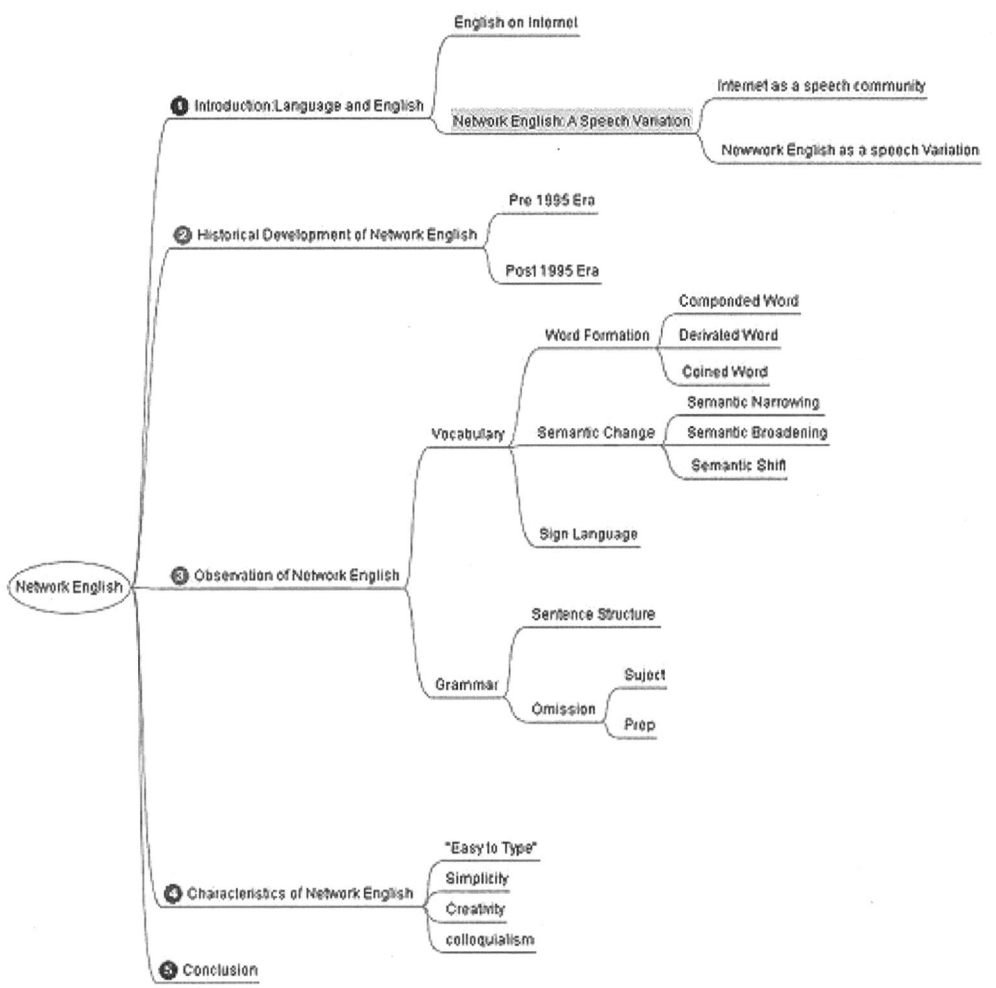

Timeline Outline

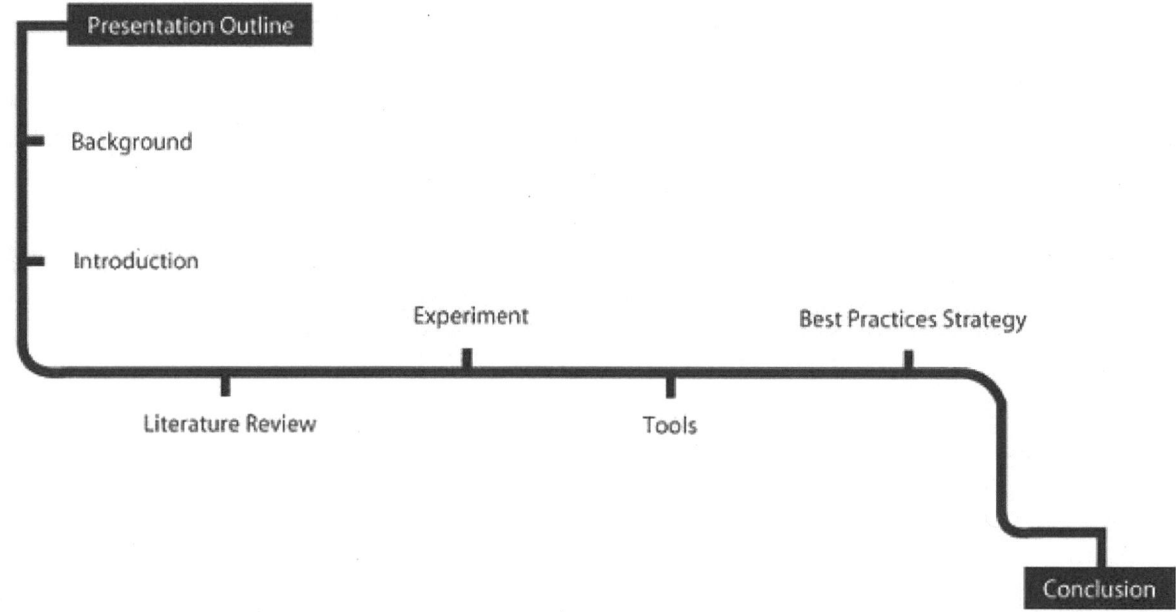

Wrap Up

Whichever outline you've started with, it can conveniently morph into an essay draft, simply by picking an area to attack. Start fleshing it out with full sentences, complete thoughts, and relevant sources.

One of the many advantages to working from an outline is that you don't have to begin your draft at the beginning of the paper. Pick a section you feel strongly about, and start there. Hopscotch around your outline in whatever order you choose, in order to keep the momentum going.

Enter Flash-Drafting

A typical expectation for an essay draft is that it will take a few days to develop. The longer the final product, the longer that time of initial development (usually).

From that perspective, it's no wonder many students are hesitant to revise later! When you invest a lot of time crafting something, you grow quite attached to it. You don't want to have that feeling of having to "start over" again with serious revision, later.

Flash Drafts

- are completed in one concentrated time period (~ 45 minutes)
- are written "fast and furious" with no time to sweat the small stuff
- contain notes where a writer might need to research or develop further later
- conform to the general structure of the final product

By adding in a timed component to the first, fast draft of an essay, you get several advantages. There's literally no time for perfection, so concerns about "doing it right" stop being a roadblock to writing anything at all. Flash drafts generate a lot of raw material that can be refined and built upon later. And these drafts boost your confidence as you realize how much you already know about the subject.

Flash drafts are effective for any writer. Proof of this comes from the following essay by Stacey Shubitz, a teacher of writing for both grade school and college students.

"Flash Drafting Leads to Large-Scale Revision"

I've been at the June Writing Institute this week. Kelly Boland Hohne has been my section leader for "Raise the Level of Literature-Based and Research-Based Argument Essays." In the past week, I've written two flash drafts, one literary essay and one research-based essay. I have found the process scary and liberating all at once. Here's why.

Flash-drafting unnerved me because I'm used to taking my time with writing. I tinker with words. I play with punctuation. I type, I cut, I paste, I cut some more, I copy, etc. I do this because I want to make sure my thoughts are as succinct as they can possibly be. This week, I learned that flash-drafting doesn't afford a writer with making it perfect. That's what revision is for!

My flash drafts and my initial revisions of my flash drafts were anything but perfect. Kelly encouraged us to use . . . a Glow and Grow. . . . That is, after we flash-drafted, we looked at what we did well as writers and marked it "glow." Then, wherever we needed to improve our writing, we marked it "grow."

Seeing as I didn't spend tons of time on my flash-drafts, I'm excited to revise because I know I need to. My flash-drafts weren't my best work. (Heck, they were all written while I was riding on mass transit balancing my iPad on my lap!) Now that I've gone through the flash-drafting process *twice* this week, I understand how it can lead to more excitement about making large-scale revisions in response to what one learns next in writing workshop (or in my case, from my session leader, Kelly).

ShareAlike

- Flash-Drafting Leads to Large-Scale Revision. **Authored by**: Stacey Shubitz. **Provided by**: Two Writing Teachers. **Located at**: https://twowritingteachers.org/2014/06/27/flash-drafting/. **License**: *CC BY-NC-SA: Attribution-NonCommercial-ShareAlike*
- Image of The Flash. **Authored by**: Robert Ball. **Located at**: https://flic.kr/p/9msAq5. **License**: *CC BY-NC-ND: Attribution-NonCommercial-NoDerivatives*
- Revision and Adaptation. **Provided by**: Lumen Learning. **License**: *CC BY-NC-SA: Attribution-NonCommercial-ShareAlike*

The Art of Re-Seeing

Revising is the rearrangement and fine tuning of a fully developed—if not totally completed—draft so that the thesis or hypothesis is aligned with the writer's purpose, the development of the argument and its persuasive conclusion, and the audience's needs and characteristics.

Often, writers perform the multiple drafting, revising, and editing stages concurrently. Similarities among these writing tasks permit such concurrent task performance.

The Art of Revision

Revising a written document sometimes closely resembles the multiple drafting stage of the writing process. The main difference between drafting and revising probably lies within the completeness of the document itself. Rough drafts are characterized by varying degrees of completeness, which the writer attempts to finish in a less-than-polished manner. The overriding need to write details down on paper or record them in electronic form drives the writer during the rough draft stage. The task during the rough draft stage is to include all the features of the proposed thesis and supporting details. These rough drafts are akin to an unformed block of stone into which the artist is chiseling an image that is not yet fully recognizable to the audience.

Revised drafts are based upon a completed rough draft that now needs to be chiseled into a fully recognizable work of art. During the revising stage, the chiseled image becomes clearer, more developed according to the controlling thesis, and less defined by unnatural, awkward angles. However, the ultimate task of the revising stage is to make that recognizable but still ill-defined image into a beautiful work of art.

The writer considers the succinctness of the thesis (meaning precise and concise wording), the adequateness and relevance of the supporting details, the fluency of development, and the concluding finishing touches during the revising stage. Paragraph structure and transitions are also considered. So too are diction and rhetorical strategies examined for appropriateness to the task. Sometimes, these considerations might lead the writer to rewrite the entire piece, including the thesis or hypothesis, once the writer realizes that the purpose and the audience require a more focused or different written expression. When such rewrites occur, many writers engage in a recursive process of drafting and revising, often simultaneously. Some writers might even begin again with the pre-writing stage as they realize that this rewrite is actually a completely different writing task.

A Critical Step

Revising, for many writers and teachers of writing, is the critical step in any writing process. It is the step that often frustrates many writers because it can be tedious and tiresome to pay such close attention to details that might become lost or unrecognizable in the repeated examination of what one has written.

Many writers at this stage find it beneficial to have someone else read a document that is too close to the writer's controlling thoughts and frayed emotions. The intellectual and emotional investment into one's writing is typically the reason why many emotionally developing students accuse an English teacher of disliking the student when the teacher critiques or grades an assignment.

The need to revise undeniably acknowledges that one's writing is not perfect as presented in the latest draft. One's willingness to revise means that the writer recognizes the dynamic nature of communication, which requires revisions in order to clearly articulate ideas and meet the expectations of the audience. Effective written expression is the result of careful revisions.

A System for Approaching Revision

Generally, revision should be approached in a top-down manner by addressing **higher-order concerns (HOCs)** before moving on to **lower-order concerns (LOCs)**. In writing studies, the term "higher order" is used to denote major or global issues such as thesis, argumentation, and organization, whereas "lower order" is used to denote minor or local issues such as grammar and mechanics.[1] The more analytical work of revising HOCs often has ramifications for the entire piece. Perhaps in refining the argument, a writer will realize that the discussion section does not fully consider the study's implications. Or, a writer will try a new organizational scheme and find that a paragraph no longer fits and should be cut. Such revisions may have far-reaching implications for the text.

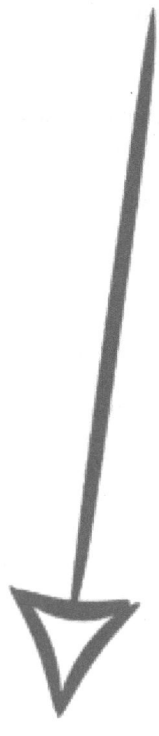

Dedicating time to tweaking wording or correcting grammatical errors is unproductive if the sentence will be changed or deleted. Focusing on HOCs before LOCs allows writers to revise more effectively and efficiently.

Revision Strategies

Bearing in mind the general system of revising from HOCs to LOCs, you can employ several revision strategies.

- **Begin by evaluating how your argument addresses your rhetorical situation**—that is, the specific context surrounding your writing, including the audience, exigence, and constraints.[2]
    - For example, you may write an article describing a new treatment. If the target journal's audience comes from a variety of disciplines, you may need to include substantial background explanation, consider the implications for practitioners and scholars in multiple fields, and define technical terms. By contrast, if you are addressing a highly specialized audience, you may be able to dispense with many of the background explanations and definitions because of your shared knowledge base. You may consider the implications only for specialists, as they are your primary audience. Because this sort of revision affects the entire text, beginning by analyzing your rhetorical situation is effective.
- **Analyze your thesis or main argument for clarity**.
- **Evaluate the global organization of your text by writing a reverse outline**. Unlike traditional outlines, which are written before drafting, reverse outlines reflect the content of written drafts.
    - In a separate document or in your text's margins, record the main idea of each paragraph. Then, consider whether the order of your ideas is logical. This method also will help you identify ideas that are out of place or digressive. You may also evaluate organization by printing the text and cutting it up so that each paragraph appears on a separate piece of paper. You may then easily reorder the paragraphs to test different organizational schemes.

McAndrew DA, Registad TJ. *Tutoring writing: a practical guide for conferences*. Portsmouth (NH): Boynton/Cook; 2001. ↵

Bitzer L. "The rhetorical situation." *Philos Rhetoric* 1968; 1 (1): 1-14. ↵

CC licensed content, Original

- Revisions and Adaptations. **Authored by**: Dann Coble. **Provided by**: Corning Community College. **Project**: ENGL 1010 OER Project. **License**: *CC BY-NC-SA: Attribution-NonCommercial-ShareAlike*

CC licensed content, Shared previously

- Revising. **Authored by**: Vinetta Bell. **Provided by**: Learn NC. **Located at**: http://www.learnnc.org/lp/editions/writing-process/5811. **Project**: A Writing Process. **License**: *CC BY-SA: Attribution-ShareAlike*
- Revision and Adaptation. **Provided by**: Lumen Learning. **License**: *CC BY-NC-SA: Attribution-NonCommercial-ShareAlike*
- Revision Strategies. **Authored by**: Kristin Messuri. **Located at**: http://pulmonarychronicles.com/ojs/index.php?journal=pulmonarychronicles&page=article&op=view&path%5B%5D=263&path%5B%5D=662. **Project**: Pulmonary Chronicles. **License**: *CC BY: Attribution*
- Post-Draft Outline. **Authored by**: Alexis McMillan-Clifton. **Provided by**: Tacoma Community College. **Located at**: http://prezi.com/ilic1tcomvne/?utm_campaign=share&utm_medium=copy&rc=ex0share. **License**: *CC BY: Attribution*
- Image of blue arrow. **Authored by**: ClkerFreeVectorImages. **Located at**: https://pixabay.com/en/arrow-down-blue-handdrawn-pointing-310601/. **License**: *CC0: No Rights Reserved*

Peer Review

Seeking Input from Others

College writers have many potential opportunities to seek out feedback on their work, at any stage of the writing process. For instance, your college's Writing Center or Tutoring Center would be happy to work with you on prewriting, early drafts, or nearly finished drafts.

Friends or family members might also be good options for feedback, if you trust that they will be genuine and helpful with their input.

You will likely also have the opportunity to participate in peer review for many courses that require writing assignments.

Peer Review

Instructors teaching a writing-intensive course, or any course that requires students to produce a substantial amount of writing, should consider creating opportunities for students to read and respond to one another's writing. Such opportunities to engage in "peer review," when well planned, can help students improve their reading and writing skills and learn how to collaborate effectively.

More specifically, participating in peer review can help students:

- Learn how to read carefully, with attention to the details of a piece of writing (whether their own or another writer's);
- Learn how to strengthen their writing by taking into account the responses of actual and anticipated readers;
- Make the transition from writing primarily for themselves or for an instructor to writing for a broader audience–a key transition for students as they learn to write university-level papers and as they prepare for post-graduate work;
- Learn how to formulate and communicate constructive feedback on a peer's work;
- Learn how to gather and respond to feedback on their own work.

Challenges in the Peer Review Process

Many instructors who have incorporated peer review into their courses report less than satisfying results. In fact, it is quite common to find that, when asked to participate in peer review, students rush through the peer-review process and offer their peers only vaguely positive comments, such as "I liked your paper," or "Good job," or "Good paper, but a few parts need more work." Furthermore, many students seem to ignore peer-reviewers' comments on their writing.

There are several possible reasons behind such responses:

Many students feel uncomfortable with the task of having to pronounce a judgment on their peers' writing. This discomfort may be the result of their maturity level, their desire not to hurt a peer's feelings (perhaps made more acute by the fact that they are anxious about having their peers read and judge their own writing), or simply their inexperience with providing constructive criticism on a peer's work. A vaguely positive response allows them to avoid a socially uncomfortable situation and to create an environment of mutual support (Nilson 2003).

If students are not given clear guidance from their instructors, they may not know how to comment on one another's writing in a specific and constructive way. In addition, it should be noted that students may not understand how to comment on their peers' writing because over the years they have not received helpful feedback from instructors who have graded their papers.

Some instructors ask their students to evaluate their peers' writing using the same criteria the instructor uses when grading papers (e.g., quality of thesis, adequacy of support, coherence, etc.). Undergraduate students often have an inadequate understanding of these criteria, and as a result, they either ignore or inappropriately apply such criteria during peer-review sessions (Nilson 2003).

Many students do not perceive feedback from peers as relevant to the process of writing a paper for a course. Especially at the beginning of their undergraduate work, students are likely to assume that it is only the instructor's feedback that "counts."

Even when they take seriously feedback provided by their peers, students often do not know how to incorporate that feedback when they revise their papers.

Responding to Input from Others

As authors, you may dread receiving reviewer comments asking for major revisions. It's daunting to rework something for which you have already taken great pains. But don't be tempted to give up. Most often, the final outcome is worth the effort. Here are some pointers on how to respond to such comments.

- **Take a break**: Initial irritation is only natural. Take time off and then read the comments again carefully and objectively to ensure that you have clearly understood the reviewers' concerns.
- **Articulate point-by-point responses**: Number the reviewers' points and respond to them sequentially. If you're required to respond to your reviewers, this makes it easier for others to follow what you have done. Even if your reviewers never see your responses, this is an effective way to inventory their advice and make sure that you've evaluated all of it.
- **Create well-reasoned responses to input**: If you do not agree with a reviewer's comment, that's only fair. However, do not simply disagree. Justify this disagreement, to yourself or to the reviewer, by providing as many details as necessary to help any reader understand your line of reasoning. Where possible, cite published studies to support your argument.
- **Pay attention to detail**: Details are important when explaining how you have addressed each concern. For example, if a reviewer has said that you need to include/reinterpret data, you can describe the tests you performed and the results you got and mention where you have added this information.
- **Watch your tone**: Remember, the reviewers are critiquing your work, not you. Do not let their feedback color any future interactions you have with them. If you disagree on some point, say so honestly but respectfully, and support your statement with a rational explanation.
- **Appreciate the reviewers' work**: Peer reviewers invest their own time in reviewing your writing. Their intention is to help you improve your writing, and hopefully earn higher grades as a result. Take advantage of their advice. In fact, a long list of detailed reviewer comments usually means that reviewer has spent considerable time evaluating your work and providing constructive feedback. Be sure to thank reviewers for their consideration and effort.

Finishing Touches

Style

The stage of proofreading is often focused solely on "correctness": making sure that all the details are right, and that language is used according to the rules. Proofreading also offers a great opportunity to address more personal concerns, however. It's a chance to focus on your **style**, and allows you to craft the final product that best represents your unique perspective.

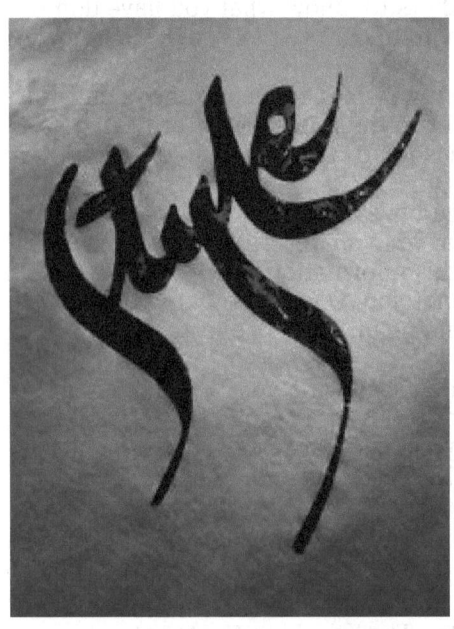

A writer's style is what sets his or her writing apart. Style is the way writing is dressed up (or down) to fit the specific context, purpose, or audience. Word choice, sentence fluency, and the writer's voice — all contribute to the style of a piece of writing. How a writer chooses words and structures sentences to achieve a certain effect is also an element of style. When Thomas Paine wrote "These are the times that try men's souls," he arranged his words to convey a sense of urgency and desperation. Had he written "These are bad times," it's likely he wouldn't have made such an impact!

Style is usually considered to be the province of literary writers. Novelists such as Ernest Hemingway and William Faulkner and poets such as Emily Dickinson and Walt Whitman are well known for their distinctive literary styles. But journalists, scientists, historians, and mathematicians also have distinctive styles, and they need to know how to vary their styles to fit different audiences. For example, the first-person narrative style of a popular magazine like *National Geographic* is quite different from the objective, third-person expository style of a research journal like Scientific American, even though both are written for informational purposes.

Not just right and wrong

Style is not a matter of right and wrong but of what is appropriate for a particular setting and audience. Consider the following two passages, which were written by the same author on the same topic with the same main idea, yet have very different styles:

"Experiments show that Heliconius butterflies are less likely to ovipost on host plants that possess eggs or egg-like structures. These egg mimics are an unambiguous example of a plant trait evolved in response to a host-restricted group of insect herbivores."

"Heliconius butterflies lay their eggs on Passiflora vines. In defense the vines seem to have evolved fake eggs that make it look to the butterflies as if eggs have already been laid on them." (Example from Myers, G. (1992). Writing biology: Texts in the social construction of scientific knowledge. Madison: University of Wisconsin Press. p. 150.)

What changed was the audience. The first passage was written for a professional journal read by other biologists, so the style is authoritative and impersonal, using technical terminology suited to a professional audience. The second passage, written for a popular science magazine, uses a more dramatic style, setting up a conflict between the butterflies and the vines, and using familiar words to help readers from non-scientific backgrounds visualize the scientific concept being described. Each style is appropriate for the particular audience.

Elements of style

Many elements of writing contribute to an author's style, but three of the most important are word choice, sentence fluency, and voice.

Word Choice

Good writers are concise and precise, weeding out unnecessary words and choosing the exact word to convey meaning. Precise words—active verbs, concrete nouns, specific adjectives—help the reader visualize the sentence. Good writers use adjectives sparingly and adverbs rarely, letting their nouns and verbs do the work.

Good writers also choose words that contribute to the flow of a sentence. Polysyllabic words, alliteration, and consonance can be used to create sentences that roll off the tongue. Onomatopoeia and short, staccato words can be used to break up the rhythm of a sentence.

Sentence Fluency

Sentence fluency is the flow and rhythm of phrases and sentences. Good writers use a variety of sentences with different lengths and rhythms to achieve different effects. They use parallel structures within sentences and paragraphs to reflect parallel ideas, but also know how to avoid monotony by varying their sentence structures.

Good writers also arrange their ideas within a sentence for greatest effect. They avoid loose sentences, deleting extraneous words and rearranging their ideas for effect. Many students initially write with a looser oral style, adding words on to the end of a sentence in the order they come to mind. This rambling style is often described as a "word dump" where everything in a student's mind is dumped onto the paper in no particular order. There is nothing wrong with a word dump as a starting point: the advantage of writing over speaking is that writers can return to their words, rethink them, and revise them for effect. Tighter, more readable style results when writers choose their words carefully, delete redundancies, make vague words more specific, and use subordinate clauses and phrases to rearrange their ideas for the greatest effect.

Voice

Because voice is difficult to measure reliably, it is often left out of scoring formulas for writing tests. Yet voice is an essential element of style that reveals the writer's personality. A writer's voice can be impersonal or chatty, authoritative or reflective, objective or passionate, serious or funny.

Strategies to Revise for Style

Read an essay draft out loud, preferably to another person. Better yet, have another person read your draft to you. Note how that person interprets your words. Does it come across as you had meant it originally? If not, revise.

Adopt a persona that's related to your topic. Write from the perspective of this person you create: what language would a young woman who'd just spent two years in the Peace Corps use, for instance, if the essay were about the value of volunteer work? How would the words on the page of a project about gun control look coming from the perspective of a very conservative gun owner?

Combine (some) short sentences, or break apart (some) long sentences. Sentence length variety is an asset to your readers, as noted above. If you find a stretch of your essay that uses many sentences of approximately the same length close together, focus on combining or breaking apart there.

Punch up the word choice. Not every word in an essay can be a "special" word, nor should they be. But if your writing in an area feels a little flat, the injection of a livelier word can have strong rhetorical and emotional impact on your reader. Think of these words as jewels in the right setting. Often swapping out "to be" verbs (is, was, were, etc.) with more action-packed verbs has immediate, positive impact. Adjectives are also good candidates for updating–look for "things" and "stuff," or "very" and "many," to replace with more precise terminology.

Lower Order Concerns

Previously we examined higher order concerns (HOCs) as part of the revision stage of the writing process. Once we move to the proofreading stage, it's time to consider the lower order concerns (LOCs). The difference is simple: HOCs are global issues, or issues that affect how a reader understands the entire paper; LOCs are issues that don't *necessarily* interrupt understanding of the writing by themselves.

HOCs	LOCs
Audience	Grammar
Thesis statement	Punctuation
Organization	Citation
Focus	Spelling
Development of ideas	Sentence structure

You may find yourself thinking, "Well, it depends," or, "But what if...?" You're absolutely right to think so. These lists are just guidelines; every writer will have a different hierarchy of concerns. Always try to think in terms of, "Does this affect my understanding of the writing?"

Are HOCs More Important than LOCs?

No, not necessarily. HOCs tend to interrupt a reader's understanding of the writing, and that's why they need to be addressed first. However, if a LOC becomes a major obstacle, then it naturally becomes a higher priority.

Think of an example of how a Lower Order Concern could become a Higher Order Concern.

Here are some other issues you might face. These may be more difficult to categorize, and they may largely depend on the writing. If you think, "It depends," make notes about the circumstances under which these issues could be a HOC or a LOC.

- Evaluating sources
- citation method
- style
- paragraph structure
- active vs. passive voice
- format

How to Address LOCs

Analyze your use of source material. Check any paraphrases and quotations against the original texts. Quotations should replicate the original author's words, while paraphrases should maintain the original author's meaning but have altered language and sentence structures. For each source, confirm that you have adhered to the preferred style guide for the target journal or other venue.

Consider individual sentences in terms of grammar, mechanics, and punctuation. Many LOCs can be revised by isolating and examining different elements of the text. Read the text sentence by sentence, considering the grammar and sentence structure. Remember, a sentence may be grammatically correct and still confuse readers.If you notice a pattern—say, a tendency to misplace modifiers or add unnecessary commas—read the paper looking only for that error. Read the document backwards, word for word, looking for spelling errors. Throughout the writing process and especially at this stage of revision, keep a dictionary, a thesaurus, and a writing handbook nearby.

Strategies such as reading aloud and seeking feedback are useful at all points in the revision process. Reading aloud will give you distance from the text and prevent you from skimming over what is actually written on the page. This strategy will help you to identify both HOCs, such as missing concepts, and LOCs, such as typos. Additionally, seeking feedback will allow you to test your ideas and writing on real readers. Seek feedback from readers both inside and outside of your target audience in order to gain different perspectives.

"Correctness" in Writing

In thinking about correctness, it's important to recognize that some rules are more important than others.

Essential Rules of the English Language

Joseph Williams helpfully distinguishes three kinds of rules in Williams and Bizup's *Style*.[1] First, there are rules that are basic to English, such as "the car" not "car the." For example,

INCORRECT: I thought whether true claims not.

CORRECT: I hadn't thought about whether the claims were true.

If you've gotten most of your formal education in English, you probably observe these rules routinely. If your writing has mismatches of number (singular/plural) or tense, it might be due to haste or carelessness rather than unawareness. Similarly, capitalizing the first word of a sentence and ending with appropriate punctuation are basic rules that most people comply with automatically when writing for a professor or in other formal situations.

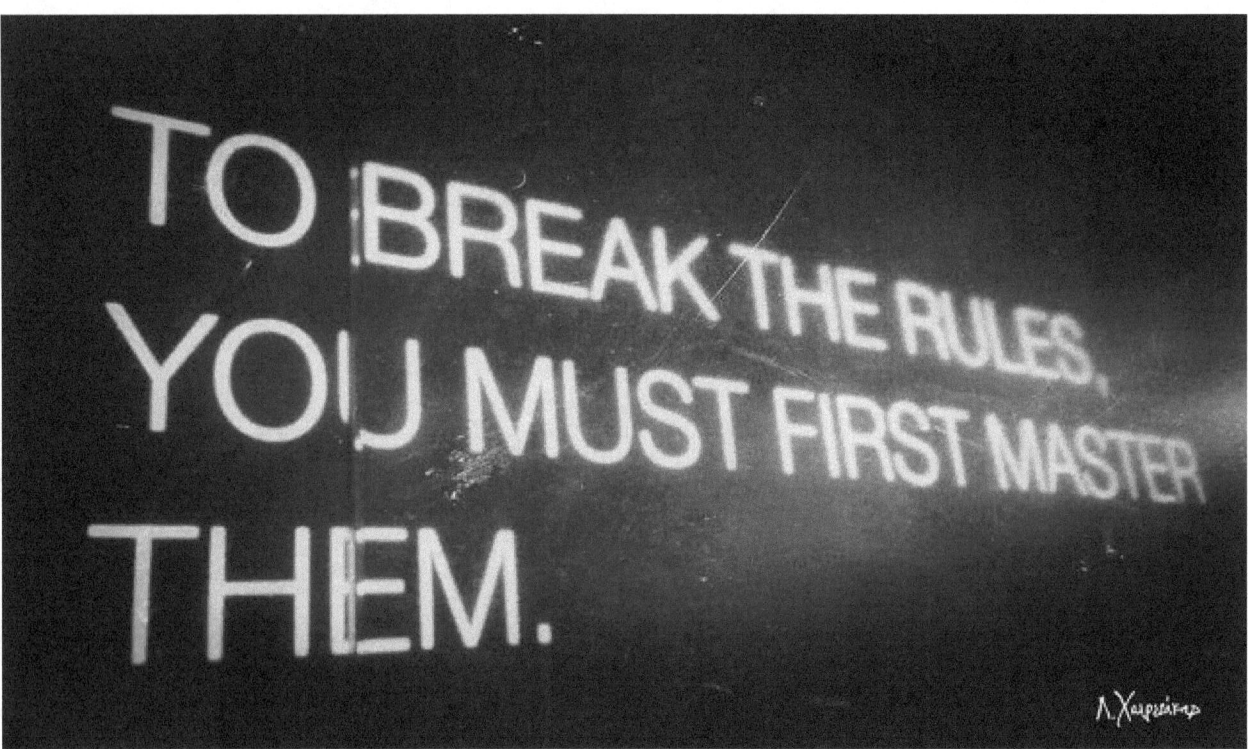

Rules of Formality

Williams' second category is comprised of rules that distinguish standard written English from the informal variants that people use in their day-to-day lives. Most students with middle-class and non-immigrant backgrounds use informal vernaculars that closely parallel standard written English. Students with working-class or more modest backgrounds or who are members of transnational and multi-lingual communities may use informal variants of English in their everyday lives that are quite different from standard written English. It's an unfortunate reality of social inequality that such students have to expend more effort than their middle-class English-speaking counterparts to master the standard conventions. It's not really fair, but at least the mechanics and rules of formal writing are documented and unambiguous. Learning to communicate effectively in different social contexts is part of becoming an educated person.

Some examples:

INFORMAL: We ain't got no more of them cookies.

FORMAL: We don't have any more of those cookies.

INFORMAL: My coat, my phone, and my keys was all lock in the car.

FORMAL: My coat, my phone, and my keys were all locked in the car.

INFORMAL: u shd go 2 café b4 wrk bc coffee

FORMAL: You should go the café before work to get some coffee.

The informal versions are clearly English, and they're widely understandable to others. The first and second examples contain choices of tense, number, and punctuation that are inappropriate in standard written English even though they don't actually impede communication. Most students already understand that these first two categories of rules (rules fundamental to English and the rules of standard written English) are obligatory for formal writing.

Rules as Folklore

There is a third category of rules that Williams notes and enthusiastically criticizes; he calls them "invented rules" because they usually arise from busybody grammarians rather than enduring patterns of customary language use. Some invented rules Williams calls "options": those that your reader will notice when you *observe* them and not care if you don't. Here's an example of the fabled don't-end-a-sentence-with-a-preposition rule:

OBSERVING THE RULE: With which concept can we analyze this problem?

IGNORING THE RULE: Which concept can we analyze this problem with?

Some grammarians would claim that only the first version is correct. However, you probably have the (accurate) impression that professional writers are much more likely to choose the second version. This rule does not reflect real-life customary practice, even in standard written English. That's why Williams calls it an "invented rule." Most of your professors are fine with the second version above, the one that ends a sentence with a preposition.

Williams calls the second sub-category of invented rules "folklore." They're invented rules (like "options") in that grammarians think writers should observe them, but, in reality, no one does. Williams gleefully lists instances in which the very grammarians who propose these rules go on to unselfconsciously violate them.[2] You may have heard of these rules, but they're widely considered absurd.

For example, some grammarians are dismayed that people use "that" and "which" interchangeably, and they argue that writers should use "that" to indicate restrictive elements and "which" to indicate non-restrictive elements. A restrictive element is one that makes a necessary specification about something; a non-restrictive element is one that simple adds extra information. Consider these two examples:

Version 1:

The party that Alex went to was shut down by the police.

Version 2:

The party which Alex went to was shut down by the police.

For almost all readers, versions 1 and 2 are saying the exact same thing. For the persnickety grammarian, version 1 is specifying the party that *Alex* went to, and not the party that, say, Jordan went to, while version 2 is simply inserting extra information about Alex's attendance at the party. According to these grammarians, "that Alex went to" adds critically needed information (restrictive) while "which Alex went to" adds bonus information (non-restrictive).

As Williams and some others explain: it's bullshit. Professional writers use commas and carefully chosen words to do the job of distinguishing restrictive and non-restrictive elements, and they choose whichever relative pronoun ("that" or "which") sounds better in context. You could observe the distinction between that and which if you like, but no one would notice. More importantly, observing this invented rule wouldn't necessarily make your writing any clearer, more concise, or more graceful.

One Particular Folklore Rule to Follow

There is one rule that Williams calls "folklore" that you probably have to observe in college papers nonetheless: that is, the rule that you can't start sentences with But, And, So, For, or Yet (or other coordinating conjunctions). Browsing through assigned readings and articles published in major newspapers and magazines will quickly lead you to texts that violate this so-called rule. Here are two examples:

> From the front page of the *New York Times* January 7, 2014:[3] "But since the financial crisis, JPMorgan has become so large and profitable that it has been able to weather the government's legal blitz, which has touched many parts of the bank's sprawling operations." And a little further down we see, "Yet JPMorgan's shares are up 28 percent over the last 12 months."

> From a news article in *Science*, December 21, 2007:[4] "Altered winds blew in more warm air from the subtropics only in models in which mid-latitude oceans warmed as observed; apparently, the warmer oceans altered the circulation. And that ocean warming is widely viewed as being driven by the strengthening greenhouse."

Whether or not to start sentences with conjunctions will ultimately come down to a matter of your instructors' preferences. Thus, you shouldn't start sentences with "And," "But" or other coordinating conjunctions unless you've been specifically invited to.

There are countless other rules beyond the ones discussed here. The point of these examples is to show that you don't have to observe every little rule you've ever heard of. There are some elements of mechanics that you have to master. These practices will gradually become second nature. It's sometimes hard to know at the outset which rules are standard, which are options, and which are folklore. With the help of a good handbook and your instructors, you'll learn them over time.

The larger point here is that that observing rules isn't about traversing a minefield of potential errors; it's just about learning and adopting the practices appropriate to your audience, which is one of the first rules of writing well.

Williams first described invented rules in J.M. Williams, "A Phenomenology of Error," *College Composition and Communication*, 32, no. 2 (1981): 152-168. ↵
J.M. Williams, *Phenomenology of Error* ↵
Peter Eavis, "Steep Penalties Taken in Stride by JPMorgan Chase," *New York Times*, January 7, 2014, page A1. ↵
Richard A. Kerr, "Global Warming Coming Home to Roost in the American Midwest," *Science* 318, no. 5858 (2007): 1859. ↵

Attribution

- Writing Center Theory and Pedagogy. **Provided by**: Missouri State University. **Located at**: https://msuwritingcenter.wikispaces.com/Writing+Center+Theory+and+Pedagogy. **Project**: MSU Writing Center Wiki. **License**: *CC BY-SA: Attribution-ShareAlike*
- Revision Strategies. **Authored by**: Kristin Messuri. **Located at**: http://pulmonarychronicles.com/ojs/index.php?journal=pulmonarychronicles&page=article&op=view&path%5B%5D=263&path%5B%5D=662. **Project**: Pulmonary Chronicles. **License**: *CC BY: Attribution*
- Image of students. **Authored by**: Anne Petersen. **Located at**: https://flic.kr/p/8NKsze. **License**: *CC BY-NC-ND: Attribution-NonCommercial-NoDerivatives*
- Revision and Adaptation. **Provided by**: Lumen Learning. **License**: *CC BY-SA: Attribution-ShareAlike*
- Correctness in Writing. **Authored by**: Amy Guptill. **Provided by**: The College at Brockport, SUNY. **Located at**: http://textbooks.opensuny.org/writing-in-college-from-competence-to-excellence/. **Project**: Writing in College: From Competence to Excellence. **License**: *CC BY-NC-SA: Attribution-NonCommercial-ShareAlike*
- Image of To Break the Rules. **Authored by**: Lefteris Heretakis. **Located at**: https://flic.kr/p/e8Lxzi. **License**: *CC BY: Attribution*
- Image of hands holding book. **Authored by**: Savannah van der Niet. **Located at**: https://flic.kr/p/devRjk. **License**: *CC BY-NC-ND: Attribution-NonCommercial-NoDerivatives*

College Writing: Argument

Introduction to Argument

All Writing is Argumentative

This chapter is about rhetoric—the art of persuasion. Every time we write, we engage in argument. Through writing, we try to persuade and influence our readers, either directly or indirectly. We work to get them to change their minds, to do something, or to begin thinking in new ways. Therefore, every writer needs to know and be able to use principles of rhetoric. The first step towards such knowledge is learning to see the argumentative nature of all writing.

I have two goals in this chapter: to explain the term rhetoric and to give you some historical perspective on its origins and development; and to demonstrate the importance of seeing research writing as a rhetorical, persuasive activity.

As consumers of written texts, we are often tempted to divide writing into two categories: argumentative and non-argumentative. According to this view, in order to be argumentative, writing must have the following qualities. It has to defend a position in a debate between two or more opposing sides; it must be on a controversial topic; and the goal of such writing must be to prove the correctness of one point of view over another.

On the other hand, this view goes, non-argumentative texts include narratives, descriptions, technical reports, news stories, and so on. When deciding to which category a given piece of writing belongs, we sometimes look for familiar traits of argument, such as the presence of a thesis statement, of "factual" evidence, and so on.

Research writing is often categorized as "non-argumentative." This happens because of the way in which we learn about research writing. Most of us do that through the traditional research report, the kind which focuses too much on information-gathering and note cards and not enough on constructing engaging and interesting points of view for real audiences. It is the gathering and compiling of information, and not doing something productive and interesting with this information, that become the primary goals of this writing exercise. Generic research papers are also often evaluated on the quantity and accuracy of external information that they gather, rather on the persuasive impact they make and the interest they generate among readers.

Having written countless research reports, we begin to suspect that all research-based writing is non-argumentative. Even when explicitly asked to construct a thesis statement and support it through researched evidence, beginning writers are likely to pay more attention to such mechanics of research as finding the assigned number and kind of sources and documenting them correctly, than to constructing an argument capable of making an impact on the reader.

Arguments Aren't Verbal Fights

We often have narrow concept of the word "argument." In everyday life, argument often implies a confrontation, a clash of opinions and personalities, or just a plain verbal fight. It implies a winner and a loser, a right side and a wrong one. Because of this understanding of the word "argument," the only kind of writing seen as argumentative is the debate-like "position" paper, in which the author defends his or her point of view against other, usually opposing points of view.

Such an understanding of argument is narrow because arguments come in all shapes and sizes. I invite you to look at the term "argument" in a new way. What if we think of "argument" as an opportunity for conversation, for sharing with others our point of view on something, for showing others our perspective of the world? What if we see it as the opportunity to tell our stories, including our life stories? What if we think of "argument" as an opportunity to connect with the points of view of others rather than defeating those points of view?

Some years ago, I heard a conference speaker define argument as the opposite of "beating your audience into rhetorical submission." I still like that definition because it implies gradual and even gentle explanation and persuasion instead of coercion. It implies effective use of details, and stories, including emotional ones. It implies the understanding of argument as an explanation of one's world view.

Arguments then, can be explicit and implicit, or implied. Explicit arguments contain noticeable and definable thesis statements and lots of specific proofs. Implicit arguments, on the other hand, work by weaving together facts and narratives, logic and emotion, personal experiences and statistics. Unlike explicit arguments, implicit ones do not have a one-sentence thesis statement. Instead, authors of implicit arguments use evidence of many different kinds in effective and creative ways to build and convey their point of view to their audience. Research is essential for creative effective arguments of both kinds.

Definitions of Rhetoric and the Rhetorical Situation

The art of creating effective arguments is explained and systematized by a discipline called rhetoric. Writing is about making choices, and knowing the principles of rhetoric allows a writer to make informed choices about various aspects of the writing process. Every act of writing takes places in a specific rhetorical situation. The three most basic and important components of a rhetorical situations are:

- Purpose of writing
- Intended audience,
- Occasion, or context in which the text will be written and read

These factors help writers select their topics, arrange their material, and make other important decisions about their work.

Before looking closely at different definitions and components of rhetoric, let us try to understand what rhetoric is not. In recent years, the word "rhetoric" has developed a bad reputation in American popular culture. In the popular mind, the term "rhetoric" has come to mean something negative and deceptive. Open a newspaper or turn on the television, and you are likely to hear politicians accusing each other of "too much rhetoric and not enough substance." According to this distorted view, rhetoric is verbal fluff, used to disguise empty or even deceitful arguments.

Examples of this misuse abound.

However, rhetoric is not a dirty trick used by politicians to conceal and obscure, but an art, which, for many centuries, has had many definitions. Perhaps the most popular and overreaching definition comes to us from the Ancient Greek thinker Aristotle. Aristotle defined rhetoric as "the faculty of observing in any given case the available means of persuasion". Aristotle saw primarily as a practical tool, indispensable for civic discourse.

Elements of the Rhetorical Situation

When composing, every writer must take into account the conditions under which the writing is produced and will be read. It is customary to represent the three key elements of the rhetorical situation as a triangle of writer, reader, and text, or, as "communicator," "audience," and "message."

The three elements of the rhetorical situation are in a constant and dynamic interrelation. All three are also necessary for communication through writing to take place. For example, if the writer is taken out of this equation, the text will not be created. Similarly, eliminating the text itself will leave us with the reader and writer, but without any means of conveying ideas between them, and so on.

Moreover, changing on or more characteristics of any of the elements depicted in the figure above will change the other elements as well. For example, with the change in the beliefs and values of the audience, the message will also likely change to accommodate those new beliefs, and so on.

In his discussion of rhetoric, Aristotle states that writing's primary purpose is persuasion. Other ancient rhetoricians' theories expand the scope of rhetoric by adding new definitions, purposes, and methods. For example, another Greek philosopher and rhetorician Plato saw rhetoric as a means of discovering the truth, including personal truth, through dialog and discussion. According to Plato, rhetoric can be directed outward (at readers or listeners), or inward (at the writer him or herself). In the latter case, the purpose of rhetoric is to help the author discover something important about his or her own experience and life.

The third major rhetorical school of Ancient Greece whose views have profoundly influenced our understanding of rhetoric were the Sophists. The Sophists were teachers of rhetoric for hire. The primary goal of their activities was to teach skills and strategies for effective speaking and writing. Many Sophists claimed that they could make anyone into an effective rhetorician. In their most extreme variety, Sophistic rhetoric claims that virtually anything could be proven if the rhetorician has the right skills. The legacy of Sophistic rhetoric is controversial. Some scholars, including Plato himself, have accused the Sophists of bending ethical standards in order to achieve their goals, while others have praised them for promoting democracy and civic participation through argumentative discourse.

What do these various definitions of rhetoric have to do with research writing? Everything! If you have ever had trouble with a writing assignment, chances are it was because you could not figure out the assignment's purpose. Or, perhaps you did not understand very well whom your writing was supposed to appeal to. It is hard to commit to purposeless writing done for no one in particular.

Research is not a very useful activity if it is done for its own sake. If you think of a situation in your own life where you had to do any kind of research, you probably had a purpose that the research helped you to accomplish. You could, for example, have been considering buying a car and wanted to know which make and model would suite you best. Or, you could have been looking for an apartment to rent and wanted to get the best deal for your money. Or, perhaps your family was planning a vacation and researched the best deals on hotels, airfares, and rental cars. Even in these simple examples of research that are far simpler than research most writers conduct, you as a researcher were guided by some overriding purpose. You researched because you had a purpose to accomplish.

How to Approach Writing Tasks Rhetorically

The three main elements of rhetorical theory are purpose, audience, and occasion. We will look at these elements primarily through the lens of Classical Rhetoric, the rhetoric of Ancient Greece and Rome. Principles of classical rhetoric (albeit some of them modified) are widely accepted across the modern Western civilization. Classical rhetoric provides a solid framework for analysis and production of effective texts in a variety of situations.

Purpose

Good writing always serves a purpose. Texts are created to persuade, entertain, inform, instruct, and so on. In a real writing situation, these discrete purposes are often combined.

Audience

The second key element of the rhetorical approach to writing is audience-awareness. As you saw from the rhetorical triangle earlier in this chapter, readers are an indispensable part of the rhetorical equation, and it is essential for every writer to understand their audience and tailor his or her message to the audience's needs.

The key principles that every writer needs to follow in order to reach and affect his or her audience are as follows:

- Have a clear idea about who your readers will be.
- Understand your readers' previous experiences, knowledge, biases, and expectations and how these factors can influence their reception of your argument.
- When writing, keep in mind not only those readers who are physically present or whom you know (your classmates and instructor), but all readers who would benefit from or be influenced by your argument.
- Choose a style, tone, and medium of presentation appropriate for your intended audience.

Occasion

Occasion is an important part of the rhetorical situation. It is a part of the writing context that was mentioned earlier in the chapter. Writers do not work in a vacuum. Instead, the content, form and reception of their work by readers are heavily influenced by the conditions in society as well as by personal situations of their readers. These conditions in which texts are created and read affect every aspect of writing and every stage of the writing process, from topic selection, to decisions about what kinds of arguments used and their arrangement, to the writing style, voice, and persona which the writer wishes to project in his or her writing. All elements of the rhetorical situation work together in a dynamic relationship. Therefore, awareness of rhetorical occasion and other elements of the context of your writing will also help you refine your purpose and understand your audience better. Similarly having a clear purpose in mind when writing and knowing your audience will help you understand the context in which you are writing and in which your work will be read better.

One aspect of writing where you can immediately benefit from understanding occasion and using it to your rhetorical advantage is the selection of topics for your compositions. Any topic can be good or bad, and a key factor in deciding on whether it fits the occasion. In order to understand whether a particular topic is suitable for a composition, it is useful to analyze whether the composition would address an issue, or a rhetorical exigency when created. The writing activity below can help you select topics and issues for written arguments.

To understand how writers can study and use occasion in order to make effective arguments, let us examine another ancient rhetorical concept. Kairos is one of the most fascinating terms from Classical rhetoric. It signifies the right, or opportune moment for an argument to be made. It is such a moment or time when the subject of the argument is particularly urgent or important and when audiences are more likely to be persuaded by it. Ancient rhetoricians believed that if the moment for the argument is right, for instance if there are conditions in society which would make the audience more receptive to the argument, the rhetorician would have more success persuading such an audience. For example, as I write this text, a heated debate about the war on terrorism and about the goals and methods of this war is going on in the US. It is also the year of the Presidential Election, and political candidates try to use the war on terrorism to their advantage when they debate each other. These are topics of high public interested, with print media, television, radio, and the Internet constantly discussing them. Because there is an enormous public interest in the topic of terrorism, well-written articles and reports on the subject will not fall on deaf ears. Simply put, the moment, or occasion, for the debate is right, and it will continue until public interest in the subject weakens or disappears.

Rhetorical Appeals

In order to persuade their readers, writers must use three types of proofs or rhetorical appeals. They are logos, or logical appeal; pathos, or emotional appeal; and ethos, or ethical appeal, or appeal based on the character and credibility of the author. It is easy to notice that modern words "logical," "pathetic," and "ethical" are derived from those Greek words. In his work Rhetoric, Aristotle writes that the three appeals must be used together in every piece of persuasive discourse. An argument based on the appeal to logic, or emotions alone will not be an effective one.

Understanding how logos, pathos, and ethos should work together is very important for writers who use research. Often, research writing assignment are written in a way that seems to emphasize logical proofs over emotional or ethical ones. Such logical proofs in research papers typically consist of factual information, statistics, examples, and other similar evidence. According to this view, writers of academic papers need to be unbiased and objective, and using logical proofs will help them to be that way.

Because of this emphasis on logical proofs, you may be less familiar with the kinds of pathetic and ethical proofs available to you. Pathetic appeals, or appeals to emotions of the audience were considered by ancient rhetoricians as important as logical proofs. Yet, writers are sometimes not easily convinced to use pathetic appeals in their writing. As modern rhetoricians and authors of the influential book Classical Rhetoric for the Modern Student (1998), Edward P.J. Corbett and Robert Connors said, "People are rather sheepish about acknowledging that their opinions can be affected by their emotions" (86). According to Corbett, many of us think that there may be something wrong about using emotions in argument. But, I agree with Corbett and Connors, pathetic proofs are not only admissible in argument, but necessary (86-89). The most basic way of evoking appropriate emotional responses in your audience, according to Corbett, is the use of vivid descriptions (94).

Using ethical appeals, or appeals based on the character of the writer, involves establishing and maintaining your credibility in the eyes of your readers. In other words, when writing, think about how you are presenting yourself to your audience. Do you give your readers enough reasons to trust you and your argument, or do you give them reasons to doubt your authority and your credibility? Consider all the times when your decision about the merits of a given argument was affected by the person or people making the argument. For example, when watching television news, are you predisposed against certain cable networks and more inclined towards others because you trust them more?

So, how can a writer establish a credible persona for his or her audience? One way to do that is through external research. Conducting research and using it well in your writing help with you with the factual proofs (logos), but it also shows your readers that you, as the author, have done your homework and know what you are talking about. This knowledge, the sense of your authority that this creates among your readers, will help you be a more effective writer.

The logical, pathetic, and ethical appeals work in a dynamic combination with one another. It is sometimes hard to separate one kind of proof from another and the methods by which the writer achieved the desired rhetorical effect. If your research contains data which is likely to cause your readers to be emotional, it data can enhance the pathetic aspect of your argument. The key to using the three appeals, is to use them in combination with each other, and in moderation. It is impossible to construct a successful argument by relying too much on one or two appeals while neglecting the others.

Research Writing as Conversation

Writing is a social process. Texts are created to be read by others, and in creating those texts, writers should be aware of not only their personal assumptions, biases, and tastes, but also those of their readers. Writing, therefore, is an interactive process. It is a conversation, a meeting of minds, during which ideas are exchanged, debates and discussions take place and, sometimes, but not always, consensus is reached. You may be familiar with the famous quote by the 20th century rhetorician Kenneth Burke who compared writing to a conversation at a social event. In his 1974 book The Philosophy of Literary Form Burke writes,

> Imagine that you enter a parlor. You come late. When you arrive, others have long preceded you, and they are engaged in a heated discussion, a discussion too heated for them to pause and tell you exactly what it is about. In fact, the discussion had already begun long before any of them got there, so that no one present is qualified to retrace for you all the steps that had gone before. You listen for a while, until you decide that you have caught the tenor of the argument; then you put in your oar. Someone answers; you answer him, another comes to your defense; another aligns himself against you, to either the embarrassment of gratification of your opponent, depending upon the quality of your ally's assistance. However, the discussion is interminable. The hour grows late, you must depart. And you do depart, with the discussion still vigorously in progress (110-111).

This passage by Burke is extremely popular among writers because it captures the interactive nature of writing so precisely. Reading Burke's words carefully, we will notice that the interaction between readers and writers is continuous. A writer always enters a conversation in progress. In order to participate in the discussion, just like in real life, you need to know what your interlocutors have been talking about. So you listen (read). Once you feel you have got the drift of the conversation, you say (write) something. Your text is read by others who respond to your ideas, stories, and arguments with their own. This interaction never ends!

To write well, it is important to listen carefully and understand the conversations that are going on around you. Writers who are able to listen to these conversations and pick up important topics, themes, and arguments are generally more effective at reaching and impressing their audiences. It is also important to treat research, writing, and every occasion for these activities as opportunities to participate in the on-going conversation of people interested in the same topics and questions which interest you.

Our knowledge about our world is shaped by the best and most up-to-date theories available to them. Sometimes these theories can be experimentally tested and proven, and sometimes, when obtaining such proof is impossible, they are based on consensus reached as a result of conversation and debate. Even the theories and knowledge that can be experimentally tested (for example in sciences) do not become accepted knowledge until most members of the scientific community accept them. Other members of this community will help them test their theories and hypotheses, give them feedback on their writing, and keep them searching for the best answers to their questions. As Burke says in his famous passage, the interaction between the members of intellectual communities never ends. No piece of writing, no argument, no theory or discover is ever final. Instead, they all are subject to discussion, questioning, and improvement.

A simple but useful example of this process is the evolution of humankind's understanding of their planet Earth and its place in the Universe. As you know, in Medieval Europe, the prevailing theory was that the Earth was the center of the Universe and that all other planets and the Sun rotated around it. This theory was the result of the church's teachings, and thinkers who disagreed with it were pronounced heretics and often burned. In 1543, astronomer Nikolaus Kopernikus argued that the Sun was at the center of the solar system and that all planets of the system rotate around the Sun. Later, Galileo experimentally proved Kopernikus' theory with the help of a telescope. Of course, the Earth did not begin to rotate around the Sun with this discovery. Yet, Kopernikus' and Galileo's theories of the Universe went against the Catholic Church's teachings which dominated the social discourse of Medieval Europe. The Inquisition did not engage in debate with the two scientists. Instead,

Kopernikus was executed for his views and Galileo was sentenced to house arrest for his views.

Although in the modern world, dissenting thinkers are unlikely to suffer such harsh punishment, the examples of Kopernikus and Galileo teach us two valuable lessons about the social nature of knowledge. Firstly, Both Kopernikus and Galileo tried to improve on an existing theory of the Universe that placed our planet at the center. They did not work from nothing but used beliefs that already existed in their society and tried to modify and disprove those beliefs. Time and later scientific research proved that they were right. Secondly, even after Galileo was able to prove the structure of the Solar system experimentally, his theory did not become widely accepted until the majority of people in society assimilated it. Therefore, new findings do not become accepted knowledge until they penetrate the fabric of social discourse and until enough people accept them as true.

Conclusions

In this chapter, we have learned the definition of rhetoric and the basic differences between several important rhetorical schools. We have also discussed how to key elements of the rhetorical situation: purpose, audience, and context. As you work on the research writing projects presented throughout this book, be sure to revisit this chapter often. Everything that you have read about here and every activity you have completed as you worked through this chapter is applicable to all research writing projects in this book and beyond. Most school writing assignments give you direct instructions about your purpose, intended audience, and rhetorical occasion. Truly proficient and independent writers, however, learn to define their purpose, audiences, and contexts of their writing, on their own. The material in this chapter is designed to enable to become better at those tasks.

When you receive a writing assignment, it is very tempting to see it as just another hoop to jump through and not as a genuine rhetorical situation, an opportunity to influence others with your writing. It is certainly tempting to see yourself writing only for the teacher, without a real purpose and oblivious of the context of your writing.

The material of this chapter as well as the writing projects presented throughout this book are designed to help you think of writing as a persuasive, rhetorical activity. Conducting research and incorporating its results into your paper is a part of this rhetorical process.

Sources

Aristotle. "Rhetoric." Aristotle's Rhetoric. June 21, 2004. http://www.public.iastate.edu/~honeyl/Rhetoric/. April 21, 2008.

Burke, Kenneth. The Philosophy of Literary Form. Berkeley: University of California Press, 1941.

Clinton, Hillary. "Scranton." Youtube. April 7, 2008. http://youtube.com/watch?v=uCQBYsoo_mc. April 21, 2008.

CNN. "N. Korea Talks On Despite Rhetoric." CNN.com. August 3, 2003. http://www.cnn.com/2003/WORLD/asiapcf/east/08/03/nkorea.talks/index.html.... April 21, 2008.

Corbett, Edward, P.J and Connors, Robert. Classical Rhetoric for the Modern Student. Oxford University Press, USA; 4 edition, 1998.

Fritz, Ben et al. "About Spinsanity." Spinsanity. 2001-2005. http://www.spinsanity.org. April 21, 2008.

Obama, Barack. "One Voice." Youtube. April 8, 2008. http://youtube.com/watch?v=AO_TfQ6hiXk. April 21, 2008.

Papakyriakou/Anagnostou, Ellen. Kairos. Ancient Greek Cities. 1998. http://www.sikyon.com/sicyon/Lysippos/lysip_kairos.jpg. April 21, 2008.

Rouzie, Albert. "The Rhetorical Triangle." Rhetoric Resources. 1998. http://www-as.phy.ohiou.edu/~rouzie/fall151/rhetriang.gif. April 21, 2008.

wafer157. "Obama Rhetoric." Youtube. February 27, 2008. http://www.youtube.com/watch?v=O6hdQtVGV_A. April 21, 2008.

The 5 Questions of Argument

The 5 Questions

Questions are at the core of arguments. In academic writing, we tend to build arguments from the answers to just five kinds of questions:

> What do you want me to do or think?
> Why should I do or think that?
> How do I know that what you say is true?
> What about this other idea, fact, or consideration?
> What general principles ground your argument?

In a Nutshell

When you ask people to do or think something they otherwise would not, they quite naturally want to know why they should do so. In fact, people tend to ask the same five questions. When you make a good argument, you anticipate and respond to each of these questions with a particular part of argument:

> The answer to *What do you want me to do or think?* is your **claim**: "I claim that you should do or think X."
> The answer to *Why should I do or think that?* states your **reasons**: "You should do or think X because . . ."
> The answer to *How do I know that what you say is true?* presents your **evidence**: "You can believe my reasons because they are supported by these facts . . ."
> The answer to *What about this other idea, fact, or conclusion?* **acknowledges** that your readers might see things differently and then **responds** to that alternative view.
> The answer to *Why should I accept that your reasons support your claim?* states your general principle of reasoning, called a **warrant**: "My specific reason supports my specific claim because whenever this general condition is true, we can generally draw a conclusion like mine."

The Principle

Academics, business people, scientists, and other professionals all make arguments to determine what to do or think, or to solve a problem by enlisting others to do or believe something they otherwise would not. What matters is not just that you believe that what you have to say is true, but that you give others good reasons to believe it as well—and also show them that you have considered the issue from multiple angles. To do that, build your argument out of the answers to the five questions any rational person will expect you to answer.

The Five Questions That Every Reader Will Ask

Question #1—"What do you want me to do or think?"

This question means that the reader is ready to hear your **claim**. You know how to answer this question because you make arguments like this every day. Suppose, for example, that Sally is having coffee with her friend Jim. Jim points out a story on the front page of his newspaper:

Jim: So did you hear about the hurricane that's headed for New Orleans?

Sally: Yes, I think they should evacuate the city as soon as possible.

Sally has made a claim: a statement of her view of what someone should do: New Orleans should be evacuated. Note that this is not a statement of fact but of Sally's idea, her judgment about the best course of action. She takes a position on a problem without an obvious solution; other rational people could disagree. Some might claim that the hurricane is not strong enough to warrant evacuation or that this time New Orleans is properly prepared for a hurricane. Sally has made a claim because her statement is up for debate.

Question #2—"Why should I think that?"

This question is about what **reasons** support your claim. Most readers won't question your argument until they know your reasons. Let's look at how Jim responds to Sally's claim:

Jim: Really? Why do you say that?

Sally: Well, New Orleans is surrounded by water and it's mostly below sea level. If a hurricane breaks the levees that keep the water out, the city will flood. Houses could be destroyed, and people would be at risk.

Sally answers Jim's question by giving him a few reasons why she thinks New Orleans should be evacuated. New Orleans is (1) surrounded by water, (2) mostly below sea level, and (3) protected by levees. So if the levees break and let the water in, (4) houses will be destroyed, and (5) people will be at risk.

Question #3—"How do I know that your reasons are true?"

This question asks for factual **evidence** to support the given reasons. Jim asks Sally a version of this question to push her for more information:

Jim: Will the levees actually break? Why do you think that they're in danger of failing?

Sally: Remember Hurricane Katrina in 2005? The levees failed then, and the city was almost ruined. It's right there in the newspaper story: many of the levees have been rebuilt or reinforced since Katrina, but the government is way behind and there are a lot of levees that are just like the ones that failed after Katrina. And even the ones that have been rebuilt will not protect against the worst storm surges.

When Jim asks what makes Sally believe that the levees are in danger of failing, she must respond with facts. For her factual evidence, Sally points to a real, historical event as a precedent, and she cites facts she found in a reliable newspaper. In an academic argument, you'll also need to give evidence that your ideas are based on real-world facts. These facts can take the form of quotations, events, statistics, dates, or other data that you found in a reliable source, but they must be something that your readers accept as true in order for your readers to see them as evidence. Taken together, your claim, reasons, and evidence make up the core of your argument. While your claims, reasons, and evidence do answer your readers' questions, they are also mostly about you, what you think and why. Your argument may be complete with just these three parts, but to fully address your readers' concerns, you also need to address what they think and why.

Question #4—"What about this other idea, fact, or conclusion? Or: What if I think about this topic differently than you do?"

You can expect that for any serious claim about a significant problem, there will be some readers who don't see things the way you do. They may take a different approach to the problem; they may want to consider different evidence; or they may even think that your reasons and evidence point to a different conclusion. If so, you have to anticipate that they will ask, "What about my way of thinking about this?" In order for your argument to be the most effective, you have to address these objections, counterarguments, varying perspectives, and so on. The best way to do this is to **acknowledge** your readers' possible alternative positions and then **respond** to them. Here, Jim raises a question based on a fact that he thinks Sally has not fully considered:

Jim: Sure, the Katrina flood was a disaster. But this new hurricane is not as strong as Katrina. It poses much less danger. And evacuation is expensive.

Sally: That's true; the hurricane is weaker than Katrina now. But hurricanes often get stronger as they approach land, and you can't wait until the last minute to evacuate—people will just get stuck out on the roads. So I think that everyone should evacuate even if it is expensive and at the moment seems that it may not be necessary. Better safe than sorry.

Sally acknowledges that Jim has a point: the current danger may in fact be less than that posed by Katrina. But she responds with more facts: hurricanes can get stronger and evacuation takes time, so that it will be too late to evacuate if the hurricane intensifies as it approaches land. She then restates her claim: people should evacuate.

Question #5—"Why should I accept that your reasons support your claim?"

This last question forces us to consider the logical assumptions on which we base our arguments. Many arguments never address these assumptions because writers assume that their readers will reason as they do. So we rarely see the answer to the fifth question, a statement of a general principle of reasoning or **warrant**. But if you think your readers may not share your general principles, you should state them in your argument. In Sally's response to Jim's point about balancing the risk of flooding against the cost of evacuation, we see that they are following different principles:

Jim: I don't know. Being too safe may not be smart. I'm not sure that the risk of flooding is enough to force an evacuation.

Sally: Well, I believe that no cost is too high to save lives. So whenever we can anticipate a reasonable possibility that lives will be endangered, we should be willing to accept a reasonable cost to avoid the loss of life. Even though the hurricane may not cause flooding, there is enough chance that it will. The cost of an evacuation is not too high a price to pay to save lives.

Jim may still not accept Sally's principle: he may think that the costs are too high. But what is important is that he can now see the complete basis of Sally's argument: he knows her claim, her reasons, her evidence, how she responds to his alternative views, and what principle she applies to connect her reasons to her claim.

CC licensed content, Shared previously

Toulmin's Schema

Stephen Edelston Toulmin (born March 25, 1922) is a British philosopher, author, and educator. Influenced by the Austrian philosopher Ludwig Wittgenstein, Toulmin devoted his works to the analysis of moral reasoning. Throughout his writings, he seeks to develop practical arguments which can be used effectively in evaluating the ethics behind moral issues. The Toulmin Model of Argumentation, a diagram containing six interrelated components used for analyzing arguments, was considered his most influential work, particularly in the field of rhetoric and communication, and in computer science.

Stephen Toulmin is a British philosopher and educator who devoted to analyzing moral reasoning. Throughout his writings, he seeks to develop practical arguments which can be used effectively in evaluating the ethics behind moral issues. His most famous work was his Model of Argumentation (sometimes called "Toulmin's Schema," which is a method of analyzing an argument by breaking it down into six parts. Once an argument is broken down and examined, weaknesses in the argument can be found and addressed.

Toulmin's Schema:

Claim: conclusions whose merit must be established. For example, if a person tries to convince a listener that he is a British citizen, the claim would be "I am a British citizen."
Data: the facts appealed to as a foundation for the claim. For example, the person introduced in 1 can support his claim with the supporting data "I was born in Bermuda."
Warrant: the statement authorizing the movement from the data to the claim. In order to move from the data established in 2, "I was born in Bermuda," to the claim in 1, "I am a British citizen," the person must supply a warrant to bridge the gap between 1 & 2 with the statement "A man born in Bermuda will legally be a British Citizen." Toulmin stated that an argument is only as strong as its weakest warrant and if a warrant isn't valid, then the whole argument collapses. Therefore, it is important to have strong, valid warrants.
Backing: facts that give credibility to the statement expressed in the warrant; backing must be introduced when the warrant itself is not convincing enough to the readers or the listeners. For example, if the listener does not deem the warrant as credible, the speaker would supply legal documents as backing statement to show that it is true that "A man born in Bermuda will legally be a British Citizen."
Rebuttal: statements recognizing the restrictions to which the claim may legitimately be applied. The rebuttal is exemplified as follows, "A man born in Bermuda will legally be a British citizen, unless he has betrayed Britain and become a spy of another country."
Qualifier: words or phrases expressing how certain the author/speaker is concerning the claim. Such words or phrases include "possible," "probably," "impossible," "certainly," "presumably," "as far as the evidence goes," or "necessarily." The claim "I am definitely a British citizen" has a greater degree of force than the claim "I am a British citizen, presumably."
The first three elements "claim," "data," and "warrant" are considered as the essential components of practical arguments, while the 4-6 "Qualifier," "Backing," and "Rebuttal" may not be needed in some arguments. When first proposed, this layout of argumentation is based on legal arguments and intended to be used to analyze arguments typically found in the courtroom; in fact, Toulmin did not realize that this layout would be applicable to the field of rhetoric and communication until later.

Here are a few more examples of Toulmin's Schema:

Suppose you see a one of those commercials for a product that promises to give you whiter teeth. Here are the basic parts of the argument behind the commercial:

Claim: You should buy our tooth-whitening product.
Data: Studies show that teeth are 50% whiter after using the product for a specified time.

Warrant: People want whiter teeth.
Backing: Celebrities want whiter teeth.
Rebuttal: Commercial says "unless you don't want to attract guys."
Qualifier: Fine print says "product must be used six weeks for results."

Notice that those commercials don't usually bother trying to convince you that you want whiter teeth; instead, they assume that you have bought into the value our culture places on whiter teeth. When an assumption–a warrant in Toulmin's terms–is unstated, it's called an implicit warrant. Sometimes, however, the warrant may need to be stated because it is a powerful part of the argument. When the warrant is stated, it's called an explicit warrant.

Another example:

Claim: People should probably own a gun.
Data: Studies show that people who own a gun are less likely to be mugged.
Warrant: People want to be safe.
Backing: May not be necessary. In this case, it is common sense that people want to be safe.
Rebuttal: Not everyone should own a gun. Children and those will mental disorders/problems should not own a gun.
Qualifier: The word "probably" in the claim.

Another example:

Claim: Flag burning should be unconstitutional in most cases.
Data: A national poll says that 60% of Americans want flag burning unconstitutional.
Warrant: People want to respect the flag.
Backing: Official government procedures for the disposal of flags.
Rebuttal: Not everyone in the U.S. respects the flag.
Qualifier: The phrase "in most cases"

Toulmin says that the weakest part of any argument is its weakest warrant. Remember that the warrant is the link between the data and the claim. If the warrant isn't valid, the argument collapses.
CC licensed content, Shared previously

- Toulmin's Schema. **Provided by**: Utah State University. **Located at**: http://www.saylor.org/courses/engl002#4.2.4. **Project**: USU OpenCourseWare. **License**: *CC BY-NC-SA: Attribution-NonCommercial-ShareAlike*

Rogerian Argument

Solving Problems by Negotiating Differences

How many times have you been in an argument that you knew you couldn't win? Are you reluctant to change your mind about certain social, political, or personal issues? Do you have an unshakable faith in a particular religion or philosophy? For example, are you absolutely certain that abortion is immoral under all circumstances? Are you categorically against animal experimentation for advancements in medicine? Do you believe that criminals who have tortured and killed people should receive the death penalty? Do you believe that parents should have no more than two children because of the world population problem? Do you believe it is your patriotic duty to buy solely American products?

Some of our beliefs and arguments are based on faith, some on emotion, and some on logic alone. We all hold different religious, political, and personal beliefs that largely define who we are and how we think. Within the past fifty years, as the size of our global village has appeared to shrink with the use of television, fax, and jets, we have become increasingly more sophisticated and knowledgeable. As a result, most educated people now realize that few significant issues have simple solutions. Thanks to modern scholarship and research, we have come to realize that our personalities and thoughts are shaped to some degree by cultural expectations. Philosophers have challenged us to recognize that our worldviews – our assumptions about reality, what is good, what is possible – are influenced by our day-to-day experiences. We have realized that truth is not a fixed, static entity that can be carried into a battle like a banner.

One wonderful aspect of your college career is meeting different worldviews through books and through discussions with people whom you otherwise would not encounter. Indeed, many college campuses offer a wonderful glimpse of the diversity of modern-day life. A wide-eyed glance at students at the university center on my campus, for instance, will show you Chinese students working alongside students from Africa and South America. Young women dressed in their power suits mix freely with returning older adult students. Fraternity brothers rush from place to place, dressed in their blue blazers and short haircuts, while male musicians, dressed in the tie-dyed fashions of the 1960s and shoulder-length hair, play guitars and sing protest songs.

One result of our increasingly sophisticated world is that you cannot assume that your readers will believe or even understand everything you say. On the contrary, you need to assume that your readers will doubt you. They will question the validity of your evidence and test the logic of your conclusions. Modern readers tend to be particularly contentious when you insist on assertions that they find objectionable. Because of this shift in audience attitude, writers need to develop compelling ways of organizing and presenting arguments.

When you wish to address an emotional and controversial issue and when your audience is likely to be threatened by your ideas, you will probably not be successful if you make your claim in the introduction of your essay (or verbal argument). No matter how thoroughly you go on to support your ideas with careful reasoning and to refute other claims (such as those held by your audience) respectfully, your readers have already decided to ignore you. For example, can you imagine how your roommate would respond if you remark that he or she is a terrible slob? Even if you follow up your comment with photographs of the dirty dishes, cluttered rooms, and soiled carpet left in his or her wake, can you imagine that the final outcome of your detailed presentation might be resolution? More likely you will face anger, bitterness, and denial. Watch your introductory prepositions!

Most of us tend to resist change and are threatened by ideas that challenge what we believe. Also, most of us dislike being told what to do and how to think, so even if our brains tell us to agree, our emotions (and egos) tell us to shut down and ignore what we are hearing. A male chauvinist who believes that women are intellectually inferior to men will be unlikely to listen to your argument that women are as intelligent as men. Your quotes from world-renowned educators and philosophers and your statistics from the Stanford-Blinet or SAT, GRE, and MCAT scores would probably be dismissed as inaccurate because they threaten his assumptions. Of course, you could hope that the chauvinist would change his mind over time when he wasn't being pressed, yet you couldn't bet on this outcome.

Because conflict is inevitable, we need to seek creative ways to solve complicated problems and to negotiate differences between opposing parties. Although there are no simple formulas for bringing opposing factions together, we do have a relatively new form of communication founded on Carl Rogers's client-centered therapeutic approach to one-on-one and group counseling. Essentially, the Rogerian problem-solving approach re-conceptualizes our goals when we argue. Instead of assuming that an author or speaker should hope to overcome an antagonistic audience with shrewd reasoning, the Rogerian approach would have the author or speaker attempt to reach some common ground with the audience. Thus, in a very real way, Rogerian "persuasion" is not a form of persuasion so much as it is a way of opening communication for negotiating common ground between divergent points of view. In terms of writing, we could say that the Rogerian approach melds the techniques of informative analyses with those of persuasive reports. Your goal when you employ the tactics of Rogerian problem-solving is not for you to win and for your opponent to lose, a scenario that more often results in both parties losing. Instead, you explore ways that will allow both you and your audience to win.

On Rogerian Argument

[adapted from Rhetoric Matters: Language and Argument in Context by Megan McIntyre and Curtis Le Van]

Rogerian argument is often difficult for students to understand because it asks them to think about controversial topics in a different way: from the perspective of someone they disagree with. The discussions that follow are meant to help you understand the reason for and the components of an argument in Rogerian style.

On Finding Common Ground

["On Finding Common Ground" is written by Jeffrey Spicer, University of South Florida]

"It is only through the clash of adverse opinions that the remainder of the truth has any chance of being supplied."

– John Stuart Mill, On Liberty, 1859

"The major barrier to mutual interpersonal communication is our very natural tendency to judge, to evaluate, to approve or disapprove, the statement of the other person or the other group."

– Carl Rogers, "Communication: Its Blocking and Its Facilitation," 1951

argue (v.) – from the Greek argos, lit. "white," or arguron, lit. "silver," and meaning "to shine forth": in contemporary usage, to present reasons for or against.

In 1951, the psychologist Carl Rogers gave a talk at the Centennial Conference on Communications at Northwestern University that changed the way we think about argument. Psychology at that time was dominated by psychologists like B.F. Skinner, who were learning to scientifically condition thoughts and feelings in the same way that Pavlov had conditioned his dogs to salivate at the sound of their dinner bell a half-century before.

Rogers, on the other hand, was a humanist. He believed that human speech and human cognition were interrelated and that the success or failure of one was related to the success or failure of the other. In "Communication: Its Blocking and Its Facilitation," he put forward as the cornerstone of his practice the belief that "the whole task of psychotherapy is the task of dealing with a failure in communication" (330).

According to Rogers, the principle difficulty preventing people from settling their differences, indeed from communicating effectively in an everyday sense, was that people couldn't stop evaluating one another. The more important a topic was to them, the more emotional the participants in a discussion became, and the more they were apt to judge what the other person was saying rather than giving it the best hearing they could. In short, Rogers noticed that when people argue, they tend to make judgments about their opponents' positions before they really understand them.

Rogers's goal, then, was to avoid this tendency to constantly evaluate and instead to "listen with understanding." By this, he meant that people should not only try to understand that someone holds a particular viewpoint but also try to get a sense of what it's like to believe that. "What does that mean? It means to see the expressed idea and attitude from the other person's point of view, to sense how it feels to him, to achieve his frame of reference in regard to the thing he is talking about" (Rogers 331-32). Rogers himself acknowledged barriers to this kind of understanding. First and foremost, you have to be willing to try it, and not many people are. Rogers's approach seems like you're giving ground to your opponents and, what's worse, sometimes you actually are. "In the first place, it takes courage [...] you run the risk of being changed yourself" (Rogers 333).

It is important to note, though, that this sort of Rogerian understanding is also itself an argumentative tactic. First, people will almost always refuse to consider something if they feel threatened by it, and Rogerian understanding reduces the threat to the opposition. Second, people reciprocate; they tend to treat others as they are treated by them.

Despite the initial difficulties, then, each new understanding of the opponent's view makes the next easier, while at the same time inviting, even obligating, the opponent to strive for a like understanding. "This procedure can deal with the insincerities, the defensive exaggerations, the lies, the 'false fronts' which characterize almost every failure in communication. These defensive distortions drop away with astonishing speed as people find that the only intent is to understand, not judge" (Rogers 336).

This Rogerian process started to make its way into textbooks in 1970. Richard E. Young, Alton L. Becker, and Kenneth L. Pike's introduction of Rogerian psychology in their book *Rhetoric: Discovery and Change* seeks to simplify some of Rogers's terminology and begin to present the process as a set of rhetorical objectives: "The writer who uses the Rogerian strategy attempts to do three things:

> to convey to the reader that he is understood
> to delineate the area within which he believes the reader's position to be valid
> to induce him to believe that he and the writer share certain moral qualities (275)

Put like this, in such a simple and reductive way, the process of attaining and expressing Rogerian understanding seems almost easy.

It is important to note that these are not developmental steps intended as heuristics, that indeed there are no sequential stages to a Rogerian argument. They are instead objectives to be pursued independently and recursively with the probably effect of facilitating communication. As Young, Becker, and Pike write, "Rogerian argument has no conventional structure; in fact, users of the strategy deliberately avoid conventional persuasive structures and techniques because these devices tend to produce a sense of threat." This is not to say the argument has no structure, but rather that "the structure is more directly the product of a particular writer, a particular topic, and a particular audience" (275). The danger of argumentative form becoming an exclusionary force, silencing rather than evoking discussion, is therefore greatly reduced.

At this point, then, you may be wondering what Rogerian argument might actually look like in terms of an essay for a composition class. An essay modeled on Rogers's approach should include a few particular parts:

- a discussion of the problem from both points of view that uses value-neutral language
- a discussion of the writer's opponent's point of view and a selection of facts or assertions the writer might be willing to concede to his opponent
- a discussion of the writer's point of view and a selection of facts or assertions the writer's opponent might be able to accept about his point of view
- a thesis that establishes a compromise between these two points of view and represents concessions from both the writer and his opponent

Analyzing Pertinent Conventions

Below are some of the strategies that you can use to negotiate consensus between opposing parties. As usual, you should not consider the following to be a rigid formula. Instead, pick and choose from these strategies in light of your audience, purpose, and intended voice.

Present the Problem

In the introduction, identify the issue and clarify its significance. Because you need to adopt a nonthreatening persona throughout your essay, however, avoid dogmatically presenting your view as the best or only way to solve the problem. Unlike your strategy for shaping a conventional persuasive text, at this point in your discussion you will not want to lay your cards on the table and summarize your presentation. Instead, explain the scope and complexity of the issue. You might want to mention the various approaches that people have taken to solve the problem and perhaps even suggest that the issue is so complicated that the best you and your readers can hope for is consensus – or agreement on some aspect of the matter.

In your introduction and throughout your essay, you will want to explain the problem in ways that will make your audience say, "Yes, this author understands my position." Because the people whom you are writing for may feel stress when you confront them with an emotionally charged issue and may already have made up their minds firmly on the subject, you should try to interest such reluctant readers by suggesting that you have an innovative way of viewing the problem. Of course, this tactic is effective only when you can indeed follow through and be as original as possible in your treatment of the subject. Otherwise, your readers may reject your ideas because they recognize that you have misrepresented yourself.

Challenge Yourself to Risk Change

Rather than masking your thoughts behind an "objective persona," the Rogerian approach allows you to express your true feelings. However, if you are to meet the ideals of Rogerian communication, you need to challenge your own beliefs; you must be so open-minded that you truly entertain the possibility that your ideas are wrong, or at least not absolutely right. According to Rogers, you must "run the risk of being changed yourself. You ... might find yourself influenced in your attitudes or your personality."

Elaborate on the Value of Opposing Positions

In this part of your argument you will want to elaborate on which of your opponent's claims about the problem are correct. For example, if your roommate's messiness is driving you crazy but you still want to live with him or her, stress that cleanliness is not the be-all-and-end-all of human life. Commend your roommate for helping you focus on your studies and express appreciation for all of the times that he or she has pitched in to clean up. And, of course, you would also want to admit to a few annoying habits of your own, such as taking thirty-minute showers or talking on your cell phone late at night while your roommate is trying to sleep! After viewing the problem from your roommate's perspective, you might even be willing to explore how your problem with compulsive neatness is itself a problem.

Show Instances When Your Assertions Are Valid

Once you have identified the problem in as nonthreatening a way as possible, established a fair-minded persona, and called for some level of consensus based on a "higher" interest, you have reached the most important stage in Rogerian negotiation: you can now present your position. At this point in your argument, you do not want to slap down a "But!" or "However!" and then come out of your corner punching. Remember the spirit of Rogerian problem solving: your ultimate goal is not to beat your audience, but to communicate with them and to promote a workable compromise. For example, in the sample argument with your roommate, rather than issuing an ultimatum such as "Unless you start picking up after yourself and doing your fair share of the housework, I'm moving out," you could say, "I realize that you view housekeeping as a less important activity than I do, but I need to let you know that I find your messiness to be highly stressful, and I'm wondering what kind of compromise we can make so we can continue living together." Yes, this statement carries an implied threat, but note how this sentence is framed positively and minimalizes the emotional intensity inherent in the situation.

To achieve the nonthreatening tone needed to diffuse emotional situations, avoid exaggerating your claims or using biased, emotional language. Also, avoid attacking your audience's claims as exaggerated. Whenever you feel angry or defensive, take a deep breath and look for points in which you can agree with or understand your opponents. When you are really emotional about an issue, try to cool off enough to recognize where your language is loaded with explosive terms. To embrace the Rogerian approach, remember that you need to defuse your temper and set your pride and ego aside.

Present Your Claim in a Nonthreatening Way

Admittedly, it is difficult to substantiate an argument while acknowledging the value of competing positions. Yet if you have done an effective job in the early part of your essay, then your audience perceives you to be a reasonable person – someone worth listening to. Consequently, you should not sell yourself short when presenting your position.

Because of the emotionally charged context of your communication situation, you still need to maintain the same open-minded persona that you established in the introductory paragraphs. Although your main focus in this section is to develop the validity of your claim, you can maintain your fair-minded persona by recalling significant counterarguments and by elaborating on a few limitations of your claim. You can also remind your readers that you are not expecting them to accept your claim completely. Instead, you are merely attempting to show that under certain circumstances your position is valid.

Search for a Compromise and Call for a Higher Interest

Near the conclusion of your essay, you may find it useful to encourage your audience to seek a compromise with you under a call for a "higher interest."

Writing Assignments

The Rogerian method of problem solving is designed for exploring controversial interpersonal, social, and political problems. You can use these techniques to help you begin or end a personal relationship or to help you effectively communicate with your professors, etc. Knowledge of the Rogerian method can help you deal with instances of sexual discrimination in the workplace or help you encourage insecure authorities to take the action that you want. You could use Rogerian approaches to encourage your classmates and other students at your school to be more sympathetic about social problems such as poverty and ecological issues. To select a subject for a Rogerian analysis, try reviewing your journal and freewrite about significant interpersonal problems you have dealt with in your life. Below are a few questions that may help you identify a subject:

> Do I want to write about an interpersonal issue? For example, am I having trouble communicating with someone? Could the breakdown be linked to my failure to employ Rogerian strategies? Are there any major differences in belief that I could bridge by communicating with him or her in a Rogerian way?
> Do I want to write about a social or political problem? Are there any on-campus or work-related problems that I wish to explore? For example, am I worried about an important national issue such as the federal deficit? Or could I promote harmony in a local or campus conflict?
> Are there any sports-related topics that I could tackle? For example, do I want to convince skiers that short skis have carved up the mountain in an ugly way? Do I want to persuade tennis players that we need to throw away the wide-body power rackets and go back to the days of wooden rackets because power tennis is killing finesse tennis?
> Consider playing the role of a marketing executive. Find a new product that you believe is superior to an established product and then write some advertising copy that explains why people should shirt their loyalty to the new product.

CC licensed content, Shared previously

Causal Arguments

"Why are things like this? What is the effect, or result, of this?" and "What causes this?"–These questions guide authors as they analyze or argue about causal relationships, such as "What is the effect of a college education on income?" View fascinating reports on various cause/effect topics and then explore your own causal relationship. Improve your critical thinking skills.

Unlike explanations of processes, which follow a chronological order of events, cause and effect texts are deeply speculative and tentative, relying on causal reasoning and argument. Your purpose is to answer

Why are things like this?
What is the effect, or result, of this?
What is the cause of this?

Analyzing cause-and-effect relationships requires you to question how different parts and sequences interact with each other over time, which is often more difficult than reporting a chronological order of events, as you do when describing a process.

Why Write About Causes and Effects?

Human beings ask why perhaps more than any other question. When we listen to the nightly news and hear about the atrocities of war, we wonder, "What causes the hatred?" When we read about the violence plaguing our country, we ask, "Why does the United States lead the world in violent crimes?" When we read studies that indicate that 28 percent of women in America have been raped and that the occurrence of date rape is rising on college campuses, we ask, "Why is this happening?" When we read about environmental problems such as the depletion of the ozone layer, we wonder, "Why don't we do something about it?" Whenever we make decisions in our daily lives, we ask ourselves, "Why should I do this?"

On a daily basis, we seek to understand why events occurred by identifying the factors that led up to them. For example, if you were not doing well in school and on homework assignments, you might ask, "Did my high school class(es) sufficiently prepare me for this class? Am I studying long enough? Am I taking effective lecture notes? Am I paying too much attention to the course texts and too little to the instructor's lectures? How is my attendance? Is my part-time job interfering too much with my school work? Am I using my time to study effectively? Are some of my friends having a negative influence on my study habits? Am I taking too many courses or putting too much time into another course? What can I do to improve my memory or study skills?" After asking these and other questions, you would eventually be able to identify a variety of causes for your poor performance, and once you recognize the causal relationship, you can set about realistically to improve your grade.

Cause-and-effect assignments are among the most interesting writing projects that you will tackle in school and in professional life. In school, teachers frequently assign process assignments. For example, humanities professors may ask for an analysis of what causes particular music genres or artistic genres to capture the imagination of popular culture; history professors, the impact of cultures on world history; social science professors, the effects of inventions on culture or the effect of gun control laws on violent homicide rates; business professors, the effects of changes in the interest rates on the economy.

Cause-and-effect texts are extremely common in professions–particularly the sciences, where researchers employ the scientific method to seek out cause-and-effect relationships. Writers commonly focus on analyzing causes or effects. A medical writer, for example, might explore the effects of a poor diet or the causes of a disease. A lawyer might argue the effect of an accident on his client. A sports writer might analyze why a team continues its losing or winning streak.

Diverse Rhetorical Situations

The purpose of many cause-and-effect texts is to explain the effects or causes of something. And the tone of these texts tends to be dispassionate and objective. In complex situations, however, the writer's purpose may shift from explaining to speculating or even arguing about an interpretation. Sometimes writers argue about a particular cause or effect because they want to sell you something or because they want to change your mind on a policy or interpretation.

People write about causes and effects for a variety of communication situations, and they employ a variety of media. The shape and content of cause-and-effect reports tend to be more diverse than the shape and content of texts that explain subjects, concepts, or processes, as suggested in the table below.

Purposes	Audiences	Voices	Media
• Speculate • Explain • Satirize • Argue • Sell	• Mass market audience • Decision makers • Researchers • Individuals • Consumers	• First person • Passionate • Objective • Academic	• Advertisements • Listserv messages • Essays • Newspapers • Magazines • Editorials • Web sites • Videos

Focus

When dealing with causes and effects, it is important to keep to a narrow topic. Time constraints and resources should always be kept in mind when pursuing a topic. Example: To find the reasons for world hunger would take years of research and/or tons of hours, so focus on a specific entity of a broad topic. Perhaps you could identify one country's efforts over the past few years.

Writers often bring focus to their work by claiming cause-and-effect relationships upfront, in their introductions. These "thesis statements" guide the writer and reader throughout the document. And they also offer clues as to the writer's voice, tone, and persona. Consider, for example, this tongue-in-cheek analysis of the The Dead Grandmother/Exam Syndrome and the Potential Downfall Of American Society.

The basic problem can be stated very simply: A student's grandmother is far more likely to die suddenly just before the student takes an exam, than at any other time of year.

While this idea has long been a matter of conjecture or merely a part of the folklore of college teaching, I can now confirm that the phenomenon is real. For over twenty years I have collected data on this supposed relationship, and have not only confirmed what most faculty had suspected, but also found some additional aspects of this process that are of potential importance to the future of the country. The results presented in this report provide a chilling picture and should waken the profession and the general public to a serious health and sociological problem before it is too late.

Development

Critical readers such as your instructors are quick to recognize shallow reasoning. College instructors expect you to cite multiple causes or effects when you are addressing a complex phenomenon. For example, if you were exploring the effects of TV on children, your readers would most likely expect you to do more than attack the violence as being unethical or immoral. Likewise, if you were analyzing the causes of our nation's high divorce rates, your instructors would expect you to do more than cite troubles with finances as the cause of divorces.

To help you develop a stronger sense of the level of detail your readers need to understand a particular cause-and-effect relationship, consider conducting research. What have others reported about the particular cause-and-effect relationship you are exploring? Read about what others have speculated or reported about your topic.

Below are some additional suggestions for developing your cause-and-effect report.

Check for Post Hoc Fallacies

Critical readers will expect you to develop the reasoning that demonstrates the cause and effect relationship isn't due to chance. Academic readers are reluctant to assume causality between two actions because they are trained to identify post hoc ("after this") fallacies. Essentially a post hoc fallacy occurs when an author assumes Event B was caused by Event A simply because it followed Event A; the connection is false because it is equally possible that Event B was caused by some other factor. For example, let us suppose that Bill has been jilted by his girlfriend Laura. Because Laura argued with Bill last Friday night that he never spent any money on her and that she always has to pay for their dates, Bill might assume that she left him because he was cheap. However, this might not be the true reason for Laura's dumping Bill. In fact, it could be that Laura was tired of Bill's negative view of life. Perhaps she truly left Bill because she found him to be insensitive, boring, and uncommunicative.

Identify Sufficient and Necessary Causes

In some instances you may be able to explain an effect by identifying sufficient causes and necessary causes.

A sufficient cause is one that can cause the effect to take place. By itself, a sufficient cause can explain a phenomenon or trend. For instance, in order for someone to contract the AIDS virus, any of the following forms of contact is a sufficient cause:

A previously infected patient's bodily fluids must enter the uninfected person's body through either an open sore, Sexual conduct, Or a contaminated instrument such as a needle.

Frequently more than one sufficient cause is necessary to explain a phenomenon or trend. Three or four causes, for example, may be necessary to explain an effect. You cannot say, for example, that all one needs is a match to start a fire. You also need oxygen and something to burn. When describing physical phenomena such as how acid rain is produced, you may have little difficulty identifying sufficient causes. Explaining human behavior is rarely so simple, of course.

Identify Remote/Speculative Causes

When we face complicated questions and problems, we often are unable to identify sufficient causes so we must speculate about necessary causes—those causes that can result in the effect. For instance, no single cause precipitated the collapse of the Soviet Union, yet we could speculate that hunger, poor economic conditions, alienation from communism, and political corruption were all remote causes.

Because academic readers are sensitive to the complexity of most issues, they generally do not expect you to offer sufficient causes for complex problems. Instead, they expect you to speculate about possible causes and effects, while limiting the scope of your claims with qualifiers such as "usually," "may," "possible," "sometimes" or "most." No simple answer, no sufficient cause, can explain, for example, why some people become violent criminals or serial killers while others devote themselves to feeding the hungry or serving the helpless.

Establish an Appropriate Voice

You can choose from a range of tones, personas and voices. Some writers choose a contentious, argumentative tone. Sometimes writers will soften their tone, perhaps assuming a milder persona than they actually feel, because they fear providing the information in a more straightforward, argumentative way would cause readers to look elsewhere. For example, in Tropical Forests and Climate Change, the Canadian Development Agency offers a terrifying, well-researched analysis of global warming, yet softens its message with this caveat in the introduction:

> Climate change predictions are difficult because of the complexity of the atmosphere and the interaction of the many variables involved.

Humanize Abstract Issues

No matter how technical your subject is, you should keep in mind that you are writing to other people. When you sense that the human story is being lost in abstract figures or academic jargon, consider adding an anecdote of how the problem you are discussing affects particular people. For example, Melissa Henderson, a student writer, began her report on the effect of crack on babies with the following portrayal of a newborn, which she composed after reading numerous essays about the effect of crack cocaine on human fetuses:

> Lying restlessly under the warm lights like a McDonald's Big Mac, Baby Doe fights with all of his three pounds of strength to stay alive. Because he was born prematurely, Baby Doe has an array of tubes and wires extending from his frail body which constantly monitor his heartbeat, drain excess fluid from his lungs and alert hospital personnel in the event he stops breathing. As he lies in the aseptic incubator his rigid little arms and legs twitch and jerk as though a steady current of electricity coursed through his veins. Suddenly, without warning or provocation, he begins to cry a mournful, inconsolable wail that continues steadily without an end in sight. As the nurses try to comfort the tiny infant with loving touches and soothing whispers, Baby Doe's over-wrought nervous system can no longer cope. Suffering from sensory overload, he withdraws into the security offered in a long, deep slumber. Welcome to the world, Baby Doe, your mother is a crack cocaine addict.

As you write drafts of your causal report, consider incorporating an anecdote—that is, a brief story about how people are influenced by your subject. For example, if you are researching the effects of a sluggish economy on our nation's poor, you might want to flesh out your statistics by depicting the story of how one homeless family lost their jobs, income, medical benefits, house, community, and hope.

Use Visuals

Although visuals are not required–in fact, many cause-and-effect texts do not use visuals–readers appreciate visuals, particularly ones that explain the cause-and-effect relationship being addressed. Consider, for example, this visual from the United States Environmental Protection Agency's Web site on Global Warming:

Readers particularly appreciate tables and graphs. Critical readers will often skim through a document's tables before reading the text:

Visuals can be used to influence readers at an emotional level. For example, at Project GHB's Tragedy Page, each picture links to an obituary, which tells the personal story of how these young people overdosed on GHB

Organization

When analyzing causal relationships, you must reveal to readers how different parts and sequences interact with each other over time. Rather than merely reporting the order of events in chronological fashion as we do when describing a process, you need to identify the specific reasons behind the effects or causes. Your organization needs to reflect the logic of your analysis. This is often difficult because a single cause can result in many different effects. Likewise, an effect can have multiple causes.

For example, even a simple effect such as a minor car accident can have multiple causes. Yes, we could say that John D. caused the accident because he was driving while intoxicated. Yet if we knew more about John D.'s state of mind—if we knew, for instance, that he wasn't watching where he was going because he was thinking about his wife's threat to leave him—then we could identify additional causes for the accident. It could very well be that he was exhausted after a sleepless night. Or perhaps his personal predicament had nothing to do with the accident: Maybe the loss of his job that morning or his failure to have faulty brakes replaced is a more significant cause for the accident. If we get really carried away with our reasoning, we could say that his former employers were responsible. After all, John D. would not have lost his job if the automobile manufacturer he worked for had not closed three of its American plants and moved manufacturing of some parts to plants in Mexico, Hong Kong, and Japan. In addition, we could also find potential causes for the accident by considering the other driver, Susan K. Maybe she rushed into the busy intersection expecting everyone else to make room for her because she was already late for an in-class exam. Perhaps if Susan K. had not consumed four pots of coffee, she would have been more mellow, more cautious, and less willing to risk her life to get to school on time.

Use Formatting to Highlight Your Organization

You can emphasize the most emphatic elements of your analysis by using headings and subheadings. A quick scan of any of the cause-and-effect readings highlights the popularity of headings. For example, below are the headings used by the Canadian International Development Agency for their essay on Tropical Forests and Climate Change

- Is the world's climate changing?
- How are we causing climate change?
- Impact of climate change on forests
- Climate change convention and the Kyoto protocol
- Forestry's role in mitigating climate change
- Carbon trading markets
- Conclusions

You may also want to play with the formatting of your text to highlight the reasoning behind your causal analysis. Consider, for example, the Canadian International Development Agency's Tropical Forests and Climate Change. These authors used callouts to define climate change terms that readers may not understand and they used call out boxes to emphasize important points in their essay:

The Sustainable Forest Management Project in Cameroon, Trees for Tomorrow in Jamaica, and the Arenal Conservation and Development Project are CIDA-supported projects that work towards enhancing forest management in developing countries.

Expanding the area of forest cover by establishing tree plantations, agroforestry plantings, or analog forests enlarges the capacity of the terrestrial carbon sink. Trees are composed of approximately 50 percent carbon which they extract from the atmosphere during photosynthesis. The rate of carbon sequestration depends on the growth characteristics of the species, the conditions for growth where the tree is planted, and the density of the tree's wood. It is greatest in the younger stages of tree growth, between 20 to 50 years. Growth rates on commercial plantations in the tropics have been improving steadily as the results of tree improvement research have been applied. The technology to establish fast-growing plantations exists, as does the global expertise for establishing them. Growth rates of more than 30 cubic metres/hectare/year are now commonplace for intensive industrial pulp plantations in the tropics and FAO estimates that there are between 1.5 million and 2.0 million hectares of tree plantations established every year.

You may find it helpful to visually represent the structure of your argument, perhaps even including your organizational map as a visual for readers. For example, consider the following screenshot from the EPA's site on global warming. From this image, you understand four topics are being addressed and you understand the questions that guide the EPA's causal analysis:

Introduce the Topic: Typically, texts that explore cause-and-effect relationships summarize the author's position upfront, in the introduction (see General to the Specific Strategies). For example, back in 1985, Joseph K. Skinner began his influential essay "Big Mac and the Tropical Forests" with this dramatic opening–two sentences that immediately focus your attention on the causal connection he explicates throughout his essay: Hello, fast-food chains. Goodbye, tropical forests. However, you may want to avoid explicit thesis sentences and forecasting statements if your subject is likely to threaten the beliefs of your audience or if it is an inherently emotional subject. You may occasionally find it important to establish a credible persona first by reviewing what your readers are likely to believe about a causal relationship and then by stating your own opinion.

For example, assume you are writing an essay against spanking children. Now if your audience believes that spanking children is the proper way to discipline them, and if you claim in the introduction of the essay that spanking children may result in their becoming criminals, then your readers might assume you are an oddball and dismiss your essay. Yet if you intelligently discuss some of the reasons why parents and psychologists recommend spanking and then introduce extensive research from prominent journals and reports that all violent criminals were spanked as children, your readers might be more willing to listen to your reasoning

Style: When grappling with difficult issues and concepts, your prose can understandably become unclear, dull, or cluttered. Eventually, though, as you continue to revise your drafts and further refine your message, you need to cut away the superfluous words, redundancies, and needless abstractions. You can make your language more interesting and more understandable by eliminating needless jargon; passive voice; lengthy, redundant sentences; or pompous and archaic language.

Provide Descriptive, Sensory Language: You can help your readers imagine your subject better by appealing to their senses. Whenever possible, describe how an object looks, sounds, tastes, feels, or smells. For example, in this excerpt from Carl Sagan's powerful essay on the effects of a nuclear war, "The Nuclear Winter," notice how Sagan appeals to our visual sense in his description of the effect of a single nuclear bomb on a city: In a 2 megaton explosion over a fairly large city, buildings would be vaporized, people reduced to atoms and shadows, outlying structures blown down like matchsticks and raging fires ignited. And if the bomb exploded on the ground, an enormous crater, like those that can be seen through a telescope on the surface of the Moon, would be all that remained where midtown once had been.

The lifeblood of effective writing is concrete and sensory language. A word, properly placed, can create a tone that angers or inspires a reader. Knowing the power of language to promote change, effective writers are selective in their use of concrete words—words that represent actual physical things like "chair" and "house"—and sensory words—words that appeal to our five senses. Selecting the right word or group of words is a crucial step in drawing your readers into your work so that they can fully understand your vision and ideas. Note the masterful use of concrete and sensory words in this passage from a Newsweek essay, "Don't Go in the Water":

"Black mayonnaise": The problem for most landlubbers, of course, is that most of the effects of coastal pollution are hard to see. Bays and estuaries that are now in jeopardy—Boston Harbor, for example, or even San Francisco Bay—are still delightful to look at from shore. What is happening underwater is quite another matter, and it is not for the squeamish. Scuba divers talk of swimming through clouds of toilet paper and half-dissolved feces, of bay bottoms covered by a foul and toxic combination of sediment, sewage and petrochemical waste appropriately known as "black mayonnaise." Fishermen haul in lobsters and crab [sic] covered with mysterious "burn holes" and fish whose fins are rotting off. Offshore, marine biologists track massive tides of algae blooms fed by nitrate and phosphate pollution—colonies of floating microorganisms that, once dead, strangle fish by stripping the water of its life giving oxygen.

In addition to selecting an abundance of distinctive concrete words (such as sediment, sewage, and nitrate) and sensory words (foul, burn holes, feces), the authors have used powerful images and metaphors. Note, for example, the clouds of toilet paper. Even more potent is the image of "black mayonnaise." Can you imagine biting into a sandwich spread with such poison?

When Speculating, Use Qualifying Language: When addressing complex issues and processes, you adopt an appropriate speculative voice by using words like "may cause" or "could also."

Useful Qualifying Words and Phrases: may, might, usually typically, perhaps, can, I believe it seems likely. As an example of carefully chosen qualifying words, consider the following passage from the US EPA's Web site on global warming impacts:

- Rising global temperatures are expected to raise sea level, and change precipitation and other local climate conditions. Changing regional climate could alter forests, crop yields, and water supplies. It could also affect human health, animals, and many types of ecosystems. Deserts may expand into existing rangelands, and features of some of our National Parks may be permanently altered.
- Most of the United States is expected to warm, although sulfates may limit warming in some areas. Scientists currently are unable to determine which parts of the United States will become wetter or drier, but there is likely to be an overall trend toward increased precipitation and evaporation, more intense rainstorms, and drier soils.
- Unfortunately, many of the potentially most important impacts depend upon whether rainfall increases or decreases, which can not be reliably projected for specific areas.

CC licensed content, Shared previously

- Causes & Effects. **Authored by**: Joe Moxley. **Provided by**: Writing Commons. **Located at**: https://writingcommons.org/causes-effects. **License**: *CC BY-NC-ND: Attribution-NonCommercial-NoDerivatives*

The Persuasive Essay

Learning Objectives

Determine the purpose and structure of persuasion in writing.
Identify bias in writing.
Assess various rhetorical devices.
Distinguish between fact and opinion.
Understand the importance of visuals to strengthen arguments.
Write a persuasive essay.

The Purpose of Persuasive Writing

The purpose of persuasion in writing is to convince, motivate, or move readers toward a certain point of view, or opinion. The act of trying to persuade automatically implies more than one opinion on the subject can be argued.

The idea of an argument often conjures up images of two people yelling and screaming in anger. In writing, however, an argument is very different. An argument is a reasoned opinion supported and explained by evidence. To argue in writing is to advance knowledge and ideas in a positive way. Written arguments often fail when they employ ranting rather than reasoning.

Tip

Most of us feel inclined to try to win the arguments we engage in. On some level, we all want to be right, and we want others to see the error of their ways. More times than not, however, arguments in which both sides try to win end up producing losers all around. The more productive approach is to persuade your audience to consider your opinion as a valid one, not simply the right one.

The Structure of a Persuasive Essay

The following five features make up the structure of a persuasive essay:

Introduction and thesis
Opposing and qualifying ideas
Strong evidence in support of claim
Style and tone of language
A compelling conclusion

Creating an Introduction and Thesis

The persuasive essay begins with an engaging introduction that presents the general topic. The thesis typically appears somewhere in the introduction and states the writer's point of view.

Tip

Avoid forming a thesis based on a negative claim. For example, "The hourly minimum wage is not high enough for the average worker to live on." This is probably a true statement, but persuasive arguments should make a positive case. That is, the thesis statement should focus on how the hourly minimum wage is low or insufficient.

Acknowledging Opposing Ideas and Limits to Your Argument

Because an argument implies differing points of view on the subject, you must be sure to acknowledge those opposing ideas. Avoiding ideas that conflict with your own gives the reader the impression that you may be uncertain, fearful, or unaware of opposing ideas. Thus it is essential that you not only address counterarguments but also do so respectfully.

Try to address opposing arguments earlier rather than later in your essay. Rhetorically speaking, ordering your positive arguments last allows you to better address ideas that conflict with your own, so you can spend the rest of the essay countering those arguments. This way, you leave your reader thinking about your argument rather than someone else's. You have the last word.

Acknowledging points of view different from your own also has the effect of fostering more credibility between you and the audience. They know from the outset that you are aware of opposing ideas and that you are not afraid to give them space.

It is also helpful to establish the limits of your argument and what you are trying to accomplish. In effect, you are conceding early on that your argument is not the ultimate authority on a given topic. Such humility can go a long way toward earning credibility and trust with an audience. Audience members will know from the beginning that you are a reasonable writer, and audience members will trust your argument as a result. For example, in the following concessionary statement, the writer advocates for stricter gun control laws, but she admits it will not solve all of our problems with crime:

Although tougher gun control laws are a powerful first step in decreasing violence in our streets, such legislation alone cannot end these problems since guns are not the only problem we face.

Such a concession will be welcome by those who might disagree with this writer's argument in the first place. To effectively persuade their readers, writers need to be modest in their goals and humble in their approach to get readers to listen to the ideas.

These phrases of concession include:

- although
- of course
- though
- granted that
- still
- yet

Bias in Writing

Everyone has various biases on any number of topics. For example, you might have a bias toward wearing black instead of brightly colored clothes or wearing jeans rather than formal wear. You might have a bias toward working at night rather than in the morning, or working by deadlines rather than getting tasks done in advance. These examples identify minor biases, of course, but they still indicate preferences and opinions.

Handling bias in writing and in daily life can be a useful skill. It will allow you to articulate your own points of view while also defending yourself against unreasonable points of view. The ideal in persuasive writing is to let your reader know your bias, but do not let that bias blind you to the primary components of good argumentation: sound, thoughtful evidence and a respectful and reasonable address of opposing sides.

The strength of a personal bias is that it can motivate you to construct a strong argument. If you are invested in the topic, you are more likely to care about the piece of writing. Similarly, the more you care, the more time and effort you are apt to put forth and the better the final product will be.

The weakness of bias is when the bias begins to take over the essay—when, for example, you neglect opposing ideas, exaggerate your points, or repeatedly insert yourself ahead of the subject by using *I* too often. Being aware of all three of these pitfalls will help you avoid them.

The Use of *I* in Writing

The use of *I* in writing is often a topic of debate, and the acceptance of its usage varies from instructor to instructor. It is difficult to predict the preferences for all your present and future instructors, but consider the effects it can potentially have on your writing.

Be mindful of the use of *I* in your writing because it can make your argument sound overly biased. There are two primary reasons:

> Excessive repetition of any word will eventually catch the reader's attention—and usually not in a good way. The use of *I* is no different.
> The insertion of *I* into a sentence alters not only the way a sentence might sound but also the composition of the sentence itself. *I* is often the subject of a sentence. If the subject of the essay is supposed to be, say, smoking, then by inserting yourself into the sentence, you are effectively displacing the subject of the essay into a secondary position. In the following example, the subject of the sentence is underlined:

Smoking is bad.

I think smoking is bad.

In the first sentence, the rightful subject, *smoking*, is in the subject position in the sentence. In the second sentence, the insertion of *I* and *think* replaces *smoking* as the subject, which draws attention to *I* and away from the topic that is supposed to be discussed. Remember to keep the message (the subject) and the messenger (the writer) separate.

Checklist

Developing Sound Arguments

Does my essay contain the following elements?

- An engaging introduction
- A reasonable, specific thesis that is able to be supported by evidence
- A varied range of evidence from credible sources
- Respectful acknowledgement and explanation of opposing ideas
- A style and tone of language that is appropriate for the subject and audience
- Acknowledgement of the argument's limits
- A conclusion that will adequately summarize the essay and reinforce the thesis

Fact and Opinion

Facts are statements that can be definitely proven using objective data. The statement that is a fact is absolutely valid. In other words, the statement can be pronounced as true or false. For example, 2 + 2 = 4. This expression identifies a true statement, or a fact, because it can be proved with objective data.

Opinions are personal views, or judgments. An opinion is what an individual believes about a particular subject. However, an opinion in argumentation must have legitimate backing; adequate evidence and credibility should support the opinion. Consider the credibility of expert opinions. Experts in a given field have the knowledge and credentials to make their opinion meaningful to a larger audience.

For example, you seek the opinion of your dentist when it comes to the health of your gums, and you seek the opinion of your mechanic when it comes to the maintenance of your car. Both have knowledge and credentials in those respective fields, which is why their opinions matter to you. But the authority of your dentist may be greatly diminished should he or she offer an opinion about your car, and vice versa.

In writing, you want to strike a balance between credible facts and authoritative opinions. Relying on one or the other will likely lose more of your audience than it gains.

Tip

The word *prove* is frequently used in the discussion of persuasive writing. Writers may claim that one piece of evidence or another proves the argument, but proving an argument is often not possible. No evidence proves a debatable topic one way or the other; that is why the topic is debatable. Facts can be proved, but opinions can only be supported, explained, and persuaded.

Using Visual Elements to Strengthen Arguments

Adding visual elements to a persuasive argument can often strengthen its persuasive effect. There are two main types of visual elements: quantitative visuals and qualitative visuals.

Quantitative visuals present data graphically. They allow the audience to see statistics spatially. The purpose of using quantitative visuals is to make logical appeals to the audience. For example, sometimes it is easier to understand the disparity in certain statistics if you can see how the disparity looks graphically. Bar graphs, pie charts, Venn diagrams, histograms, and line graphs are all ways of presenting quantitative data in spatial dimensions.

Qualitative visuals present images that appeal to the audience's emotions. Photographs and pictorial images are examples of qualitative visuals. Such images often try to convey a story, and seeing an actual example can carry more power than hearing or reading about the example. For example, one image of a child suffering from malnutrition will likely have more of an emotional impact than pages dedicated to describing that same condition in writing.

Writing at Work

When making a business presentation, you typically have limited time to get across your idea. Providing visual elements for your audience can be an effective timesaving tool. Quantitative visuals in business presentations serve the same purpose as they do in persuasive writing. They should make logical appeals by showing numerical data in a spatial design. Quantitative visuals should be pictures that might appeal to your audience's emotions. You will find that many of the rhetorical devices used in writing are the same ones used in the workplace. For more information about visuals in presentations, see Chapter 14 "Creating Presentations: Sharing Your Ideas".

Writing a Persuasive Essay

Choose a topic that you feel passionate about. If your instructor requires you to write about a specific topic, approach the subject from an angle that interests you. Begin your essay with an engaging introduction. Your thesis should typically appear somewhere in your introduction.

Start by acknowledging and explaining points of view that may conflict with your own to build credibility and trust with your audience. Also state the limits of your argument. This too helps you sound more reasonable and honest to those who may naturally be inclined to disagree with your view. By respectfully acknowledging opposing arguments and conceding limitations to your own view, you set a measured and responsible tone for the essay.

Make your appeals in support of your thesis by using sound, credible evidence. Use a balance of facts and opinions from a wide range of sources, such as scientific studies, expert testimony, statistics, and personal anecdotes. Each piece of evidence should be fully explained and clearly stated.

Make sure that your style and tone are appropriate for your subject and audience. Tailor your language and word choice to these two factors, while still being true to your own voice.

Finally, write a conclusion that effectively summarizes the main argument and reinforces your thesis. See Chapter 15 "Readings: Examples of Essays" to read a sample persuasive essay.

Key Takeaways

- The purpose of persuasion in writing is to convince or move readers toward a certain point of view, or opinion.
- An argument is a reasoned opinion supported and explained by evidence. To argue, in writing, is to advance knowledge and ideas in a positive way.
- A thesis that expresses the opinion of the writer in more specific terms is better than one that is vague.
- It is essential that you not only address counterarguments but also do so respectfully.
- It is also helpful to establish the limits of your argument and what you are trying to accomplish through a concession statement.
- To persuade a skeptical audience, you will need to use a wide range of evidence. Scientific studies, opinions from experts, historical precedent, statistics, personal anecdotes, and current events are all types of evidence that you might use in explaining your point.
- Make sure that your word choice and writing style is appropriate for both your subject and your audience.
- You should let your reader know your bias, but do not let that bias blind you to the primary components of good argumentation: sound, thoughtful evidence and respectfully and reasonably addressing opposing ideas.
- You should be mindful of the use of *I* in your writing because it can make your argument sound more biased than it needs to.
- Facts are statements that can be proven using objective data.
- Opinions are personal views, or judgments, that cannot be proven.
- In writing, you want to strike a balance between credible facts and authoritative opinions.
- Quantitative visuals present data graphically. The purpose of using quantitative visuals is to make logical appeals to the audience.
- Qualitative visuals present images that appeal to the audience's emotions.

CC licensed content, Shared previously

Mechanics: Punctuation

End Punctuation

There are three punctuation marks that come at the end of a sentence: the period (.), the question mark (?), and the exclamation point (!). A sentence is always followed by a single space, no matter what the concluding punctuation is.

Periods

Periods indicate a neutral sentence, and as such are by far the most common ending punctuation mark. They've been at the end of every sentence on this page so far. They occur at the end of statements.

Question Marks

A question mark comes at the end of a question (How was class today?). A rhetorical question is asked to make a point, and does not expect an answer. Some questions are used principally as polite requests (Would you pass the salt?).

All of these questions can be categorized as direct questions, and all of these questions require a question mark at their ends.

Indirect Questions

Indirect questions do not have question marks at their ends. They can be used in many of the same ways as declarative ones, but they often emphasize knowledge or lack of knowledge:

- I can't guess **how Tamika managed it**.
- I wonder **whether I looked that bad**.
- Cecil asked **where the reports were**.

Notice how different word order is used in direct and indirect questions: in direct questions the verb usually comes before the subject, while indirect questions the verb appears second.

Exclamation Points

The exclamation point is a punctuation mark usually used after an interjection or exclamation to indicate strong feelings or high volume, and often marks the end of a sentence. You've likely seen this overused on the internet.

While this kind of statement is excessive, there are appropriate ways to use exclamation points. A sentence ending in an exclamation mark may be an exclamation (such as "Wow!" or "Boo!"), or an imperative ("Stop!"), or may indicate astonishment: "They were the footprints of a gigantic duck!"

The exclamation mark is sometimes used in conjunction with the question mark. This can be in protest or astonishment ("Out of all places, the water-hole?!").

Informally, exclamation marks may be repeated for additional emphasis ("That's great!!!"), but this practice is generally considered only acceptable in casual or informal writing, such as text messages or online communication with friends and family.Punctuation Clusters

Occasionally, you'll come across an instance that seems to require multiple punctuation marks right next to each other. Sometimes you need to keep all the marks, but other times, you should leave some out.

You should never use more than one ending punctuation mark in a row (period, question mark exclamation point). When quoting a question, you would end with a question mark, not a question mark and a period. If an abbreviation, like *etc.*, ends a sentence, you should only use one period.

> Carlos leaned forward and asked, "Did you get the answer to number six?"
> I think we'll have enough food. Mary bought the whole store: chips, soda, candy, cereal, etc.

However, you can place a comma immediately after a period, as you can see above with *etc.* This rule also applies to the abbreviations *e.g.* and *i.e.*

Note: For those who are curious, *e.g.* stands for *exempli gratia*, which means "for example," and *i.e.* stands for *id est*, which means "that is."

Periods and parentheses can also appear right next to each other. Sometimes the period comes after the closing parenthesis (as you can see earlier in this section), but sometimes it appears inside the parentheses.
CC licensed content, Shared previously

Commas

Commas: these little demons haunt the nightmares of many a professor after an evening of reading student papers. It seems nearly impossible to remember and apply the seventeen or so comma rules that seem to be the standard.

Perhaps the best and most instructive way for us to approach the comma is to remember its fundamental function: *it is a separator.* Once you know this, the next step is to determine what sorts of things generally require separation. This includes most transition words, descriptive words or phrases, adjacent items, and complete ideas (complete ideas contain both a subject and a verb). Commas are also used to separate similar items in lists.

Transition Words

Transition words add new viewpoints to your material; commas before and after transition words help to separate them from the sentence ideas they are describing. Transition words tend to appear at the beginning or in the middle of a sentence:

- *Therefore*, the natural gas industry can only be understood fully through an analysis of these recent political changes.
- The lead prosecutor was prepared, *however*, for a situation like this.

Note: As was mentioned, these words require commas at the beginning or middle of a sentence. When they appear between two complete ideas, however, a period or semicolon is required beforehand:

- Clint had been planning the trip with his kids for three months; *however*, when work called he couldn't say no.
- Sam was retired. *Nevertheless*, he wanted to help out.

As you can see from these examples, comma is *always* required after transition words.

Descriptive Phrases

Descriptive phrases often need to be separated from the things that they describe. Descriptive phrases tend to come at the very beginning of a sentence, right after the subject of a sentence, or at the very end of a sentence:

- **Near the end of the eighteenth century**, James Hutton introduced a point of view that radically changed

scientists' thinking about geologic processes.
- James Lovelock, **who first measured CFCs globally**, said in 1973 that CFCs constituted no conceivable hazard.
- All of the major industrialized nations approved, **making the possibility a reality**.

In each example, the phrase separated by the comma could be deleted from the sentence without destroying the sentence's basic meaning. If the information is necessary to the primary sentence meaning, it should **not** be set off by commas. Let's look at a quick example of this:

- Jefferson's son, Miles, just started college.
- Jefferson's son Miles just started college

You would write the first sentence if Jefferson only has one son and his name is Miles. If Jefferson only has one son, then *Miles* is not needed information and should be set off with commas.

You would write the second sentence if Jefferson has multiple sons, and it is his son Miles who just got into college. In the second sentence, *Miles* is necessary information, because until his name is stated, you can't be sure which of Jefferson's sons the sentence is talking about.

This test can be very helpful when you're deciding whether or not to include commas in your writing.

Adjacent Items

Adjacent items are separated so that the reader can consider each item individually.

The river caught fire on July 4, 1968, in Cleveland, Ohio.

The dates (July 4, 1968) and places (Cleveland, Ohio) are juxtaposed, and commas are needed because the juxtaposed items are clearly different from each other. This applies to countries as well as states: "Paris, France, is beautiful this time of year."

Coordinating Conjunctions: FANBOYS

We learned about coordinating conjunctions earlier in the course. These are words that join two words or phrases of equal importance. The mnemonic FANBOYS helps us remember the seven most common: *for, and, nor, but, or, yet,* and *so.*

When these conjunctions join two words or phrases, no comma is necessary (for more than two, take a look at "Commas in Lists" just below). However, when these conjunctions are used to join two complete ideas, a comma is required:

- Paula and Lucca had a great time on their date.
- Danny studied the lifespan of rhinoceroses in their native Kenya and the lifespan of rhinoceroses in captivity.
- Minh turned off the lights but left the door unlocked.
- We could write this as two separate sentences, but we've chosen to join them together here.

Commas in Lists

Perhaps one of the most hotly contested comma rules is the case of the **serial comma**. MLA style (as well as APA and *Chicago*) requires the use of the serial comma—AP style highly recommends leaving it out. But what is the serial comma?

The serial comma is the comma before the conjunction (*and, or,* and *nor*) in a series involving a parallel list of three or more things. For example, "I am industrious, resourceful, **and** loyal." The serial comma can provide clarity in certain situations. For example, if the *and* is part of a series of three or more phrases (groups of words) as opposed to single words:

Medical histories taken about each subject included smoking history, frequency of exercise, current height and weight, and recent weight gain.

The serial comma can also prevent the end of a series from appearing to be a parenthetical:

I'd like to thank my sisters, Beyoncé and Rhianna.

Without the serial comma, it may appear that the speaker is thanking his or her two sisters, who are named Beyoncé and Rhianna (which could be possible, but isn't true in this case). By adding the serial comma, it becomes clear that the speaker is thanking his or her sisters, as well as the two famous singers: "I'd like to thank my sisters, Beyoncé, and Rhianna."

By always using a comma before the *and* in any series of three or more, you honor the distinctions between each of the separated items, and you avoid any potential reader confusion.

Note: Some professors and many academic journals prefer to leave out the serial comma (for the journals, it is literally cheaper to print fewer commas). Because of this, the serial comma is not recommend in AP style.

Just as it is common for someone to have to look up the same tricky word dozens of times before committing its proper spelling to memory, you may need to reference comma rules multiple times before they feel natural to use. As with spelling, commas (or the absence of commas) must be repeatedly challenged in your writing.

As you perfect your comma usage, you will learn to recognize and reevaluate your sentence patterns, and the rewards are numerous. There is no foolproof or easy way to exorcise all of your comma demons, but a great place to start is reminding yourself of the comma's basic function as a separator and justifying the separation of elements. In the end, you simply must make a habit of reading, writing, and revising with comma correctness in mind.

Hyphens and Dashes

Hyphens

The Oxford Manual of Style once stated, "If you take hyphens seriously you will surely go mad." Hyphens belong to that category of punctuation marks that will hurt your brain if you think about them too hard, and, like commas, people disagree about their use in certain situations. Nevertheless, you will have to use them regularly because of the nature of academic and professional writing. If you learn to use hyphens properly, they help you to write efficiently and concretely.

The Hyphen's Function

Fundamentally, the hyphen is a joiner. It can join several different types of things:

- two nouns to make one complete word (kilogram-meter)
- an adjective and a noun to make a compound word (accident-prone)
- two words that, when linked, describe a noun (agreed-upon sum, two-dimensional object)
- a prefix with a noun (un-American)
- double numbers (twenty-four)
- numbers and units describing a noun (1000-foot face; a 10-meter difference)
- "self" words (self-employed, self-esteem)
- new word blends (cancer-causing, cost-effective)
- prefixes and suffixes to words, in particular when the writer wants to avoid doubling a vowel or tripling a consonant (anti-inflammatory; shell-like)
- multiple adjectives with the same noun (blue- and yellow-green beads; four- and five-year-olds)

A rule of thumb for the hyphen is that the resulting word must act as one unit; therefore, the hyphen creates a new word that has a single meaning. Usually, you can tell whether a hyphen is necessary by applying common sense and mentally excluding one of the words in question, testing how the words would work together without the hyphen. For example, the phrases "high-pressure system," "water-repellent surface," and "fuel-efficient car" would not make sense without hyphens, because you would not refer to a "high system," a "water surface," or a "fuel car." As your ears and eyes become attuned to proper hyphenation practices, you will recognize that both meaning and convention dictate where hyphens fit best.

Examples of Properly Used Hyphens

Some examples of properly used hyphens follow:

- small-scale study
- two-prong plug
- strength-to-weight ratio
- high-velocity flow

- frost-free lawn
- self-employed worker
- one-third majority
- coarse-grained wood
- decision-making process
- blue-green algae
- air-ice interface
- silver-stained cells
- protein-calorie malnutrition
- membrane-bound vesicles
- phase-contrast microscope
- long-term-payment loan
- cost-effective program
- time-dependent variable
- radiation-sensitive sample
- long-chain fatty acid

Note how the hyphenated word acts as a single unit carrying a meaning that the words being joined would not have individually.

When Hyphens Are Not Needed

By convention, hyphens are not used after words ending in –*ly*, nor when the words are so commonly used in combination that no ambiguity results. In these examples, no hyphens are needed:

- finely tuned engine
- blood pressure
- sea level
- real estate
- census taker
- atomic energy
- civil rights law
- public utility plant
- carbon dioxide

Note: Phrases like containing the word *well* like *well known* are contested. *Well* is an adverb, and thus many fall into the school of thought that a hyphen is unnecessary. However, others say that leaving out the hyphen may cause confusion and therefore include it (*well-known*). The standard in MLA is as follows: When it appears before the noun, *well known* should be hyphenated. When it follows the noun, no hyphenation is needed.

- She is a **well-known** person.
- She is **well known**.

Prefixes and Suffixes

Most prefixes do not need to be hyphenated; they are simply added in front of a noun, with no spaces and no joining punctuation necessary. The following is a list of common prefixes that do not require hyphenation when added to a noun:

- after
- anti
- bi
- bio
- co

- cyber
- di
- down
- hetero
- homo
- infra
- inter
- macro
- micro
- mini
- non
- photo
- poly
- stereo
- thermo

When prefixes are added to a proper noun, they require a hyphen (e.g., *nonviolent*, but *non-European*).

> **Note:** The prefix *re* generally doesn't require a hyphen. However, when leaving out a hyphen will cause confusion, one should be added. Look at the following word pairs, for example:
>
> - *resign* (leave a position) v. *re-sign* (sign the paper again)
> - *recreation* (an activity of leisure) v. *re-creation* (create something again)

Common suffixes also do not require hyphenation, assuming no ambiguities of spelling or pronunciation arise. Typically, you do not need to hyphenate words ending in the following suffixes:

- able, less, fold, like, wise

Commonly Used Word Blends

Also, especially in technical fields, some words commonly used in succession become joined into one. The resulting word's meaning is readily understood by technical readers, and no hyphen is necessary. Here are some examples of such word blends, typically written as single words:

- blackbody
- groundwater
- airship
- downdraft
- longwall
- upload
- setup
- runoff
- blowout

Dashes

The dash functions almost as a colon does in that it adds to the preceding material, but with extra emphasis. Like a caesura (a timely pause) in music, a dash indicates a strong pause, then gives emphasis to material following the pause. In effect, a dash allows you to *redefine* what was just written, making it more explicit. You can also use a dash as it is used in the first sentence of this paragraph: to frame an interruptive or parenthetical-type comment that you do not want to de-emphasize.

Jill Emery confirms that Muslim populations have typically been ruled by non-Muslims—specifically Americans, Russians, Israelis, and the French.
The dissolution took 20 minutes—much longer than anticipated—but measurements were begun as soon as the process was completed.

There is no "dash" button on a computer keyboard. Instead, create it by typing the hyphen button twice in a row; or use the "symbol" option in your word processor; or use the Mac shortcut option + shift + —.

The dash we typically use is technically called the "em dash," and it is significantly longer than the hyphen. There is also an "en dash"—whose length is between that of the hyphen and the em dash, and its best usage is to indicate inclusive dates and numbers:

- July 6–September 17
    - The date range began on July 6 and ended on September 17.
- Barack Obama (1961–)
    - This indicates the year a person was born, as well as the fact that he or she is still alive.
- pp. 148–56
    - This indicates pages 148 through 156. With number ranges, you can remove the first digit of the second number if it's the same as the first number's.

It can also be used for flight or train routes.

- The London–Paris train will be running thirty minutes late today.

Like the em dash, the en dash is not on the standard computer keyboard. Select it from word processor's symbol map (or if you have a Mac, you can type **option + -**), or it may even be inserted automatically by your word processor when you type inclusive numbers or dates with a hyphen between them. In most contexts, a hyphen can serve as an en dash, but in professional publications—especially in the humanities—an en dash is correct.

When you type the hyphen, en dash, and em dash, no spaces should appear on either side of the punctuation mark.

Apostrophes and Quotation Marks

Apostrophes

Possession

With possessives, the apostrophe is used in combination with an *s* to represent that a word literally or conceptually possesses what follows it. Singular words whether or not they end in *s*, are made possessive by adding an apostrophe + *s*. For plural words, we typically indicate possession simply by adding the apostrophe without an additional *s*. However, a plural that does not end in an *s* (e.g., *bacteria*), we would add an apostrophe + *s*.

- a student's paper
- one hour's passing
- Illinois's law
- interviewees' answers
- her professors' office (an office shared by two of her professors; if it were just one professor we would write *her professor's office*)

Note: Practices vary from style to style, so be sure to check the rules in your course's discipline for this.

Contractions

A contraction is a shortened phrase. *He will* becomes *he'll*, *are not* becomes *aren't*, *would have* becomes *would've*, and *it is* becomes *it's*. In all of these cases, the apostrophe stands in for the missing letters.

You may find yourself being steered away from using contractions in your papers. While you should write to your teacher's preference, keep in mind that leaving out contractions can often make your words sound over formal and stilted. (And you shouldn't eliminate contractions in your papers just to up your word count!)

Your versus *You're*

Your versus *You're*

- Your v. you're
- Its v. it's
- Their v. they're

All three of these pairs are the same kind of pair: a possessive pronoun and a contracted version of a pronoun + *to be* (*you're = you are*; *it's = it is*; *they're = they are*). These are easy to mix up (especially *its/it's*) because—as we've learned—an apostrophe + *s* indicates possession. The best way to use these correctly is to remember that possessive pronouns never have an apostrophe: if there's an apostrophe with a pronoun, it's a contraction, not a possessive.

Acronyms and Numbers

In technical writing, acronyms and numbers are frequently pluralized with the addition of an apostrophe *s*, but this is falling out of favor, and there is typically no need to put an apostrophe in front of the *s*. Therefore, *SSTs* (sea surface temperatures) is more acceptable than *SST's* when your intention is simply to pluralize.

Ideally, use the apostrophe before the *s* with an acronym or a number only to show possession (i.e., "an 1860's law"; "DEP's testing") or when confusion would otherwise result ("mind your *p*'s and *q*'s").

When talking about a specific decade *the 1920s* should be shortened to *the '20s*. Notice that the apostrophe curls away from the numbers, indicating that the missing characters originally appeared prior to the apostrophe.

Quotation Marks

There are three typical ways quotation marks are used. The first is pretty self-explanatory: you use quotation marks when you're making a direct quote.

- He said "I'll never forget you." It was the best moment of my life.
- Yogi Berra famously said, "A nickel ain't worth a dime anymore."

If you're just writing an approximation of something a person said, you would *not* use quotation marks:

- She told me about Pizza the three-toed sloth yesterday.
- He said that he would be late today.

The second is when you're calling attention to a word. For example:

- I can never say "Worcestershire" correctly.
- How do you spell "definitely"?

Note: It is this course's preference to use italics in these instances:

- I can never say *Worcestershire* correctly.
- How do you spell *definitely*?

However, using quotes is also an accepted practice.

The last use is scare quotes. This is the most misused type of quotation marks. People often think that quotation marks mean emphasis.

- Buy some "fresh" chicken today!
- We'll give it our "best" effort.
- Employees "must" wash their hands before returning to work.

However, when used this way, the quotation marks insert a silent "so-called" into the sentence, which is often the opposite of the intended meaning.

Where do Quotation Marks Go?

Despite what you may see practiced, the fact is that the period and comma always go inside the quotation marks. (The rules in British English are different, which may be where some of the confusion arises.)

- Correct: The people of the pine barrens are often called "pineys."
- Incorrect: The people of the pine barrens are often called "pineys".

The semicolon, colon, dash, question mark, and exclamation point can fall insider outside of the quotation marks, depending on whether the punctuation is a part of the original quote:

- This measurement is commonly known as "dip angle"; dip angle is the angle formed between a normal plane and a vertical.
- Built only 50 years ago, Shakhtinsk—"minetown"—is already seedy.
- When she was asked the question "Are rainbows possible in winter?" she answered by examining whether raindrops freeze at temperatures below 0 °C. (Quoted material has its own punctuation.)
- Did he really say "Dogs are the devil's henchmen"? (The quote is a statement, but the full sentence is a question.)

Brackets, Parentheses, and Ellipses

Parentheses

Parentheses are most often used to identify material that acts as an aside (such as this brief comment) or to add incidental information.

Other punctuation marks used alongside parentheses need to take into account their context. If the parentheses enclose a full sentence beginning with a capital letter, then the end punctuation for the sentence falls *inside* the parentheses. For example:

> Typically, suppliers specify air to cloth ratios of 6:1 or higher. (However, ratios of 4:1 should be used for applications involving silica or feldspathic minerals.)

If the parentheses indicate a citation at the end of a sentence, then the sentence's end punctuation comes after the parentheses are closed:

> In a study comparing three different building types, respirable dust concentrations were significantly lower in the open-structure building (Hugh et al., 2005).

Finally, if the parentheses appear in the midst of a sentence (as in this example), then any necessary punctuation (such as the comma that appeared just a few words ago) is delayed until the parentheses are closed.

You can also use parentheses to provide acronyms (or full names for acronyms). For example, "We use the MLA (Modern Language Association) style guide here" or "The Modern Language Association (MLA) style guide is my favorite to use."

Remember, parentheses always appear in pairs. If you open a parenthesis, you need another to close it!

> **Note:** In technical writing, there are additional rules for using parentheses, which can be more nuanced. While we won't discuss those rules here, it's important to bear their existence in mind, especially if you're considering going into a more technical field.

Brackets

Brackets are a fairly uncommon punctuation mark. Their main use is in quotations: they can be used to clarify quotes. For example, say you want to quote the following passage:

> "I finally got to meet Trent today. I had a really great time with him. He was a lot taller than expected, though."

However, you only want to relay the fact that Trent was taller than the speaker expected him to be. In order to do this, you would write the following: "[Trent] was a lot taller than expected."

The brackets let the reader know that while the word *Trent* wasn't in the original quote, his name was implied there. When using brackets, you need to be careful not to change the original meaning of the quote.

Another use of brackets is when there is a spelling or informational error in the original quote. For example, "Gabriel sat down on the river bank to fed [*sic*] the ducks." (The term *sic* means that the typo was in the original source of this quote.)

Ellipses

An ellipsis (plural *ellipses*) is a series of three periods, as you can see in the icon to the right.

As with most punctuation marks, there is some contention about its usage. The main point of contention is whether or not there should be a space between the periods (. . .) or not (...). MLA, APA, and *Chicago*, the most common style guides for students, support having spaces between the periods. Others you may encounter, such as in journalism, may not.

Quotes

Like the brackets we just learned about, you will primarily see ellipses used in quotes. They indicate a missing portion in a quote. Look at the following quote for an example:

Camarasaurus, with its more mechanically efficient skull, was capable of generating much stronger bite forces than *Diplodocus*. This suggests that *Camarasaurus* was capable of chomping through tougher plant material than *Diplodocus*, and was perhaps even capable of a greater degree of oral processing before digestion. This actually ties in nicely with previous hypotheses of different diets for each, which were based on apparent feeding heights and inferences made from wear marks on their fossilized teeth.

Diplodocus seems to have been well-adapted, despite its weaker skull, to a form of feeding known as branch stripping, where leaves are plucked from branches as the teeth are dragged along them. The increased flexibility of the neck of *Diplodocus* compared to other sauropods seems to support this too.

It's a lengthy quote, and it contains more information than you want to include. Here's how to cut it down:

Camarasaurus, with its more mechanically efficient skull, was capable of generating much stronger bite forces than *Diplodocus*. This suggests that *Camarasaurus* was capable of chomping through tougher plant material than *Diplodocus*. . . . This actually ties in nicely with previous hypotheses of different diets for each, which were based on apparent feeding heights and inferences made from wear marks on their fossilized teeth.

Diplodocus seems to have been well-adapted . . . to a form of feeding known as branch stripping, where leaves are plucked from branches as the teeth are dragged along them.

In the block quote above, you can see that the first ellipsis appears to have four dots. ("They are instantly recognized by their long, sweeping necks and whiplashed tails. . . .") However, this is just a period followed by an ellipsis. This is because ellipses **do not** remove punctuation marks when the original punctuation still is in use; they are instead used in conjunction with original punctuation. This is true for all punctuation marks, including periods, commas, semi-colons, question marks, and exclamation points.

By looking at two sympatric species (those that lived together) from the fossil graveyards of the Late Jurassic of North America . . . , [David Button] tried to work out what the major dietary differences were between sauropod dinosaurs, based on their anatomy.

One of the best ways to check yourself is to take out the ellipsis. If the sentence or paragraph is still correctly punctuated, you've used the ellipsis correctly. (Just remember to put it back in!).

The Pause

The ellipsis can also indicate . . . a pause. This use is typically informal, and is only be used in casual correspondence (e.g., emails to friends, posts on social media, texting) or in literature. Because this use occurs in literature, you may find yourself quoting a passage that already has an ellipsis in it. For example, look at this passage spoken by Lady Bracknell, in *The Importance of Being Ernest*.

Well, I must say, Algernon, that I think it is high time that Mr. Bunbury made up his mind whether he was going to live or to die. This shilly-shallying with the question is absurd. Nor do I in any way approve of the modern sympathy with invalids. I consider it morbid. Illness of any kind is hardly a thing to be encouraged in others. Health is the primary duty of life. I am always telling that to your poor uncle, but he never seems to take much notice . . . as far as any improvement in his ailment goes. I should be much obliged if you would ask Mr. Bunbury, from me, to be kind enough not to have a relapse on Saturday, for I rely on you to arrange my music for me. It is my last reception, and one wants something that will encourage conversation, particularly at the end of the season when every one has practically said whatever they had to say, which, in most cases, was probably not much.

If you were to quote the passage, it may appear that something has been removed from the quote. So how can we indicate that this is not the case? If you think back to the bracket rules we just discussed, you may remember that [*sic*] can be used to show that an error was in the original. In a similar practice, we can enclose the ellipsis in brackets to show it appeared in the original work:

Well, I must say, Algernon, that I think it is high time that Mr. Bunbury made up his mind whether he was going to live or to die. This shilly-shallying with the question is absurd. Nor do I in any way approve of the modern sympathy with invalids. I consider it morbid. Illness of any kind is hardly a thing to be encouraged in others. Health is the primary duty of life. I am always telling that to your poor uncle, but he never seems to take much notice [. . .] as far as any improvement in his ailment goes. I should be much obliged if you would ask Mr. Bunbury, from me, to be kind enough not to have a relapse on Saturday, for I rely on you to arrange my music for me. It is my last reception, and one wants something that will encourage conversation, particularly at the end of the season when every one has practically said whatever they had to say, which, in most cases, was probably not much.

Semicolons and Colons

Semicolons

The semicolon is one of the most misunderstood and misused punctuation marks; in fact, it is often mistaken for the colon (which we'll discuss next). However, these two punctuation marks are not interchangeable. A semicolon connects two complete ideas (a complete idea has a subject and a verb) that are connected to each other. Look at this sentence for example:

> Anika's statue is presently displayed in the center of the exhibit; this location makes it a focal point and allows it to direct the flow of visitors to the museum.

The first idea tells us where Anika's statue is, and the second idea tells us more about the location and its importance. Each of these ideas could be its own sentence, but by using a semicolon, the author is telling the reader that the two ideas are connected. Often, you may find yourself putting a comma in the place of the semicolon; this is incorrect. Using a comma here would create a run-on sentence. Remember: a comma can join a complete idea to other items while a semicolon needs a complete idea on either side.

The semicolon can also be used to separate items in a list when those items have internal commas. For example, say you're listing a series of cities and their states, or you're listing duties for a resume:

- As a photographer for National Geographic, Renato had been to a lot of different places including São Paulo, Brazil; Kobe, Japan; Kyiv, Ukraine; and Barcelona, Spain.
- As an engineering assistant, I had a variety of duties: participating in pressure ventilation surveys; completing daily drafting, surveying, and data compilation; and acting as a company representative during a roof-bolt pull test.

Colons

The colon: well-loved but, oh, so misunderstood. The colon is not just used to introduce a list; it is far more flexible. The colon can be used after the first word of a sentence or just before the final word of a sentence. The colon can also be used to introduce a grammatically independent sentence. Thus, it is one of the most powerful punctuation marks.

The colon is like a sign on the highway, announcing that something important is coming. It acts as an arrow pointing forward, telling you to read on for important information. A common analogy used to explain the colon is that it acts like a flare in the road, signaling that something meaningful lies ahead.

Use the colon when you wish to provide pithy emphasis.

- To address this problem, we must turn to one of the biologist's most fundamental tools: the Petri dish.

Use the colon to introduce material that explains, amplifies, or summaries what has preceded it.

- The Petri dish: one of the biologist's most fundamental tools.
- In low carbon steels, banding tends to affect two properties in particular: tensile ductility and yield strength.

The colon is also commonly used to present a list or series:

- A compost facility may not be located as follows: within 300 feet of an exceptional-value wetland, within 100 feet of a perennial stream, or within 50 feet of a property line.

Mechanics: Style

Parts of a Sentence

Every sentence has a subject and a predicate. The **subject** of a sentence is the noun, pronoun, or phrase or clause the sentence is about, and the <u>predicate</u> is the rest of the sentence after the subject:

- Einstein's general **theory** of relativity <u>has been subjected to many tests of validity over the years.</u>
- In a secure landfill, the **soil** on top and the **cover** <u>block storm water intrusion into the landfill</u>. *(compound subject)*
  - There are two subjects in this sentence: *soil* and *cover*.
  - Notice that the introductory phrase, "In a secure landfill," is not a part of the subject or the predicate.
- The **pressure** <u>is maintained at about 2250 pounds per square inch</u> then <u>lowered to form steam at about 600 pounds per square inch</u>. *(compound predicate)*
  - There are two predicates in this sentence: "is maintained at about 2250 pounds per square inch" and "lowered to form steam at about 600 pounds per square inch"
- <u>Surrounding the secure landfill on all sides are</u> impermeable barrier **walls**. *(inverted sentence pattern)*
  - In an inverted sentence, the predicate comes before the subject. You won't run into this sentence structure very often as it is pretty rare.

A predicate can include the verb, a direct object, and an indirect object.

Direct Object

A direct object—a noun, pronoun, phrase, or clause acting as a noun—takes the action of the main verb (e.g., the verb is happening to the object). A direct object can be identified by putting *what?*, *which?*, or *whom?* in its place.

- The housing assembly of a mechanical pencil contains the mechanical **workings** of the pencil.
- Lavoisier used curved glass **discs** fastened together at their rims, with wine filling the space between, to focus the sun's rays to attain temperatures of 3000° F.
- The dust and smoke lofted into the air by nuclear explosions might cool the earth's **atmosphere** some number of degrees.
- A 20 percent fluctuation in average global temperature could reduce biological **activity**, shift weather **patterns**, and ruin **agriculture**. *(compound direct object)*

Indirect Object

An indirect object—a noun, pronoun, phrase, or clause acting as a noun—receives the action expressed in the sentence. It can be identified by inserting *to* or *for*.

- The company is designing senior **citizens** a new walkway to the park area.
  - The company is not designing new models of senior citizens; they are designing a new walkway *for* senior citizens. Thus, senior citizens is the indirect object of this sentence.
- Please send the personnel **office** a resume so we can further review your candidacy.
  - You are not being asked to send the office somewhere; you're being asked to send a resume *to* the office. Thus, the personnel office is the indirect object of this sentence.

Note: Objects can belong to any verb in a sentence, even if the verbs aren't in the main clause. For example, let's look at the sentence "When you give your teacher your assignment, be sure to include your name and your class number."

- *Your teacher* is the indirect object of the verb *give*.
- *Your assignment* is the direct object of the verb *give*.
- *Your name* and *your class number* are the direct objects of the verb *include*.

Phrases and Clauses

Phrases and clauses are groups of words that act as a unit and perform a single function within a sentence. A phrase may have a partial subject or verb but not both; a dependent clause has both a subject and a verb (but is not a complete sentence). Here are a few examples (not all phrases are highlighted because some are embedded in others):

Phrases	Clauses
Electricity has to do **with those physical phenomena** involving electrical charges and their effects when **in motion** and when **at rest** (*involving electrical charges and their effects* is also a phrase).	Electricity manifests itself as a force of attraction, independent of gravitational and short-range nuclear attraction, **when two oppositely charged bodies are brought close to one another**.
In 1833, Faraday's experimentation **with electrolysis** indicated a natural unit **of electrical charge**, thus **pointing to a discrete rather than continuous charge**. (*to a discrete rather than continuous charge* is also a phrase.)	**Since the frequency is the speed of sound divided by the wavelength**, a shorter wavelength means a higher wavelength.
The symbol that denotes a connection **to the grounding conductor** is three parallel horizontal lines, each of the lower ones **being shorter than the one above it**.	Nuclear units planned or in construction have a total capacity of 186,998 KW, **which, if current plans hold, will bring nuclear capacity to about 22% of all electrical capacity by 1995**. (*if current plans hold* is a clause within a clause)

There are two types of clauses: dependent and independent. A dependent clauses is dependent on something else: it cannot stand on its own. An independent clause, on the other hand, is free to stand by itself.

So how can you tell if a clause is dependent or independent? Let's take a look at two the clauses from the table above:

- when two oppositely charged bodies are brought close to one another
- Since the frequency is the speed of sound divided by the wavelength
- which, if current plans hold, will bring nuclear capacity to about 22% of all electrical capacity by 1995

These are all dependent clauses. Any clause with a subordinating conjunctions (like *when* or *since*) is a dependent clause. For example "I was a little girl in 1995" is an independent clause, but "Because I was a little girl in 1995" is a dependent clause. Clauses that start with relative pronouns, like *which*, also become dependent clauses.
CC licensed content, Shared previously

Common Sentence Structures

Basic Sentence Patterns

Subject + verb

The simplest of sentence patterns is composed of a **subject** and **verb** without a direct object or subject complement. It uses an <u>intransitive verb</u>, that is, a verb requiring no direct object:

- Control **rods remain** inside the fuel assembly of the reactor.
- The **development** of wind power practically **ceased** until the early 1970s.
- The **cross-member** exposed to abnormal stress eventually **broke**.
- Only two **types** of charge **exist** in nature.

Subject + verb + direct object

Another common sentence pattern uses the **direct object**:

- **Silicon conducts electricity** in an unusual way.
- The anti-reflective **coating** on the silicon cell **reduces reflection** from 32 to 22 percent.

Subject + verb + indirect object + direct object

The sentence pattern with the **indirect object** and **direct object** is similar to the preceding pattern:

- **I am writing her** about a number of **problems** that I have had with my computer.
- **Austin, Texas, has** recently **built** its **citizens** a **system** of bike lanes.

Sentence Types

Simple Sentences

A simple sentence is one that contains a **subject** and a **verb** and no other independent or dependent clause.

- **One** of the tubes **is attached** to the manometer part of the instrument indicating the pressure of the air within the cuff.
- There **are** basically two **types** of stethoscopes.
  - In this sentence, the subject and verb are inverted; that is, the verb comes before the subject. However, it is still classified as a simple sentence.
- To measure blood pressure, a **sphygmomanometer** and a **stethoscope are needed**.
  - This sentence has a compound subject—that is, there are two subjects—but it is still classified as a simple sentence.

Command sentences are a subtype of simple sentences. These sentences are unique because they don't actually have a subject:

- **Clean** the dishes.
- **Make** sure to take good notes today.
- After completing the reading, **answer** the following questions.

In each of these sentences, there is an implied subject: *you*. These sentences are instructing the reader to complete a task. Command sentences are the only sentences in English that are complete without a subject.

Compound Predicates

A **predicate** is everything in the verb part of the sentence after the subject (unless the sentence uses inverted word order). A *compound predicate* is two or more predicates joined by a coordinating conjunction. Traditionally, the conjunction in a sentence consisting of just two compound predicates is not punctuated.

- Another library media specialist **has been using Accelerated Reader for ten years** and **has seen great results**.
- This cell phone app lets users **share pictures instantly with followers** and **categorize photos with hashtags**.

Compound Sentences

A compound sentence is made up of two or more *independent clauses* joined by a <u>coordinating conjunction</u> (and, or, nor, but, yet, for) and a comma, an adverbial conjunction and a semicolon, or just a semicolon.

- In sphygmomanometers, too narrow a cuff can result in erroneously high readings, <u>and</u> too wide a cuff can result in erroneously low readings.
- Some cuff hook together<u>;</u> others wrap or snap into place.

Command sentences can be compound sentences as well:

- Never give up<u>;</u> never surrender.
- Turn the handle 90 degrees <u>and</u> push the button four times.

When you have a compound command sentence with a coordinating conjunction, you do not need to include a comma, because the two have the same subject.

Punctuation Patterns

While your sentence's punctuation will always depend on the content of your writing, there are a few common punctuation patterns you should be aware of.

Simple sentences have these punctuation patterns:

- _____.
- _____, _____.

Compound predicate sentences have this punctuation pattern: _____ _____ and _____.

Compound Sentences have these punctuation patterns:

- _____, and _____.
- _____; _____.

As you can see from these common patterns, periods, commas, and semicolons are the punctuation marks you will use the most in your writing. As you write, it's best to use a variety of these patterns. If you use the same pattern repeatedly, your writing can easily become boring and drab.

Run-on Sentences

Run-on sentences occur when two or more independent clauses are improperly joined. One type of run-on that you've probably heard of is the *comma splice*, in which two independent clauses are joined by a comma without a coordinating conjunction (*and, or, but*, etc.).

Let's look at a few examples of run-on sentences:

- Choosing a topic for a paper can be the hardest part but it gets a lot easier after that.
- Sometimes, books do not have the most complete information, it is a good idea then to look for articles in specialized periodicals.

All three of these have two independent clauses. Each clause should be separated from another with a period, a semicolon, or a comma and a coordinating conjunction:

- Choosing a topic for a paper can be the hardest part, but it gets a lot easier after that.
- Sometimes, books do not have the most complete information; it is a good idea then to look for articles in specialized periodicals.

> **Note:** Caution should be exercised when defining a run-on sentence as a sentence that just goes on and on. A run-on sentence is a sentence that goes on and on **and** isn't correctly punctuated. Not every long sentence is a run-on sentence. For example, look at this quote from *The Great Gastby*:
>
> Its vanished trees, the trees that had made way for Gatsby's house, had once pandered in whispers to the last and greatest of all human dreams; for a transitory enchanted moment man must have held his breath in the presence of this continent, compelled into an aesthetic contemplation he neither understood nor desired, face to face for the last time in history with something commensurate to his capacity for wonder.
>
> If you look at the punctuation, you'll see that this quote is a single sentence. F. Scott Fitzgerald used commas and semicolons is such a way that, despite its great length, it's grammatically sound, as well. Length is no guarantee of a run-on sentence.

Common Causes of Run-Ons

We often write run-on sentences because we sense that the sentences involved are closely related and dividing them with a period just doesn't seem right. We may also write them because the parts seem too short to need any division, like in "She loves skiing but he doesn't." However, "She loves skiing" and "he doesn't" are both independent clauses, so they need to be divided by a comma and a coordinating conjunction—not just a coordinating conjunction by itself.

Another common cause of run-on sentences is mistaking adverbial conjunctions for coordinating conjunctions. For example if we were to write, "She loved skiing, however he didn't," we would have produced a comma splice. The correct sentence would be "She loved skiing; however, he didn't."

Fixing Run-On Sentences

Before you can fix a run-on sentence, you'll need to identify the problem. When you write, carefully look at each part of every sentence. Are the parts independent clauses, or are they dependent clauses or phrases? Remember, only independent clauses can stand on their own. This also means they have to stand on their own; they can't run together without correct punctuation.

Let's take a look at a few run-on sentences and their revisions:

> Most of the hours I've earned toward my associate's degree do not transfer, however, I do have at least some hours the University will accept.
> The opposite is true of stronger types of stainless steel they tend to be more susceptible to rust.
> Some people were highly educated professionals, others were from small villages in underdeveloped countries.

Let's start with the first sentence. This is a comma-splice sentence. The adverbial conjunction *however* is being treated like a coordinating conjunction. There are two easy fixes to this problem. The first is to turn the comma before *however* into a period. If this feels like too hard of a stop between ideas, you can change the comma into a semicolon instead.

- Most of the hours I've earned toward my associate's degree do not transfer. However, I do have at least some hours the University will accept.
- Most of the hours I've earned toward my associate's degree do not transfer; however, I do have at least some hours the University will accept.

The second sentence is a run-on as well. "The opposite is true of stronger types of stainless steel" and "they tend to be more susceptible to rust." are both independent clauses. The two clauses are very closely related, and the second clarifies the information provided in the first. The best solution is to insert a colon between the two clauses:

> The opposite is true of stronger types of stainless steel: they tend to be more susceptible to rust.

What about the last example? Once again we have two independent clauses. The two clauses provide contrasting information. Adding a conjunction could help the reader move from one kind of information to another. However, you may want that sharp contrast. Here are two revision options:

- Some people were highly educated professionals, while others were from small villages in underdeveloped countries.
- Some people were highly educated professionals. Others were from small villages in underdeveloped countries.

CC licensed content, Shared previously

Sentence Fragments

Fragments are simply grammatically incomplete sentences—they are phrases and dependent clauses. These are grammatical structures that cannot stand on their own: they need to be connected to an independent clause to work in writing. So how can we tell the difference between a sentence and a sentence fragment? And how can we fix fragments when they already exist?

As you learn about fragments, keep in mind that length is not very helpful when determining if a sentence is a fragment or not. Both of the items below are fragments:

- Before you go.
- Ensuring his own survival with his extensive cache of supplies (food, water, rope, tarps, knives, and a first aid kit).

Let's dive in and see just what makes these both fragments.

Common Causes of Fragments

Part of the reason we write in fragments is because we often speak that way. However, there is a difference between writing and speech, and it is important to write in full sentences. Additionally, fragments often come about in writing because a fragment may already seem too long.

Non-finite verbs (gerunds, participles, and infinitives) can often trip people up as well. Since non-finite verbs don't act like verbs, we don't count them as verbs when we're deciding if we have a phrase or a clause. Let's look at a few examples of these:

- Running away from my mother.
- To ensure your safety and security.
- Beaten down since day one.

Even though all of the above have non-finite verbs, they're phrases, not clauses. In order for these to be clauses, they would need an additional verb that acts as a verb in the sentence.

Words like *since*, *when*, and *because* turn an independent clause into a dependent clause. For example "I was a little girl in 1995" is an independent clause, but "Because I was a little girl in 1995" is a dependent clause. This class of word includes the following: after, although, as, as far as, as if, as long as, as soon as, as though, because, before, even if, even though, every time, if, in order that, since, so, so that, than, though, unless, until, when, whenever, where, whereas, wherever, and while.

Relative pronouns, like *that* and *which*, do the same type of thing as those listed above.

Coordinating conjunctions (our FANBOYS) can also cause problems. If you start a sentence with a coordinating conjunction, make sure that it is followed a complete clause, not just a phrase!

As you're identifying fragments, keep in mind that command sentences are *not* fragments, despite not having a subject. Commands are the only grammatically correct sentences that lack a subject:

- Drop and give me fifty!
- Count how many times the word *fragrant* is used during commercial breaks.

Fixing Sentence Fragments

Let's take a look at a couple of examples:

> Ivana appeared at the committee meeting last week. And made a convincing presentation of her ideas about the new product.
> The committee considered her ideas for a new marketing strategy quite powerful. The best ideas that they had heard in years.
> She spent a full month evaluating his computer-based instructional materials. Which she eventually sent to her supervisor with the strongest of recommendations.

Let's look at the phrase "And made a convincing presentation of her ideas about the new product" in example one. It's just that: a phrase. There is no subject in this phrase, so the easiest fix is to simply delete the period and combine the two statements:

> Ivana appeared at the committee meeting last week and made a convincing presentation of her ideas about the new product.

Let's look at example two. The phrase "the best ideas they had heard in years" is simply a phrase—there is no verb contained in the phrase. By adding "they were" to the beginning of this phrase, we have turned the fragment into an independent clause, which can now stand on its own:

> The committee considered her ideas for a new marketing strategy quite powerful; they were the best ideas that they had heard in years.

What about example three? Let's look at the clause "Which she eventually sent to her supervisor with the strongest of recommendations." This is a dependent clause; the word *which* signals this fact. If we change "which she eventually" to "eventually, she," we also turn the dependent clause into an independent clause.

> She spent a full month evaluating his computer-based instructional materials. Eventually, she sent the evaluation to her supervisor with the strongest of recommendations.

CC licensed content, Shared previously

Parallel Structure

What exactly is parallel structure? It's simply the practice of using the same structures or forms multiple times: making sure the parts are parallel to each other. Parallel structure can be applied to a single sentence, a paragraph, or even multiple paragraphs. Compare the two following sentences:

- Yara loves running, to swim, and biking.
- Yara loves running, swimming, and biking.

Was the second sentence a smoother read than the first? The second sentence uses parallelism—all three verbs are gerunds—whereas in the first sentence two are gerunds and one is an infinitive. While the first sentence is technically correct, it's easy to trip up over the mismatching items. The application of parallelism improves writing style and readability, and it makes sentences easier to process.

Compare the following examples:

- Lacking parallelism: "She likes cooking, jogging, and to read."
- Parallel: "She likes cooking, jogging, and reading."
- Parallel: "She likes to cook, jog, and read."

Once again, the examples above combine gerunds and infinitives. To make them parallel, the sentences should be rewritten with just gerunds or just infinitives. Note that the nonparallel example, while inelegantly worded, is grammatically correct: "cooking," "jogging," and "to read" are all grammatically valid conclusions to "She likes."

- Lacking parallelism: "The dog ran across the yard and jumped over the fence, and **down the alley he sprinted**."
- Parallel: "The dog ran across the yard, jumped over the fence, and **sprinted down the alley**."

The nonparallel example, is grammatically valid; "down the alley he sprinted" is an entirely separate clause. However, it is not parallel. You may find that the parallel example sounds much better to your ears.

Parallelism can also apply to names. If you're writing a research paper that includes references to several different authors, you should be consistent in your references. For example, if you talk about Jane Goodall and Henry Harlow, you should say "Goodall and Harlow," not "Jane and Harlow" or "Goodall and Henry." This is something that would carry on through your entire paper: you should use the same mode of address for every person you mention.

You can also apply parallelism across a passage:

> Manuel painted eight paintings in the last week. Jennifer sculpted five statues in the last month. Zama wrote fifteen songs in the last two months.

Each of the sentences in the preceding paragraph has the same structure: Name + *-ed* verb + number of things + *in the* past time period. When using parallelism across multiple sentences, be sure that you're using it well. If you aren't careful, you can stray into being repetitive. Unfortunately, really the only way to test this is by re-reading the passage and seeing if it "feels right." While this test doesn't have any rules to it, it can often help.

Rhetoric and Parallelism

Parallelism can also involve repeated words or repeated phrases. These uses are part of "rhetoric" (a field that focuses on persuading readers) Here are a few examples of repetition:

- "**The inherent vice** of capitalism is the unequal sharing of blessings; **the inherent virtue** of socialism is the equal sharing of miseries." —Winston Churchill

- "Let every nation know, whether it wishes us well or ill, that we shall **pay any price, bear any burden, meet any hardship, support any friend, oppose any foe** to assure the survival and the success of liberty." —John F. Kennedy
- "And that government **of the people, by the people, for the people**, shall not perish from the earth." —Abraham Lincoln, *Gettysburg Address*

When used this way, parallelism makes your writing or speaking much stronger. These repeated phrases seem to bind the work together and make it more powerful—and more inspiring. This use of parallelism can be especially useful in writing conclusions of academic papers or in persuasive writing.

Active and Passive Voice

There are two main "voices" in English writing: the active voice and the passive voice. You've probably heard a lot about them—and you've probably been warned away from the passive voice. But what exactly are they?

In the simplest terms, an active voice sentence is written in the form of "A does B." (For example, "Carmen sings the song.") A passive voice sentence is written in the form of "B is done by A." (For example, "The song is sung by Carmen.") Both constructions are grammatically sound and correct. Let's look at a couple more examples of the passive voice:

- I've been hit! (*or*, I have been hit!)
- Jasper was thrown from the car when it was struck from behind.

You may have noticed something unique about the previous two sentences: the subject of the sentence is not the person (or thing) performing the action. The passive voice "hides" who does the action. Despite these sentences being completely grammatically sound, we don't know who hit "me" or what struck the car.

The passive is created using the verb *to be* and the past participle. When identifying passive sentences, remember that *to be* has other uses than just creating the passive voice. "She was falling" and "His keys were lost" are not passive sentences. In the first, *to be* is a continuous past verb, and in the second *to be* is past tense linking verb. There are two key features that will help you identify a passive sentence:

Something is happening (the sentence has a verb that is not a linking verb).
The subject of the sentence is not doing that thing.

Usage

As you read at the two sentences below, think about the how the different voice may affect the meaning or implications of the sentence:

- **Passive voice:** The rate of evaporation is controlled by the size of an opening.
- **Active voice:** The size of an opening controls the rate of evaporation.

The passive choice slightly emphasizes "the rate of evaporation," while the active choice emphasizes "the size of an opening." Simple. So why all the fuss? Because passive constructions can produce grammatically tangled sentences such as this:

Groundwater flow is influenced by zones of fracture concentration, as can be recognized by the two model simulations (see Figures 1 and 2), by which one can see . . .

The sentence is becoming a burden for the reader, and probably for the writer too. As often happens, the passive voice here has smothered potential verbs and kicked off a runaway train of prepositions. But the reader's task gets much easier in the revised version below:

Two model simulations (Figures 1 and 2) illustrate how zones of fracture concentration influence groundwater flow. These simulations show . . .

To revise the above, all we did was look for the two buried things (simulations and zones) in the original version that could actually *do* something, and we made the sentence clearly about these two nouns by placing them in front of active verbs. This is the general principle to follow as you compose in the active voice: Place concrete nouns that can perform work in front of active verbs.

Revise Weak Passive-Voice Sentences

As we've mentioned, the passive voice can be a shifty operator—it can cover up its source, that is, who's doing the acting, as this example shows:

- **Passive:** The papers **will be graded** according to the criteria stated in the syllabus.
  - *Graded by whom though?*
- **Active: The teacher** will grade the papers according to the criteria stated in the syllabus.

It's this ability to cover the actor or agent of the sentence that makes the passive voice a favorite of people in authority—policemen, city officials, and, yes, teachers. At any rate, you can see how the passive voice can cause wordiness, indirectness, and comprehension problems.

Passive	Question	Active
Your figures **have been reanalyzed** in order to determine the coefficient of error. The results **will be announced** when the situation is judged appropriate.	Who analyzes, and who will announce?	**We** have reanalyzed your figures in order to determine the range of error. **We** will announce the results when the time is right.
With the price of housing at such inflated levels, those loans **cannot be paid** off in any shorter period of time.	Who can't pay the loans off?	With the price of housing at such inflated levels, **homeowners** cannot pay off those loans in any shorter period of time.
After the arm of the hand-held stapler **is pushed** down, the blade from the magazine **is raised by** the top-leaf spring, and the magazine and base.	Who pushes it down, and who or what raises it?	After **you** push down on the arm of the hand-held stapler, **the top-leaf spring** raises the blade from the magazine, and the magazine and base move apart.
However, market share **is being lost by** 5.25-inch diskettes as is shown in the graph in Figure 2.	Who or what is losing market share, who or what shows it?	However, **5.25-inch diskettes** are losing market share as the graph in **Figure 2** shows.
For many years, federal regulations concerning the use of wire-tapping **have been ignored**. Only recently **have** tighter restrictions **been imposed** on the circumstances that warrant it.	Who has ignored the regulations, and who is now imposing them?	For many years, **government officials** have ignored federal regulations concerning the use of wire-tapping. Only recently has **the federal government** imposed tighter restrictions on the circumstances that warrant it.

Don't get the idea that the passive voice is always wrong and should never be used. It is a good writing technique when we don't want to be bothered with an obvious or too-often-repeated subject and when we need to rearrange words in a sentence for emphasis. The next page will focus more on how and why to use the passive voice.

There are several different situations where the passive voice is more useful than the active voice.

- When you don't know who did the action: *The paper had been moved.*
  - The active voice would be something like this: "Someone had moved the paper." While this sentence is technically fine, the passive voice sentence has a more subtle element of mystery, which can be especially helpful in creating a mood in fiction.
- When you want to hide who did the action: *The window had been broken.*
  - The sentence is either hiding who broke the window or they do not know. Again, the sentence can be reformed to say "Someone had broken the window," but using the word *someone* clearly indicates that someone (though we may not know who) is at fault here. Using the passive puts the focus on the window rather than on the person who broke it, as he or she is completely left out of the sentence.

- When you want to emphasize the person or thing the action was done to: *Caroline was hurt when Kent broke up with her.*
  - We automatically focus on the subject of the sentence. If the sentence were to say "Kent hurt Caroline when he broke up with her," then our focus would be drawn to Kent rather than Caroline.
- A subject that can't actually *do* anything: *Caroline was hurt when she fell into the trees.*
  - While the trees hurt Caroline, they didn't actually do anything. Thus, it makes more sense to have Caroline as the subject rather than saying "The trees hurt Caroline when she fell into them."

Note: It's often against convention in scholarly writing to use *I*. While this may seem like a forced rule, it also stems from the fact that scholars want to emphasize the science or research as opposed to the author of the paper. This often results in the passive voice being the best choice. This is not the case in other formal settings, such as in resumes and in cover letters.

Using the Passive

Now that we know there are some instances where passive voice is the best choice, how do we use the passive voice to its fullest? The answer lies in writing direct sentences—in passive voice—that have simple subjects and verbs. Compare the two sentences below:

- Photomicrographs were taken to facilitate easy comparison of the samples.
- Easy comparison of the samples was facilitated by the taking of photomicrographs.

Both sentences are written in the passive voice, but for most ears the first sentence is more direct and understandable, and therefore preferable. Depending on the context, it does a clearer job of telling us what was done and why it was done. Especially if this sentence appears in the "Experimental" section of a report (and thus readers already know that the authors of the report took the photomicrographs), the first sentence neatly represents what the authors actually did—took photomicrographs—and why they did it—to facilitate easy comparison.

AThe passive voice can also be used following relative pronouns like *that* and *which*.

- I moved into the house **that was built** for me.
- Adrián's dog loves the treats **that are given** to him.
- Brihanna has an album **that was signed** by the Beastie Boys.

In each of these sentences, it is grammatically sound to omit (or *elide*) the pronoun and *to be*. Elision is used with a lot of different constructions in English; we use it shorten sentences when things are understood. However, we can only use elision in certain situations, so be careful when removing words! You may find these elided sentences more natural:

- I moved into the house **built** for me.
- Adrián's dog loves the treats **given** to him.
- Brihanna has an album **signed** by the Beastie Boys

CC licensed content, Shared previously

Mechanics: Word Choice

Nouns

Nouns are a diverse group of words, and they are very common in English. Nouns are a category of words defining **things**—the name of people (Dr. Sanders, lawyers), places (Kansas, factory, home), things (scissors, sheet music, book), or ideas (love, truth, beauty, intelligence).

Pluralization

English has both regular and irregular plural nouns. Regular plurals follow this rule (and other similar rules), but irregular plurals are, well, not regular and don't follow a "standard" rule.

Regular Plurals

Let's start with regular plurals: **regular plural nouns** use established patterns to indicate there is more than one of a thing. As was mentioned earlier, we add the plural suffix –s or –es to most words (*cats*, *zebras*, *classes*, *foxes*, *heroes*). Remember that when words have a foreign origin (e.g.,Latin, Greek, Spanish), we just add the plural suffix –s (*tacos*, *avocados*, *maestros*).

When a word ends in *y* and there is a consonant before *y*, we change the *y* to *i* and add –es. Thus *sky* becomes *skies*. However, if the *y* follows another vowel, you simply add an –s. (*donkeys*, *alloys*). When a word ends in –*f* or –*fe*, we change the *f* to *v* and add –es (*calves*, *leaves*). However, if there are two terminal *f*s or if you still pronounce the *f* in the plural, you simply add an –s (*cliffs*, *chiefs*).

Irregular Plurals

Irregular plurals, unlike regular plurals, don't necessarily follow any particular pattern—instead, they follow a lot of *different* patterns. Because of this, irregular plurals require a lot of memorization. If you're ever in doubt, the dictionary is there for you.

The first kind of irregular plural we'll talk about is the **no-change** or **base plural**. In these words, the singular noun has the exact same form as the plural (*sheep*, *fish*, *deer*, *moose*). Most no-change plurals are types of animals. The next type of irregular is the **mid-word vowel change**. This includes words like *tooth*, *man*, and *mouse*, which become *teeth*, *men*, and *mice*.

> **Note:** The plural for a computer mouse (as opposed to the fuzzy animal) can either be *mice* or *mouses*. Some people prefer *mouses* as it creates some differentiation between the two words.

We also have the **plural –en.** In these words –en is used as the plural ending instead of –s or -es.

- child → children
- ox → oxen
- brother → brethren
- sister → sistren

> **Note:** *Brethren* and *sistren* are antiquated terms that you're unlikely to run into in your life; however, since these are the only four words in English that use this plural, all four have been included above.

The last category of irregular plurals is borrowed words. These words are native to other languages (e.g., Latin, Greek) and have retained the pluralization rules from their original tongue.

Singular -us; Plural -i	cactus → cacti	fungus → fungi	syllabus → syllabi
Singular -a; Plural -ae	formula → formulae	vertebra → vertebrae	larva → larvae
Singular -ix, -ex; Plural -ices, -es	appendix → appendices	matrix → matrices	index → indices
Singular -on, -um; Plural -a	bacterium → bacteria	criterion → criteria	medium → media
Singular -is; Plural -es	thesis → theses	analysis → analyses	crisis → crises

The rules presented in the table above are almost always followed, but as a borrowed word becomes more popular in its usage, it can be adopted into regular pluralization. For example, *formulas* and *appendixes* are accepted words in formal situation. Additionally, in informal speech, *cactuses* and *funguses* are acceptable.

> **Note:** Because of the word's history, *octopuses* is preferred to *octopi*, but *octopi* is an accepted word.

Practice

Look at each word in the table below. Identify if the words is singular or plural, then write the other version of the word and explain which rule the plural has used in its formation. For example:

- *stimuli* is the plural of *stimulus*. The singular ends with a *-us*, so the plural ends with an *-i*.
- *ox* is the singular of *oxen*. This is an *-en* noun. To form the plural, an *-en* was added.

reefs		boys		waltz	
memorandum		hypothesis		phenomena	
focus		vertebra		appendices	

children		squid		man

Show Answer

There are a lot of ways to categorize nouns: concrete vs. abstract nouns, common vs. proper nouns, count vs. non-count nouns, and compound vs. non-compound nouns. Let's take a look at each of these kinds of categorization and see exactly what they each mean.

Concrete vs. Abstract Nouns

Concrete nouns are things you can hold, see, or otherwise sense, like *book*, *light*, or *warmth*.

Abstract nouns, on the other hand, are (as you might expect) abstract concepts, like *time* and *love*.

- concrete noun: rock
- abstract noun: justice

Common vs. Proper Nouns

Common nouns are generic words, like *tissue* or *watch*. They are lower-cased (unless they begin a sentence). A proper noun, on the other hand, is the name of a specific thing, like the brand name *Kleenex* or *Rolex*. Proper nouns are always capitalized.

- common noun: name
- proper noun: Ester

> **Note:** This rule also applies to adjectives that are based on proper nouns:
>
> - It's often difficult to understand Shakespearian language.
> - After her encounter with Lukas, Elisa vowed to hate all Swiss men.
>
> However, when you're talking about *swiss cheese*, *pasteurized milk*, and *french fries*, these adjectives lower-cased. They have a non-literal meaning: the cheese isn't really from Switzerland, Louie Pasteur didn't treat the milk himself, and the fries aren't really from France.

Count vs. Non-Count Nouns

A **count noun** (also **countable noun**) is a noun that can be modified by a numeral (*three chairs*) and that occurs in both singular and plural forms (*chair, chairs*). The can also be preceded by words such as *a, an,* or *the* (*a chair*). Quite literally, count nouns are nouns which can be counted.

A **non-count noun** (also **mass noun**), on the other hand, has none of these properties. It can't be modified by a numeral (*three furniture* is incorrect), occur in singular/plural (*furnitures* is not a word), or co-occur with *a, an,* or *the* (*a furniture* is incorrect). Again, quite literally, non-count nouns are nouns which cannot be counted.

Less or Fewer? Many or Much?

The adjectives *less* and *fewer* are both used to indicate a smaller amount of the noun they modify. *Many* and *much* are used to indicate a large amount of something. People often will use these words interchangeably; however, the words *fewer* and *many* are used with count nouns, while *less* and *much* are used with non-count nouns:

- The pet day care has **fewer** dogs than cats this week.
- Next time you make these cookies, you should use **less** sugar.
- **Many** poets struggle when they try to determine if a poem is complete or not.
- There's too **much** goodness in her heart for her own good.

You may have noticed that *much* has followed the adverb *too* in this example (*too much*). This is because you rarely find *much* by itself. You don't really hear people say things like "Now please leave me alone; I have *much* research to do." The phrase "a lot of" has taken its place in current English: "I have a lot of research to do." *A lot of* can be used in the place of either *many* or *much*:

- **A lot of** poets struggle when they try to determine if a poem is complete or not.
- There's **a lot of** goodness in her heart for her own good.

Compound Nouns

A **compound noun** is a noun phrase made up of two nouns, e.g. *bus driver*, in which the first noun acts as a sort of adjective for the second one, but without really describing it. (For example, think about the difference between *a black bird* and *a blackbird*.)

Figure 1. A crow is a black bird, while a blackbird is a specific species of bird.

Compound nouns can be made up of two or more other words, but each compound has a single meaning. There are three typical structures of compound nouns.

Types of Compound Nouns

Compounds may be written in three different ways:

- **The solid or closed forms** in which two usually moderately short words appear together as one: *housewife, lawsuit, wallpaper, basketball*, etc.
- **The hyphenated form** in which two or more words are connected by a hyphen: *house-builder, single-mindedness, rent-a-cop*, and *mother-of-pearl*.
- **The open or spaced form** consisting of newer combinations of usually longer words, such as *distance learning, player piano, lawn tennis*, etc.

Hyphens are often considered a squishy part on language (we'll discuss this further in Text: Hyphens and Dashes). Because of this, you can encounter open, hyphenated, and closed forms for the same compound noun, such as the triplets *container ship/container-ship/containership* and *particle board/particle-board/particleboard*.

If you're ever in doubt whether a compound should be closed, hyphenated, or open, dictionaries are your best reference.

Plurals

The process of making compound nouns plural has its own set of conventions to follow. In all forms of compound nouns, we pluralize the chief element of a compound word (i.e., we pluralize the primary noun of the compound).

- fisher**man** → fisher**men**
- black **bird** → black **birds**
- **passer**by → **passers**by

The word *hand-me-down* doesn't have a distinct primary noun, so its plural is *hand-me-downs*.
CC licensed content, Shared previously

- Text: Pluralization. **Provided by**: Lumen Learning. **License**: *CC BY: Attribution*
- Image of two men. **Authored by**: Gregor Cresnar. **Provided by**: The Noun Project. **Located at**: https://thenounproject.com/search/?q=people&i=176708. **License**: *CC BY: Attribution*
- Text: Common vs. Proper Nouns and Concrete vs. Abstract Nouns. **Provided by**: Lumen Learning. **License**: *CC BY: Attribution*
- Count noun. **Provided by**: Wikipedia. **Located at**: https://en.wikipedia.org/wiki/Count_noun. **License**: *CC BY-SA: Attribution-ShareAlike*
- Mass noun. **Provided by**: Wikipedia. **Located at**: https://en.wikipedia.org/wiki/Mass_noun. **License**: *CC BY-SA: Attribution-ShareAlike*
- English compound. **Provided by**: Wikipedia. **Located at**: https://en.wikipedia.org/wiki/English_compound. **License**: *CC BY-SA: Attribution-ShareAlike*
- Compound noun. **Provided by**: Teflpedia. **Located at**: http://teflpedia.com/Compound_noun. **License**: *CC BY-SA: Attribution-ShareAlike*
- Crow. **Authored by**: Valters Krontals. **Located at**: https://flic.kr/p/ayxZnp. **License**: *CC BY: Attribution*
- Common Blackbird. **Authored by**: Andreas Trepte. **Located at**: https://commons.wikimedia.org/wiki/File:Common_Blackbird.jpg. **License**: *CC BY-SA: Attribution-ShareAlike*
- Revision and Adaptation. **Provided by**: Lumen Learning. **License**: *CC BY-SA: Attribution-ShareAlike*

Pronoun Cases and Types

A pronoun stands in the place of a noun. Like nouns, pronouns can serve as the subject or object of a sentence: they are the things sentences are about. Pronouns include words like *he*, *she*, and *I*, but they also include words like *this*, *that*, *which*, *who*, *anybody*, and *everyone*. Before we get into the different types of pronouns, let's look at how they work in sentences.

Because a pronoun is replacing a noun, its meaning is dependent on the noun that it is replacing. This noun is called the **antecedent**. Let's look at the first sentence of this paragraph again:

Because a pronoun is replacing a noun, **its** meaning is dependent on the noun that **it** is replacing.

There are two pronouns here: *its* and *it*. *Its* and *it* both have the same antecedent: "a pronoun." Whenever you use a pronoun, you must also include its antecedent. Without the antecedent, your readers (or listeners) won't be able to figure out what the pronoun is referring to. Let's look at a couple of examples:

- Jason likes it when people look to him for leadership.
- Trini does her hair and makeup every day—with no exceptions.

So, what are the antecedents and pronouns in these sentences?

- *Jason* is the antecedent for the pronoun *him*.
- *Trini* is the antecedent for the pronoun *her*.

So far, we've only looked at personal pronouns, but there are a lot of other types, including demonstrative, and indefinite pronouns. Let's discuss each of these types in further depth:

Personal Pronouns

The following sentences give examples of personal pronouns used with antecedents:

- **That man** looks as if **he** needs a new coat. (the noun phrase *that man* is the antecedent of *he*)
- **Kat** arrived yesterday. I met **her** at the station. (*Kat* is the antecedent of *her*)
- When **they** saw us, **the lions** began roaring (*the lions* is the antecedent of *they*)
- **Adam and I** were hoping no one would find **us**. (*Adam and I* is the antecedent of *us*)

> **Note:** Pronouns like *I*, *we*, and *you* don't always require an explicitly stated antecedent. When a speaker says something like "I told you the zoo was closed today," it's implied that the speaker is the antecedent for *I* and the listener is the antecedent for *you*.

Reflexive pronouns are a kind of pronoun that are used when the subject and the object of the sentence are the

same.   **Jason** hurt **himself**. (*Jason* is the antecedent of *himself*)
              We were teasing **each other**. (*we* is the antecedent of *each other*)

This is true even if the subject is only implied, as in the sentence "Don't hurt yourself." *You* is the unstated subject of this sentence.

Reflexive pronouns include *myself, ourselves, yourself, yourselves himself, herself, itself, themselves*. They can only be used as the object of a sentence—not as the subject. You can say "I jinxed myself," but you can't say "Myself jinxed me."

Note: When the first- or second-person reflexive pronoun is appropriate, object-case and reflexive pronouns can often be used interchangeably:

The only person I'm worrying about today is **me**.
The only person I'm worrying about today is **myself**.
You don't need to make anyone happy except **you**.
You don't need to make anyone happy except **yourself**.

Why do you think this is? When would you use one or the other?

Pronouns may be classified by three categories: person, number, and case.

Person refers to the relationship that an author has with the text that he or she writes, and with the reader of that text. English has three persons (first, second, and third):

First-person is the speaker or writer him- or herself. The first person is personal (*I*, *we*, etc.)
Second-person is the person who is being directly addressed. The speaker or author is saying this is about you, the listener or reader.
Third-person is the most common person used in academic writing. The author is saying this is about other people. In the third person singular there are distinct pronoun forms for male, female, and neutral gender.

There are two **numbers**: **singular** and **plural**. As we learned in nouns, singular words refer to only one a thing while plural words refer to more than one of a thing (*I* stood alone while *they* walked together).

English personal pronouns have two **cases**: **subject** and **object**. Subject-case pronouns are used when the pronoun is doing the action (*I* like to eat chips, but *she* does not). Object-case pronouns are used when something is being done to the pronoun (John likes *me* but not *her*).

Possessive pronouns are used to indicate possession (in a broad sense). Some must be accompanied by a noun: e.g., *my* or *your*, as in "I lost **my** wallet." This category of pronouns behaves similarly to adjectives. Others occur as independent phrases: e.g., *mine* or *yours*. For example, "Those clothes are **mine**."

The table below includes all of the personal pronouns in the English language. They are organized by person, number, and case:

Person	Number	Subject	Object	Possessive	
First	Singular	I	me	my	mine
	Plural	we	us	our	ours
Second	Singular	you	you	your	yours
	Plural	you	you	your	yours
Third	Singular	he	him	his	his
		she	her	her	hers
		it	it	its	its
	Plural	they	them	their	theirs

Demonstrative Pronouns

Demonstrative pronouns substitute for things being pointed out. They include *this, that, these*, and *those*. *This* and *that* are singular; *these* and *those* are plural.

The difference between *this* and *that* and between *these* and *those* is a little more subtle. *This* and *these* refer to something that is "close" to the speaker, whether this closeness is physical, emotional, or temporal. *That* and *those* are the opposite: they refer to something that is "far."

- Do I actually have to read all of *this*?
  - The speaker is indicating a text that is close to her, by using "this."
- *That* is not coming anywhere near me.
  - The speaker is distancing himself from the object in question, which he doesn't want to get any closer. The far pronoun helps indicate that.
- You're telling me you sewed all of *these*?
  - The speaker and her audience are likely looking directly at the clothes in question, so the close pronoun is appropriate.
- *Those* are all gross.
  - The speaker wants to remain away from the gross items in question, by using the far "those."

Note: these pronouns are often combined with a noun. When this happens, they act as a kind of adjective instead of as a pronoun.

- Do I actually have to read all of *this* contract?
- *That* thing is not coming anywhere near me.
- You're telling me you sewed all of *these* dresses?
- *Those* recipes are all gross.

The antecedents of demonstrative pronouns (and sometimes the pronoun *it*) can be more complex than those of personal pronouns:

- **Animal Planet's puppy cam has been taken down for maintenance.** I never wanted *this* to happen.
- I love Animal Planet's panda cam. **I watched a panda eat bamboo for half an hour.** *It* was amazing.

In the first example, the antecedent for *this* is the concept of the puppy cam being taken down. In the second example, the antecedent for *it* in this sentence is the experience of watching the panda. That antecedent isn't explicitly stated in the sentence, but comes through in the intention and meaning of the speaker.

Indefinite Pronouns

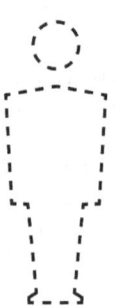

Indefinite pronouns, the largest group of pronouns, refer to one or more unspecified persons or things, for example: **Anyone** can do that.

These pronouns can be used in a couple of different ways:

- They can refer to members of a group separately rather than collectively. (To **each** his or her own.)
- They can indicate the non-existence of people or things. (**Nobody** thinks that.)
- They can refer to a person, but are not specific as to first, second or third person in the way that the personal pronouns are. (**One** does not clean **one's** own windows.)

Please note that all of these pronouns are singular. The table below shows the most common indefinite pronouns:

anybody	anyone	anything	each	either	every
everybody	everyone	everything	neither	no one	nobody
nothing	nobody else	somebody	someone	something	one

> **Note:** Sometimes third-person personal pronouns are sometimes used without antecedents—this applies to special uses such as dummy pronouns and generic *they*, as well as cases where the referent is implied by the context.
>
> - You know what *they* say.
> - *It's* a nice day today.

Singular *They*

As we've just seen, indefinite pronouns demand singular pronouns, like in "To each his or her own." However, in informal speech, you'll often hear things like "To each their own" or "Someone is singing in the hallway. If they haven't stopped in five minutes, I'm going to have to take drastic measures." If you think about your own speech, it's very likely that you use *they* as a singular pronoun for someone whose gender you don't know.

So why do people use *they* this way, even though it's a plural? It likely stems from the clunkiness of the phrase "he or she." It is also possible that *they* is following the same evolution as the word *you*. In Early Modern English, *you* was used as either a plural, second-person pronoun or as a polite form for the more common, singular *thee*. However, *you* eventually overtook almost all of the second-person pronouns, both singular and plural.

While this use of the singular *they* is still not "officially" correct—and you definitely shouldn't use this in your English papers—it's interesting to watch English change before our very eyes.

Relative Pronouns

There are five relative pronouns in English: *who, whom, whose, that*, and *which*. These pronouns are used to connect different clauses together. For example:

- Belen, **who** had starred in six plays before she turned seventeen, knew that she wanted to act on Broadway someday.
- My daughter wants to adopt the dog **that** doesn't have a tail.

These pronouns behave differently from the other categories we've seen. However, they are pronouns, and it's important to learn how they work.

Pronoun Antecedents

Antecedent Clarity

We've already defined an **antecedent** as the noun (or phrase) that a pronoun is replacing. The phrase "antecedent clarity" simply means that is should be clear who or what the pronoun is referring to. In other words, readers should be able to understand the sentence the first time they read it—not the third, forth, or tenth. In this page, we'll look at some examples of common mistakes that can cause confusion, as well as ways to fix each sentence.

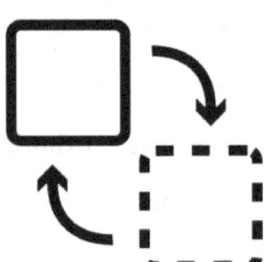

Let's take a look at our first sentence:

> Rafael told Matt to stop eating his cereal.

When you first read this sentence, is it clear if the cereal Rafael's or Matt's? Is it clear when you read the sentence again? Not really, no. Since both Rafael and Matt are singular, third person, and masculine, it's impossible to tell whose cereal is being eaten (at least from this sentence).

How would you best revise this sentence? Let's assume the cereal is Rafael's:

- Rafael told Matt to stop eating Rafael's cereal.
- Matt was eating Rafael's cereal. Rafael told him to stop it.

What if the cereal is Matt's?

- Rafael told Matt to stop eating Matt's cereal.
- Matt was eating his own cereal when Rafael told him to stop.

These aren't the only ways to revise the sentence. However, each of these new sentences has made it clear whose cereal it is.

Were those revisions what you expected them to be?

Let's take a look at another example:

> Katerina was really excited to try French cuisine on her semester abroad in Europe. They make all sorts of delicious things.

When you read this example, is it apparent who the pronoun *they* is referring to? You may guess that *they* is referring to the French—which is probably correct. However, this is not actually stated, which means that there isn't actually an antecedent. Since every pronoun needs an antecedent, the example needs to be revised to include one.

How would you best revise this sentence? Type your ideas in the text frame below, and then look at the suggested revisions.

As you write, keep these two things in mind:

- Make sure your pronouns always have an antecedent.
- Make sure that it is clear what their antecedents are.

Antecedent Agreement

As you write, make sure that you are using the correct pronouns. When a pronoun matches the person and number of its antecedent, we say that it **agrees** with it antecedent. Let's look at a couple of examples:

- I hate it when Zacharias tells me what to do. **He**'s so full of **himself**.
- The Finnegans are shouting again. I swear you could hear **them** from across town!

In the first sentence, *Zacharias* is singular, third person, and masculine. The pronouns *he* and *himself* are also singular, third person, and masculine, so they agree. In the second sentence, *the Finnegans* is plural and third person. The pronoun *them* is also plural and third person.

When you select your pronoun, you also need to ensure you use the correct case of pronoun. Remember we learned about three cases: subject, object, and possessive. The case of your pronoun should match its role in the sentence. For example, if your pronoun is doing an action, it should be a subject:

- **He** runs every morning.
- **I** hate it when **she** does this.

However, when something is being done to your pronoun, it should be an object:

- Birds have always hated **me**.
- My boss wanted to talk to **him**.
- Give **her** the phone and walk away.

However, things aren't always this straightforward. Let's take a look at some examples where things are a little more confusing.

Person and Number

Some of the trickiest agreements are with indefinite pronouns:

- Every student should do his or her best on this assignment.
- If nobody lost his or her scarf, then where did this come from?

As we learned earlier in this outcome, words like *every* and *nobody* are singular, and demand singular pronouns. Here are some of the words that fall into this category: anybody, anyone, anything, each, either, every, everybody, everyone, everything, neither, no one, nobody, nothing, one, somebody, someone, something.

Some of these may feel "more singular" than others, but they all are technically singular. Thus, using "he or she" is correct (while *they* is incorrect).

- Anyone going on this hike should plan on being in the canyon for at least seven hours; he or she should prepare accordingly.
- I know somebody has been throwing his or her trash away in my dumpster, and I want him or her to stop.

However, as you may have noticed, the phrase "he or she" (and its other forms) can often make your sentences clunky. When this happens, it may be best to revise your sentences to have plural antecedents. Because "he or she" is clunky, you'll often see issues like this:

The way each individual speaks can tell us so much about him or her. It tells us what groups they associate themselves with, both ethnically and socially.

As you can see, in the first sentence, *him or her* agrees with the indefinite pronoun *each*. However, in the second sentence, the writer has shifted to the plural *they*, even though the writer is talking about the same group of people. When you write, make sure your agreement is correct and **consistent**.

Case

You and I versus *You and Me*

Some of the most common pronoun mistakes occur with the decision between "you and I" and "you and me." People will often say things like "You and me should go out for drinks." Or—thinking back on the rule that it should be "you and I"—they will say "Susan assigned the task to both you and I." However, both of these sentences are wrong. Remember that every time you use a pronoun you need to make sure that you're using the correct case.

Let's take a look at the first sentence: "You and me should go out for drinks." Both pronouns are the subject of the sentence, so they should be in subject case: "You and I should go out for drinks."

In the second sentence (Susan assigned the task to both you and I), both pronouns are the object of the sentence, so they should be in object case: "Susan assigned the task to both you and me."

CC licensed content, Shared previously

- Text: Pronoun Antecedents. **Provided by**: Lumen Learning. **License**: *CC BY: Attribution*
- Image of two squares. **Authored by**: Didzis Gruznovs. **Provided by**: The Noun Project. **Located at**: https://thenounproject.com/search/?q=replace&i=201238. **License**: *CC BY: Attribution*
- Image of handshake. **Authored by**: Lauren Manninen. **Provided by**: The Noun Project. **Located at**: https://thenounproject.com/search/?q=agree&i=11865. **License**: *CC BY: Attribution*

Articles

There are three articles in the English language: *the, a,* and *an.* These are divided into two types of articles: definite (*the*) and indefinite (*a, an*). The definite article indicates a level of specificity that the indefinite does not. "An apple" could refer to any apple; however "the apple" is referring back to a specific apple. There are also cases where no article is required:

- with generic nouns (plural or uncountable): *cars have accelerators, happiness is contagious,* referring to cars and happiness in general (compare *the happiness I felt yesterday,* specifying particular happiness)
- with most proper names: *Sabrina, France, London,* etc.

Indefinite Article

The indefinite article of English takes the two forms *a* and *an.* These can be regarded as meaning "one," usually without emphasis.

Distinction between *a* and *an*

You've probably learned the rule that *an* comes before a vowel, and that *a* comes before a consonant. While this is generally true, it's more accurate to say that *an* comes before a vowel *sound*, and *a* comes before a consonant *sound*. Let's look at a couple of examples with *a*:

- *a box*
- *a HEPA filter* (HEPA is pronounced as a word rather than as letters)
- *a one-armed bandit* (pronounced "won. . . ")
- *a unicorn* (pronounced "yoo. . . ")

Let's try it again with *an*:

- *an apple*
- *an EPA policy* (the letter *E* read as a letter still starts with a vowel sound)
- *an SSO* (pronounced "es-es-oh")

- *an hour* (the *h* is silent)
- *an heir* (pronounced "air")

Note: Some speakers and writers use *an* before a word beginning with the sound *h* in an unstressed syllable: *an historical novel, an hotel.* However, where the *h* is clearly pronounced, this usage is now less common, and *a* is preferred.

Definite Article

The definite article *the* is used when the referent of the noun phrase is assumed to be unique or known from the context. For example, in the sentence "The boy with glasses was looking at the moon," it is assumed that in the context the reference can only be to one boy and one moon.

The can be used with both singular and plural nouns, with nouns of any gender, and with nouns that start with any letter. This is different from many other languages which have different articles for different genders or numbers. *The* is the most commonly used word in the English language.

Word Order

In most cases, the article is the first word of its noun phrase, preceding all other adjectives and modifiers.

> *The* little old red bag held *a* very big surprise.

There are a few exceptions, however:

> Certain determiners, such as *all, both, half, double,* precede the definite article when used in combination (*all the team, both the girls, half the time, double the amount*).
> *Such* and *what* precede the indefinite article (*such an idiot, what a day!*).
> Adjectives qualified by *too, so, as* and *how* generally precede the indefinite article: *too great a loss, so hard a problem, as delicious an apple as I have ever tasted, I know how pretty a girl she is.*
> When adjectives are qualified by *quite* (particularly when it means "fairly"), the word *quite* (but not the adjective itself) often precedes the indefinite article: *quite a long letter*. **Note:** the phrase *a quite long letter* is also a correct construction. However the two have different meanings:

> > In *quite a long letter, quite* modifies *letter*: it's quite a letter.
> > In *a quite long letter, quite* modifies *long*: the letter is quite long.

Prepositions

Prepositions are relation words; they can indicate location, time, or other more abstract relationships. A preposition combines with another word (usually a noun or pronoun) called the complement. Prepositions are still in bold, and their complements are in italics:

- The woods **behind** *my house* are super creepy **at** *night*.
- She sang **until** *three in the morning*.
- They were happy **for** *him*.
- He counted **to** *three*.

Prepositions generally come before their complements (e.g., **in** England, **under** the table, **of** Elena). However, there are a small handful of exceptions, including **notwithstanding** and **ago**:

- *Financial limitations* **notwithstanding**, Phil paid back his debts.
- He was released *three days* **ago**.

Prepositions of location are pretty easily defined (*near, far, over, under*, etc.), and prepositions about time are as well (*before, after, at, during*, etc.). Prepositions of "more abstract relationships," however, are a little more nebulous in their definition.

So far, all of the prepositions we've looked at have been one word (and most of them have been one syllable). The most common prepositions are one-syllable words. According to one ranking, the most common English prepositions are *on, in, to, by, for, with, at, of, from, as*.

There are also some prepositions that have more than one word:

- in spite of (She made it to work in spite of the terrible traffic.)
- by means of (He traveled by means of boat.)
- except for (Joan invited everyone to her party except for Ben.)
- next to (Go ahead and sit down next to Jean-Claude.)

Using Prepositions

A lot of struggles with prepositions come from trying to use the correct preposition. Some verbs require specific prepositions. Here's a table of some of the most commonly misused preposition/verb pairs:

different from	comply with	dependent on	think of or about
need of	profit by	glad of	bestow upon

Some verbs take a different preposition, depending on the object of the sentence:

agree with a person	agree to a proposition	part from (a person)	part with (a thing)
differ from (person or thing)	differ from or with an opinion	confide in (to trust in)	confide to (to entrust to)
reconcile with (a person)	reconcile to (a statement or idea)	confer on (to give)	confer with (to talk with)
compare with (to determine value)	compare to (because of similarity)	convenient to (a place)	convenient for (a purpose)

When multiple objects take the same preposition, you don't need to repeat the preposition. For example, in the sentence "I'll read any book by J.K. Rowling or R. L. Stine," both *J. K. Rowling* and *R. L. Stine* are objects of the preposition *by*, so it only needs to appear once in the sentence. However, you can't do this when you have different prepositions. Let's look at this using a common phrase: "We fell out of the frying pan and into the fire." If you leave out one of the prepositions, as in "We fell out of the frying pan and the fire," the sentence is saying that we fell out of the frying pan *and* out of the fire, which would be preferable, but isn't the case in this idiom.

Prepositions in Sentences

You'll often hear about **prepositional phrases**. A prepositional phrase includes a preposition and its complement (e.g., "**behind** *the house*" or "*a long time ago*"). These phrases can appear at the beginning or end of sentences. When they appear at the beginning of a sentence, they typically need a comma afterwards:

- You can drop that off behind the house.
- A long time ago, dinosaurs roamed the earth.
- As the saying goes, hard work always pays off.

Ending a Sentence with a Preposition

It is 100 percent okay to end a sentence with a preposition. The rule against doing so stems from Latin, which belongs to a completely different language family than English. Using a terminal preposition can often make your writing smoother and more concise. Winston Churchill is credited with saying "This is the sort of English up with which I will not put," when he was criticized for his use of terminal prepositions. (A more natural way to phrase Churchill's glib quote would be "This is the sort of English I will not put up with.")

However, it's still best to avoid using terminal prepositions unnecessarily. If your sentence ends with a preposition and would still mean the same thing without the preposition, take it out. For example:

- Where are you at?
- That's not what it's used for.

If you remove *at*, the sentence becomes "Where are you?" This means the same thing, so removing *at* is a good idea. However, if you remove *for*, the sentence becomes "That's not what it's used," which doesn't make sense.

- Practical Grammar and Composition. **Authored by**: Thomas Wood. **Located at**: http://www.gutenberg.org/ebooks/22577. **Project**: Project Gutenberg. **License**: *Public Domain: No Known Copyright*

Conjunctions

Conjunctions are the words that join sentences, phrases, and other words together. Conjunctions are divided into several categories, all of which follow different rules. We will discuss coordinating conjunctions, adverbial conjunctions, correlative conjunctions, and subordinating conjunctions.

Coordinating Conjunctions

The most common conjunctions are *and*, *or*, and *but*. These are all **coordinating conjunctions**. Coordinating conjunctions are conjunctions that join, or coordinate, two or more equivalent items (such as words, phrases, or sentences). The mnemonic acronym *FANBOYS* can be used to remember the most common coordinating conjunctions: *for*, *and*, *nor*, *but*, *or*, *yet*, and *so*. Here are some examples of these used in sentences:

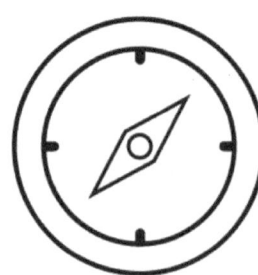

- Nuclear-powered artificial hearts proved to be complicated, bulky, **and** expensive.
- Any external injury **or** internal injury put patients at risk of uncontrolled bleeding because the small clots that formed throughout the circulatory system used up so much of the clotting factor.
- The current from the storage batteries can power lights, **but** the current for appliances must be modified within an inverter.

Rule 1: Joining Two Complete Ideas

Let's look back at one of our example sentences:

> The current from the storage batteries can power lights, but the current for appliances must be modified within an inverter.

There are two complete ideas in this sentence (a complete idea has both a subject and a verb). Because each of these ideas could stand alone as a sentence, the coordinating conjunction that joins them must be preceded by a comma. Otherwise you'll have a run-on sentence.

> Run-on sentences are one of the most common errors in college-level writing. Mastering the partnership between commas and coordinating conjunctions will go a long way towards resolving many run-on sentence issues in your writing.

Rule 2: Joining Two Similar Items

So what if there's only one complete idea, but two subjects or two verbs?

> Any external injury or internal injury put patients at risk of uncontrolled bleeding because the small clots that formed throughout the circulatory system used up so much of the clotting factor.
> In the 1960s, artificial heart devices did not fit well and tended to obstruct the flow of venous blood into the right atrium.

The first sentence has two subjects: *external injury* and *internal injury*. They are joined with the conjunction *and*. The second sentence has two verbs: *did not fit well* and *tended to obstruct*. They are joined with the conjunction *and*. In both sentences, we don't need any additional punctuation.

Rule 3: Joining Three or More Similar Items

What do you do if there are three or more items?

- Anna loves to run, David loves to hike, and Luz loves to dance.
- Fishing, hunting, and gathering were once the only ways for people do get food.
- Emanuel has a very careful schedule planned for tomorrow. He needs to work, study, exercise, eat, and clean.

As you can see in the examples above, there is a comma after each item, including the item just prior to the conjunction. There is a little bit of contention about this, but overall, most styles prefer to keep the additional comma (also called the serial comma).

Starting a Sentence

Many students are taught—and some style guides maintain—that English sentences should not start with coordinating conjunctions. However, this is not true. Students are often advised away from this in order to prevent sentence fragments, but there is nothing wrong with starting a sentence with a coordinating conjunction.

Adverbial Conjunctions

Adverbial conjunctions link two separate thoughts or sentences. When used to separate thoughts, as in the example below, a comma is required on either side of the conjunction. When used to separate complete ideas (items with both a subject and a verb), a semi-colon is required before the conjunction and a comma after.

- The first artificial hearts were made of smooth silicone rubber, which apparently caused excessive clotting and, **therefore**, uncontrolled bleeding.
- The Kedeco produces 1200 watts in 17 mph winds using a 16-foot rotor; **on the other hand**, the Dunlite produces 2000 watts in 25 mph winds.

Adverbial conjunctions include the following words; however, it is important to note that this is by no means a complete list.

therefore	however	in other words
thus	then	otherwise
nevertheless	on the other hand	in fact

Correlative Conjunctions

Correlative conjunctions are word pairs that work together to join words and groups of words of equal weight in a sentence.

The table below shows some examples of correlative conjunctions being used in a sentence:

Correlative Conjunction	Example
either . . . or	You **either** do your work **or** prepare for a trip to the office. (Either do, or prepare)
neither . . . nor	**Neither** the basketball team **nor** the football team is doing well.
not only . . . but (also)	He is **not only** handsome, **but also** brilliant. (Not only A, but also B)
	Not only is he handsome, **but also** he is brilliant. (Not only is he A, but also he is B.)
both . . . and	**Both** the cross country team **and** the swimming team are doing well.
whether . . . or	You must decide **whether** you stay **or** you go. (It's up to you)
	Whether you stay **or** you go, the film must start at 8 pm. (It's not up to you)
just as . . . so	**Just as** many Americans love basketball, **so** many Canadians love ice hockey.
as much . . . as	Football is **as much** an addiction **as** it is a sport.
no sooner . . . than	**No sooner** did she learn to ski, **than** the snow began to thaw.
rather . . . than	I would **rather** swim **than** surf.
the . . . the	**The** more you practice dribbling, **the** better you will be at it.
as . . . as	Football is **as** fast **as** hockey (is (fast)).

Subordinating Conjunctions

Subordinating conjunctions, are conjunctions that join an independent clause and a dependent clause. Here are some examples of subordinating conjunctions:

- The heart undergoes two cardiac cycle periods: diastole, **when** blood enters the ventricles, and systole, **when** the ventricles contract and blood is pumped out of the heart.
- **Whenever** an electron acquires enough energy to leave its orbit, the atom is positively charged.
- She did the favor **so that** he would owe her one.

Let's take a moment to look back at the previous examples. Can you see the pattern in comma usage? The commas aren't dependent on the presence subordinating conjunctions—they're dependent on the placement of clauses they're in. Let's revisit a couple examples and see if we can figure out the exact rules:

- The heart undergoes two cardiac cycle periods: diastole, **when** blood enters the ventricles, and systole, **when** the ventricles contract and blood is pumped out of the heart.
  - These clauses are both extra information: information that is good to know, but not necessary for the meaning of the sentence. This means they need commas on either side.
- **Whenever** an electron acquires enough energy to leave its orbit, the atom is positively charged.
  - In this sentence, the dependent clause comes before an independent clause. This means it should be followed by a comma.
- She did the favor **so that** he would owe her one.
  - In this sentence, the independent clause comes before a dependent clause. This means no comma is required.

The most common subordinating conjunctions in the English language are shown in the table below:

after	although	as	as far as	as if	as long as	as soon as
as though	because	before	even if	even though	every time	if
in order that	since	so	so that	than	though	unless
until	when	whenever	where	whereas	wherever	while

CC licensed content, Shared previously

Verb Types

Active Verbs

Active verbs are the simplest type of verb: they simply express some sort of action: e.g., *contain, roars, runs, sleeps.*

Transitive and Intransitive Verbs

Active verbs can be divided into two categories: transitive and intransitive verbs. A **transitive verb** is a verb that requires one or more objects. This contrasts with intransitive verbs, which do not have objects.

It might be helpful to think of it this way: transitive verbs have to be *done to* something or someone in the sentence. Intransitive verbs only have to be done *by* someone.

Let's look at a few examples of transitive verbs:

- We are going to **need** a bigger boat.
  - The object in this sentence is the phrase "a bigger boat." Consider how incomplete the thought would be if the sentence only said "We are going to need." Despite having a subject and a verb, the sentence is meaningless without the object phrase.
- She hates **filling out** forms.
  - *Hates* is also a transitive verb. Without the phrase "filling out forms," the phrase "She hates" doesn't make any sense.

Intransitive verbs, on the other do not take an object.

- John **sneezed** loudly.
  - Even though there's another word after *sneezed*, the full meaning of the sentence is available with just the subject *John* and the verb *sneezed*: "John sneezed." Therefore, *sneezed* is an intransitive verb. It doesn't have to be done to something or someone.
- My computer completely **died**.
  - Again, *died* here is enough for the sentence to make sense. We know that the computer (the subject) is what died.

Note: there are some verbs that can act as both transitive and intransitive verbs. Here are a few examples:

Intransitive	Transitive
The fire has **burned** for hundreds of years.	Miranda **burned** all of her old school papers.
Don't let the engine stop **running**!	Karl **ran** the best horse track this side of the river.
The vase **broke**.	She **broke** the toothpick.

Multi-Word Verbs

Multi-word verbs a subclass of active verbs. They are made up of multiple words, as you might have guessed. They include things like *stirfry*, *kickstart*, and *turn in*. Multi-word verbs often have a slightly different meaning than their base parts. Take a look at the difference between the next two sentences:

- Ben carried the boxes out of the house.
- Ben carried out the task well.

The first sentence uses a single word verb (*carried*) and the preposition *out*. If you remove the preposition (and its object), you get "Ben carried the boxes," which makes perfect sense. In the second sentence, *carried out* acts as a single entity. If you remove *out*, the sentence has no meaning: "Ben carried the task well" doesn't make sense.
Let's look at another example:

- She's been shut up in there for years.
- Dude, shut up.

Can you see how the same principles apply here? Other multi-word verbs include *find out*, *make off with*, *turn in*, and *put up with*.

Linking Verbs

A linking verb is a verb that links a subject to the rest of the sentence. There isn't any "real" action happening in the sentence. Sentences with linking verbs become similar to math equations. The verb acts as an equal sign between the items it links.

While *to be* verbs are the most common linking verbs (*is*, *was*, *were*, etc.), there are other linking verbs as well. Here are some illustrations of other common linking verbs:

- Over the past five days, Charles **has become** a new man.
  - It's easy to reimagine this sentence as "Over the past five days, Charles = a new man."
- Since the oil spill, the beach **has smelled** bad.
  - Similarly, one could also read this as "Since the oil spill, the beach = smelled bad."
- That word processing program **seems** adequate for our needs.
  - Here, the linking verb is slightly more nuanced than an equals sign, though the sentence construction overall is similar. (This is why we write in words, rather than math symbols, after all!)

Helping Verbs

Helping verbs (sometimes called *auxiliary verbs*) are, as the name suggests, verbs that help another verb. They provide support and add additional meaning. Here are some examples of helping verbs in sentences:

- Mariah **is** looking for her keys still.
- Kai **had** checked the weather three times already.

As you just saw, helping verbs include things like *is* and *had* (we'll look at a more complete list later). Let's look at some more examples to examine exactly what these verbs do. Take a look at the sentence "I have finished my dinner." Here, the main verb is *finish*, and the helping verb *have* helps to express tense. Let's look at two more examples:

- By 1967, about 500 U.S. citizens **had** received heart transplants.
  - While *received* could function on its own as a complete thought here, the helping verb *had* emphasizes the distance in time of the date in the opening phrase.
- **Do** you want tea?
  - *Do* is a helping verb accompanying the main verb *want*, used here to form a question.
- Researchers **are** finding that propranolol is effective in the treatment of heartbeat irregularities.
  - The helping verb *are* indicates the present tense, and adds a sense of continuity to the verb *finding*.

The following table provides a short list of some verbs that can function as helping verbs, along with examples of the way they function.

Helping Verb	Function	Examples
be	Express tense and a sense of continuity.	He **is** sleeping.
	Express tense and indicate the passive voice	They **were** seen.
can	Express ability	I **can** swim. Such things **can** help.
could	Express possibility	That **could** help.
do	Express negation (requires the word *not*)	You **do** not understand.
	Ask a question	**Do** you want to go?
have	Express tense and a sense of completion	They **have** understood.
might	Express possibility	We **might** give it a try.
must	Express confidence in a fact	It **must** have rained.
should	Express a request	You **should** listen.
	Express likelihood	That **should** help.
will	Express future tense	We **will** eat pie. The sun **will** rise tomorrow at 6:03.

would	Express future likelihood	Nothing **would** accomplish that.

The negative forms of these words (*can't*, *don't*, *won't*, etc.) are also helping verbs.

> **Note:** The helping verbs *to be*, *to have*, and *would* are used to indicate tense.

Verb Tenses and Agreement

Tenses

There are three standard tenses in English: past, present and future. All three of these tenses have simple and more complex forms. For now we'll just focus on the simple present (things happening now), the simple past (things that happened before), and the simple future (things that will happen later).

- **Simple Present:** work(s)
- **Simple Past:** worked
- **Simple Future:** will work

The singular third person requires a slightly different present then other persons. Look at the tables below to see the correct tenses for each person:

Person	Past	Present	Future
I	verb + *ed*	verb	will verb
We	verb + *ed*	verb	will verb
You	verb + *ed*	verb	will verb
He, She, It	verb + *ed*	verb + *s* (or *es*)	will verb
They	verb + *ed*	verb	will verb

Let's look at the verb *to walk* for an example:

Person	Past	Present	Future
I	walked	walk	will walk
We	walked	walk	will walk
You	walked	walk	will walk
He, She, It	walked	walks	will walk
They	walked	walk	will walk

Irregular Verbs

There are a lot of irregular verbs. Unfortunately, there's a lot of memorization involved in keeping them straight.

Here are the tables for *to be* and *to have* for a quick reference:

To be

Person	Past	Present	Future
I	was	am	will be
We	were	are	will be
You	were	are	will be
He, She, It	was	is	will be
They	were	are	will be

To have

Person	Past	Present	Future
I	had	have	will have
We	had	have	will have
You	had	have	will have
He, She, It	had	has	will have
They	had	have	will have

Tense Agreement

The basic idea behind sentence agreement is pretty simple: all the parts of your sentence should match (or **agree**). Verbs need to agree with their subjects in **number** (singular or plural) and in **person** (first, second, or third). In order to check agreement, you simply need to find the verb and ask who or what is doing the action of that verb, for example:

- **I** really **am** (first-person singular) vs. **We** really **are** (first-person plural)
- The **boy sings** (third-person singular) vs. The **boys sing** (third-person plural)

Compound subjects are plural, and their verbs should agree. Look at the following sentence for an example:

A pencil, a backpack, and a notebook **were** issued to each student.

Verbs will never agree with nouns that are in phrases. To make verbs agree with their subjects, follow this example:

The direction of the three plays **is** the topic of my talk.

The subject of "my talk" is *the direction,* not *plays*, so the verb should be singular.

In the English language, verbs usually come after subjects. But when this order is reversed, the writer must make the verb agree with the subject, not with a noun that happens to precede it. For example:

Beside the house **stand** sheds filled with tools.

The subject is *sheds*; it is plural, so the verb must be *stand*.

Consistency

One of the most common mistakes in writing is a lack of tense consistency. Writers often start a sentence in one tense but ended up in another. Look back at that sentence. Do you see the error? The first verb *start* is in the present tense, but *ended* is in the past tense. The correct version of the sentence would be "Writers often start a sentence in one tense but end up in another."

These mistakes often occur when writers change their minds halfway through writing the sentence, or when they come back and make changes but only end up changing half the sentence. It is very important to maintain a consistent tense, not just in a sentence but across paragraphs and pages. Decide if something happened, is happening, or will happen and then stick with that choice.

Read through the following paragraphs. Can you spot the errors in tense?

If you want to pick up a new outdoor activity, hiking is a great option to consider. It's a sport that is suited for a beginner or an expert—it just depended on the difficulty hikes you choose. However, even the earliest beginners can complete difficult hikes if they pace themselves and were physically fit.

Not only is hiking an easy activity to pick up, it also will have some great payoffs. As you walked through canyons and climbed up mountains, you can see things that you wouldn't otherwise. The views are breathtaking, and you will get a great opportunity to meditate on the world and your role in it. The summit of a mountain is unlike any other place in the world.

As we mentioned earlier, you want to make sure your whole passage is consistent in its tense. You may have noticed that the most of the verbs in this passage are in present tense; we've edited the passage be consistently in the present tense. All edited verbs have been bolded:

If you want to pick up a new outdoor activity, hiking is a great option to consider. (1) It's a sport that can be suited for a beginner or an expert—it just **depends** on the difficulty hikes you choose. However, even the earliest beginners can complete difficult hikes (2) if they pace themselves and **are** physically fit.

(3) Not only is hiking an easy activity to pick up, it also **has** some great payoffs. (4) As you **walk** through canyons and **climb** up mountains, you can see things that you wouldn't otherwise. (5) The views are breathtaking, and you **get** a great opportunity to meditate on the world and your role in it. The summit of a

mountain is unlike any other place in the world.

Here's each original sentence, along with an explanation for the changes:

It's a sport that is suited for a beginner or an expert—it just **depended** on the difficulty hikes you choose.
- *depended* should be the same tense as *is*; it just **depends** on the difficulty

if they pace themselves and **were** physically fit.
- *were* should be the same tense as *pace*; if they pace themselves and **are** physically fit.

Not only is hiking an easy activity to pick up, it also **will have** some great payoffs.
- *will have* should be the same tense as *is*; it also **has** some great pay offs

As you **walked** through canyons and **climbed** up mountains
- *walked* and *climbed* are both past tense, but this doesn't match the tense of the passage as a whole. They should both be changed to present tense: As you **walk** through canyons and **climb** up mountains.

The views are breathtaking, and you **will get** a great opportunity to meditate on the world and your role in it.
- *will get* should be the same tense as *are*; you **get** a great opportunity

Non-Finite Verbs

Just when we thought we had verbs figured out, we're brought face-to-face with a new animal: non-finite verbs. These words *look* similar to verbs we've already been talking about, but they *act* quite different from those other verbs.

By definition, a non-finite verb cannot serve as the main verb in an independent clause. In practical terms, this means that they don't serve as the action of a sentence. They also don't have a tense. While the sentence around them may be past, present, or future tense, the non-finite verbs themselves are neutral. There are three types of non-finite verbs: gerunds, participles, and infinitives.

Gerunds

Gerunds all end in *-ing*: *skiing, reading, dancing, singing,* etc. Gerunds **act like nouns** and can serve as subjects or objects of sentences. They can be created using active or helping verbs:

- I like **swimming**.
- **Being loved** can make someone feel safe.
- Do you fancy **going out**?
- **Having read the book once before** makes me more prepared.

Often the "doer" of the gerund is clearly signaled:

- We enjoyed **singing** yesterday (we ourselves sang)
- Tomás likes **eating** apricots (Tomás himself eats apricots)

However, sometimes the "doer" must be overtly specified, typically in a position immediately before the non-finite verb:

- We enjoyed their **singing.**
- We were delighted at Bianca **being** awarded the prize.

Participles

A **participle** is a form of a verb that is used in a sentence to modify a noun, noun phrase, verb, or verb phrase, and then plays a role similar to an adjective or adverb. It is one of the types of nonfinite verb forms.

The two types of participle in English are traditionally called the **present participle** (forms such as *writing, singing* and *raising*) and the **past participle** (forms such as *written, sung* and *raised*).

The Present Participle

Even though they look exactly the same, gerunds and present participles do different things. As we just learned, the gerund acts as a noun: e.g., "I like *sleeping*"; "*Sleeping* is not allowed." Present participles, on the other hand, act similarly to an adjective or adverb: e.g., "The *sleeping* girl over there is my sister"; "*Breathing* heavily, she finished the race in first place."

The present participle, or participial phrases (clauses) formed from it, are used as follows:

- as an adjective phrase modifying a noun phrase: *The man **sitting** over there is my uncle.*

- adverbially, the subject being understood to be the same as that of the main clause: **Looking** at the plans, I gradually came to see where the problem lay. He shot the man, **killing** him.
- more generally as a clause or sentence modifier: Broadly **speaking**, the project was successful.

The present participle can also be used with the helping verb to be to form a type of present tense: Marta was **sleeping**. This is something we learned a little bit about in helping verbs and tense.

The Past Participle

Past participles often look very similar to the simple past tense of a verb: finished, danced, etc. However, some verbs have different forms. Reference lists will be your best help in finding the correct past participle. Here's a short list of some of the most common irregular past participles you'll use:

Verb	Simple Past	Past Participle
to be	was/were	been
to become	became	become
to do	did	done
to go	went	gone
to know	knew	know
to see	saw	seen
to speak	spoke	spoken
to take	took	taken
to write	wrote	written

Past participles are used in a couple of different ways:

- as an adjective phrase: The chicken **eaten** by the children was contaminated.
- adverbially: **Seen** from this perspective, the problem presents no easy solution.
- in a nominative absolute construction, with a subject: The task **finished**, we returned home.

The past participle can also be used with the helping verb to have to form a type of past tense: The chicken has **eaten**. It is also used to form the passive voice: Tianna was **voted** as most likely to succeed. When the passive voice is used following a relative pronoun (like that or which) we sometimes leave out parts of the phrase:

- He had three things **that were** taken away from him
- He had three things taken away from him

In the second sentence, we removed the words that were. However, we still use the past participle taken. The removal of these words is called elision. Elision is used with a lot of different constructions in English; we use it shorten sentences when things are understood. However, we can only use elision in certain situations, so be careful when removing words!

Infinitives

To be or not to be, that is the question.

—Hamlet

The infinitive is the basic dictionary form of a verb, usually preceded by *to* (when it's not, it's called the **bare infinitive**, which we'll discuss more later). Thus *to go* is an infinitive. There are several different uses of the infinitive. They can be used alongside verbs, as a noun phrase, as a modifier, or in a question.

With Other Verbs

The *to*-infinitive is used with other verbs (we'll discuss exceptions when we talk about the bare infinitive):

- I aim **to convince** him of our plan's ingenuity.
- You already know that he'll fail **to complete** the task.

You can also use multiple infinitives in a single sentence: "Today, I plan **to run** three miles, **to clean** my room, and **to update** my budget." All three of these infinitives follow the verb *plan*. Other verbs that often come before infinitives include *want, convince, try, able,* and *like.*

As a Noun Phrase

The infinitive can also be used to express an action in an abstract, general way: "**To err** is human"; "**To know** me is **to love me**." No one in particular is completing these actions. In these sentences, the infinitives act as the subjects.

Infinitives can also serve as the object of a sentence. One common construction involves a dummy subject (*it*): "It was nice **to meet** you."

As a Modifier

Infinitives can be used as an adjective (e.g., "A request **to see** someone" or "The man **to save** us") or as an adverb (e.g., "Keen **to get** on," "Nice **to listen** to," or "In order **to win**").

In Questions

Infinitives can be used in elliptical questions as well, as in "I don't know where **to go**."

> **Note:** The infinitive is also the usual dictionary form or citation form of a verb. The form listed in dictionaries is the bare infinitive, although the *to*-infinitive is often used in referring to verbs or in defining other verbs: "The word *amble* means 'to walk slowly'"; "How do we conjugate the verb *to go*?"
> Certain helping verbs do not have infinitives, such *will, can,* and *may.*

Split Infinitives?

One of the biggest controversies among grammarians and style writers has been the appropriateness of separating the two words of the *to*-infinitive as in "to *boldly* go." Despite what a lot of people have declared over the years, there is absolutely nothing wrong with this construction. It is 100 percent grammatically sound.

Part of the reason so many authorities have been against this construction is likely the fact that in languages such as Latin, the infinitive is a single word, and cannot be split. However, in English the infinitive (or at least the *to*-infinitive) is two words, and a split infinitive is a perfectly natural construction.

> ### *Try to* versus *Try and*
>
> One common error people make is saying *try and* instead of *try to*, as in "I'll try and be there by 10:00 tomorrow." However, *try* requires a to-infinitive after it, so using *and* is incorrect. While this construction is acceptable in casual conversation, it is not grammatically correct and should not be used in formal situations.

The Bare Infinitive

As we mentioned previously, the infinitive can sometimes occur without the word *to*. The form without *to* is called the **bare infinitive** (the form with *to* is called the ***to*-infinitive**). In the following sentences both *sit* and *to sit* would each be considered an infinitive:

- I want **to sit** on the other chair.
- I can **sit** here all day.

Infinitives have a variety of uses in English. Certain contexts call for the *to*-infinitive form, and certain contexts call for the bare infinitive; they are not normally interchangeable, except in occasional instances like after the verb *help*, where either can be used.

As we mentioned earlier, some verbs require the bare infinitive instead of the *to*-infinitive:

- The helping verb *do*
    - Does she **dance**?
    - Zi doesn't **sing**.
- Helping verbs that express tense, possibility, or ability like *will, can, could, should, would,* and *might*
    - The bears will **eat** you if they catch you.
    - Lucas and Gerardo might **go** to the dance.
    - You should **give** it a try.
- Verbs of perception, permission, or causation, such as *see, watch, hear, make, let, and have* (after a direct object)
    - Look at Caroline **go**!
    - You can't make me **talk**.
    - It's so hard to let someone else **finish** my work.

The bare infinitive can be used as the object in such sentences like "What you should do is **make** a list." It can also be used after the word *why* to ask a question: "Why **reveal** it?"

The bare infinitive can be tricky, because it often looks exactly like the present tense of a verb. Look at the following sentences for an example:

- You **lose** things so often.
- You can **lose** things at the drop of a hat.

In both of these sentences, we have the word *lose*, but in the first sentence it's a present tense verb, while in the second it's a bare infinitive. So how can you tell which is which? The easiest way is to try changing the subject of the sentence and seeing if the verb should change:

- She **loses** things so often.
- She can **lose** things at the drop of a hat.

Now that we've learned how to use each of the different non-finite verbs, let's take a look at how they're used together. This practice will help you distinguish non-finite verbs from each other (as well as distinguishing them from the "normal" verbs we learned about previously in this outcome).

Complex Verb Tenses

We've finally learned the different pieces that we need to understand in order to discuss some more advanced tenses.

These tenses include things like "We had been going to the same restaurant for five years." What's the difference between this sentence and "We went to the same restaurant for five years?" While both sentences have the same meaning, the first sentence creates a sense of continuity: it's something that happened repeatedly. There's an even bigger difference when you look at future tenses:

- She will eat 500 gummy bears.
- She will have eaten 500 gummy bears.

In the first sentence, the entirety of the action takes place in the future. In the second sentence, we get a sense that the action will be complete some time in the future.

Was working	Is working	Will be working
WORKED	**WORK**	**WILL WORK**
Had been working	Has been working	Will have been working
Had worked	Has worked	Will have worked

These forms are created with different forms of *to be* and *to have*. When you combine a form of *to be* with the present participle, you create a **continuous tense**; these tenses indicate a sense of continuity. The subject of the sentence was (or is, or will be) doing that thing for awhile.

- **Present:** is working
- **Past:** was working
- **Future:** will be working (You can also say "is going to be working.")

When you combine a form of *to have* with the past participle of a verb, you create a **perfect tense**; these tenses indicate a sense of completion. This thing had been done for a while (or has been, or will have been).

- **Present:** has worked
- **Past:** had worked
- **Future:** will have worked

You can also use these together. *To have* must always appear first, followed by the past participle *been*. The present participle of any verb can then follow. These **perfect continuous tenses** indicate that the verb started in the past, and is still continuing:

- **Present:** has been working
- **Past:** had been working
- **Future:** will have been working

Sometimes these verb tenses can be split by adverbs: "Zachi has been **studiously** reading all of the latest articles on archeology."

Adjectives and Adverbs

Adjectives

An adjective modifies a noun; that is, it provides more detail about a noun. This can be anything from color to size to temperature to personality. Adjectives usually occur just before the nouns they modify, but they can also follow a linking verb (in these instances, adjectives can modify pronouns as well):

- The generator is used to convert **mechanical** *energy* into **electrical** *energy*.
- The kids' *schoolhouse* was **red**.

Numbers can also be adjectives in some cases. When you say "Seven is my lucky number," *seven* is a noun, but when you say "There are seven cats in this painting," *seven* is an adjective because it is modifying the noun *cats*.

Comparable Adjectives

Some adjectives are **comparable**: they exist on a scale. For example, a person may be polite, but another person may be more polite, and a third person may be the most polite of the three. The word *more* here modifies the adjective *polite* to indicate a comparison is being made (a **comparative**), and *most* modifies the adjective to indicate an absolute comparison (a **superlative**).

There is another way to compare adjectives in English. Many adjectives can take the suffixes *–er* and *–est* to indicate the comparative and superlative forms, respectively (e.g., *great, greater, greatest*). Some adjectives are *irregular* in this sense (*good, better, best; bad, worse, worst*).

There is no simple rule to decide which means is correct for any given adjective; however, the general tendency is for shorter adjectives to take the suffixes, while longer adjectives do not.

- *hotter* (not *more hot*)
- *more beautiful* (not *beautifuller*)
- *more pretentious* (not *pretentiouser*)

A Note about *Fun*

The adjective *fun* is one of the most notable exceptions to the rules. You might expect the comparative to be *funner* and the superlative to be *funnest*. However, for a long time, these words were considered non-standard, with *more fun* and *most fun* acting as the correct forms.
The reasoning behind this rule is now obsolete (it has a lot to do with the way *fun* became an adjective), but the stigma against *funner* and *funnest* remains. While the tides are beginning to change, it's safest to stick to *more fun* and *most fun* in formal situations (such as in academic writing or in professional correspondence).

When you use comparative adjectives, the adjective is often accompanied by the word *than* (e.g., "He is taller than me"). When using *than*, there are two things you should keep in mind:

You should use *than*, not the word *then*. *Then* indicates time, rather than comparison.
When you're trying to emphasize just how "adjective" a thing is, you shouldn't follow *than* with a second instance of the comparative. "She is shorter than shorter," is incorrect. The emphatic phrase "She is shorter than short," would be correct.

Non-Comparable Adjectives

Non-comparable adjectives, on the other hand, are not measured on a scale, but are binary. Either something is "adjective," or it is not. For example, some English speakers would argue that it does not make sense to say that one thing is "more ultimate" than another, or that something is "most ultimate," since the word *ultimate* is already an absolute. Other examples include *dead*, *true*, and *unique*.

Native speakers will frequently play with non-comparable adjectives. Although *pregnant* is logically non-comparable (someone is pregnant or she is not), you may hear a sentence like "She looks more and more pregnant each day." Likewise *extinct* and *equal* appear to be non-comparable, but one might say that a language about which nothing is known is "more extinct" than a well-documented language with surviving literature but no speakers, and George Orwell once wrote "All animals are equal, but some are more equal than others."

Adverbs

Adverbs can perform a wide range of functions: they can modify verbs, adjectives, and other adverbs. They can come either before or after the word they modify. An adverb may provide information about the manner, place, time, frequency, certainty, or other circumstances of the activity indicated by the verb:

- Suzanne sang **loudly** (*loudly* modifies the verb *sang*, indicating the manner of singing)
- We left it **here** (*here* modifies the verb phrase *left it*, indicating place)
- I worked **yesterday** (*yesterday* modifies the verb *worked*, indicating time)
- You **often** make mistakes (*often* modifies the verb phrase *make mistakes*, indicating frequency)
- He **undoubtedly** did it (*undoubtedly* modifies the verb phrase *did it*, indicating certainty)

They can also modify noun phrases, prepositional phrases, or whole clauses or sentences, as in the following examples. Once again the adverbs are in bold, while the words they modify are in italics.

- I bought **only** the fruit (*only* modifies the noun phrase *the fruit*)
- Roberto drove us **almost** to the station (*almost* modifies the prepositional phrase *to the station*)
- **Certainly** we need to act (*certainly* modifies the sentence as a whole)

Intensifiers and Adverbs of Degree

Adverbs can also be used as modifiers of adjectives, and of other adverbs, often to indicate degree. Here are a few examples:

- You are **quite** right (the adverb *quite* modifies the adjective *right*)
- Milagros is **exceptionally** pretty (the adverb *exceptionally* modifies the adjective *pretty*)
- She sang **very** loudly (the adverb *very* modifies another adverb—*loudly*)
- Wow! You ran **really** quickly! (the adverb *really* modifies another adverb—*quickly*)

Adverbs may also undergo comparison, taking comparative and superlative forms. This is usually done by adding *more* and *most* before the adverb (*more slowly, most slowly*). However, there are a few adverbs that take non-standard forms, such as *well*, for which *better* and *best* are used (i.e., "He did **well**, she did **better**, and I did **best**").

> **Note:** When using intensifiers alongside the adverb *also*, *also* should always appear first: "He also really loved pie" is correct, while "He really also loved pie" is not.

Very

Some people are of the opinion that the words *very* and *really* indicate weak writing. You've probably seen lists of adjectives to use instead of these adverbs (along with an adjective). While this can be true in some cases (*enormous* or *gigantic* would probably serve better than "really big"), *very* and *really* aren't terrible words. As in most cases, you just need to be conscious of your choices. When you use these adverbs, pause and see if

---

there's a better way to word what you're saying.

Common Mistakes

Only

Have you ever noticed the effect the word *only* can have on a sentence, especially depending on where it's placed? Let's look at a simple sentence:

- She loves horses.

Let's see how *only* can influence the meaning of this sentence:

- *Only* she loves horses.
    - No one loves horses but her.
- She *only* loves horses.
    - The one thing she does is love horses.
- She loves *only* horses.
    - She loves horses and nothing else.

Only modifies the word that directly follows it. Whenever you use the word *only* make sure you've placed it correctly in your sentence.

Literally

A linguistic phenomenon is sweeping the nation: people are using *literally* as an intensifier. How many times have you heard things like "It was literally the worst thing that has ever happened to me," or "His head literally exploded when I told him I was going to be late again"?

So what's the problem with this? According to *Merriam-Webster's Dictionary*, the actual definition of *literal* is as follows:

- involving the ordinary or usual meaning of a word
- giving the meaning of each individual word
- completely true and accurate : not exaggerated[1]

According to this definition, *literally* should be used only when something actually happened. Our cultural usage may be slowly shifting to allow *literally* as an intensifier, but it's best to avoid using *literally* in any way other than its dictionary definition, especially in formal writing.

"Literal." *Merriam-Webster.com.* Merriam-Webster, n.d. Web. 20 June 2016. ↵

College Success Strategies

Strategies to Improve Your Vocabulary

There are several proven benefits in improving your vocabulary, but how should we go about learning new words in the most effective way? By using the following ten vocabulary-building strategies, you are guaranteed to develop a strong vocabulary and keep improving it every day.

1. Read Voraciously

It's undeniable that reading is the most effective way to get new vocabulary. When you read, you see **words being used in context** — and that's what makes it much more effective than, for example, merely memorizing word lists.

With context information surrounding each new word, there's a good chance you can guess its meaning just by understanding the overall text. Finding out the meaning of words in such a way is the natural way of learning language–and reading provides the best opportunity to get exposed to this natural way of learning.

If you're not able to infer the meaning of new words when reading, it's probably because there are too many unknown words in the text. In that case, try reading easier materials. The key to good reading is making it a pleasurable activity. Don't be afraid of coming across unknown words, but make sure the text is appropriate for your reading level.

2. Make Friends with the Dictionary

A dictionary is the first indispensable resource to improve your vocabulary. It's only by looking up a word in a dictionary that you will learn its precise meaning, spelling, alternate definitions, and find additional useful information about it. A thesaurus is also a valuable resource for learning by finding connections between words, such as their synonyms and antonyms.

Consider adding a good dictionary and thesaurus to your bookshelf. Here are some recommendations:

- Oxford Advanced Learner's Dictionary
- The New Oxford American Dictionary
- The Oxford American Writer's Thesaurus

For online dictionaries, there are many free options with great extra features. Even if you have a good dictionary in print already, you can't miss having a good online dictionary at your disposal:

- OneLook: has a reverse lookup function (get the word from its definition) and works as a "meta-dictionary," showing you definitions from other major online dictionaries
- Merriam-Webster's Online Dictionary: a well-established and well-regarded name in the realm of dictionaries
- Ninjawords: searches the free dictionary Wiktionary. What makes this site interesting is that you can look up multiple words simultaneously. Moreover, the results pages can be bookmarked – making them good personal reference pages
- Thinkmap Visual Thesaurus: if you're a fan of mind mapping, you will certainly enjoy viewing related words represented in a visual map format

- Answers.com, Dictionary.com, The Free Dictionary and many others: all of them are good resources – try each one at least once to help you make up your mind.

3. Use It or Lose It

Don't settle after you learn a new word by reading it or looking it up in the dictionary: these are good starts, but it's by **using the new words** that you truly commit them to your long-term memory.

Be creative and try to use your newly learned words in as many ways as possible:

- Write them down
- Say them aloud
- Create sentences with them, mentally or in writing
- Try to use them in a conversation
- Discuss them with friends

It's also important to be aware of your own language style: every time you catch yourself saying common or nonspecific words such as "nice," try coming up with richer and more precise expressions instead.

4. Learn One New Word a Day

If you learn just one new word every day, you'll soon notice they add up pretty quickly.

Many websites provide free word-of-the-day services. Here are some to try:

- Merriam-Webster's Online Word of the Day: this is the website that delivers the most useful words of all. It's also the most feature-rich: it provides audio explanation, pronunciation, and word history.
- WordSmart Wordcast: provides difficulty level, comprehensive details, and audio pronunciation for the word.
- Dictionary Word of the Day: another fine service, perhaps not as complete as Merriam-Webster's or WordSmart, but still worth checking out.

5. Understand the True Meaning of Words

By deeply understanding words, you can make your vocabulary grow exponentially. Instead of just memorizing words, try to really understand them by looking at their etymology, word roots, prefixes, and suffixes. At least half of English words are derived from Greek and Latin roots, so enormous benefits come from being familiar with them.

Just to pick an example, when you understand that the prefix "ortho" means *straight* or *right*, you start to find connections between seemingly unrelated words, such as *orthodontist* (a specialist who straightens teeth) and *orthography* (the correct, or straight way of writing).

Understanding the logic behind words always pays off in terms of learning and recalling. Consider the examples: "breakfast" meaning "interrupt the night's fast," or "rainbow" meaning "bow or arc caused by rain." While these meanings may be trivial to native English speakers, having such insights about words, foreign or otherwise, never fails to deepen your connection to them.

6. Maintain a Personal Lexicon

By keeping a personalized list of learned words, you'll have a handy reference you can use to review these words later. It's very likely you'll want to go back and refresh your memory on recent words, so keeping them in your own list is much more efficient than going back to the dictionary every time.

Even if you never refer back to your lexicon again, writing words down at least once will greatly enhance your ability to commit them to your permanent memory. Another excellent learning aid is to write an original sentence containing the word — and using your lexicon to do that is a great way of enforcing this habit. You can also add many other details as you see fit, such as the date you first came across the word or maybe a sequential number to help you reach some word quota you define.

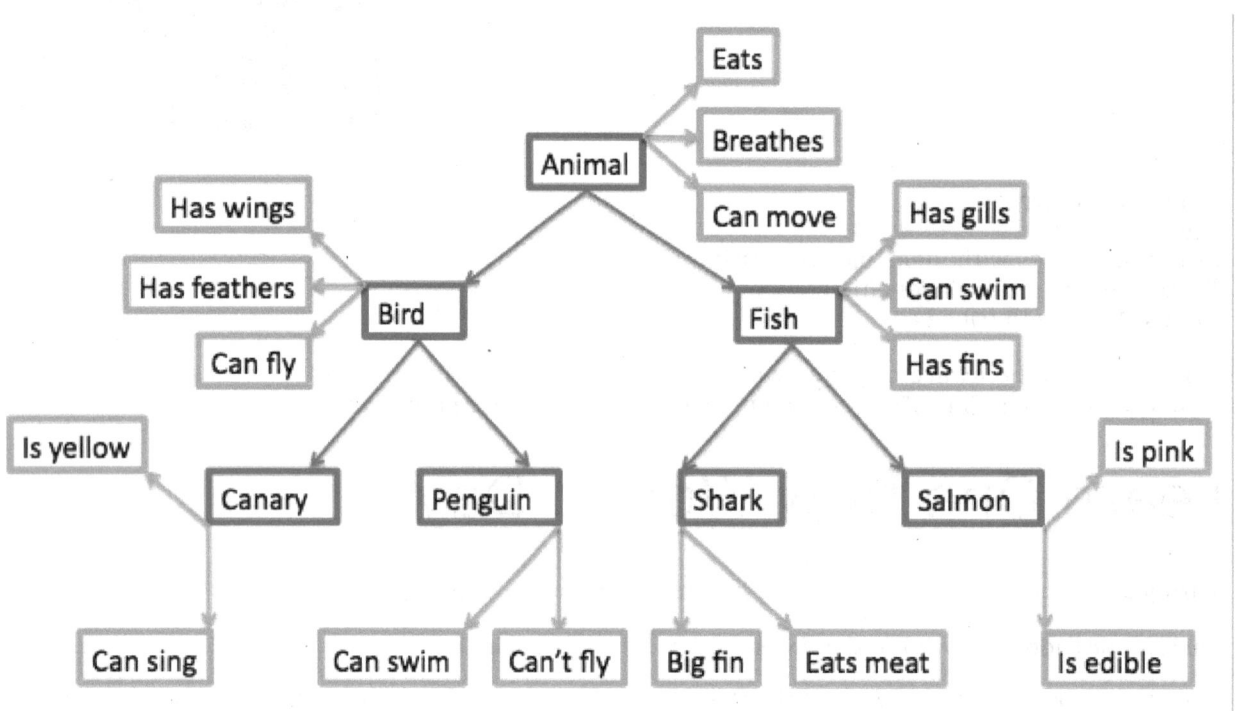

There are many ways you can keep your personal word list; each has its own advantages and disadvantages, so make sure to pick the format that works best for you. You may prefer to keep it as a simple text file in the computer, or in a regular paper notebook, or maybe as flash cards in a shoe box.

One option is a computer spreadsheet, for its handy features such as searching, sorting, and filtering.

7. Follow a Process

To make vocabulary improvement a permanent habit in your everyday life, you should make it as habitual, automatic, and tightly integrated in your daily workflow as possible-otherwise you won't do it when your days get too busy.

In that regard, one particularly useful concept is the one of maintaining a "Word Inbox." By having a predefined place you use to capture the words you come across, you can process them much more efficiently.

Your process can be as simple as you wish–the key is to define it beforehand and then follow it. By knowing exactly how and how often to process your inbox, you stay on top of your vocabulary improvement process, even when there are other pressing matters crying out for your attention.

8. Play and Have Fun

Playing games and engaging in group activities are useful in any kind of learning, but particularly effective for language-related learning. Gather your family and friends and play word games together. Some interesting options are Quiddler, as well as the classics Scrabble and Boggle.

If you don't want to spend money on boxed games, it's easy to come up with your own word activities. You may, for example, try your own variation of "Word Evening": at a specific day of each week, a different person brings a new word to the meal. The person reads the word, defines it, and the others must come up with a sentence using the word.

If you don't have time or don't want to engage in group activities, there are numerous options of word games in the Internet. You can either play them when you're bored, or integrate them in your daily routine, such as playing a quick game after lunch, for example. Consider the following recommendations:

- Merriam Webster's Daily Word Game
- Merriam Webster's Daily Crossword
- Word Games on Yahoo! Games

9. Leverage Every Resource You Can

The Internet is a gold mine of resources for vocabulary building. Here are a few to get you started, though many more exist:

There are plenty of vocabulary applications you can try. There are many vocabulary-related books you can explore. There is a wealth of free literature on sites such as Project Gutenberg. If you use the Firefox browser, there are many ways to integrate dictionary lookup functions, such as the plug-ins Answers.com and DictionarySearch.

The point is that you're only limited by your willingness to learn: let curiosity be your guide and you will never run out of resources to learn from.

10. Diversify

Do something different from your daily routine: hunting, fishing, or blogging–any activity that is not a part of your normal life can become a great way to learn new words, as every niche has its own jargon and unique ways of communicating. Read different books and magazines than the ones you're used to. Watch foreign-language movies. Take up new hobbies, hang out with different people.

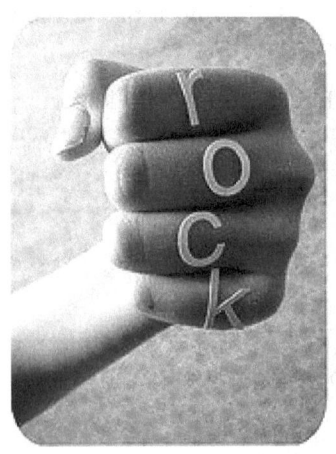 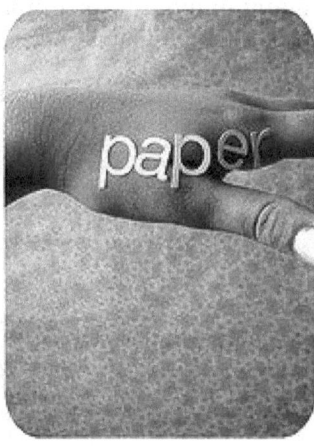 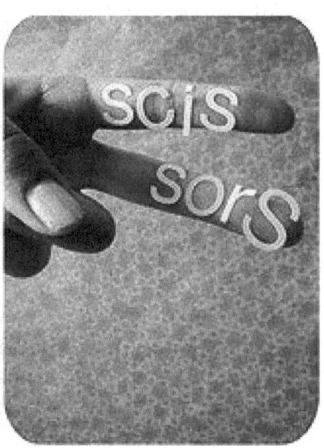

By doing things out of the ordinary you will not only improve your vocabulary but also make your life much more interesting.

CC licensed content, Shared previously

- 10 Sure-Fire Strategies to Improve Your Vocabulary. **Authored by**: Luciano Passuello. **Provided by**: Litemind. **Located at**: https://litemind.com/10-strategies-improve-vocabulary/. **License**: *CC BY-NC: Attribution-NonCommercial*
- Image of people talking. **Authored by**: Pedro Ribeiro Simoes. **Located at**: https://flic.kr/p/rgC6nQ. **License**: *CC0: No Rights Reserved*
- Image of Animal Concept Map. **Authored by**: Nathanael Crawford. **Located at**: https://commons.wikimedia.org/wiki/File:Hierarchical_Model_Mental_Lexicon.png. **License**: *CC BY-SA: Attribution-ShareAlike*
- Image of rock, paper, scissors. **Authored by**: nikki. **Located at**: https://flic.kr/p/4opHEk. **License**: *CC BY-NC: Attribution-NonCommercial*
- Revision and Adaptation. **Provided by**: Lumen Learning. **License**: *CC BY-NC: Attribution-NonCommercial*

Habits for Success

Introduction

Learning Objectives

- develop a personal definition of success
- identify specific strategies to achieve success
- identify support network options

A college education is aligned with greater success in many areas of life. While enrolled in college, most students are closely focused on making it through the next class or passing the next test. It can be easy to lose sight of the overall role that education plays in life. But sometimes it helps to recall what a truly great step forward you are taking!

It's also important to recognize, though, that some students do not succeed; they drop out within the first year. Sometimes this is due to financial problems or a personal or family crisis. But too frequently, students drop out because they're having trouble passing their courses.

In this section, we examine the elements of college success. Are there patterns of success you strive for but aren't yet reaching? Where might you shore up your support? What strategies can you use to achieve success in your college endeavors?

A Personal Definition for Success

How do you define college success? The definition really depends on you. You might think that "success" is earning an associate's degree or attending classes in a four-year college. Maybe success is a bachelor's or master's degree or a PhD. Maybe success means receiving a certificate of completion or finishing skill-based training.

You might be thinking of other measures of college success, too—like grades. For instance, you might be unhappy with anything less than an A in a course, although maybe this depends on the difficulty of the subject. As long as you pass with a C, you might be perfectly content. But no matter how you define success personally, you probably wouldn't think it means earning a D or lower grade in a class.

To help you start to define what success means to you, take this quick self-assessment about your college goals and beyond. How many of these items are important to you?

I Want to Be Able to . . .	Yes	No
Change my major during my college years		
Have good relationships with my professors		
Be eligible for financial aid		
Be eligible for scholarships		
Get awards		
Get reductions on my car insurance		
Prove to my employer that I can work hard		
Keep my parents happy		
Make connections to get a job after graduation		

Finally, consider that we can't be successful all the time at everything. We have to balance our energy and our focus, to get what we really want.

Strategies to Achieve Success

If most students believe that passing a class is the minimum requirement for "success," and if most students want to be successful in their courses, why aren't more college students consistently successful in the classroom?

Perhaps some common misconceptions are at play. For example, we often hear students say, "I just can't do it!" or "I'm not good at math," or "I guess college isn't for me...," or "I'm not smart enough." But these explanations for success or failure aren't necessarily accurate. Considerable research into college success reveals that **intellect usually has nothing to do with having difficulty in or failing college courses**. More often, success depends on how fully you embrace and master the following seven strategies:

Learn how to take effective notes in class.
Review the text and your reading notes prior to class.
Participate in class discussion and maybe even join a study group.
Go to office hours and ask your instructor questions.
Give yourself enough time to research, write, and edit your essays in manageable stages.
Take advantage of online or on-campus academic support resources.
Spend sufficient time studying.

So if you feel you are not smart enough for college, ask yourself if you can implement some of these skills. Can you make more time for learning? One approach is to create a regular study schedule and make sure you allow yourself ample time. Most college success experts agree that students should study two hours outside of class for every hour in class. Only break away from your committed schedule if an extreme situation prevents you from sticking to it.

Another strategy to consider implementing is group study. For example, rather than relying just on your own knowledge, notes, and skills, try studying with other students in your difficult classes. Studying in a group gives every group member a chance to ask questions and talk about concepts.

You can also add a tutor to your study group. You will really be able to notice a positive difference. Tutoring is generally free in college, and the strategies and knowledge you gain will be invaluable. Usually tutors have taken the class you are currently enrolled in, and they are trained to get the best out of you.

Overall, students struggle in college not because of natural intellect or smarts, but because of poor time management, disorganization, and lack of quality study time. The good news is that there are ways to combat this, specifically by doing things like creating a regular study schedule, studying in groups, and taking advantage of your school's academic resources, like a tutoring center, instructor office hours, and any available online help.

Campus Support Networks

Whether your campus is small, tall, *grande*, or *venti*, you are probably amazed by the array of institutionally supported student activities available for your enrichment and enjoyment. Perhaps your biggest challenge is deciding how much extra time you have after studying and which added activities yield the greatest reward.

Benefits of Participating in Student Life

How is it that becoming fully involved in student life can have such a positive impact on student satisfaction and

academic success?

The National Survey of Student Engagement—a survey measuring student involvement in academic and cocurricular activities—shows that student success is directly linked to student involvement in the institution. In fact, survey results show that the higher the level of student involvement is, the higher student grades are and the more likely students are to reenroll the next term. All of this seems to translate to satisfaction. The following lists some of the many benefits and rewards that result from active participation in campus and student life.

- **Personal interests are tapped**: Cocurricular programs and activities encourage students to explore personal interests and passions. As students pursue these interests, they learn more about their strengths and possible career paths. These discoveries can be lasting and life-changing.
- **A portfolio of experience develops**: Experience with just about any aspect of college life maybe relevant to a prospective employer. Is freshman year too soon to be thinking about résumés? Definitely not! If you gain leadership experience in a club, for example, be sure to document what you did so you can refer back to it (you might want to keep track of your activities and experiences in a journal, for instance).
- **Fun leads to good feelings**: Students typically pursue cocurricular activities because the activities are enjoyable and personally rewarding. Having fun is also a good way to balance the stress of meeting academic deadlines and studying intensely.
- **Social connections grow**: When students are involved in cocurricular activities, they usually interact with others, which means meeting new people, developing social skills, and being a part of a community. It's always good to have friends who share your interests and to develop these relationships over time.
- **Awareness of diversity expands**: The multicultural nature of American society is increasingly reflected and celebrated on college campuses today. You will see this not only in the classroom but also in the cocurricular activities, clubs, organizations, and events. For example, your college might have a Black Student Union, an Asian Pacific Student Union, a Japanese Student Association, a Chinese Student Association, and many others. Having access to these resources gives students the opportunity to explore different cultures and prepare to live, work, and thrive in a vibrantly diverse world.
- **Self-esteem grows**: When students pursue their special interests through cocurricular activities, it can be a real boost to self-esteem. Academic achievement can certainly be a source of affirmation and satisfaction, but it's nice to have additional activities that validate your special contributions in other ways.

All in all, being involved in the campus community is vital to every student, and it's vital to the college, too. It's a symbiotic relationship that serves everyone well.

The key to getting the most out of college is to take advantage of as many facets of student life as possible while still keeping up with your academic commitments. That's pretty obvious, right? What may be less obvious is that focusing exclusively on your academic work and not getting involved in any of the rich and diverse cocurricular activities on campus can come at a real price and even hamper your success.

Major College Resources and How To Use Them

> Professors do care about how you are doing in their class; they genuinely want you to succeed, but they will give you the grade you earn. There are people and resources on campus for you to utilize so you can earn the grade you want. Your professors are one of those resources, and are perhaps the most important. Go see them during office hours, ask them questions about the material and get extra help if you need it. ... Another resource to utilize can be found in the campus learning center. ... The first time I took a paper there, I recall standing outside the door for about ten minutes thinking of an excuse not to go in. Thankfully I saw a classmate walk in and I followed suit. ... Thanks to that first visit, I received an A- on the paper! –Kristen Mruk, "The Student Experience"

College resources to help you reach your educational and career goals are plentiful on most campuses. Here are several campus resources to know about and find early in your college career. You may not need them right away; some you may not need at all. But you will at least find several to be vital. Be familiar with your options. Know where to find the services. Have contact information. Be prepared to visit for help.

Advising

Most colleges and universities assign an academic adviser to each student. The adviser may be associated with your major. There may also be an office or department that provides advising. Call upon your adviser or the advising office if you have an issue with your adviser or you need other help.

Tutoring and Writing Centers

Tutoring and writing centers are established for all students, and seeking help from them is expected and to your advantage. Such services are covered by your tuition dollars, and they can richly enhance performance in any area of your studies. Know where to find these centers and how to schedule appointments.

Other Academic Support Facilities

Your college may also offer academic support in various other forms: for example, computer labs with trained assistants, tutors, mentors, peer advisers, and more. You can research what kinds of special support are available and be ready to take advantage of them.

Library Reference Desk

College libraries are staffed with professionals whose main function is to assist you and the college community in finding needed resources. Don't hesitate to find the reference desk and get to know the reference librarians. Invariably you will learn about valuable resources—many of them online—that you didn't know existed. Reference librarians are also educators, and they're there to help you.

Campus Health Center

In the event that you need any health services whatsoever, the campus health center can be your first destination. Stop into the center and learn about the services offered, the hours of operation, emergency provisions, and routine health services available.

Campus Counseling

Counseling is an essential service that colleges and universities invariably provide. Services can ranges from life-saving care to assistance with minor concerns. Life stressors, such as deaths and divorces in the family, issues with friends, substance abuse, and suicide are just a few of the many issues that college students may experience or witness others struggling with. Don't take matters into your own hands. Get help! The counseling center can help you and support you in gaining solid footing during difficult times. Don't hesitate to take full advantage of the services and help they offer.

Career Services

One of the most important purposes of college is to prepare students for a career. All colleges and universities have a career office that can assist you with many critical aspects of finding a suitable career. It may also help you find a campus job or review options for your major, help you get an internship, draft your résumé, and practice interview skills. Visiting the career office is a must for every student, and it's worth doing early and often (rather than waiting until you're about to graduate).

Spiritual Life

Most college campus have interfaith facilities to meet the spiritual-life needs of the entire college community. You may find these facilities to be a refuge in special moments of need or resources for your ongoing involvement. A healthy spiritual life can bring greater balance to your student life.

Additional support centers that students may wish to visit include offices for financial aid, students with disabilities, housing, diversity, student organizations, athletics, continuing education, international students, child care, and many others. Refer to your college Web site or other college directory for information about the many, many services that can be part of your college experience.

Time Management

Introduction

> ### Learning Objectives
>
> - define your current uses of time in daily life
> - explore time management strategies to add time for college success activities
> - identify procrastination behaviors and strategies to avoid them

The two areas most students struggle with when acclimating to college life are studying and time management. These issues arise from trying to manage newfound freedoms in college and from misunderstanding expectations of college classes. Time management is a means to build a solid foundation for college success.

How You Use Your Time

As most students discover, time in college is not the same as it was in high school. There are many more "unscripted" hours of the day. Fewer hours are devoted to sitting in a classroom, but more hours are expected to be devoted to classwork, on your own. While this can be liberating, you may find that social opportunities conflict with academic expectations. For example, a free day before an exam, if not wisely spent, can spell trouble for doing well on the exam. It is easy to fall behind when there are so many choices and opportunities.

In the next few sections, we'll take three steps towards learning to effectively manage our time. First, we have to see where we are, currently, with our use of time.

Step 1: Identify Your Time Management Style

The following self-assessment survey can help you determine your time-management personality type. Read each question in the Questions column. Then read the possible responses. Select one response for each question. Each response should reflect what you probably would do in a given situation, not what you think is the "right" answer. Put a checkmark in the My Time Management Type column next to your likely response.

	QUESTIONS	RESPONSES: Which response most closely matches what you would do? In the right column, check one response (a, b, c or d) for each question.	MY TIME MANAGEMENT TYPE
1	Your instructor just gave your class the prompts for your first essay, which is due in two weeks. How do you proceed from here?	a. Choose a prompt and begin working on a thesis immediately. Better to get it out of the way!	O Early bird
		b. Read over the prompts and let them sink in for a week or so. You'll still have one more week to finish the assignment, right?	O Balancing act
		c. Read the prompts and maybe start playing around with ideas, but wait to really start writing until the day before. You swear it's all in your head somewhere!	O Pressure cooker
		d. Definitely last. You'll wait until everyone else has done their work, so you can make sure you are not duplicating efforts. Whatever, this is why you hate group work.	O Improviser
2	You are working on a group assignment that requires you to split up responsibilities with three other classmates. When would you typically finish your part?	a. First. Then you're done and don't have to worry about it. Plus it could give you time in case you want to tweak anything later.	O Early bird
		b. After one or two of the others have submitted their materials to the group, but definitely not last. You wanted to see how they approached it first.	O Balancing act
		c. Maybe last, but definitely before the assignment due date and hopefully before any of the other group members ask about it.	O Pressure cooker
		d. Definitely last. You'll wait until everyone else has done their work, so you can make sure you are not duplicating efforts. Whatever, this is why you hate group work.	O Improviser

	QUESTIONS	RESPONSES: Which response most closely matches what you would do? In the right column, check one response (a, b, c or d) for each question.	MY TIME MANAGEMENT TYPE
3	Your instructor just shared the instructions for your next assignment and you read them but don't quite understand what he's asking for in a certain part. What would you probably do?	a. Send the instructor an email that afternoon. When he doesn't respond that night, email him again. This is your worst nightmare—you just want to know what he wants!!	O Early bird
		b. Send him an email asking for clarification, giving yourself enough time to wait for his response and then complete the assignment. Better to be safe than sorry.	O Balancing act
		c. Try to figure it out for yourself. You're pretty sure what he's trying to say, and you'll give it your best shot.	O Pressure cooker
		d. Don't say anything until after the assignment is due. Other people in the class felt the same way too, probably!	O Improviser
4	The course you are taking requires you to post in a weekly discussion forum by Sunday night each week so the class can talk about everyone's posts on Monday. When do you submit your posts?	a. Tuesday night, after the first day of class that week. Then it's out of the way.	O Early bird
		b. Thursday or Friday night. You want to let the week's discussion sink in a little so you can collect your thoughts.	O Balancing act
		c. Sunday night. You always forget during the weekend!	O Pressure cooker
		d. Monday at 3 AM. That still counts as Sunday night, right?	O Improviser

QUESTIONS	RESPONSES: Which response most closely matches what you would do? In the right column, check one response (a, b, c or d) for each question.	MY TIME MANAGEMENT TYPE
5 You have an important assignment due Monday morning, and you have a social/work/family obligation that will keep you busy for most of the weekend. It is now the Wednesday before the assignment is due. How would you approach this dilemma?	a. You already finished it yesterday, the day it was assigned. Done!	O Early bird
	b. You tell yourself that you'll finish it by Friday night, and you manage this by chipping away at it over those 3 days. ...Little. By. Little.	O Balancing act
	c. You tell yourself that you'll finish it by Friday night, so you can have your weekend free, but you still have a little left to do on Sunday—no big deal.	O Pressure cooker
	d. You tell yourself that you'll take the weekend off, then stay up late on Sunday or wake up early on Monday to finish it. It's not a final or anything, and you have a life.	O Improviser
6 You have to read 150 pages before your next class meeting. You have 4 days to do so. What would you most likely do?	a. 150 pages divided by 4 days means... a little less than 40 pages a day. You like to chunk it this way because then you'll also have time to go over your notes and highlights, and come up with questions for the instructor.	O Early bird
	b. 150 pages divided by...well ... 2 days (because it's been a long week), means 75 pages a day. Totally doable.	O Balancing act
	c. 150 pages, the day before it is due. You did this to yourself, it's fine.	O Pressure cooker
	d. How much time does it take to skim the text for keywords and/or find a summary online?	O Improviser

Assessing Your Responses

Which of the four basic time-management personality types did you select the most? Which did you select the least? Do you feel like these selections match the student you have been in the past? Has your previous way of doing things worked for you, or do you think it's time for a change? Remember, we can all always improve!

Learn more below about your tendencies. Review traits, strengths, challenges, and tips for success for each of the four time-management personality types.

The Early Bird

- **Traits**: You like to make checklists and feel great satisfaction when you can cross something off of your to-do list. When it comes to assignments, you want to get started as soon as possible (and maybe start brainstorming before that), because it lets you stay in control.

- **Strengths**: You know what you want and are driven to figure out how to achieve it. Motivation is never really a problem for you.
- **Challenges**: Sometimes you can get more caught up in getting things done as quickly as possible and don't give yourself enough time to really mull over issues in all of their complexity.
- **Tips for Success**: You're extremely organized and on top of your schoolwork, so make sure you take time to really enjoy learning in your classes. Remember, school isn't all deadlines and checkboxes—you also have the opportunity to think about big-picture intellectual problems that don't necessarily have clear answers.

The Balancing Act

- **Traits**: You really know what you're capable of and are ready to do what it takes to get the most out of your classes. Maybe you're naturally gifted in this way or maybe it's a skill that you have developed over time; in any case, you should have the basic organizational skills to succeed in any class, as long as you keep your balance.
- **Strengths**: Your strength really lies in your ability to be well rounded. You may not always complete assignments perfectly every time, but you are remarkably consistent and usually manage to do very well in classes.
- **Challenges**: Because you're so consistent, sometimes you can get in a bit of a rut and begin to coast in class, rather than really challenging yourself.
- **Tips for Success**: Instead of simply doing what works, use each class as an opportunity for growth by engaging thoughtfully with the material and constantly pushing the boundaries of your own expectations for yourself.

The Pressure Cooker

- **Traits**: You always get things done and almost always at the last minute. Hey, it takes time to really come up with good ideas!
- **Strengths**: You work well under pressure, and when you do finally sit down to accomplish a task, you can sit and work for hours. In these times, you can be extremely focused and shut out the rest of the world in order to complete what's needed.
- **Challenges**: You sometimes use your ability to work under pressure as an excuse to procrastinate. Sure, you can really focus when the deadline is tomorrow, but is it really the best work you could produce if you had a couple of days of cushion?
- **Tips for Success**: Give yourself small, achievable deadlines, and stick to them. Make sure they're goals that you really could (and would) achieve in a day. Then don't allow yourself to make excuses. You'll find that it's actually a lot more enjoyable to not be stressed out when completing schoolwork. Who would have known?

The Improviser

- **Traits**: You frequently wait until the last minute to do assignments, but it's because you've been able to get away with this habit in many classes. Sometimes you miss an assignment or two, or have to pretend to have done reading that you haven't, but everyone does that sometimes, right?
- **Strengths**: You think quickly on your feet, and while this is a true strength, it also can be a crutch that prevents you from being really successful in a class.
- **Challenges**: As the saying goes, old habits die hard. If you find that you lack a foundation of discipline and personal accountability, it can be difficult to change, especially when the course material becomes challenging or you find yourself struggling to keep up with the pace of the class.
- **Tips for Success**: The good news is you can turn this around! Make a plan to organize your time and materials in a reasonable way, and really stick with it. Also, don't be afraid to ask your instructor for help, but be sure to do it before, rather than after, you fall behind.

Create A Schedule

Once you've evaluated how you have done things in the past, you'll want to think about how you might create a schedule for managing your time well going forward. The best schedules have some flexibility built into them, as unexpected situations will always pop up along the way.

Your schedule will be unique to you, depending on the level of detail you find helpful. There are some things—due dates and exam dates, for example—that should be included in your schedule no matter what. But you also might find it helpful to break down assignments into steps (or milestones) that you can schedule, as well.

Again, this is all about what works best for you. Do you want to keep a record of only the major deadlines you need to keep in mind? Or does it help you to plan out every day so you stay on track? Your answers to these questions will vary depending on the course, the complexity of your schedule, and your own personal preferences.

Your schedule will also vary depending on the course you're taking. So pull out your syllabus and try to determine the rhythm of the class by looking at the following factors:

- Will you have tests or exams in this course? When are those scheduled?
- Are there assignments and papers? When are those due?
- Are there any group or collaborative assignments? You'll want to pay particular attention to the timing of any assignment that requires you to work with others.

You can find many useful resources online that will help you keep track of your schedule. Some are basic, cloud-based calendars (like Google calendar, iCal, Outlook), and some (like iHomework) are specialized for students.

We all have exactly 168 hours per week. How do you spend yours? How much time will you be willing to devote to your studies?

Questions and Answers About Schedules

Student 1: Do I really need to create a study schedule? I can honestly keep track of all of this in my head.
    Answer: Yes, you really should create a study schedule. Your instructors may give you reminders about what you need to do when, but if you have multiple classes and other events and activities to fit in, it's easy to lose track. A study schedule helps you carve out sufficient time—and stick to it.

Student 2: Realistically, how much time should I spend studying for class?
    Answer: This is a good question and a tough one to answer. Generally speaking, for each hour of class, you should spend a minimum of two to three hours studying. Thus, a typical three-hour class would require a minimum of six to nine hours of studying per week. If you are registered for 15 credits a semester, then you would need to spend 30 to 45 hours each week studying for your classes, which can be as much time needed for a full-time job. If you think of college as a "job," you will understand that it takes work to succeed.
    One important college success skill is learning how to interact with the course materials. Think about learning a sport or playing a game. How do you learn how to play it? With lots of practice and engagement. The more you play, the better you get. The same applies to learning. You need to engage with the course material and concentrate on learning.

Student 3: Aside from class time requirements, should I account for anything else as I draw up my schedule?
    Answer: This depends on how detailed you want your schedule to be. Is it a calendar of important dates, or do you need a clear picture of how to organize your entire day? The latter is more successful, so long as you stick with it. This is also where it will be helpful to determine when you are most productive and efficient. When are you the most focused and ready to learn new things? In the morning, afternoon, or evening?

Student 4: My life and school requirements change on a week-to-week basis. How can I possibly account for this when making a schedule?
    Answer: Try creating a variable schedule in case an event comes up or you need to take a day or two off.

Student 5: I'm beginning to think that scheduling and time management are good ideas, but on the other hand they seem unrealistic. What's wrong with cramming? It's what I'll probably end up doing anyway . . .
    Answer: Cramming, or studying immediately before an exam without much other preparation, has many disadvantages. Trying to learn any subject or memorize facts in a brief but intense period of time is

basically fruitless. You simply forget what you have learned much faster when you cram. Instead, study in smaller increments on a regular basis: your brain will absorb complex course material in a more profound and lasting way because it's how the brain functions.

Get Better at Prioritizing

Due dates are important. Set your short and long-term goals accordingly. Ask yourself the following:

- What needs to get done today?
- What needs to get done this week?
- What needs to get done by the end the first month of the semester?
- What needs to get done by the end the second month of the semester?
- What needs to get done by the end of the semester?

Your time is valuable. Treat it accordingly by getting the most you can out of it.

Above all, avoid procrastination. Procrastination is the kiss of death, because it's difficult to catch up once you've fallen behind. Do you have a problem with procrastination? Be on your guard so that it doesn't become an issue for you.

Procrastination Checklist

Do any of the following descriptions apply to you?

- My paper is due in two days and I haven't really started writing it yet.
- I've had to pull an all-nighter to get an assignment done on time.
- I've turned in an assignment late or asked for an extension when I really didn't have a good excuse not to get it done on time.
- I've worked right up to the minute an assignment was due.
- I've underestimated how long a reading assignment would take and didn't finish it in time for class.
- I've relied on the Internet for information (like a summary of a concept or a book) because I didn't finish the reading on time.

If these sound like issues you've struggled with in the past, you might want to consider whether you have the tendency to procrastinate and how you want to deal with it in your future classes. You're already spending a lot of time, energy, and money on the classes you're taking—don't let all of that go to waste!

Strategies to Combat Procrastination

Below are some effective strategies for overcoming procrastination:

Keep your studying "bite-sized." When confronted with 150 pages of reading or 50 problems to solve, it's natural to feel overwhelmed. Try breaking it down: What if you decide that you will read for 45 minutes or that you will solve 10 problems? That sounds much more manageable.
Turn off your phone, close your chat windows, and block distracting Web sites. The best advice we've ever heard is to treat your studying as if you're in a movie theater—just turn it off.
Set up a reward system. If you read for 40 minutes, you can check your phone for 5 minutes. But keep in mind that reward-based systems only work if you stick to an honor system.
Study in a place reserved for studying ONLY. Your bedroom may have too many distractions (or temptations, such as taking a nap), so it may be best to avoid it when you're working on school assignments.
Use checklists. Make your incremental accomplishments visible. Some people take great satisfaction and motivation from checking items off a to-do list. Be very specific when creating this list, and clearly describe each task one step at a time.

- Foundations of College Success: Words of Wisdom. **Authored by**: Thomas C. Priester, editor. **Provided by**: Open SUNY Textbooks. **Located at**: http://textbooks.opensuny.org/foundations-of-academic-success/. **License**: *CC BY-NC-SA: Attribution-NonCommercial-ShareAlike*
- Your Use of Time. **Authored by**: Linda Bruce. **Provided by**: Lumen Learning. **Located at**: https://courses.candelalearning.com/lumencollegesuccess/chapter/your-use-of-time/. **License**: *CC BY: Attribution*
- Image of deadlines. **Authored by**: Cinty Ionescu. **Located at**: https://flic.kr/p/7eUCbm. **License**: *CC BY-NC: Attribution-NonCommercial*
- Outcome: Time Management. **Provided by**: Lumen Learning. **License**: *CC BY: Attribution*
- Introduction to Time Management for Success. **Authored by**: Ronda Dorsey Neugebauer. **Provided by**: Chadron State College. **Project**: Kaleidoscope Open Course Initiative. **License**: *CC BY: Attribution*
- Online Study Skills and Managing Time. **Provided by**: California Community Colleges Online Education Initiative. **Located at**: https://apps.3cmediasolutions.org/oei/04-Online-Study-Skills-and-Managing-Time/index.html. **License**: *CC BY: Attribution*
- Overcome Procrastination For Good!. **Authored by**: Joseph Clough. **Located at**: https://youtu.be/JjU0GbUDtrk. **License**: *CC BY: Attribution*
- Self-Check. **Provided by**: Lumen Learning. **License**: *CC BY: Attribution*